CHAD CARGILL'S
ACT®

By Chad Cargill, Lee Ann Cavener, Betsy Easley, Bill Meek & Katina Skinner

MILL CITY PRESS

Mill City Press, Inc.
2301 Lucien Way #415
Maitland, FL 32751
407.339.4217
www.millcitypress.net

© 2021 by Chad Cargill
Lee Ann Cavener, Betsy Easley, Bill Meek & Katina Skinner

All rights reserved solely by the author. The author guarantees all contents are original and do not infringe upon the legal rights of any other person or work. No part of this book may be reproduced in any form without the permission of the author. The views expressed in this book are not necessarily those of the publisher.

Due to the changing nature of the Internet, if there are any web addresses, links, or URLs included in this manuscript, these may have been altered and may no longer be accessible. The views and opinions shared in this book belong solely to the author and do not necessarily reflect those of the publisher. The publisher therefore disclaims responsibility for the views or opinions expressed within the work.

All rights reserved. No part of this book may be reproduced in any form or by any means, electronic or mechanical, including photocopying, without permission from Cargill Consulting®, Inc. All inquiries should be addressed to Cargill Consulting®, Inc., PO Box 160, Harrah, OK 73045-0160.
www.chadcargill.com

ACT® is the registered trademark of ACT, Inc. Cargill Consulting®, Inc., has no affiliation with ACT, Inc., and is not approved or endorsed (nor would we want to be) by ACT, Inc.

Paperback ISBN-13: 978-0-9743-7802-2

For my family: Shellie, Camden, Cayce, Creed, Clarity, Cai, Carli, Crosby, and Cat.

ABOUT THE AUTHORS

Chad Cargill is the founder of Cargill Consulting. During high school Chad knew he needed to win scholarships in order to attend Oklahoma State University. Chad's freshman year in high school, he discovered that many scholarships were based solely on ACT scores and the journey was on. He took the ACT a total of 18 times in high school raising his score 13 points and reaching the 99.5 percentile. This increase was simply due to him learning what was on the test and how to take it. After graduating high school, Chad went back to his high school to tell some of the students what he learned. When the results of those students' tests were very positive, the counselor asked if he would come back to tell more students. After a few cycles of helping students at his alma mater, other schools began hearing about the workshop. Soon he began giving workshops around the country. Chad graduated from Oklahoma State with a B.S. in Industrial Engineering and Management. He worked 5 years in Oklahoma City at Lucent Technologies as a manufacturing planning engineer. He now travels through the school year speaking to high school students across the country. Chad has personally given his test prep workshop to over 150,000 students. You can view his upcoming schedule at chadcargill.com. His podcast can be found at podcast.chadcargill.com. If you are interested in having Chad present his workshop at your high school, call for details (405) 454-3233.

In addition to giving workshops, Chad is the founder and president of Echo Replay the nation's top sideline replay company for high school and college sports. You can read more about this on the Echo website echo1612.com. Chad loves to work on his family orchard, Smith Ferry Farm (SmithFerryFarm.com).

Chad and Shellie have 8 kids Camden, Cayce, Creed, Clarity, Cai, Carli, Crosby, and Cat. Creed and Clarity were born in the Democratic Republic of Congo, and Cai, Carli, and Crosby were born in Uganda. Cat was an adopted frozen embryo. Learn more at EmbryoDonation.org. Chad is passionate about adoption and missions both local and abroad.

Lee Ann Cavener recently retired after a 39-year career in education. Most of those years were at Ponca City High School in Oklahoma where she taught English and ACT prep. She finished her career at Cascia Hall Preparatory School where she taught English and worked with students in ACT test preparation. Lee Ann stays busy with family, golf, and volunteer work.

Betsy Easley graduated from Fort Gibson High School in Fort Gibson, Oklahoma in 1986. She received an Associate of Arts degree from Connors State College in 1988 and graduated in 1993 from Oklahoma State University with a Bachelor of Science in Secondary Education with an English emphasis. In 2005 after completing the rigorous program requirements, Betsy became a National Board Certified Teacher. Betsy has been teaching at Ponca City High School since 1993. She is currently teaching Pre AP English 2, English 2 and ACT Preparation. She has been the Po-Hi Student Council Advisor since 1996. She has been a Ponca City High School teacher of the year twice and was chosen as the Ponca City Public Schools district Teacher of the Year in 2013.

Bill Meek graduated from Hobart High School in Hobart, Oklahoma salutatorian in 1961. He received his Bachelors degree from the University of Oklahoma in 1965. He was awarded grants from the National Science Foundation to do research at the Oklahoma University Biological research station in 1966 and Seattle Pacific College in 1968 and attained a Masters degree in Natural Science in 1977 from Oklahoma University. Bill taught science for 29 years with the last 22 years at Harrah High School. He served as head of the science department at Harrah where he designed and implemented an advanced Biology program which helped put Harrah's ACT composite and science scores highest in Eastern Oklahoma County for numerous years. He was also head boys basketball coach leading the boys to 21 consecutive winning seasons and being named conference coach of the year 13 times. At Harrah, Coach Meek had the best record of any team in his class for the decade of the 80's and 2nd in the decade of the 70's with an overall record of 420-147 in 21 years. He also coached 15 AAU state champion girls teams which also won numerous national championships and national medalist awards in AAU, YBOA and BCI tournaments. His achievements on the court were only second to those as a biology teacher. He was always a teacher first and coach second.

Dr. Katina Skinner has a PhD in Industrial Engineering with an emphasis on Quality and Reliability Engineering from Arizona State University. She has taught Engineering Statistics and Design of Engineering Experiments at Arizona State University and Business Statistics at Grand Canyon University. Currently she lives in Tempe, Arizona where she still loves math. She also teaches Bible classes to women.

TABLE OF CONTENTS

PREFACE
General Test Taking Tips and Strategies 1
ENGLISH – General Tips and Strategies 8
ENGLISH CONCEPTS 12
    Adjective Use 12
    Adverb Use 14
    Conjunction Use 18
    Verb Use 23
    Subject/Verb Agreement I 27
    Subject/Verb Agreement II 30
    Subject/Verb Agreement III 31
    Pronoun Usage 33
    Pronoun and Antecedent Agreement 37
    Who and Whom 39
    Comma Usage I 41
    Comma Usage II 44
    Comma Usage III 45
    Comma Usage IV 47
    Semicolon Use 49
    Colon Use I 52
    Colon Use II 54
    Using the Dash 56
    Using Apostrophes 58
    Dangling and Misplaced Modifiers 60
    Parallel Structure 63
    Rhetorical Skills 64
        Content Discussion 64
        Transitions 65
        Coherence 67
        Computer Passage 68
        Frankenstein Passage 69
        Practical Joke Passage 71
    Substandard English 74
    Appendix 77
        Conjunctions 77
        Irregular Verbs 78
        Linking Verbs 78
        Prepositions 79
        Pronouns 80
        Transitions 82
ENGLISH PRACTICE TEST 1 83
ENGLISH PRACTICE TEST 2 103
ENGLISH WRITING TEST 125
ENGLISH KEYS 130
MATH – General Tips and Strategies 160
MATH LESSONS 166
    Angles Add to 180°/Equilateral/Isosceles/Right Triangles 166
    Area of a Triangle/Terms: Altitude, Median, Base 168
    Area of a Circle/Radius/Diameter/Circumference 170
    Midpoint Formula 172
    Parallel Lines Divided by a Transversal 173
    Inscribed Angles/Interior Angles 176
    Percents 177
    Square Roots and Exponents 178

Rational and Irrational Numbers...180
Similar Triangles 181
Common Right Triangles 183
Word Problems 185
Geometry- Acute, Obtuse, Right, Complementary and Supplementary Angles 187
Quadratic Equation 189
Inequalities 191
Logarithms 193
Pythagorean Theorem 194
Absolute Values 195
Averages/Terms: Sum, Difference, Product, and Quotient 197
Trigonometry 199
Algebra 203
Distance Formula 204
Equation of a Circle 206
Functions/Polynomials 208
Greatest Common Factor/Least Common Multiple 209
General Equation of a Line..210
Graphing and the (X,Y) Coordinate System 213
Perimeter 215
Area of Irregular Shapes..217
Area of a Trapezoid 219
Polygons and Angles 220
Simplification and Factoring 223
Sequences and Series 224
Probability and Proportions 226
Expressions 228

MATH WORKSHEETS 230
Angles add to 180° 230
Area of a Triangle 233
Area of a Circle 236
Midpoint Formula 239
Parallel Lines Divided by a Transversal 242
Inscribed Angles 245
Percents 248
Squareroots 251
Irrational Numbers 254
Similar Triangles 256
Common Right Triangles 260
Word Problems 263
Geometry 269
Quadratic Equations 272
Inequalities 275
Logarithms 280
Pythagorean Theorem 282
Absolute Values 285
Averages 288
Trigonometry 292
Algebra 298
Distance Formula 301
Equation of a Circle 306
Functions/Polynomials 311
Greatest Common Factor/Least Common Multiple...313
General Equation of a Line...316
Graphing and the (X,Y) Coordinate System 322
Perimeter 326

    Area 331
    Polygons and Angles 336
    Simplification and Factoring 339
    Sequences and Series 343
    Probability and Proportions 346
    Expressions 350
MATH PRACTICE TEST 1 354
MATH PRACTICE TEST 2 370
MATH KEYS 387

READING COMPREHENSION – General Tips and Strategies 402
READING COMPREHENSION EXERCISES 408
    Types of Questions 408
    Visualization Exercises 414
    Speed Reading – Word Grouping 415
    Speed Reading – Eye Movement 418
READING COMPREHENSION PRACTICE TEST I 420
READING COMPREHENSION PRACTICE TEST II 428
READING COMPREHENSION PRACTICE TEST III 436
READING COMPREHENSION PRACTICE TEST IV 444
READING COMPREHENSION KEYS 452

SCIENCE REASONING – General Tips and Strategies 468
SCIENCE REASONING EXERCISES 476
    Logical Reasoning Exercise 1 (Basic Logic) 476
    Logical Reasoning Exercise 2 (Investment Challenge) 477
    Logical Reasoning Exercise 3 (The Stock Market) 478
    Logical Reasoning Exercise 4 (Win/Loss Records) 481
    Logical Reasoning Exercise 5 (The Quiz) 482
    Logical Reasoning Exercise 6 (Get Home Quick) 483
    Table Trend Exercises 484
    Making Notes Exercise 485
    Comprehensive Science Activity 490
    Science Data Collection and Presentation Project Report 501
SCIENCE REASONING KEYS - Activities 502
SCIENCE REASONING PRACTICE TEST 1 517
SCIENCE REASONING PRACTICE TEST 2 525
SCIENCE REASONING KEYS - Practice Tests 537

REVIEW PAGE 541

HOW TO PRACTICE

If you attended the workshop given by Chad Cargill:

- ✓ Review bullet lists for each item in the general idea sections.
- ✓ Follow the recommended practice outlined in the workshop for each section.
- ✓ Focus on your weakness areas, and complete all associated lessons and exercises.
- ✓ Reinforce your areas of strength with a quick review of the concepts.
- ✓ Highlight key points and formulas in the lessons for a quick review before each test.
- ✓ Review all workshop notes.
- ✓ Study the review page at the end of this book.

If you are working on this individually and have not attended the workshop by Chad Cargill:

- ✓ Read general idea sections focusing on the key points in the bullet lists for each item.
- ✓ For English and math, complete a practice test untimed. Work about 5 questions at a time. Check your answers for each group of five as you go. Don't worry about speed. Just try to understand the concept being tested. The goal on every question is to understand why you got it right or why you got it wrong. Genuinely practice! Complete the lessons and associated exercises for all concepts that you missed or need reinforced. Finally, work a timed practice test. Then check your answers. For every question that you miss, determine why. Review concepts again as necessary.
- ✓ For reading comprehension, you should complete the visualization and speed reading exercises. Take time to endure the speed reading exercises. If you are a slow reader, you should do the card sliding exercise a little each day for about 2 weeks prior to the test. To determine your reading method, read at least two passages using each of the three methods outlined on in the reading methods section. Then using the method that works best for you, take an entire 35 minute practice test giving yourself 8 minutes and 45 seconds per passage. Some passages may take you a little more or less time, but in general you want to average 8 minutes and 45 seconds each.
- ✓ For science reasoning, complete all exercises. The comprehensive science activity can help you if you are struggling with a variety of graphs and tables. Work both practice tests using the skills emphasized in the exercises.
- ✓ Study the review page at the end of this book.
- ✓ Get to one of Chad's workshops as soon as possible.

If you are working on this as curriculum in a school semester preparation class:

- ✓ Follow your teacher's lesson plans.
- ✓ Highlight key points in lessons for quick review before each test.
- ✓ Take notes for each concept so you can review before you take the test.
- ✓ Study the review page at the end of this book.

SCORING YOUR ACT TESTS

Use this table to determine your approximate score on the ACT. Scores vary by test. These numbers are approximately what your score would be based on the number you get correct in each section.

Find the number you got correct in the column corresponding with the test you took. Then read the associated scale score listed in the far left and far right columns. Once you have taken all four sections, add your scale scores. Divide the total by four. If the result ends in a fraction, round to the nearest whole number. If the fraction is greater than or equal to 1/2, round up; otherwise, round down.

Scale Score	Raw Scores				Scale Score
	Test 1 English	Test 2 Math	Test 3 Reading	Test 4 Science	
36	75	60	40	40	36
35	74	-	39	-	35
34	72-73	59	38	39	34
33	71	58	37	-	33
32	70	57	-	38	32
31	68-69	55-56	36	37	31
30	67	54	35	-	30
29	66	52-53	-	36	29
28	65	50-51	33-34	35	28
27	63-64	48-49	32	34	27
26	61-62	45-47	31	33	26
25	59-60	42-44	30	31-32	25
24	56-58	40-41	28-29	29-30	24
23	54-55	37-39	27	27-28	23
22	51-53	35-36	25-26	25-26	22
21	49-50	33-34	24	23-24	21
20	46-48	31-32	22-23	21-22	20
19	43-45	28-30	21	19-20	19
18	40-42	25-27	20	17-18	18
17	38-39	22-24	19	15-16	17
16	35-37	19-21	17-18	13-14	16
15	32-34	15-18	16	12	15
14	29-31	12-14	15	10-11	14
13	26-28	10-11	13-14	9	13
12	23-25	8-9	11-12	8	12
11	20-22	6-7	9-10	6-7	11
10	17-19	5	7-8	5	10
9	15-16	4	-	4	9
8	12-14	-	6	3	8
7	10-11	3	5	-	7
6	8-9	2	-	2	6
5	6-7	-	4	-	5
4	5	-	3	-	4
3	3-4	1	2	1	3
2	2	-	1	-	2
1	0-1	0	0	0	1

GENERAL TEST TAKING TIPS AND STRATEGIES

1. Take as many ACT tests as you can.

- Keep taking the test.
- Take the test at least once your sophomore, junior, and senior years.
- Get familiar with the test by taking the test.

When I was in high school, I took the ACT test eighteen times. I raised my score from a nineteen to a thirty-two. At that time, a 32 ACT was the 99th percentile, and that score turned into a ton of scholarship money. I was not able to raise my score thirteen points because I was a genius. I simply took the test as many times as I possibly could in order to reach my goal of thirty-two. I realize the test is expensive, but the higher your score, the more money in scholarships you will win and the more likely you are to qualify for the school you want to attend. Taking the test multiple times allows you to learn, as I did, what is on the test, how to recognize certain common aspects of the test, and how to improve your score. Many students take the test a few times without raising or even dropping their score, so they never take it again. This is absolutely ridiculous! Just because your score drops does not mean you can not raise your score. My score dropped several times, but I kept taking the test because I was determined to reach a goal. Also, taking the test as many times as you can allows you the highest probability of taking "your" test. For example, in a single elimination spelling bee you may be the best speller participating, but if you get a word that you simply do not know regardless of all the others that you do know, you will be eliminated. The ACT test follows the same principle. The test you took may have contained certain questions or passages you simply could not understand. Thus, you have to find "your" test. You will never know how high you could have scored unless you try. Keep taking the test.

2. The ACT test is beatable.

- You <u>CAN</u> raise your score.
- Don't let anyone tell you because of who you are, where you are from, or how much money your parents make that you can't raise your score.
- Think positively and be persistent.

The bottom line is you CAN raise your score. I don't care how many times you have taken the test, you can do it. If you quit taking the test, you won't raise your score. I took the test five times in a row my senior year and didn't raise my score. But the last three times my senior year, I went from a 29 to a 32. You can do the same. Dream big dreams and set high goals. Don't be satisfied with your score. Press for a higher score. Those few points may get you admitted to the college of your dreams or win you a few extra scholarships.

3. There are generalities to every test.

- The same people make the test every time.
- Every time they make the test, they test the same concepts.
- Learn the concepts – raise your score.

The people who make the ACT put the same questions on every test only with different numbers and wording. For example, on almost every ACT math section you will have to find the midpoint or distance between two points. Also, on almost every English section you will have to apply the dash as it relates to an abrupt change in sentence structure or thought. These are just a few examples of common generalities on every ACT. This book covers the topics, concepts, and ideas that can be used on every ACT. If you learn these topics, rules, and ideas, you will put yourself in a position to raise your score.

4. Take a practice test before the real thing and consider residual testing.

- Residual tests are actual ACT tests.
- Residual tests are given at most colleges and universities.
- Residual tests count the same as national ACT tests at most schools and for most scholarships.
- Take residual tests every 60 days.

Prepare for the test by taking a practice test before the national test. This allows you to get accustomed to the endurance and concentration that the test requires. This will also allow you to see how the generalities discussed in this workbook actually apply to the test. Taking practice tests before the real thing will help you to find out what works best for you. This workbook discusses many concepts that will help you, but there is no correct way to take the test. The correct way for you may be different than that for another student; therefore, it is important that you study the test and decide what works best for you.

Another effective way of preparing for the ACT test is to take a residual test. A residual test is an actual ACT test that you can take at most colleges and universities. These tests are usually given on weekdays, but you may find a few schools that give them on Saturdays. You usually get your residual test score very quickly. At most testing centers, you get your score the next day. This provides quick feedback and shows how well prepared you are for the national test. The residual test score may not be used for some national or state scholarships; however, colleges and universities will accept these for most scholarships they award as well as most independent scholarships. I took several residual tests when I was in high school. I used the residual test not only as a practice test, but also as a score to submit to the universities for scholarships. I would encourage you to check with the college or university you are considering as to whether they accept residual scores. Not every high school senior has the financial resources to take multiple residual tests, but if you possibly can, I would. Residual ACT costs vary widely from as low as $30 to over $100. Residual tests can be taken every sixty days. You should research the policy of the residual testing centers in your area before you start taking the tests in order to maximize the number of tests that you can take and to allow you to use your scores for qualifying and scholarships. Let me challenge you and your friends to go take a residual test every sixty days for one year. I think you will be surprised with the results. Finally, try to remember any concepts that were difficult. Write them down immediately after the test. Ask your teachers to help with them. Go to any college website search bar and type, "Residual ACT testing." If they offer this test, their link should appear.

5. Don't stay up late the night before cramming for the test.

- Start studying **NOW**!
- The night before should only be a quick review.
- Please don't stay out late the night before the test.

Please don't wait to start studying until the week of the test. If you do, you will not be ready. This test is complex, and it covers a wide range of topics. You really need to start reviewing the concepts, rules, and formulas several weeks before the test. The night before, you should briefly review the basic rules outlined in this workbook, but your previous knowledge from studying this workbook should be sufficient enough that you do not have to spend much time that night. It always seems that the night before the test (especially the October test) is a big event like homecoming. I encourage you to go to your school's activities, but after the game, go home and sleep. Rest will help more than last minute cramming. Finally, don't wait until the week of the test to start practicing with your calculator. Get your calculator as soon as possible and practice with it regularly.

6. Treat the ACT test morning like a regular school day.

- If you eat breakfast on a school day, eat breakfast on the ACT morning.
- Shower, eat, put on make-up, etc., just like you would on a school day.
- Dress warmly but comfortably.

The ACT test is very long and extremely difficult. One of the hardest things to do while taking the test is to stay focused. If you are hungry, you will be distracted. This distraction will be compounded by other distractions, thus, reducing your concentration level and affecting your score. On a Saturday morning, you will not be happy being in a school taking a four-hour test. If you don't shower and brush your teeth that morning, by the end of the test you will not only be miserable, you'll feel like you have things growing on you. Get ready for an ACT like you get ready for an important school day. Dress in layers so you can adjust clothing based on the temperature of the room. Just treat the ACT morning like a regular school day.

7. Use the bathroom before the test.

- Reduce distractions by using the bathroom before the test.
- Try to use the bathroom at the break between the math and reading sections.
- If you have to use the bathroom during the test, raise your hand.

A friend of mine, who scored in the upper twenties on his ACT, learned this lesson the hard way. The science section is one of the hardest sections to understand, and it requires a high level of concentration. Typically, my friend's science ACT score was around thirty-three. Once during the science section, he had to use the bathroom. Because of this, his concentration was so bad he set his pencil down and concentrated on not going to the bathroom rather than taking the test. Needless to say, his score for that section dropped about eight points. Use the bathroom before the test and during intermission.

You have the right to go to the bathroom during the test. Simply raise your hand and tell the test administrator you are going to the bathroom. Your test-taking time continues while you go to the bathroom, so hurry. My friend should have raised his hand and simply gone to the bathroom.

8. Answer every question.

- Guess on every question if you do not know the answer or are about out of time – there is no penalty for guessing.
- Choose whatever letter you want although *A/F* or *D/J* may be better than *B/G* or *C/H* near the end of a section.
- Make sure you go back and answer questions you skipped.

You are not penalized for guessing. In order to give yourself the highest score possible, answer every question. When the test administrator is about to call time, you should fill in an oval on each question you have not already answered. Most "experts" say when guessing, you should always guess the same letter. Their argument is if you randomly guess, you will have no more than a 1 in 4 chance (1 in 5 chance for math) getting the question right. However, by guessing the same choice repeatedly, there is an additional chance the same answer will be used more than once and it may be quicker. Most "experts" follow by saying you should choose *B/G* or *C/H*. I think statistically it makes no difference if you choose the same letter or a different letter each time. I do like putting the same letter on every question because I think it is simpler and quicker. As far as which letter to put, I suspect the people who make the ACT probably know about the *B* or *C* philosophy, so I always chose *A* or *D*. For example, on the 2017-2018 released tests *A/F*, *D/J*, and *E/K* (*E/K* for math only) were correct 45% more on the last 10 questions of each section. I have also seen the letter frequency almost even, but I have never seen a distinct advantage to *B* and *C* on the last 10 questions of each section. Finally, make sure you do a quick review of each section before they call time and guess on any questions you may have skipped.

GENERAL TEST TAKING TIPS AND STRATEGIES

9. Always have a watch and keep exact time while taking the test.

- Always know how much time remains.
- Use your watch to make the time remaining obvious.
- Ignore the "five-minute" announcement.
- Don't focus on the time so much that it hinders your ability to focus.

One of the downfalls of being an inexperienced ACT test taker is you may not know how much time you have left. The tests are very long and difficult to finish. As mentioned earlier, you should always answer every question. If you run out of time without every question answered, your score will not be as high as it could be. Time seems to pass very quickly during a difficult section. Be aware of the time but not terrified of it. Using a wall clock in the testing center may not be the best method. I found that trying to keep time on my watch or a simple wall clock often confused me. Concentrating solely on the test often caused me to forget when the test started and when it was supposed to end. In order to prevent this unnecessary confusion, I created my own method of time keeping. I wore a simple three-handed (hour, minute, and second) watch. Before a section began, I let the second hand on my watch rotate until it pointed to the twelve. Then, I stopped the second hand from moving by pulling out the crown. Next, I adjusted the other hands so that the clock read exactly noon. Then, I backed the time from noon for the amount of time allotted for the section. For example, on the English test which lasts 45 minutes, I moved the clock to read 11:15. When the test administrator said, "Go," I started the clock. I knew when my watch read noon, the test was over. No questions. No confusion. This method may seem somewhat ridiculous, but if you want to reduce confusion and improve your score, master a time keeping method. A digital watch can also be used if you want to purchase one, but it can not make noise or communicate such as an Apple watch.

Finally, when the test administrators announce "five minutes" remaining in each section, you should ignore them. Using this method, you already know the time because you are keeping time on your watch. Also, five minutes is a lot of time. For example, the science test is six passages designed to be of approximately equal length and difficulty. The science test as a whole is 35 minutes long. Thirty-five minutes divided by six equal passages is five minutes and 50 seconds. At the five-minute call, if you think your test is over and you panic, you are greatly reducing your score. Many students start guessing in all four sections when the test administrator calls five-minutes. If you do that, you are going to guess on approximately 24 questions total in English, math, reading, and science. If the guessing odds play out, you will get about 6 of the 24 correct. Consider the following: if you score a 19, you are getting about half the questions correct. If you do this while guessing when they call five minutes, you got 6 out of 24 rather than 12 out of 24. That is a difference of 6 questions spread over the four sections of the ACT. Did you know that a difference of 6 questions spread over the four sections of the ACT is over a one composite score increase? If you are guessing at 5 minutes and scoring a 19, try the method described above, and your composite ACT score should increase to at least a 20 doing this alone!

10. If you think you are doing badly, <u>don't worry</u>; everyone else is too.

- Quit worrying about those so-called geniuses around you.
- Your friends that look like they know what they are doing in math are missing questions just like you.
- Keep testing. Don't quit because you think you are too dumb to take the test.

Have you ever been taking the math test and freaked out because everyone around you was pounding away on those big screen TV calculators? You just sat there and said to yourself something like, "Oh, my gosh. I am so stupid, and they are so smart!" Did you know that in many states, the average student misses about half the math questions? The next time you catch yourself looking at all your friends pounding their calculators, rest assured, they probably don't know what they are doing either. Just relax and do your best. If you prepared with this book, you are going to be in great shape.

There will be many distractions around you. Students will speed through different sections. Don't worry about the pace of other students. Remember that the test is hard for everyone. Just keep doing your best while ignoring the distractions.

Each section of the ACT test is graded comparatively across the nation. In a general sense, this test is curved. Although the curving is a little different than the method most teachers use, the same concepts apply. Once all the tests have been graded, ACT then decides how many you could miss to make a certain score. Just because you miss a lot of questions does not mean that your score will decrease. Typically, if you think a particular section is hard, then probably the rest of America does also. Don't worry about it. Do your best, and that is all that you can do.

11. Do not read the directions before each section.

- Don't waste time reading the directions.
- Read the directions the night before.
- If you do the practice tests in this book, you will be familiar with the directions.

When the test administrator begins each section, he/she may say something like, "The English section contains 75-questions and you will have 45-minutes to complete it. Turn to page 2. Read the directions carefully, and you may begin." The directions at the top of each section on an actual test are the exact same directions that are printed in your practice test that ACT provides to you free of charge titled "Preparing for the ACT Assessment." You should read the directions before you take the actual test. Wasting time reading directions during your actual test will only penalize you the amount of time it takes to read them.

GENERAL TEST TAKING TIPS AND STRATEGIES

12. Always order a copy of your tests and answers when available.

- For an additional fee you can order your answers, the correct answers, and the test questions.
- This is only available on the December, April, and June national ACT tests.
- Identify what concepts you missed.
- Donate to school when you graduate.

For an additional fee ($30 at time of printing, up from $22), you can order your answers, the correct answers, and the test questions on the December, April, and June national ACT tests. This allows you to see what questions and associated concepts you missed. You will receive this typically 3-4 weeks following the test. You can order this when you register for the test, online up to the day of the test, or by mail up to six months after you test. ACT embracing inflation, now charges $40 (up from $22) if you order after the test. What a joke! When you receive your test, study every question you missed. Then practice those weakness areas. After you graduate, give these tests to your teachers. Your teachers will greatly appreciate you helping them and the future students.

If you can afford this, do it. This gives you a huge advantage.

ENGLISH – GENERAL TIPS AND STRATEGIES

| 45 Minutes | 75 Questions |

TYPES OF QUESTIONS

➥ **Grammar/Usage/ Mechanics**
➥ **Rhetorical**

About 55 of the 75 questions require you to make a change to a word or group of words that are underlined in a passage. The changes may include words and punctuation or only words. Each question has four possible answers, the first of which will usually be *No Change*. On these questions you must determine the following two things:
  ➢ Are the words correct or appropriate?
  ➢ Are they punctuated correctly?

If the sentence is correct as written, you can choose *No Change*, but be careful with this choice (see English rule 5).

The remaining 20 or so questions of the English test are questions concerning writing techniques and strategies that generally pertain to the passage as a whole or segments of the passage. There are several different types of these questions. Some examples include the following:
  ➢ Style of passage
  ➢ Purpose of passage
  ➢ Transitions from one paragraph to the next
  ➢ Summary of the passage
  ➢ Order of paragraphs

There is a different method to answering rhetorical questions than answering grammar/usage/mechanics questions (see English rule 6).

Rules for Grammar/Usage/Mechanics Questions

1. Choose the answer that is the most simple.

- On a grammar/usage/mechanics question, when you narrow it down to two or more choices that are all grammatically correct and punctuated correctly, choose the simplest answer.
- This rule will apply to as much as 30% of the grammar/usage/mechanics questions.

<u>This is the most important rule for the English test</u>! On a grammar/usage/mechanics question when you narrow it down to more than one choice that is grammatically correct, punctuated correctly, and sounds good in the sentence, choose the simplest answer. Usually, it will be the right answer. Somewhere between 6 and 8 times per test, there will be grammar/usage/mechanics questions with more than one correct answer. Most students freeze on these. When in doubt, choose the simplest answer.

ENGLISH – GENERAL TIPS AND STRATEGIES

For example, in math 1/2 is better than 4/8. Why? 1/2 is better because it is simplified or reduced. They are both correct, but 1/2 is better. The same concept applies in English. In general, I would rather choose *the door* instead of *the seven-foot, pine door*.

Also, there are an additional 3-4 questions with answers that contain redundancies. So out of 55 or so grammar/usage/mechanics questions, you could see as many as 12 questions which the simplest answer is best. On some tests, almost 22% of the grammar/usage/mechanics questions follow the simple and redundancy rules.

2. Always re-read your choice in the complete sentence.

- Take time to verify your answer makes sense by re-reading the entire sentence using the choice you selected.
- Replace any underlined punctuation as well as the words with the choice you selected.
- Verify that your choice contains correct grammar, punctuation, and usage.
- Verify your choice fits the style and flow of the passage.

On every grammar/usage/mechanics question you need to go back and re-read the entire sentence containing the choice you selected to make sure it contains correct grammar, punctuation, and usage. If there is a transition to a sentence before or after the sentence containing the underlined part, make sure the sentence flows smoothly and logically. Keep in mind that the choice you select cannot simply fit into the sentence with the underlined part. It must fit into the entire passage.

3. Try each choice in the sentence.

- Re-read the complete sentence with the underlined part for each choice.
- Eliminate all words and punctuation that are underlined.
- When you know a choice is incorrect, mark it out in your test booklet.
- Use reasoning.

When answering a grammar/usage/mechanics question, try each choice in the sentence. Read the complete sentence containing the underlined part, eliminate anything underlined (including all words and punctuation). Try each choice to see if the new sentence contains correct grammar, punctuation and usage. When you try a choice and you know it is incorrect, mark through that letter in the test booklet. If you do this, you can eliminate wrong answers and increase your probability of getting the correct answer.

Use reasoning as much as possible. Reasoning means not necessarily looking for the right answers but eliminating the wrong answers.

NOTE: You CAN write in your test booklet. Many students think you are not supposed to write in the test booklet, but that is simply not true. One exception is residual tests. On residual tests, the testing centers will make you write on scrap paper they give you.

4. Read all of the passage.

- Read the passage as you go.
- Quickly read from one underlined part to the next underlined part.
- Try to understand the main idea of the passage.

When I first started taking the ACT, I never read the entire passage in English. I believed I needed to jump from one underlined part to the next in order to finish. I really didn't see the point in reading all that verbiage between the underlined parts. Then, I would come to a rhetorical style question. This is a question like "Would the essay successfully…" or "The author's main point…" Then, I would need to go back and re-read the passage, so I could answer the question. The best strategy is to read the passage as you go.

This is not a reading comprehension test. You do not have to know all the details, but you do need to quickly read the passage as you go. While reading, ask yourself, *in general what is happening here?* If you do this, you will find the questions about the passage as a whole become much easier to answer. If you don't read the passage, it's difficult to answer questions about the passage.

Yet, many teach not to read the passage. They say in order to save time, you should jump from one underline to the next. Don't do this. ACT makers will underline a verb only in a sentence but change the tense of the verb. You will know the correct tense if you read the passage. They will use incorrect indefinite pronouns. You won't know the pronoun references if you don't read the passage. In conclusion, the general questions about the passage are *much* easier if you read the passage.

5. Don't be afraid of putting *No Change* too many times.

- *No Change* is a correct answer about 15 times on the ACT English test.
- When you answer *No Change*, a second look is okay, but don't dwell on it until you invent something wrong.

No Change is a correct answer on the ACT. You may have a tendency to think something has to be wrong with each sentence until you try to invent something wrong. You should always give a second look when the answer is *No Change*, but the bottom line is that *No Change* is a correct answer about 15 times per test. If you start putting *No Change* too many times, you may begin to lose confidence. On one test I put *No Change* about 6 of the first 10 questions, and I am fairly certain I got all of them right. How do I know? Well, my friend with a 36 in English said he did the exact same thing. Once again, if you think the answer is *No Change*, then put *No Change*.

ENGLISH – GENERAL TIPS AND STRATEGIES

Rules for Rhetorical Questions

6. Read the passage as you go and focus on the keywords.

- Read the passage as you go.
- Focus on keywords in the question.
- Do not follow the "most simple" rule (see Rule 1) on rhetorical questions.

In this book, we define a rhetorical question as a question about the writing strategies for the passage as a whole or segment of the passage. Most students who have not prepared for the ACT feel rhetorical questions are the most difficult. However, students who have prepared typically find rhetorical questions quite easy.

The number one reason why students miss rhetorical questions is they don't read the passage. It's difficult to summarize, conclude, or know the main point of a passage you didn't read. You must read the passage as you go.

Most rhetorical style questions contain keywords relating directly to the correct answer. For example, on some questions many or all of the choices could be successfully added to a passage, but only one can be added to meet the specific criteria asked. Consider the following example question:

Ex. Which of the following emphasizes the author's _____ tone in the essay?

The keyword in the blank could be a word like gentle, aggressive, friendly, or sinister. In this example, the correct answer will greatly focus on characteristics of the keyword. If these key words are noted when you read the question, you are more likely to select the correct answer.

One very important note is that you do not want to follow the "simple" rule (see English rule 1) on rhetorical questions. The simple rule is the most important rule on the English test, but not for rhetorical questions.

CONCEPT: ADJECTIVE USE

⇨ **Adjectives modify nouns or pronouns by answering one of the following questions: Which one? What kind? How many?**

EXAMPLE: As Jonathan entered the room, he smelled the **fragrant** flowers.

The adjective *fragrant* modifies the noun *flowers* by telling what kind of flowers they are.

⇨ **Often, words that can be used as pronouns may function in some sentences as adjectives because they modify rather than take the place of a noun.**

EXAMPLE: The gardener carried the shovel but put the **other** tools in the wheelbarrow.

Other modifies the noun *tools*, so in this sentence it is an adjective rather than a pronoun.

⇨ **Words that can be used as nouns may function in some sentences as adjectives.**

EXAMPLE: Avery caught her foot on the **chair** leg and fell to the floor.
In this sentence *chair* is an adjective which modifies the noun *leg*.

⇨ **The words *a*, *an*, and *the* (articles) function as adjectives. *A* and *an* are indefinite articles. Use these when referring to one of a group. *The* is a definite article; use it when referring to a specific item or person.**

EXAMPLE: I could not complete the assignment without **a** book on my topic.
My mother offered me **an** orange from the fruit basket.
The photographer asked me to hold **the** flower next to my face.

 **NOTE:** Although the usual position for an adjective is before the noun or pronoun it modifies, it can come after the noun or pronoun. The adjective may also be separated from the noun by other words.

EXAMPLE: A. Usual position: Lacey wanted a **scarlet** formal for the prom.
B. Adjective following noun: The chair, **scarred** and **wobbly**, belonged to my grandmother.
C. Adjective separated from noun: **Angry** and **militant**, the crowd moved closer to the picket line.

STUDENT PRACTICE
DIRECTIONS: Underline the adjectives in the following paragraph. Draw an arrow from each adjective to the noun or pronoun it modifies.
Don't forget the articles.
The first adjective has been marked as an example.

Because she was interested in the tragic history of World War II, Shelly decided to attend a historical lecture offered at her local university. Several WWII veterans were to discuss their experiences during the war and would answer questions following the two-hour program. As she entered the chilly lecture hall, she observed a group of men and women seated on the stage; they were dressed in uniforms from each of the branches of the armed forces. She made her way through the crowded room and found a single, empty seat toward the front. An elderly, stooped gentleman stepped to the podium and introduced himself as Nathan Gray, an Air Force pilot who had served from 1942 until January of 1945 when he was severely injured by a hidden land mine. Shelly was shocked to realize that this stoic stranger had sacrificed his left hand and most of his left leg in the service of his country. One by one, the people on the stage stepped forward to offer their incredible stories of fierce bravery, intense hardship and unfaltering courage. By the time the mesmerizing program was over, Shelly was convinced that present-day Americans truly owe an enormous debt of gratitude to what has been called the "Greatest Generation."

ACT TEST SAMPLE QUESTIONS:

1. As the tornado screamed through the neighborhood, my terrify family ran for the storm shelter. Thankfully, we made it in time, slamming the shelter door as the winds increased.

   A. NO CHANGE
   B. my terrifying family
   C. the terrify family
   D. my terrified family

2. We had seen accounts on the nightly news of the tornado damage <u>which can be severely.</u> Wondering what would happen to us, we closed our eyes and tried to be calm.

   A. NO CHANGE
   B. which can be severe.
   C. who can be severe.
   D. which can be advantageous.

3. The librarian handed me <u>a largely book</u> about muscular dystrophy, the topic I was researching for my essay.

   A. NO CHANGE
   B. largest book
   C. a large book
   D. the largely book

4. Janelle chose the <u>pretty, attractive, red dress</u> to wear to the prom.

   A. NO CHANGE
   B. pretty; attractive; red dress
   C. pretty—attractive, red dress
   D. pretty red dress

5. Many people long to become <u>American citizens</u> in order to enjoy the freedom and economic opportunity available in this country.

   A. NO CHANGE
   B. an America citizen
   C. the American citizen
   D. an American citizens

CONCEPT: ADVERB USE

➥ **Adverbs modify verbs, adjectives, or other adverbs by answering one of the following questions: Where? When? How? To what extent?**

> EXAMPLE: I have always wanted to live **there**. (where?)
> We can meet **later** at the library. (when?)
> Marci finished the test **quickly**, but took time to review her answers. (how?)
> The props for the play are **completely** finished. (to what extent?)

TIP: Many adverbs end in –ly: *completely, frequently, firmly, obviously, carefully.* **Remember that not all words that end in** –ly **are adverbs (***daily* **news,** *early* **appointment,** *only* **message), and that not all adverbs must end in** –ly *(best, now, fast, ever, not).*

↪ **Adverbs modify adjectives:**

EXAMPLE: I picked up the surprisingly dusty book and began to look through it.
Tara is especially interested in being a page in the state's congress.

↪ **Adverbs modify verbs:**

EXAMPLE: Albert sighed longingly as he watched Sara dance with Jason.
Banging the pans together loudly, the children marched smartly around the living room.

TIP: Never use an adverb to modify a noun or pronoun. Never use an adjective to modify a verb.

POOR: He drives bad.
  (using an adjective to modify the verb *drives*)
BETTER: He drives badly.
  (using an adverb to modify the verb *drives*)

↪ **Adverbs modify other adverbs:**

EXAMPLE: Thomas did extremely well on his college entrance exams.

Kristin realized rather quickly that she would need to have more help cleaning her bedroom.

TIP: Adverbs should be placed as close as possible to the words they modify to ensure that the meaning is clear.

EXAMPLE: I have almost seen all of the soccer games this year.
  (Have I seen any?)
I have seen almost all of the soccer games this year.
  (I have seen most of the games.)

✋ **Adverbs have three forms: regular, comparative, and superlative.**

Comparative form: compares two persons, places, things or ideas. The adverb will usually end in *–er* or be coupled with the word *more*.

EXAMPLE: Studying effectively instead of wasting time will enable the student to do **better**.

Superlative: compares three or more persons, places, things or ideas. The adverb will usually end in *–est* or be coupled with the word *most*.

EXAMPLE: Studying effectively, participating actively in class and completing all assignments on time will help a student's grade **best** of all.

TIP: In general use *more* and *most* for adverbs that end in *–ly*, and use *–er* and *–est* for other adverbs.

<u>Regular</u>	<u>Comparative</u>	<u>Superlative</u>
fluently	more fluently	most fluently
quickly	more quickly	most quickly
fast	faster	fastest
early	earlier	earliest

✋ **Avoid the double negative (using two negative words in the same sentence).**

EXAMPLE: INCORRECT: Mary and Beth **don't** do **nothing** to make people think they are arrogant.
　　　　　　BETTER:　　　Mary and Beth **don't** do **anything** to make people think they are arrogant.

STUDENT PRACTICE
　　DIRECTIONS: Read each of the following sentences carefully, and decide if the adverb is used correctly or incorrectly, and in the space provided after each sentence, correct the mistake and explain your change.

EXAMPLE:

The <u>correctly</u> copy of the document was submitted to the judge.

A. *Incorrect*

B. *The adverb incorrectly cannot modify a noun (copy). Change the adverb to an adjective which can modify a noun: correct copy.*

ENGLISH

1. The school's production of *Guys and Dolls* is <u>certain</u> entertaining.

    A. _____   B. _____

2. As the nurses stood by the patient's bed, they spoke <u>softly</u> to avoid disturbing the gravely ill man.

    A. _____   B. _____

3. Our trip from Santa Monica to Phoenix took too <u>longer</u>.

    A. _____   B. _____

4. Of the twins, Jennifer has been <u>most</u> ill than Jered.

    A. _____   B. _____

5. Because it is necessary for their survival, deer have learned to run very <u>swift</u>.

    A. _____   B. _____

ACT TEST SAMPLE QUESTIONS

1. The accident <u>occurred so quick:</u> one minute the toddler was playing next to the swimming pool, and the next minute he had fallen into the water.

    A. NO CHANGE
    B. occurred so quick,
    C. occurred so quickly:
    D. occurred so quicker:

2. Meghan believes she <u>has done extreme well</u> on the chemistry test.

    A. NO CHANGE
    B. has done extremely well
    C. have done extremely well
    D. has done extremely good

3. I wished to <u>be completely finished</u> with my homework before I went out for the evening.

    A. NO CHANGE
    B. be complete finished
    C. been completely finished
    D. be completely finish

ENGLISH

4. Even after all the practice he has had, Albert <u>sings bad</u>.

   A. NO CHANGE
   B. sings well.
   C. sings badly.
   D. sing badly.

5. Colette tries <u>to never do nothing</u> to disappoint her parents.

   A. NO CHANGE
   B. to never does nothing
   C. never to do anything
   D. to not do nothing

CONCEPT: CONJUNCTION USE

▷ A conjunction joins words or groups of words. For a list of the types of conjunctions discussed in this section, see page 77.

▷ Coordinating conjunctions may connect words or groups of words. They always connect items of the same kind. When a coordinating conjunction connects two independent clauses, place a comma directly before the conjunction.

   EXAMPLE: As I lie on the grass, I enjoyed the cool, calm **and** peaceful day.
   (The conjunction *and* connects three equal adjectives)
   Jeannie agreed to attend the prom with David, **so** she shopped for a dress on Saturday.
   (The conjunction *so* connects two equal clauses.)

▷ Correlative conjunctions also connect words or groups of words of equal value, but these conjunctions are used in pairs. See page 77.

   EXAMPLE: I decided that I would like to have not only the sweater but also the skirt.

NOTE: Notice that no comma is used after *sweater*. Do not use punctuation to separate the two parts of the correlative conjunction.

➥ Subordinating conjunctions introduce adverb clauses. Adverb clauses that appear at the beginning of a sentence are followed by a comma. Adverb clauses at the end of a sentence do not require a comma. See page 77.

    EXAMPLE: Before I can go to the movies with Carli, I must clean my bedroom.
                     I told my niece that I would take her wherever she wanted to go.

➥ **Conjunctive adverbs are used to clarify the relationship between main clauses. Always use a semicolon before and a comma after the conjunctive adverb.**

    EXAMPLE: Rock climbing can be dangerous and difficult; **however,** it can also be exhilarating.

                     I have saved over five thousand dollars during the last two years; **consequently,** I am able to make a substantial down payment on a car.

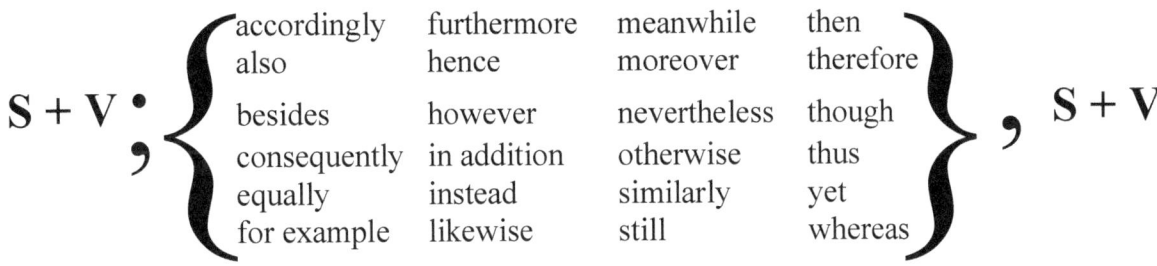

Independent Clause   Independent Clause

TIP: Make sure you use a conjunction that correctly conveys the meaning you wish. For example, you wouldn't use the conjunction *and* to show a contradiction. Read the following examples of how to use conjunctions correctly.

    Incorrect: Clarice asked to attend the music camp at the university, **but** her mother said yes.

    Better: Clarice asked to attend the music camp at the university, **and** her mother said yes.

Incorrect: I compete in the two-mile event **although** I enjoy running long distances.

Better: I compete in the two-mile event **because** I enjoy running long distances.

Incorrect: I dislike working with animals; **similarly,** my brother enjoys being a veterinarian's assistant.

Better: I dislike working with animals; **however,** my brother enjoys being a veterinarian's assistant.

 **TIP:** For more information on the correct punctuation to use with conjunctions, see the section on comma and semicolon use. (p. 41-52)

STUDENT PRACTICE
DIRECTIONS: Fill in each of the blanks with a conjunction of the type indicated in the parentheses. More than one conjunction could be correct.

1) Bryan would like to buy a new car, _____ he knows he cannot afford a car payment. (use a coordinating conjunction)

2) _____ Lisa _____ Lauren thoroughly enjoyed attending Girl's State. (use a correlative conjunction)

3) _____ we return from the tennis match, we will meet Brittney and Aaron for dinner. (use a subordinating conjunction)

4) My brother applied and was accepted to Rice University; _____, he will be moving to Houston in August. (use a conjunctive adverb)

5) _____ Pam's parents _____ my parents would miss watching us perform in the school's production of *A Midsummer Night's Dream*. (use a correlative conjunction)

6) I did very well on the latest essay in my English class; _____, my overall grade has improved. (use a conjunctive adverb)

7) Halli will not be able to drive to the dance tonight _____ she obtains her driver's license today. (use a subordinating conjunction)

8) Brandon is faced with a decision: attend the awards assembly and accept his scholarship _____ report for his first evening of work. (use a coordinating conjunction)

9) The yearbook company has lost _____ our homecoming pictures _____ all the pictures and text for the junior/senior prom. (use a correlative conjunction)

10) My grandfather promised me that if I maintained a 4.0 GPA throughout my high school career, he would pay for college; _____, he will be paying my way to Harvard in the fall. (use a conjunctive adverb)

STUDENT PRACTICE
   DIRECTIONS: Combine sentences using appropriate conjunctions.

1. Unfortunately, I did poorly on my Algebra exam.
   I did not study my notes at all.
   _____
   _____.

2. It was pouring rain.
   The game was canceled.
   We were ahead by four runs.
   _____
   _____.

3. The music was very loud.
   My mom asked us to turn it down.
   _____
   _____.

4. Mr. Quigley is a good teacher.
   His classes are usually full.
   He tells entertaining stories.
   _____
   _____.

5. Miranda has always wanted to travel to Europe.
   She would love to see the Eiffel Tower and Big Ben.
   She has very little money in her savings account.
   _____
   _____.

6. I had an unusual party.
   It was my birthday.
   My dad dressed up like a duck.
   _____
   _____.

7. The wind was howling from the north.
   The rain began to fall.
   The soldiers were soaking wet.
   _____
   _____.

8. Coretta Scott King was a fascinating woman.
   She organized many protests and marches.
   Few knew of her work.
   _____
   _____.

9. I had always wanted to read *The Hobbit*.
   I wanted to read *The Fellowship of the Ring*.
   I liked them both immensely.
   _____
   _____.

10. My brother called.
    Lindsay answered the phone.
    She told him I was mowing the lawn.
    _____
    _____.

ACT TEST SAMPLE QUESTIONS

1. Scientists at the research laboratory are concerned about the new virus that has appeared in their latest <u>experiment; accordingly they</u> must proceed with the testing or the entire project will be jeopardized.

   A. NO CHANGE
   B. experiment, accordingly they
   C. experiment; nevertheless, they
   D. experiment, nevertheless, they

2. Living in a rural area has several advantages over living in crowded <u>urban areas although people</u> who live in big cities would doubtless disagree with that theory.

   A. NO CHANGE
   B. urban areas: although people
   C. urban areas; although people
   D. urban areas because people

ENGLISH

3. Most people relish the free time they have on the <u>weekends yet few</u> would give up their jobs in order to have an abundance of free time every day.

   A. NO CHANGE
   B. weekends; yet
   C. weekends: yet
   D. weekends, yet

4. Before my first visit to the campus, I thought I wanted to attend Duke <u>University. If I</u> saw the dorms and the student center, I knew without a doubt it was the place for me.

   A. NO CHANGE
   B. University. If, I
   C. University. As soon as I
   D. University. As soon as, I

5. Because Carlos was determined to save enough money to buy new tires for <u>his truck he decided</u> not to eat out at all for an entire month.

   A. NO CHANGE
   B. his truck, he decided
   C. his truck; he decided
   D. his truck, and he decided

CONCEPT: VERB USE

Correct verb use can involve a variety of concepts; it is important to understand the principal parts of the verb as well as number, person and voice. Using each correctly is crucial to communicating your meaning.

▷ **The principal parts of the verb are the present, the present participle, the past and the past participle.**

Present	Present Participle	Past	Past Participle
talk	talking	talked	talked
learn	learning	learned	learned
fall	falling	fell	fallen

NOTE: Verbs are divided into two groups, regular and irregular, according to the way they form their past tense and past participle. Both the past tense and past participle forms of regular verbs end in *–ed*. Irregular verbs form their past tense and past participle in a variety of ways. It is a good idea to become familiar with how those irregular verbs change in order to avoid mistakes on the ACT test and in composition and speech. Below is a brief list of irregular verbs. For a more complete listing, see page 78.

Present	Present Participle	Past	Past Participle
ride	riding	rode	(have) ridden
begin	beginning	began	(have) begun
break	breaking	broke	(have) broken
burst	bursting	burst	(have) burst
choose	choosing	chose	(have) chosen
do	doing	did	(have) done
drive	driving	drove	(have) driven
eat	eating	ate	(have) eaten
freeze	freezing	froze	(have) frozen
give	giving	gave	(have) given

↪ The number of the verb (singular or plural) must be consistent with the number of the subject. See the section on subject/verb agreement for more information (p. 27-33).

↪ The person of a verb refers to whether the subject of the verb is first, second or third person and whether the subject is singular or plural.

	Singular	Plural
First person	I sing	We sing
Second person	You sing	You sing
Third person	He/she/it sings	They sing

↪ Typically the only change in the verb is in the third person.

↪ Voice indicates whether the subject is acting (active voice) or being acted upon (passive voice).

    EXAMPLE: Active voice: Mary **works** diligently at improving her free throw skills.
              Passive voice: The information **will be sent** sometime next week.
              (A passive verb pairs a *be* verb with a past participle.)

STYLE NOTE: When writing, try to avoid using passive tense too often. A series of passive sentences has an ineffectual and awkward tone that weakens your composition.
        PASSIVE: The case was handled by the detective in charge.
        BETTER: The detective in charge handled the case.

STYLE NOTE: Be aware of unnecessary shifts in verb tense. For example, when writing about events in the past, do not suddenly shift to present tense. This is a common concept tested on the ACT test. When taking the test, be sure to read ahead in the passage to determine what the correct tense is, then determine if the verb underlined matches that tense.

> **EXAMPLE:** INCORRECT: Jason threw the football then runs down field.
> BETTER: Jason threw the football then ran down field.
> INCORRECT: My nephew, Andy, yells and screamed when he doesn't get his way.
> BETTER: My nephew, Andy, yells and screams when he doesn't get his way.

STUDENT PRACTICE
  DIRECTIONS: Read each sentence carefully, then write the correct form of the verb given at the beginning of the sentence.

1. Choose   I have _____ engineering as my major.
2. Break   The vase _____ after I knocked it to the floor.
3. Drive   None of us have _____ in a crowded, metropolitan area before.
4. Speak   Jeanne will be _____ at her cousin's graduation ceremony.
5. Take   I realized I had _____ more of the chips and dip than I should have.
6. Fly   We watched the airplane as it _____ through the fog.
7. Teach   I tried to _____ my niece how to tie her shoe.
8. Talk   Marie grew calm as we _____ quietly to her about the car wreck.
9. Cry   The baby began _____ as soon as we sat down for dinner.
10. See   I have _____ this movie at least a dozen times.

ENGLISH

EXTENDED PRACTICE

DIRECTIONS: Read the following passage carefully. Decide if the underlined verbs are correct. If they are, write *correct* in the space provided. If they are not, write the correct form in the space.

My brother is five years older than I am, and when we were growing up, he never wanted to spend time with me. I idolized him and <u>following</u> him everywhere he went. One day he decided that he had had enough of my tagging along, so he <u>locks</u> me in the feed room in the barn. I was <u>terrified</u> of being in the feed room alone because it was full of mice. Worst of all, the light switch was on the outside of the room, so when my brother pushed me in, <u>slamming</u> the door shut, and <u>turns</u> off the light, I was <u>trap</u> in total darkness. I screamed and <u>cried</u> for what seemed like hours before someone heard me. In reality, my father <u>rescue</u> me after only a few minutes. As punishment, my parents made my brother take me along on his first date with his new girlfriend. He <u>spends</u> the entire evening glaring at me, but he never <u>says</u> a word.

1. _____.
2. _____.
3. _____.
4. _____.
5. _____.
6. _____.
7. _____.
8. _____.
9. _____.
10. _____.

ACT TEST SAMPLE QUESTIONS

1. Malinda woke up late, rushed through getting <u>ready and races out</u> the door, hoping to make it to work on time.

    A. NO CHANGE
    B. ready, and races out
    C. ready and have raced out
    D. ready and raced out

ENGLISH

2. Jeremy felt like he had done his best on the test. He wished, however, that he had studied the third formula a bit more.

   A. NO CHANGE
   B. that, he had studied
   C. that he had studying
   D. that he have studied

3. Mr. Westman give us permission to go to the library. We left the room and walked quickly down the stairs.

   A. NO CHANGE
   B. Westman is giving us
   C. Westman gave us
   D. Westman given us

4. My family gathered to watch my niece blow out the candles on her birthday cake. As she took a deep breath, she lost her balance, fell off the chair she was standing on and land face first in the cake.

   A. NO CHANGE
   B. on and landed
   C. on, landing
   D. on and lands

5. I watched as the blue jay chattered at the squirrel. The squirrel ignored the bird until it chased him across the yard, trying to peck him on the head.

   A. NO CHANGE
   B. squirrel ignores the bird
   C. squirrel, ignored the bird
   D. squirrel has ignored the bird

CONCEPT: SUBJECT/VERB AGREEMENT I

When a word refers to one person or thing, it is singular in number. When a word refers to more than one, it is plural in number.

Singular	**Plural**
boy	boys
watch	watches
basketball	basketballs
person	people

✎ **A verb agrees with its subject in number: singular subjects take singular verbs, and plural subjects take plural verbs. Most plural nouns end in *s*, but verbs that end in *s* are singular.**

    EXAMPLE: **Mary scores** high on tests because she studies the material.
                            (The singular verb *scores* agrees with the singular subject *Mary*.)

                            The **students** in Ms. Benson's class **practice** good study and test taking skills.
                            (The plural verb *practice* agrees with the plural subject *students*.)

✎ **The number of the subject is not affected by a phrase following the subject. Remember that the subject of a sentence is never part of a prepositional phrase.**

    EXAMPLE: The **purpose** of the meetings **was** to choose a new student council president.
                            (The singular subject *purpose* agrees with the singular verb *was*. *Of the meetings* is a prepositional phrase that does not affect the choice of the verb.)

                            Books of that kind **are** very rare and can be extremely expensive.
                            (The plural subject *Books* agrees with the plural verb *are*. *Of that kind* is a prepositional phrase that does not affect the number of the verb.)

✎ **The following indefinite pronouns are singular and take a singular verb:** *each, either, neither, one, everyone, everybody, no one, nobody, anyone, anybody, someone, somebody, everything, anything, something, nothing.*

➤ **An easy way to remember these indefinite singular pronouns is to simply memorize *each*, *either*, *neither*, and every word that ends in *thing*, *one*, and *body*.**

    EXAMPLE: **Everyone is** welcome to attend the end of the year picnic on Saturday afternoon.
                            Neither of the girls **was** ready when the boys arrived to pick them up.
                            One of the ways that I try to improve my grades **is** to take thorough notes in class and re-read them when I get home.

✎ **The following pronouns are plural and take a plural verb:** *several, few, both, many.*

    EXAMPLE: **Few** of the protesters **agree** with the president's decision to encourage increased nuclear testing.
                            Many of them **want** him to recant his statement that nuclear testing is safe.

ENGLISH

↳ **The pronouns *some*, *all*, *most*, *any*, and *none* may be either singular or plural depending on the number of the word to which they refer.**

EXAMPLE: **Some** of the court documents **were** lost, slowing the progress of the case.

Some of the testimony **is** biased because the witnesses are employees of the defendant.

NOTE: The indefinite pronouns are easy to remember. If you memorize which are singular and which may be either (the plural are obvious), you will never miss a verb choice with an indefinite pronoun on an ACT test.

↳ **Mnemonic device for always singular indefinite pronouns:** *Each, either, neither*, and all the *–ones, –bodies,* and *–things*.

↳ **Mnemonic device for indefinite pronouns which may be either singular or plural:**

ALL	M	A	N	S
	O	N	O	O
	S	Y	N	M
	T		E	E

Or, make up your own acronym that works for you.

STUDENT PRACTICE

DIRECTIONS: Choose the correct subject or verb for the following sentences.

1. None of the players (need/needs) any instruction on how to complete the play the coach called.

2. My (sister/sisters) talk constantly about their desire to start a new career.

3. The officers of the club (call/calls) the meeting to order by filing into the room.

4. No one (say/says) what he wants to say at the meeting for fear of being ridiculed.

5. After the race, the runners (begin/begins) to cool down by walking around the track.

6. The (boy/boys) throw snowballs at Jennie every time she tries to step out of the door.

7. Speaking quickly, Samuel (try/tries) to calm the fears of the parents whose children are missing.

8. Brandy and Jason (swim/swims) competitively and are ranked in the top ten in their state.

9. My dog (eat/eats) so quickly that I worry about her choking.

10. The (producer/producers) of the movie take all the credit for its success.

CONCEPT: SUBJECT/VERB AGREEMENT II

☞ **Subjects joined by *and* take a plural verb.**

> EXAMPLE: **Swimming** and **running are** two kinds of exercise I enjoy.

☞ **Singular subjects joined by *or* or *nor* take a singular verb.**

> EXAMPLE: In spite of their busy schedule, **Annie** or **Melody** always **checks** on their grandmother every day.

☞ **When a singular subject and a plural subject are joined by *or* or *nor*, the verb agrees with the subject nearer the verb.**

> EXAMPLE: Neither the secretaries nor the **principal knows** what happened to Joe's phone message.

☞ *Don't* (do not) and *doesn't* (does not) must agree with their subjects. With the subjects *I* and *you* and with plural subjects, use *don't*. With other subjects, use the singular *doesn't*.

> EXAMPLE: **You don't** want to attend the meeting?
> **I don't** have enough time to pick up my sister before I go to work.
> **Jim and Mary don't** enjoy babysitting their younger siblings.
>
> This **book doesn't** help with my research at all.
> **He doesn't** know what to study for the final because he has missed so many classes.

☞ **Collective nouns may be either singular or plural. Use a collective noun with a plural verb when it refers to the individual parts or members of a group acting separately. Use a collective noun with a singular verb when it refers to the group acting together as a unit.**

team	family	flock	group
class	herd	swarm	jury
army	fleet	faculty	committee

> EXAMPLE: The **herd** of horses **was** galloping across the plain.
> (The herd is acting as a group.)
>
> Our Armed Forces needs our support.
> (We are supporting each branch individually. If we support the Armed Forces as a group, *needs* would be changed to *need*.)

ENGLISH

▷ **A verb agrees with its subject, not its predicate nominative.**

    EXAMPLE: Hurt **feelings are** one problem that can't be ignored.
                            His biggest **challenge is** his mounting debts.

STUDENT PRACTICE
    DIRECTIONS: Circle the correct subject or verb in each of the following sentences.

1. Because of the potential for danger, my father (don't/doesn't) want my friends and me to drive from Oklahoma City to Los Angeles by ourselves.
2. Neither my friend's parents nor my mother (disagree/disagrees) with him, so it is becoming increasingly clear that the trip will not take place.
3. Skiing with the church or a family vacation (is/are) our other option.
4. The church's youth group (is/are) going to Colorado for a week.
5. My family (is/are) thinking of spending the day at Six Flags Over Texas in Arlington.
6. My (problem/problems) is my siblings.
7. I (don't/doesn't) enjoy a car trip with screaming three-year-old twins.
8. My parents and I (have/has) agreed that we will drive in the evening so the twins can sleep all the way to Texas.
9. Even though I had been planning the trip with my friends for months, my family (think/thinks) I will have a fabulous time at Six Flags with them.
10. The jury (is/are) still out on that question.

CONCEPT: SUBJECT/VERB AGREEMENT III

▷ **Words stating amount are usually singular unless the amount is thought of as individual pieces or parts.**

    ▷EXAMPLE: **Seventy-five dollars is** too much to pay for a hair cut.
                                Five days is the length of most schools' spring breaks.
                                Two thirds of the game **was** over before I even noticed the score.

                                Four days of my spring break **were** spent traveling.
                                Two thirds of the clothing **were** on sale.

▷ **The title of a work of art, literature, or music, even when plural in form, takes a singular verb.**

    EXAMPLE: *Fences*, a play by August Wilson, **is** about an African-American family living in Pittsburgh.
                              "Metaphors" **was** the first poem by Sylvia Plath I had ever read.

⇨ *Every* or *many* before a subject calls for a singular verb.

> EXAMPLE: **Every phone call** I get **interrupts** my work.
> **Many** a soldier in the war **has sacrificed** life and limb for victory.

⇨ A few nouns, although plural in form, take a singular verb. Names of certain diseases also end in s but are considered singular: *measles, mumps, scabies*. Words that end in –*ics* are usually paired with a singular verb.

> EXAMPLE: The **news** of casualties we suffered in the battle **was** hard to bear.
> **Measles is** a disease that in modern times is rarely life threatening.
> **Athletics is** a large, vital part of any high school's curriculum.

⇨ When the subject follows the verb as in sentences beginning with *there* and *here* and in questions, be certain that the verb agrees with the subject and not some other word in the sentence.

> EXAMPLE: There **are** no **questions** that are too silly to ask.
> There **is** no **question** that congress will pass the bill.
> Where **are** the **dogs** that Mr. Jackson purchased?

STYLE NOTE: In formal composition, avoid writing sentences that begin with *there is/are* or *it is*. Those words are considered expletives and are, therefore, not needed in a sentence.

INFORMAL: There are several reasons I need to go to the bank today.
BETTER: I need to go to the bank today for several reasons.

ACT TEST SAMPLE QUESTIONS

1. Working quickly in the heat, the workers in the <u>fields, throws</u> the completed bales of hay onto the flat bed trailer.

    A. NO CHANGE
    B. field, throws
    C. field throws
    D. fields throw

2. In large part due to the global community we live in, our <u>society has become</u> increasingly diverse.

    A. NO CHANGE
    B. society, has become
    C. society have become
    D. society is became

ENGLISH

3. Every person knocking on <u>the door want</u> Mr. Smith who is gone for the day.

   A. NO CHANGE
   B. the door wants
   C. the door, wants
   D. the doors want

4. A <u>collector of rare dolls have</u> multiple opportunities to meet with other collectors at conventions and toy fairs.

   A. NO CHANGE
   B. collector of rare doll have
   C. collectors of rare dolls have
   D. collector of rare dolls has

5. Delaying the trial will only postpone the verdict and upset the victims of the alleged crime. Most of the <u>attorneys believes that</u> the case should proceed immediately.

   A. NO CHANGE
   B. attorney believes that
   C. attorneys believe that
   D. attorneys will believe that

CONCEPT: PRONOUN USAGE

▷ **Personal pronouns pose a unique problem because of their shift in form depending on their use in a sentence. To understand and use pronouns correctly, you must know and be able to use the correct case forms.**

▷ **Personal pronouns have three case forms: nominative, objective and possessive.**

		Nominative Case	Objective Case	Possessive Case
Singular	First person	I	me	my, mine
	Second person	you	you	your, yours
	Third person	he, she, it	him, her, it	his, her, hers, its
Plural	First person	we	us	our, ours
	Second person	you	you	your, yours
	Third person	they	them	their, theirs

▷ **The pronouns *you* and *it* have the same form in both the nominative and objective case.**

NOMINATIVE CASE

▷ **The subject of a verb should be in the nominative case.**

   EXAMPLE: **He** and **she** will work the concession stand.
   I am excited about my upcoming vacation.
   They will meet us at the restaurant.

NOTE: If you are confused about which pronoun to use in a compound subject, try each pronoun individually with the verb.

> **He** will sing the National Anthem tonight.
> **They** will sing the National Anthem tonight.
> **He** and **they** will sing the National Anthem tonight.

➪ A predicate nominative should be in the nominative case. A predicate nominative is a noun or pronoun that follows a linking verb and renames or explains the subject of the sentence.

> The woman on the phone was **she**.
> (*She* is a predicate nominative that renames *woman*.)

EXAMPLE: I was afraid it was **she** on the telephone.
I am looking for Mr. Jeffers; are you **he**?

➪ Most likely, the examples for the predicate nominative sound odd to you. In casual conversation, many people use the objective case for predicate nominatives instead of the nominative. (I was afraid it was *her* on the telephone.) This may be acceptable in conversation, but you should use the correct form in writing and on the ACT.

OBJECTIVE CASE

➪ The direct object of a verb should be in the objective case. A direct object is a noun or pronoun that receives the action of the verb.

> Marlena presented her **report** to the class.
> (*Report* is the direct object of the verb *presented*.)

EXAMPLE: INCORRECT: Shannon paid Leland and **I** for the tickets.
BETTER: Shannon paid Leland and **me** for the tickets.

It wouldn't make sense to say *Shannon paid I for the tickets*, so it is incorrect to use *I* when paired with *Leland*.

NOTE: When the sentence is compound, remember to try the pronoun by itself to determine if it is in the correct form.

➪ The indirect object of the verb should be in the objective case. An indirect object is a word that tells *to whom* or *for whom* something is done.

> Beverly gave **Kristin** the money for the plane fare.
> (The indirect object *Kristin* tells to whom Beverly gave the money.)

EXAMPLE: Raoul handed **me** the assignment sheet.
           Ms. Arthur told **us** the secret to solving the puzzle.

➥ **The object of a preposition should be in the objective case. The object of a preposition is the noun or pronoun that ends a prepositional phrase.**

           The postman gave the package (to **me**).
           (The pronoun *me* is the object of the prepositional phrase *to me*.)

EXAMPLE: I wrote letters (to my parents and **her**).
           The pitcher threw the ball toward (Mason and **me**).

POSSESSIVE CASE

➥ **Pronouns that show ownership are in the possessive case. These possessive pronouns are divided into two categories: ones that you use before a noun and ones that you use alone.**

Use Before a Noun	Use Alone
my	mine
your	yours
his, her, its	his, hers, its
our	ours
yours	yours
their	theirs

EXAMPLE: The notebook is **mine**.
           The jet ski that is at the dock is **ours**.
           Are these **your** hunting boots?

STUDENT PRACTICE
      DIRECTIONS: In the space provided, write the correct pronoun(s) for the underlined portions of each sentence.

1. <u>Paul</u> prefers swimming to water skiing.

   _____

2. I purchased birthday presents for <u>Syndi and Charley</u>.

   _____

3. If you need to, you can use <u>my running shoes</u> for the race.

   _____

4. <u>Both Jasper and Brandon</u> want to meet us for lunch.

   _____

5. When are you planning to visit your parents?

   _____

6. My grandparents often eat dinner with my family and me.

   _____

7. The resident director for the homeless center is Ms. Cookson.

   _____

8. On your way to school, give Mr. Brownlee the cookies I made for him.

   _____

9. Afraid of my father's reaction, I carefully washed the mud from his new car.

   _____

10. Barbara and Jason's dog is a purebred Irish Wolfhound.

    _____

ACT TEST SAMPLE QUESTIONS

1. Which of they are ready to attend college?

   A. NO CHANGE
   B. of there are
   C. of them are
   D. of their are

2. I love the summer time, especially it's warm, sunny weather.

   A. NO CHANGE
   B. especially their warm
   C. especially my warm
   D. especially its warm

3. Linda gave I the reports for the committee meeting.

   A. NO CHANGE
   B. gave she the reports
   C. gave me the reports
   D. gave my the reports

ENGLISH

4. The chairman of the group <u>selected me for</u> the fundraising committee.

   A. NO CHANGE
   B. selected she for
   C. selected we for
   D. selected me, for

5. <u>They have decided</u> not to travel with a group to Europe; they prefer to go alone.

   A. NO CHANGE
   B. Them have decided
   C. Their have decided
   D. They're have decided

CONCEPT: PRONOUN AND ANTECEDENT AGREEMENT

➢ The word to which the pronoun refers is called its antecedent. In the following sentence, the noun *book* is the antecedent of the pronoun *it*.

   EXAMPLE: Janice handed the **book** to the librarian so that **it** could be replaced on the shelf.

➢ A pronoun agrees with its antecedent in number and gender. If the antecedent is singular, the pronoun should also be singular. The same theory applies to plural antecedents; they will take plural pronouns.

   EXAMPLE: The little **boy** is looking for **his** toy truck.
                    (Singular antecedent with a singular pronoun)
              All **students** will be picking up **their** diplomas on Monday.
                    (Plural antecedent with plural pronoun)

➢ The antecedent and the pronoun will not always appear in the same sentence. In the following sentences, the noun *Rosie* in the first sentence is the antecedent of the pronoun *she* in the second sentence.

   EXAMPLE: Brandon asked **Rosie** to go with him to the movies.
              She agreed, and they went last night.

➢ Some singular personal pronouns indicate a specific gender. Use *he, his* and *him* if the antecedent is masculine. Use *she, her* and *hers* if the antecedent is feminine. *It* and *its* are used if the antecedent is neither masculine nor feminine.

   EXAMPLE: **Bob** is proud of **his** new car. (masculine)
              Has **Laura** turned in **her** application? (feminine)
              The **tree** outside my window is loosing **its** leaves. (neither)

↪ Two or more antecedents joined by *and* are considered plural; two or more singular antecedents joined by *or* or *nor* are referred to by a singular pronoun.

>   EXAMPLE: **Juan and Julia** will present **their** project to the class. (plural)
>   Neither **Jonathon nor Raymond** left **his** phone number for Jamie. (singular)

↪ If one of the antecedents joined by *or* or *nor* is singular and one is plural, the pronoun should agree with the nearer antecedent. If one of the antecedents is masculine and one feminine, the pronouns must also be masculine and feminine.

>   EXAMPLE: **Neither** Mary **nor her friends** want to give up **their** chance to win the tournament.
>   Will **Kelby or Leanne** type **his or her** assignment before turning it in?

STUDENT PRACTICE
DIRECTIONS: In the space provided write a pronoun that agrees with its antecedent. Then underline the antecedent for each pronoun.

1. My daughter demands my undivided attention when _____ is telling me about her day.
2. When the boys arrived at the concert, _____ were amazed to see the number of people who were trying to buy tickets at the last minute.
3. Both Jessica and Raelynn have decided to color _____ hair red this weekend.
4. The speaker introduced herself to the waiting audience. _____ was there to talk about the death of her sister who was killed by a drunk driver.
5. After my parents picked me up at school, _____ took me to Smith Automotive to choose a car for my birthday.
6. One thing I like about AnnMarie is that _____ is always kind to other people, no matter what they say to her.
7. Oklahomans proved _____ ability to overcome adversity during the Oklahoma City bombing.
8. Knowing that I have always wanted to travel to Europe, my fiancée arranged for the two of _____ to go to Paris for our honeymoon.
9. My brother or my sister will certainly donate _____ time to our school project.
10. Neither my aunt nor my sister considers _____ cooking skills exceptional.

ENGLISH

ACT TEST SAMPLE QUESTIONS

1. In many large urban residential areas, neighbors have formed neighborhood coalitions in order to protect his property, socialize and maintain the appearance and quality of life on their streets.

    A. NO CHANGE
    B. protect their property
    C. protect her property
    D. protect my property

2. Jared decided to buy three new shirts. He needed it to wear for work.

    A. NO CHANGE
    B. needed them to
    C. needed it; to
    D. needed its to

3. Carlos and Jenni told the mayor that their would be delighted to serve on his task force.

    A. NO CHANGE
    B. that he and she would
    C. that they would
    D. that he would

4. Neither the young lady in the group nor the mothers thought she should attend every meeting.

    A. NO CHANGE
    B. thought he should
    C. thought she and they should
    D. thought they should

CONCEPT: PRONOUNS (WHO AND WHOM)

↪ The pronoun *who* also has different forms in the nominative and objective cases. *Who (whoever)* is the nominative form; *whom (whomever)* is the objective form.

↪ *Who* and *whom* appear most often in subordinate adjective or noun clauses. To choose the correct form, you must identify the use of the pronoun in the clause. If it is the subject or the predicate nominative of the clause, use *who (whoever)*; if it is the direct object or the object of a preposition, use *whom (whomever)*.

> EXAMPLE: Mr. Tilley knows **who hit the homerun** because he keeps track of the statistics.
> (Use *who* because it is the subject of the underlined clause.)
>
> My older brother, to **whom I sent the card**, has a birthday on Friday.
> (Use *whom* because it is the object of the preposition *to*.)

NOTE: An easy way to determine if a pronoun is correct is to replace *who* with *he* and *whom* with *him*. If the sentence sounds correct, you have chosen the correct pronoun. At times it will be easier to choose the pronoun if you reverse the order of the clause (put it in subject-verb order).

> **EXAMPLE:** I know whom you invited.
> Say: you invited whom. When you reverse the order, it is clear that the pronoun is the direct object of the clause; therefore, *whom* is the correct pronoun.

STUDENT PRACTICE
DIRECTIONS: Write *who* or *whom* in each of the following blanks, as appropriate.

1. Louis Zamporini is a man _____ I respect.
2. It was King Henry VIII _____ had six wives.
3. I talked with Teresa _____ was trying to paint the walls of her new living room.
4. There is the new student _____ you were asking about.
5. For _____ did Molly vote?
6. My parents wonder _____ my new boyfriend is.
7. _____ will give the graduation speech on Friday evening?
8. Our new neighbor, _____ we met yesterday morning, works at Conoco.
9. With _____ are you rooming with for your freshman year at college?
10. The president of the club is not _____ you think it is.

ACT TEST SAMPLE QUESTIONS

1. Any businessman today <u>which</u> does not understand the tax law will quickly find himself in distress.

    A. NO CHANGE
    B. who
    C. whom
    D. whose

2. Knowing for <u>who</u> the gift is intended makes shopping much easier.

    A. NO CHANGE
    B. whom
    C. that
    D. him

ENGLISH

3. <u>Whoever wishes</u> to attend the workshop may; we have several spots still open.

    A. NO CHANGE
    B. Whomever wishes
    C. Whoever wish
    D. Who wishes

4. My grandfather always said that <u>those they work</u> diligently and efficiently will reap the rewards.

    A. NO CHANGE
    B. those whom work
    C. those who work
    D. those who works

5. The <u>manager who I</u> spoke to assured me that his company was hiring immediately.

    A. NO CHANGE
    B. manager whose I
    C. managers whom I
    D. manager whom I

CONCEPT: COMMA USAGE I

☞ **Set off independent clauses in a compound sentence when they are joined by a coordinating conjunction (p. 18,77).**

    EXAMPLES: The patrol planes were delayed by a heavy rain**,** **but** they succeeded in making safe landings on the carrier deck.

    Tom has dedicated himself to a strict regimen of healthy diet, weight training, and aerobic workouts**,** **and** the hard work has paid off with amazing results.

(The independent clauses are separated by a comma and a coordinating conjunction.)

☞ **Do not use a comma to separate unequal grammatical constructions.**

    EXAMPLE:

        INCORRECT: I stayed up late last night, because I wanted to see the end of the scary movie. (This sentence contains an independent clause followed by a subordinate clause.)

        BETTER: I stayed up late last night because I wanted to see the end of the scary movie.

Note: The compound sentence may be correctly punctuated one of two ways: a comma and a coordinating conjunction or a semicolon if the conjunction is omitted.

STUDENT PRACTICE
DIRECTIONS: Insert commas as needed.

1. Joe decided not to run for the morning was icy cold.

2. I ran over some broken glass in the school parking lot so I had to change the flat before work.

3. My friend loves to eat spaghetti so I bought him a pasta maker for his birthday.

4. I desperately needed to finish my five-paragraph research paper yet I couldn't make myself stay awake.

5. Two top athletes were given highest recognition at the banquet for each had demonstrated excellence in sportsmanship and skill.

6. Monique may disagree strongly with the new student council guidelines for skirt length for she likes to wear very short skirts.

7. Jack and Jill went up the hill to fetch a pail of water but Jack refused to carry the bucket back down the hill for fear of falling.

8. Did you want to fight the crowds and heat to attend the U.S. Open or did you want to stay and watch in the comfort of your own home?

9. John will explain to the policeman why he was speeding down the dirt road with incriminating evidence in the back of his pickup or he will face the consequences of a fine and the wrath of his parents.

10. Debbie recently purchased a darling new schnauzer puppy and she will name him *Aspen* after her home in Colorado.

ACT TEST SAMPLE QUESTIONS

1. Sue was proud of the accomplishments of her three-year old daughter and she frequently, I'm ashamed to say, monopolized conversations with glowing re-enactment of her feats.

   A. NO CHANGE
   B. daughter, and she frequently, I'm
   C. daughter, however, she frequently, I'm
   D. daughter, and frequently I'm

2. Adding more fuel to the gas tank was, however, effective, and soon we were on our way again.

   A. NO CHANGE
   B. was, however; effective
   C. was however, effective,
   D. was however effectively

3. Patients are the real pioneers when they receive experimental treatment for formerly untreatable diseases so it is ironic that their names are less well known than the doctor's.

   A. NO CHANGE
   B. diseases; on the other hand
   C. diseases, in other words,
   D. diseases, so

4. I had met a new friend on the trip, and she had offered to take me on a side trip to places tourists rarely get to visit.

   A. NO CHANGE
   B. trip and
   C. trip
   D. trip,

5. The golf video game was difficult for Tiger for he discovered no correlation between skill on the course and skill with the mouse.

   A. NO CHANGE
   B. Tiger; irregardless,
   C. Tiger, for,
   D. Tiger, for

CONCEPT: COMMA USAGE II

↬ **Set off words, phrases, and clauses that are not needed (nonessential). Use commas around nonessential, transitional, or contrasting information.**

EXAMPLES:

Intense preparation, then, is known to produce higher test scores. (transitional)

Robert Frost, a Pulitzer Prize winner, is known for his poem "Birches." (nonessential)

His research paper analyzed the controversy surrounding Pete Rose, who he feels should be selected to the Baseball Hall of Fame. (nonessential)

Barbara Kingsolver, not Toni Morrison, is my favorite author. (contrasting)

Punctuation note: Do not use commas with correlative conjunctions (p. 77). Example: Liz ate not only mangos but also papayas.

STUDENT PRACTICE
DIRECTIONS: Insert commas as needed.

1. I did mention that I keyed your new car on the way out of the gymnasium didn't I?

2. Matt LeBlanc who played Joey on <u>Friends</u> is still one of my favorite comedians.

3. The <u>Iliad</u> and the <u>Odyssey</u> epic poems attributed to the poet Homer provide insight into the lives of the ancient Greeks not actual history.

4. Astronomers have been fascinated by Saturn the ringed planet.

5. His excellent work in accelerated classes moreover has enabled him to improve his class rank.

6. The poet Homer not the cartoon character Homer Simpson provides insight into the lives of the ancient Greeks.

7. Now is the time my fellow citizens to step up and do what is right for the cause.

8. The class lecture concerned Poe's definition of poetry the rhythmical creation of beauty.

9. The book that I didn't read was on the test, and <u>Bean Trees</u> which I did read was not.

10. Karen Carpenter who many teenagers today would not recognize was one of the first public figures known to have died from anorexia.

ENGLISH

ACT TEST SAMPLE QUESTIONS

1. Every <u>fisherman I suppose</u> should have his own rod and reel and bait.

   A. NO CHANGE
   B. fisherman I suppose,
   C. fisherman, I suppose,
   D. fisherman; I suppose,

2. Some professional <u>athletes, disdainful</u> of drug tests, choose to risk their careers to improve their performance at the risk of their health and reputation.

   A. NO CHANGE
   B. athletes which are disdainful
   C. athletes disdain
   D. athletes, disdainful as to the existence

3. Most reptiles, <u>of course have</u> the uncanny ability to survive.

   A. NO CHANGE
   B. of course, have
   C. of course, thus
   D. of course, since have

4. The correct answers to the <u>test to my chagrin</u> were written on the blackboard at the back of the room.

   A. NO CHANGE
   B. test, to my chagrin
   C. test, to my chagrin and embarrassment
   D. test, to my chagrin,

5. I heard the debaters argue that <u>Ford, not Chevy,</u> made the best truck.

   A. NO CHANGE
   B. Ford, not Chevy
   C. Ford, not only Chevy,
   D. Ford; however, Chevy

CONCEPT: COMMA USAGE III

↪ **Use a comma after an introductory phrase, clause, and adverb. Short introductory prepositional phrases do not require commas unless needed for clarity.**

EXAMPLES: To be able to compete on the collegiate level, many high school athletes practice their sport all year.

If you are counting on a college scholarship, pay attention to your grades, class rank, community service, and standardized test scores.

Occasionally, the person actually responsible for the vandalism will be caught and will pay the damage.

STUDENT PRACTICE
DIRECTIONS: Insert commas as needed.

1. When I write I try to pay attention to unity support and coherence.

2. After having lived on the coast for several years I have a new appreciation for life in the Midwest.

3. Furthermore the information I gave you about computer programming may be obsolete by the time I install the new software.

4. With one hand on the steering wheel and the other on the radio dial Jane made me nervous as we drove through rush-hour traffic.

5. Walking on the course before golfers arrive I appreciate the tranquility and beauty of unspoiled solitude.

6. Because lightening can be very dangerous the golf professional sounds a siren to get everyone off the course in hazardous weather.

7. Swimming at a slow and steady pace Jocelyn slowly overtook her competitors in the triathlon.

8. Frantically Joseph waved at the oncoming traffic to get them to stop before the accident.

9. Shortly you will be asked to clear off your desk and put away your notes to prepare for the test.

10. Even after a grueling 5-set match professional tennis players have to face the media or risk a hefty fine.

ACT TEST SAMPLE QUESTIONS

1. John was concerned that the national test date was the morning after he had a football game. Nevertheless his preparation and confidence allowed him to significantly improve his score.

    A. NO CHANGE
    B. Nevertheless, his
    C. Nevertheless: his
    D. Nevertheless; his

ENGLISH 47

2. Once they have read the <u>study they</u> will no longer be able to say they didn't understand the implications of pollution.

    A. NO CHANGE
    B. study. They
    C. study, they
    D. study; they

3. Rather than spending a few minutes reviewing and preparing for a <u>quiz, amazingly,</u> some students will spend twice as much time and effort devising a method to cheat.

    A. NO CHANGE
    B. quiz amazingly,
    C. quiz; amazingly,
    D. quiz, amazing,

4. John learned after his interview that he was about to face the terrifying prospect of his first job of teaching kindergarten. <u>Then,</u> the teacher's nightmares would start.

    A. NO CHANGE
    B. To begin with,
    C. Once
    D. First of all

5. Surrounded by freshmen who came from all parts of the <u>country Sal</u> was looking forward to his new adventures at the university.

    A. NO CHANGE
    B. country, Sal
    C. country, however, Sal
    D. country, but Sal

CONCEPT: COMMA USAGE IV

Use a comma to separate items in a series.

EXAMPLES: I selected my Shih Tzu because of her color, her attentiveness and her disposition.

Sue was infatuated with the attractive, tall stranger.

Jill received the promotion because she is efficient, because she is punctual and because she is the most qualified for the job.

Note: Adjectives in a series (coordinate adjectives) that can be switched or are of equal rank should be separated by commas. Adjectives that cannot be reversed (cumulative adjectives) require no commas.

The ACT does not require a comma before the conjunction when separating items in a series.

No commas:
    Sid looked smart in his **red plaid** jacket.
    Sal performed **many successful** dives in the competition.

Commas:
    Visiting the bomb site was a **powerful, meaningful** experience.

STUDENT PRACTICE
    DIRECTIONS: Insert commas as needed.

1. A good fishing lure floats bobs and wiggles in the water.

2. Excited cheerful and boisterous children at playgrounds often pay little attention to their surroundings.

3. The president had the rare combination of power principle and commitment.

4. Joseppi could not decide which car to purchase which finance arrangement was the best or which dealer offered the best service.

5. What to wear to school what to eat for breakfast and who to call for a ride are daily questions Chelsea has to consider.

6. Percy gave a quick decisive answer to the professor's question.

7. Most visitors find the Holocaust Memorial to be a powerful memorable experience.

8. Most children like watermelon because it is cold sweet and juicy.

9. As a college-bound teenager I am faced with the issues of where I should go to school how much money it will take to get my degree and what my major area of study will be.

10. Walking along the rushing cascading stream I slipped and fell into the cold icy water.

ENGLISH

ACT TEST SAMPLE QUESTIONS

1. The convention consisted of <u>many successful motivational</u> speakers in one huge gathering.

    A. NO CHANGE
    B. many, successful, motivational
    C. many; successful motivational
    D. many successful, motivational,

2. Below the <u>rushing, churning waters,</u> marine life barely notices the raging storm on the surface.

    A. NO CHANGE
    B. rushing, churning:
    C. rushing, churning, waters
    D. waters which are rushing and churning

3. The loan shark said he was not willing to postpone payment of the debt for a month, a week, <u>a day or even an hour.</u>

    A. NO CHANGE
    B. a 24-hour day or even an hour.
    C. a day; or even an hour.
    D. a day, or hourly.

4. April 19, 1995, was a <u>disastrous tragic</u> day for the people of Oklahoma.

    A. NO CHANGE
    B. disastrous; tragic
    C. disastrous, and also tragic
    D. tragic

5. Common stereotypes include <u>old women</u> drivers and wild, crazy teenagers.

    A. NO CHANGE
    B. old, women
    C. old, elderly
    D. old, women,

CONCEPT: SEMICOLON USE

➪ Use a semicolon to join independent clauses in a compound sentence without a coordinating conjunction. For a list of coordinating conjunctions, see p. 77.

    EXAMPLE: After winter break, John was happy to see Mary; Mary, who had met several interesting skiers, was not so happy to see John.

↪ **Use a semicolon to join two independent clauses joined with a conjunctive adverb. For a list of conjunctive adverbs, see p. 77.**

   EXAMPLE: Seats in the front row are expensive**;** however, balcony seats usually cost much less.

↪ **Use a semicolon to join two independent clauses combined with a transitional expression. For a list of transitions, see p. 82.**

   EXAMPLE: Jill would be thrilled to shoot two over par on the front nine of the golf tournament**;** on the other hand, Rickie Fowler would not.

NOTE: Use a comma after the conjunctive adverb and the transitional expression that joins two independent clauses.

EXAMPLE: The war may be raging; however, the games will continue.

↪ **Use a semicolon to join independent clauses or items in a series that contain commas.**

   EXAMPLE: The nominees for Sportsman of the Year did not include John Daly, professional golfer**;** Dennis Rodman, ex-professional basketball player**;** or John McEnroe, retired professional tennis player.

NOTE: Do not use a semicolon between an independent clause and a dependent clause or phrase. (This is a trick to test your knowledge of clauses and phrases.) They are of unequal grammatical rank. The following sentence shows the INCORRECT way to use a semicolon.

INCORRECT: This shirt is really too tight; although I can still wear it.

STUDENT PRACTICE
   DIRECTIONS: Insert semicolons and commas into the following sentences.

1. In her research paper on high school sports Mechelle cited Elliot Eisner a leading educational researcher Bobby Knight a notoriously aggressive coach and David Ledbetter a golf instructor who works on the mental aspects of the game.

2. Oddly enough Dennis subscribes to <u>Prevention</u> a magazine about health <u>Seventeen</u> a trendy magazine for fashion-conscious teenagers and <u>Sports Illustrated</u> a sports magazine with great photographs.

3. San Bernardino is unique among American cities indeed it is the site of a terrible terrorist act against Americans.

4. Politicians may initially refrain from negative campaigning however personal attacks seem to become more frequent as the election draws near.

5. Watching college basketball football and other sports on television renting action-packed suspenseful movies and eating junk food like chips dip buttered popcorn chocolate candy bars and brownies are my favorite weekend activities.

6. The Best Picture award went to Casablanca in 1943 however none of its legendary stars received any personal awards.

7. The De La Salle High School football team has a long history of excellence it will probably contend for the high school state title again this year.

8. In the playoffs the outstanding pitcher threw his fast ball curve ball and slider moreover he threw them with more power and finesse than ever before.

9. Jerome brought leftovers from last night's steak dinner for his school lunch he had to eat it with his fingers because he couldn't cut it with the plastic knives in the cafeteria.

10. Joan was excited about her improved ACT test score indeed her confidence grew on every test she took thereafter.

ACT TEST SAMPLE QUESTIONS

1. John's driving had endangered <u>others; the police</u> arrived to impound his car.

    A. NO CHANGE
    B. others, the police
    C. others; however, the police
    D. others, on the other hand, the police

2. <u>Kiko, however</u> reached his destination way before the others.

    A. NO CHANGE
    B. Kiko, however,
    C. Kiko: however,
    D. Kiko, moreover

3. The accused man presented his <u>evidence;</u> an affidavit declaring his presence 10 miles from the scene of the crime.

    A. NO CHANGE
    B. evidence; however,
    C. evidence
    D. evidence—

4. Annie filled her office with the latest technology—miniature fax machines, video phones and a scanner.

    A. NO CHANGE
    B. technology;
    C. technology; its
    D. technology—you now have

5. I have worked on this project for hours; consequently, I am totally exhausted.

    A. NO CHANGE
    B. hours, however,
    C. hours,
    D. hours, but,

CONCEPT: COLON USE I

⇨ Use a colon to set off a summary sentence. A summary sentence amplifies, restates, explains or emphasizes the meaning of the previous sentence.

EXAMPLE: His explanation for not having his homework was believable: He had had his car towed away with his schoolwork in the back seat.

 **Style note:** Style manuals differ on capitalization of the summary sentence. Most prefer capitalization; however, capitalization will not be used in the practice so as not to tip off the answers.

STUDENT PRACTICE
DIRECTIONS: Insert colons as needed.

1. Her excuse for missing curfew was plausible the 15-car pile up on the interstate took two hours to clear.

2. The doctor said I had nothing wrong with me at all the aches were simply growing pains.

3. The Chris Brown concert was laced with violence fourteen people were arrested and dozens were injured.

4. John's difficult academic load in his last semester had an unexpected reward he enjoyed his summer break all the more.

5. Sue has eclectic taste in music she likes Casting Crowns, Adele and Brad Paisley.

6. She found the main character in the movie to be much like her boyfriend he was handsome, charming and incredibly arrogant.

7. Langston Hughes was a great poet of the Harlem Renaissance: two well-known poems are "Homecoming" and "Dream Deferred."

8. Some critics argue that part-time work helps teens they learn discipline and respect for the value of a dollar.

9. Many educators vehemently oppose businesses who allow teens to work more than twenty hours per week they decry the extra stress and time pressures.

10. Studies have shown the benefits of a summer reading program students improve their reading scores and perform better academically.

ACT TEST SAMPLE QUESTIONS

1. Joe's metamorphosis happened so <u>suddenly; one day</u> he was a polite responsible young man, and the next he was a rude disrespectful teenager.

    A. NO CHANGE
    B. sudden: one day
    C. suddenly, because
    D. suddenly: one day

2. Not all visitors to the summer camp have been <u>welcome,</u> two years ago a grizzly bear had made his way to the camp and ransacked the tent where our food was stored.

    A. NO CHANGE
    B. welcome:
    C. welcome; since
    D. welcome, although

3. The type of pepper used in Debbie's salsa is <u>jalapeno, it's</u> very hot.

    A. NO CHANGE
    B. jalapeno; its
    C. jalapeno, its
    D. jalapeno: it's

4. Jack had decided to attend Harvard, Jill favored Yale.

   A. NO CHANGE
   B. Harvard:
   C. Harvard;
   D. Harvard; consequently

5. Jessie is a beautiful, playful puppy: however, she is no match for my Coco.

   A. NO CHANGE
   B. puppy, in addition,
   C. puppy; however,
   D. puppy—as a result

CONCEPT: COLON USE II

Use a colon to introduce a list following a complete thought (independent clause) or a formal or lengthy quote or appositive. Use a colon after *the following items*, *as follows* or *the following*.

> EXAMPLE: I have three reasons for being angry: my coach, my teacher and my parents.
>
> He ended his patriotic speech by quoting John F. Kennedy: "Ask not what your country can do for you--ask what you can do for your country."
>
> I only have one thing to say about the Most Valuable Player of the 2014 NBA playoffs: Kawhi Leonard.
>
> Among the after-school jobs some students hold are the following: baby sitter, waiter or waitress and salesperson.

Note: Do not use an unnecessary colon between a verb and its complement or object, between a preposition and its object or after words like *such as*, *including*, or *especially*. In other words, use a colon after a complete thought.

INCORRECT: The winners were: Joan, Betty, and Sue.
She likes spicy foods: like chili, salsa and fried peppers.

STUDENT PRACTICE
   DIRECTIONS: Insert colons as needed. Think about the rule as you add the punctuation.

1. My summer plans include the following rest, relaxation and recreation.

2. The school policy for appropriate dance behavior included the following regulation no freak dancing.

3. Among the most scantily clad at the awards ceremony were several gorgeous actresses Jennifer Lopez, Wynona Ryder and Charlize Theron.

4. I find several restaurant cleanup chores to be absolutely the most repugnant brushing the toilet, scrubbing the floors, scouring the sinks.

5. Teenagers cite the following as concerns about school demanding teachers and administrators, too much homework, difficult tests.

6. The politician confidently began his speech "The party in power has betrayed us. It has not only failed to keep its election promise but has sold out to the moneyed powers."

7. I finally decided on a career paleontology.

8. "I had three chairs in my house one for solitude, two for friendship, three for society." -- Thoreau

9. The following students should report immediately to the main office Michaela Green, Kim Evans, Heather Young.

10. My favorite Robert Frost poem is "Stopping By Woods on a Snowy Evening"; my favorite passage goes as follows "The woods are lovely, dark and deep./ But I have promises to keep,/ And miles to go before I sleep,/ And miles to go before I sleep."

ACT TEST SAMPLE QUESTIONS

1. One night we noticed the graffiti with the following message, "Be cool; stay in school."

    A. NO CHANGE
    B. the following message: "Be cool
    C. the following message, be cool
    D. the message that followed, "be cool

2. Many country singers are crossover artists, especially: Taylor Swift, Carrie Underwood, and Shania Twain.

    A. NO CHANGE
    B. especially
    C. however,
    D. in other words

3. My brother always <u>said, using</u> bad language was a sign of a weak vocabulary.

   A. NO CHANGE
   B. said: using
   C. said using
   D. said, "Using

4. We attended the <u>concert, and—lucky</u> for me—I was selected to receive backstage passes.

   A. NO CHANGE
   B. concert and—lucky
   C. concert: lucky
   D. concert; however,

5. Many possible hypotheses were offered for the student's strange <u>behavior; he</u> had too much to drink, he had not enough sleep and he was just plain weird.

   A. NO CHANGE
   B. behavior; such as
   C. behavior; consequently, he
   D. behavior: he

CONCEPT: USING THE DASH

↪ **Use a dash or a pair of dashes to show an abrupt change of thought or dramatic effect or to set off an introductory list or series.**

> EXAMPLES: The dilapidated truck shook and rumbled its way slowly up the hill—it must have been at least thirty years old.
>
> It was a desperate gamble—she stood little chance at winning—but she risked it anyway.
>
> Suave, debonair, athletic, irreverent—Jose is all of these.

 STYLE NOTE: Dashes are considered "strong commas." Use them sparingly and only when the context calls for special drama or for obvious interruption of thought.

STUDENT PRACTICE
   DIRECTIONS: Insert dashes into the following sentences as needed.
1. Last Saturday night at the rave have you ever seen so much skin? I danced all evening long.

2. The May 3rd, 1999 Oklahoma tornado struck early in the evening to this day the survivors gasp as they retell the story.

3. The excessive slaughter in this war was caused by an enhancement of what we learned in the Civil War the increased lethal power of explosives.

4. The cause of her debilitating illness a strange virus affecting her nervous system remains undiagnosed by her doctors.

5. Some of my friends for example Keith Lakesta and Sorrell waste too much time watching TV.

6. Modesty, honesty, loyalty, bravery, sincerity these are the traits I admire in my heroes.

7. Even his Superbowl MVP trophy his most prized possession was lost in the fire.

8. Here's how to learn study.

9. Documentary novels two of the more successful are *An American Tragedy* and *In Cold Blood* are fictionalized accounts of events based upon newspaper reports.

10. Some boisterous pranks cow tipping, for example don't seem much fun to me.

ACT TEST SAMPLE QUESTIONS

1. The professional athlete—already infamous for his off-court <u>antics; made millions</u> from his best selling novel.

    A. NO CHANGE
    B. antics who made millions
    C. antics—made millions
    D. antics which made him notorious—made millions

2. Leopard prints, polka dots, fishnet <u>hose</u> some fashion trends are destined to be repeated.

    A. NO CHANGE
    B. hose are
    C. hose—
    D. hose; consequently,

3. My brother Jim—what was he <u>thinking:</u> abruptly questioned the policeman as to how fast he had been driving before he pulled Jim over.

    A. NO CHANGE
    B. thinking?—
    C. thinking?;
    D. thinking,

4. After years of study and research, Professor Smart at last arrived at one common denominator for why many bright students fail—apathy.

   A. NO CHANGE
   B. fail;
   C. fail; its
   D. fail

5. Heather, evergreen, mauve—these are the colors I chose to decorate my bedroom.

   A. NO CHANGE
   B. mauve;
   C. mauve,
   D. mauve, however,

CONCEPT: USING APOSTROPHES

 Use an apostrophe to show possession and mark omissions in contractions.

Possessives:

1. Add an apostrophe and *s* to singular nouns and plural nouns that do not end in *s*.

   Jill's skirt
   Hemingway's novels
   women's clothes

2. Add only an apostrophe to a plural noun that ends in *s*.

   kids' trophies
   students' homework

3. Make both nouns possessive to signal individual possession; make only the final noun possessive to show joint possession.

   Butch's and Ben's coats were both dirty.   Luann and Mia's joint project won.
         (individual possession)   (joint possession)

Contractions:

1. Add an apostrophe to indicate letters omitted in contractions.

   don't   they'll   should've

 Style note: Contractions should be avoided in academic writing. Use of contractions in an ACT test indicates a lower level of sophistication of the selection.

STUDENT PRACTICE
DIRECTIONS: Write the contraction or possessive for these words.

1. she would _____

2. an album of Elvis Presley _____

3. a paper co-written by Garth and Ted _____

4. the friends of Mary and Joe _____

5. the labors of Hercules _____

6. tickets of Hoss and Pete _____

7. books belonging to anyone _____

8. the talking in class of Karlos _____

9. the writing of Shakespeare _____

10. will not _____

11. has not _____

12. have not _____

13. it is _____

ACT TEST SAMPLE QUESTIONS

1. A shocked, glazed look came over the <u>people's</u> faces at the concert last night.

    A. NO CHANGE
    B. peoples
    C. peoples'
    D. people

2. The high winds created havoc with the thatched roofs of the <u>villagers' houses.</u>

    A. NO CHANGE
    B. villagers house's.
    C. villagers' houses'.
    D. villagers houses.

3. Thunderstorms were present in the area on <u>Mark's daily</u> departure for his summer vacation.

   A. NO CHANGE
   B. the day of Marks
   C. the day of Mark's
   D. their

4. Joah listened to the outline of <u>Foster's principals</u> presented by the professor.

   A. NO CHANGE
   B. Fosters principles:
   C. Fosters' principles:
   D. Foster's principals in that they were

5. <u>Victorian writers</u> had a brief but powerful contribution to classical literature.

   A. NO CHANGE
   B. Victorians writer's
   C. Victorian's writers
   D. Victorian writer's

CONCEPT: DANGLING AND MISPLACED MODIFIERS

Dangling modifiers are modifiers that either appear to modify the wrong word or modify a word that is not included in the sentence. Dangling modifiers can be phrases, clauses or single words.

Dangling: **Walking down the street**, the wind blew me over.
(The wind is not walking down the street.)

Correct: **Walking down the street**, I was blown over by the wind.
(The phrase now correctly modifies I.)

Dangling: Malinda heated up the bottle of milk **as he cried loudly in the other room**.
(The phrase doesn't modify anything in the sentence.)

Correct: Malinda heated up the bottle of milk for the baby **as he cried loudly in the other room.**
(Now the phrase correctly modifies baby.)

NOTE: To correct a dangling modifier, rearrange the words in the sentence or add words to make the meaning apparent and logical.

ENGLISH

👉 **Misplaced modifiers are modifiers that have been placed incorrectly; therefore, they appear to modify words that they should not. Place the modifying phrase, clause or word as close as possible to the word or words it modifies so that the meaning of the sentence is clear. Many times a misplaced modifier can make the structure of the sentence awkward. Try reading the sentence out loud to hear how it sounds. At times your ear will tell you that the sentence sounds incorrect.**

EXAMPLE:
Misplaced: Joshua **only** wanted a hamburger and milkshake.
(In this sentence, *only* modifies wanted. According to this sentence, Joshua only wanted a burger and shake. Perhaps he didn't intend to get them.)

Correct: Joshua wanted **only** a hamburger and milkshake.
(In this sentence, *only* modifies hamburger and milkshake. According to this sentence, a hamburger and milkshake were all he wanted.)

Misplaced: The teacher returned the essays to the students **marked with her comments.**
(The students are not marked with comments.)

Correct: The teacher returned the essays **marked with her comments** to the students.
(Now it is clear that the essays are marked, not the students.)

STUDENT PRACTICE
DIRECTIONS: Read the following sentences carefully. If the underlined phrase or clause appears to modify the correct word or words, write *correct* in the space provided. If the underlined phrase or clause does not modify the correct word or any word in the sentence, rewrite the sentence to correct the mistake.

1. On the top shelf of the bookcase, Louie could not find his dictionary anywhere.
   _____
   _____.

2. Jesse always wants to eat leftovers from my dinner under the table.
   _____
   _____.

3. As the man walked up the drive, Bowser started barking wildly.
   _____
   _____.

4. Aware that he couldn't jump the fence without hurting himself, Mark instead walked through the gate.
   _____
   _____.

5. The elderly neighbor gave my son a new coloring book that lives three doors down.
   _____
   _____.

6. Looking for the buried bone, the dog dug frantically in the flowerbed.
   _____
   _____.

7. My husband yelled at the dog who was angry that the flowers had been ruined.
   _____
   _____.

8. Licking quickly, the ice cream cone dripped on the sidewalk.
   _____
   _____.

9. Having been in Europe for two months, home looked very inviting.
   _____
   _____.

10. Hearing the children coming up the sidewalk, the Christmas presents were hurriedly stuffed into the closet.
    _____
    _____.

ACT TEST SAMPLE QUESTIONS

1. Winning the final game of the tournament was amazing completely after working so diligently all year long.

   A. NO CHANGE
   B. completely amazing after
   C. amazing, completely after
   D. amazing after completely

2. Working frantically, the gifts were wrapped before the birthday girl arrived.

   A. NO CHANGE
   B. The gifts, working frantically were wrapped
   C. Working frantically, I wrapped the gifts
   D. The gifts were working frantically and wrapped

3. Only I was another statistic; evidently, most small businesses fail within the first year.

   A. NO CHANGE
   B. place *only* before *fail*
   C. place *only* after *year*
   D. place *only* after *was*

4. The giggling children <u>floating in the air</u> swatted at the soap bubbles.

   A. NO CHANGE
   B. place *floating in the air* after *bubbles*
   C. place *floating in the air* before *giggling*
   D. place *floating in the air* at the beginning of the sentence

5. <u>Sweating profusely</u>, Ben carefully colored in the bubble sheet for the test.

   A. NO CHANGE
   B. place *sweating profusely* after *sheet*
   C. place *sweating profusely* after *colored*
   D. place *sweating profusely* before *bubble*

CONCEPT: PARALLEL STRUCTURE

⇨ Use the same grammatical structure for two or more similar ideas.

EXAMPLES:

INCORRECT: The students enjoyed **listening to Mozart, viewing the artwork, and to read**.

BETTER: The students enjoyed **listening to Mozart, viewing the artwork, and reading Shakespeare**.

CORRECT:
The teacher said that I should **write more** and **talk less**.

After you finish your schoolwork, you can **drive along the riverfront, check out the jet skis**, and **explore the latest beachwear**.

ACT TEST SAMPLE QUESTIONS

1. History has proven that large forces can be defeated by smaller forces with determination, superior strategy and <u>with a fighting spirit.</u>

   A. NO CHANGE
   B. a fighting spirit.
   C. however, a fighting spirit.
   D. thus, a fighting spirit.

2. Many Americans risk working for oil companies in the Middle East for the lifestyle and because they like the money.

   A. NO CHANGE
   B. lifestyle; and they like
   C. lifestyle, however, they like
   D. lifestyle and

3. Unless the city leaders invest money in the west side of town, it will become dangerous, dilapidated and people won't want to live there.

   A. NO CHANGE
   B. dilapidated, and, consequently, people won't want to live there.
   C. dilapidated, and dangerously run down.
   D. dilapidated and unlivable.

4. Remembering the accident, he recalled the screech of tires, the clash of metal and smelling gasoline.

   A. NO CHANGE
   B. the fact that you could smell gasoline.
   C. smelling, gasoline.
   D. the smell of gasoline.

5. Thinking logically, organizing ideas coherently and clear expression are the bases of effective writing.

   A. NO CHANGE
   B. and clearly expression
   C. and expressing ideas clearly
   D. and writing clear expressions

CONCEPT: RHETORICAL SKILLS
CONTENT DISCUSSION

Unity--Some ACT questions will ask about unity. To answer unity questions correctly, it is important to consider the main idea of the passage and ask yourself if the sentences or ideas the question asks you to consider are consistent with the purpose of the passage. The choices in the question will contain ideas that are irrelevant to the main idea of the passage.

Style and Tone--Some ACT questions ask that you determine the appropriate level of language to use. For example a passage might begin in a very casual, conversational manner. A shift to a highly sophisticated or highly technical word choice would not be appropriate for the previously established style of the passage. The word choice and style of a passage should be consistent. Also, some passages have a predominant feeling that the author is trying to convey. This predominant feeling is called the tone of the piece. You may need to identify the tone to answer the question correctly. Again, analyze the word choice, descriptive details and the level of language to answer.

Coherence--Some ACT questions ask you to judge the manner a passage flows from one idea to the next. A common way coherence is tested is by asking you to choose the best transitional devices. (In choosing the correct transition, be sure to analyze the relationship the author is trying to establish between ideas). Transitional expressions may indicate additional, contrasting or increasingly important information will be provided. Transitions are also needed to show chronology of events, especially in a narrative. An additional way to maintain coherence is to eliminate any redundancy. The ACT wants you to choose the answer that is both clear and concise. "Keep it simple" is a good rule to remember when analyzing choices. Eliminate any choices which are needlessly wordy, ambiguous or redundant.

Support--Some ACT questions ask you to evaluate the effect of adding, deleting or revising support information. These questions usually occur at the end of a passage. Reread the section of the passage with the underlined part, substituting the suggested choices. Then determine which choice provides information that is most relevant and specific to the point being made.

TRANSITIONS

Transitions are words or phrases that connect ideas. Think of transitions as bridges between one point or idea and another. They help your reader "cross over" from one point to your next thought. Without these bridges, your writing can be confusing and unstructured.

Writers have a variety of transitions to choose from, and each of them provides a specific meaning or purpose. Look at page 82 for a list of common words and phrases; familiarize yourself with these common transitional expressions and the meaning they convey. When writing, you should choose your transitions carefully to give the exact meaning you intend. For example, you wouldn't use the transition *however* to link two similar ideas because *however* signals a contradiction. A better transition to use would be *in the same way* because this transitional phrase clearly shows the relationship you are trying to convey.

As a reader, you should look for the transitional phrases in the writing. These will help you be aware of the writer's intent and any shift in attitude. These shifts, moving from one idea, attitude, type of language or purpose to another, can be very significant in understanding the meaning of the writing. Readers who miss the shifts very often miss the point of the writing.

The English section of the ACT will test you on your knowledge of how transitions should be used. The most common question on the test concerns the choice of transitions. Be sure to read carefully before and after the passage that is underlined to make sure you understand what the writer is attempting to convey.

STUDENT PRACTICE
DIRECTIONS: Provide an appropriate transition for each of the following blanks.

Watching the sinister Badley Mansion from the safety of the dirt road which curved in front of it, Michael and James were determined that this night would be the night they stayed in the haunted house until dawn. They had tried on three previous occasions, but had not yet been successful. This time, _____, they had come prepared. _____, they had carefully considered the equipment they would need: sleeping bags, water, food, cell phones and, _____, flashlights and extra batteries. They had _____ brought a camera and several rolls of film in order to document their stay. _____, they had researched the history of the Badley family so they would be prepared for any ghosts or haunts that still resided in the mansion. _____, they had let their parents know exactly where they would be and had charged the batteries of their cell phones just in case they needed help. Taking a deep breath, Michael and James began the long, lonely walk to the front door. _____ their fears, they were going to make it. They believed that until the front door swung open and an unseen, menacing voice whispered, "Welcome to my home." _____, the boys never made it up the sidewalk or into the house. They were too busy racing for the car, frantically dialing their cell phones.

EXTENDED PRACTICE
DIRECTIONS: The following paragraph contains several underlined transitions that are used incorrectly. Correct the mistakes by marking through the incorrect transition and writing a better one above it.

In the play *Antigone*, the pride of the main characters, Creon and Antigone, serves as the source of the main conflict while also giving meaning to the play. Each character believes in a different set of ethical standards, and the choices made <u>meanwhile</u> of these standards contribute to the conflict. Creon's decision to have his law preside over the laws of the gods reveals his pride. <u>Nevertheless</u>, Antigone's decision to bury her brother, Polyneices, according to her own personal ethics reflects a comparable stubbornness. <u>On the other hand</u>, the meaning of the work lies at the heart of this conflict. Stubbornness and the inability to consider other's motives bring about tragic consequences to the principle characters and their loved ones. Consequently, the conflict reveals the true meaning of the play: Pride without restraint produces disastrous results. <u>However</u>, both Antigone and Creon are punished for their arrogance by the loss of their families and, in Antigone's case, her life.

COHERENCE
STUDENT PRACTICE
PARAGRAPH A
DIRECTIONS: Unscramble the following sentences to form a coherent paragraph. First, locate the main idea and then use transitions and repetition of ideas to determine the correct order for the paragraph. Write the sentence number from the left by the appropriate order in the paragraph. For example, place a *4* by *1st* if sentence 4 should be the 1st sentence of the paragraph.

1. After a period of time, amethysts start to form in these holes.   1st _____

2. An amethyst is a member of the quartz rock family.   2nd _____

3. It is the most valuable of the quartz gemstones.   3rd _____

4. Next, these dissolved gasses in the air get trapped in rocks.   4th _____

5. Soon these air bubbles of gasses then form holes and crevices in the rock.   5th _____

6. The result is a coarse-grained amethyst stone.   6th _____

7. Their formation begins after volcanoes erupt, and all of the gasses are in the air.   7th _____

8. Then the gasses become air bubbles in the rocks.   8th _____

STUDENT PRACTICE: UNITY
PARAGRAPH B
DIRECTIONS: Underline the two sentences that do not belong in this paragraph.

Amethysts are interesting gems. The color of amethysts ranges from red-purple to blue-violet and from pale lilac to a purplish-pink. The color comes from impurities of iron and manganese in the stone. They are mined in Sri Lanka, Uruguay and Madagascar. These stones are fairly durable with a hardness of 7. They are durable enough to be worn for every day use. They can be cut into various shapes and sizes such as ovals, hearts, squares and marquis. Diamonds are especially popular in marquis cuts. They are often used in rings, necklaces, broaches and other kinds of jewelry.

STUDENT PRACTICE: STYLE AND TONE
PARAGRAPH C
DIRECTIONS: Underline redundancies in the following paragraph. Mark out cliches and sub-standard English.

Amethysts have an old and ancient history. Amethysts were once thought to improve gross complexions and prevent hair loss and baldness. Irregardless, my father always says, however, that "beauty is only skin deep." *Amethyst* is a word taken from the Greek, meaning "not drunken." The amethyst guarded its wearer from intoxication according to alot of old folklore stories and tales. Amethysts, nowdays, represent the February birthstone.

STUDENT PRACTICE

DIRECTIONS: Read the passage below and answer the following questions.

COMPUTER PASSAGE

[1] Many inventions have impacted society in the twentieth century, but few have made as much difference as the computer. [2] IBM is a well-known computer corporation. [3] I think the most important invention of the twentieth century is the computer.

[4] Computers have brought about important advancements in technology. [5] For example, they'll make businesses faster and easier to run. [6] They enable quick filing systems and access to important information about clients. [7] Also, computers allow information to be stored and sent out more efficiently. [8] I can order Beanie Babies from several websites. [9] Information processing impacts all aspects of our lives by providing important information at the touch of a finger. [10] Computers also have improved safety. [11] Today there're computerized burglar alarms, timers, and safety features on all types of transportation. [12] Another area of large impact is the field of medicine. [13] Computers allow doctors to diagnose illnesses more accurately and find out about treatments. [14] Very few people now days haven't been changed by computers. [15] My grandmother can't work her email very well. [16] However, utilization of computer technology reflects the oppressive socioeconomic division rampant in this country. [17] This "Digital Divide" impacts all facets of modern society.

[18] Computers make our lives easier. [19] First of all, they provide modern convenience in almost everything we do. [20] Also, computers provide easy ways of communicating with others. [21] And finally, computers are just plain fun.

1. Which sentence contains the main idea of the passage?

2. Which three sentences should be eliminated from the passage because they interfere with unity?

3. The last paragraph of the passage lacks specific detail. Add your own specific examples to support sentences 19, 20 and 21.

4. List the contractions in the passage. They are examples of substandard English and should not be used in formal composition.
   _____
   _____

5. Which two sentences are not consistent with the style and purpose of the passage?
   _____
   _____
   _____
   _____

STUDENT PRACTICE
   DIRECTIONS: Read the passage below and answer the following questions.

FRANKENSTEIN PASSAGE

¹The destruction of Dr. Victor Frankenstein's world began when he went beyond the bounds of ethical science and created a monster. ²First, the horrible monster assembled by Frankenstein nearly scares people to death. ³Victor describes the creature's frightening appearance: his yellow skin inadequately covers the muscles and veins of his face and body, and he has a withered complexion and dark black lips. ⁴Besides being very ugly and distorted, Victor also comes to realize that the creature is also evil. ⁵As a result of his appearance and increasingly aggressive behavior, society rejects the monster. ⁶This lack of acceptance makes the monster furious at Victor. ⁷In return, Victor doesn't accept the monster because he wasn't even close to what he wanted to create. ⁸Blinded by his despair and disgust, Victor doesn't realize that it is the monster that killed his brother William. ⁹His brother always enjoyed flying kites down by the lake. ¹⁰He finds out only after the monster also kills his wife on their wedding night. ¹¹Dr. Frankenstein soon realized that his horrible, evil creation was out of control. ¹²How out of control was he? ¹³Well, he was so out of control that he had killed Victor's wife! ¹⁴Victor is haunted by the image of his wife murdered by the creature and finally realizes he must do something to stop the monster. ¹⁵Unfortunately, the monster wants Victor to create a female companion for him because he's lonely. ¹⁶In a moment of weakness, Dr. Frankenstein consents to making another creature to stop the monster from destroying him. ¹⁷He soon realizes the danger of creating an additional monster, however, and refuses to continue. ¹⁸Victor is deeply devastated over what has happened to his life and now realizes he has surpassed the ethical boundaries of science.

1. Correct the misplaced modifier in sentence 4.

2. From the details in this passage, how would you describe Victor's feelings toward the monster? List the details that give you that impression.

3. Identify the sentence that contains the cliché and rewrite it to maintain consistency of style of the passage.

4. Identify three sentences that are not consistent with the style and/or purpose of the passage.

5. List the contractions in this passage. They are examples of substandard English and should not be used in formal composition.

6. Write a sentence that would serve as a summary for this passage.

7. Choose an appropriate transition to add before sentence 18.

STUDENT PRACTICE
DIRECTIONS: Read the following paragraph carefully, then answer the questions.

PRACTICAL JOKE PASSAGE

¹Having previously been the victim of numerous practical jokes perpetrated by my college roommate, I decided the time had arrived to put an end to her pranks: I devised the ultimate practical joke to put an end to any doubt that I would be the victor of our unofficial competition. ²First, I painstakingly waited until my intended victim had stayed up all night studying for a Chemistry II exam, knowing that she would require a long afternoon nap to recover. ³Then on the long-awaited afternoon I meticulously threaded needle after needle with the length of thread that I could skillfully handle while my roomie slipped into the deepest of slumber. ⁴When I was convinced that she was practically unconscious, I methodically began the long and arduous process of sewing her to the bed. ⁵With brain-surgeon-like precision I carefully connected each roller to her pillow, thus immobilizing her head. ⁶I started with the brush rollers in her hair. ⁷I can really be a good seamstress when I want. ⁸Then in much longer and faster strokes I bound her T-shirt to the sheets, carefully binding around each arm and down each side. ⁹Next, moving ever so quickly in much broader strokes, I stitched my way down her pajama legs, stopping only to race down the hall to laugh hysterically at the victim I was about to revive. ¹⁰Not surprisingly, my laughter attracted the attention of many other girls in my dorm, most of whom wanted to view "the body." ¹¹With my prey thoroughly secured to the bed and still in a coma-like sleep which made her look almost dead, we amassed a large crowd of girls in the dorm to view the awakening. ¹²We waited not so patiently, barely able to contain our snickers, before I decided we would wait no longer. ¹³Fortunately, shaving cream on the toes had just the tickling effect to revive Sleeping Beauty. ¹⁴She looked pretty stupid just

laying there, but I didn't feel sorry for her cause the creep had it coming. [15]Finally, she awoke and found herself unable to move. [16]The expression on her face was a combination of terror, wonder, and total shock. [17]We could see her mind racing, searching for answers to the all-important questions—Where am I? Why are these people in my room? [18]The laughing crowd only served to further confuse and confound. [19]As I proudly proclaimed my victory as the ultimate practical joker, I was careful to make sure the message was heard loudly and clearly with my dorm mates. [20]Don't mess with me—revenge will be swift and final!

1. Write a sentence that would serve as a summary of this paragraph.

2. List the words used as transitions in the paragraph.

3. Write the sentence that contains the main idea of the paragraph (topic sentence).

4. Which sentences should be reversed to maintain coherence in the paragraph?

5. Identify the sentence that is not consistent in tone with the rest of the paragraph.

6. Suppose you want to add a sentence describing how the girl escaped from her predicament. Write a sentence you could add and indicate where you might put it.

7. Which sentence interferes with the unity of the paragraph and should be omitted?

8. Suppose you wanted to add descriptive details about what practical jokes had been played before the incident described. Would those details most likely be included in this paragraph, in a preceding paragraph or in a following paragraph?
   _____.

9. Which sentence contains an example of redundant word choice? What word/idea is repeated?
   _____
   _____
   _____.

10. In order to summarize and write a new clincher for the paragraph, the writer is considering adding the following sentence:
    Be careful when you do practical jokes because they can have serious consequences.
    Explain why this sentence would or would not be an appropriate final sentence.
    _____
    _____
    _____.

11. Suppose the writer had been assigned a personal essay about humorous aspects of her college experience? Explain why this would or would not be an appropriate paragraph to include.
    _____
    _____
    _____.

12. Write an additional "all-important question" for the roommate.
    _____
    _____
    _____.

13. The writer was careful to avoid redundancy in referring to the girl being sewn to the bed. Indicate the various ways the writer identified the girl without using her real name *Nancy*.
    _____
    _____
    _____.

14. Circle the titles that would best capture the main idea of the paragraph.
    A. Sweet Revenge
    B. Dorm Survival Tips
    C. A Stitch in Time Saves Nine
    D. Needling Nancy

CONCEPT: SUBSTANDARD ENGLISH

CONTRACTIONS
Avoid using contractions in formal writing or speaking.
   INFORMAL: They **don't** want to meet us for dinner.
   BETTER: They **do not** want to meet us for dinner.

INFINITIVES
Do not split the infinitive. An infinitive is a verbal construction consisting of the word *to* immediately followed by a verb: to read; to think; to sing. It is improper to place a word between the word *to* and its verb.

   INCORRECT: to simply read; to quietly think; to loudly sing.
   BETTER: simply to read; to think quietly; to sing loudly.

The modifier is placed either before or after the infinitive:

THAN/THEN
The word *than* is used for comparison. The word *then* is used to express time.
   I like this movie more **than** that one.
   I must finish dinner first, **then** I can go to your house.

FARTHER/FURTHER
Farther indicates distance. *Further* indicates additional time, quantity or degree.
   The women walk **farther** than I thought they did.
   Further research is required on this subject before I decide what I believe.

BETWEEN/AMONG
Between is used when referring to two individuals. *Among* is used when referring to three or more people or items.
   The mother split the sandwich **between** the two small children.
   The students whispered **among** themselves as the teacher decided who could leave early.

COULD OF/SHOULD OF
Do not use *could of* or *should of* in place of *could have* or *should have*.
   INCORRECT: Hilary **could of** won the spelling bee.
   BETTER: Hilary **could have** won the spelling bee.

FEWER/LESS
Use *fewer* when referring to items that can be counted individually (dollars, rocks, people).
Use *less* when referring to items that can not be separated (anger, time, money).
   Mr. Smithson would be happy if he had **fewer** rocks in his pasture.
   People would be happier if they spent **less** time complaining and more time appreciating the good things in their lives.

Alot/A Lot

Alot should not be one word. *A lot* (two words) is a descriptive phrase that should be avoided, especially in formal writing.

ITS/IT'S

Its is a possessive pronoun; it shows ownership of an item. *It's* is a contraction meaning it is.
    INCORRECT: The dog brought me **it's** bone.
    BETTER: The dog brought me **its** bone.

DOUBLE PREPOSITIONS

Avoid the use of certain double prepositions: *off of, off to, from off*.
    INFORMAL: I picked up the clothes **from off** the floor of my bedroom.
    BETTER: I picked up the clothes **from** the floor of my bedroom.

IRREGARDLESS/REGARDLESS

Irregardless is not a word. Use *regardless*.
    INCORRECT: Irregardless of the misinformation, the play will go on as scheduled.
    BETTER: Regardless of the misinformation, the play will go on as scheduled.

TO/TOO

To is a preposition. *Too* means *also* or *very*.

ACT TEST SAMPLE QUESTIONS

1. The story told by the second suspect had more holes <u>than</u> the story told by the first.

   A. NO CHANGE
   B. like
   C. then
   D. as when

2. Jane slipped and fell when making her grand entrance. Then she gracefully arose <u>up from off of</u> the floor.

   A. NO CHANGE
   B. from
   C. up off
   D. from off

3. A row of fir trees on the golf course marks <u>it's</u> boundaries.

   A. NO CHANGE
   B. its
   C. his
   D. its'

4. Upon her arrival in the United States, Valerie was amazed at the variety of fine dining choices.

   A. NO CHANGE
   B. a lot
   C. alot
   D. a bunch

5. Jerry was anxious to hopefully complete his project by August.

   A. NO CHANGE
   B. to complete
   C. to complete hopefully
   D. to complete hopeful

6. Lester was emphatic in the point he made before the subcommittee: Don't underestimate the power of Alan Greenspan.

   A. NO CHANGE
   B. Do not underestimate
   C. Dont' underestimate
   D. Does not underestimate

7. Monica's mother advised her not to take her argumentative behavior any further than she already had.

   A. NO CHANGE
   B. any farther than
   C. further then
   D. any farther then

8. The rivalry among the two rival gang members was becoming intense.

   A. NO CHANGE
   B. among the two
   C. between the two
   D. between the two rival

9. Looking back on the accident, Jed had no idea how he could of prevented the crash.

   A. NO CHANGE
   B. could
   C. could have
   D. couldn't of

10. Homer remarked that he would be happy if he could spend <u>fewer amounts of time</u> commuting to work.

   A. NO CHANGE
   B. fewer times
   C. lesser time
   D. less time

APPENDIX

CONJUNCTIONS

Coordinating
Conjunctions

and
but
or
nor
for
yet
so

Correlative
Conjunctions

both…and
not only…but also
either…or
neither…nor
whether…or
as…so

Subordinating
Conjunctions

after	before	unless
although	if	until
as	in order that	when
as if	since	whenever
as long as	so	where
as soon as	so that	whereas
as though	than	wherever
because	though	while

Conjunctive
Adverbs

accordingly	furthermore	meanwhile	then
also	hence	moreover	therefore
besides	however	nevertheless	though
consequently	in addition	otherwise	thus
equally	instead	similarly	yet
for example	likewise	still	whereas

IRREGULAR VERBS

Present	Past	Past Participle	Present	Past	Past Participle
beat	beat	beaten	hurt	hurt	hurt
become	became	become	keep	kept	kept
begin	began	begun	know	knew	known
blow	blew	blown	leave	left	left
break	broke	broken	mean	meant	meant
burst	burst	burst	read	read	read
buy	bought	bought	ride	rode	ridden
catch	caught	caught	ring	rang	rung
choose	chose	chosen	rise	rose	risen
come	came	come	run	ran	run
dive	dived, dove	dived	see	saw	seen
do	did	done	shake	shook	shaken
draw	drew	drawn	shine	shone	shone
drink	drank	drunk	sink	sank	sunk
drive	drove	driven	speak	spoke	spoken
eat	ate	eaten	spin	spun	spun
fall	fell	fallen	spring	sprang	sprung
feel	felt	felt	strike	struck	struck
find	found	found	swear	swore	sworn
fly	flew	flown	swim	swam	swum
forget	forgot	forgotten	swing	swung	swung
forgive	forgave	forgiven	take	took	taken
get	got	gotten	tear	tore	torn
give	gave	given	throw	threw	thrown
go	went	gone	wear	wore	worn
grow	grew	grown	weep	wept	wept
hang(suspended)	hung	hung	write	wrote	written
hide	hid	hidden			

LINKING VERBS

☞ **The most common linking verbs are the various forms of be.**

be
being
is
am
are
was
were
shall be
will be
can be
could be
should be
would be
may be

might be
must be
have been
has been
had been
could have been
should have been
would have been
might have been
must have been

ADDITIONAL LINKING VERBS

⇨ Some of these can be linking verbs in one sentence and action verbs in another. Ask yourself if the verb expresses a state of being or an action.

The cookies **smell** wonderful.

Are the cookies doing the smelling? Of course not. This verb is a linking verb because it expresses a state of being not a physical or mental action.

appear
become
feel
grow
look
remain
seem
smell
sound
stay
taste
turn

PREPOSITIONS

⇨ An easy way to remember most of the commonly used preposition is the squirrel metaphor. A preposition is anywhere a squirrel can go in relation to a log. He can go above it, around it, after it, through it, over it, under it, etc. This mnemonic device will not reveal all of the prepositions, but it will work with most of them.

aboard
about
above
across
after
against
along
among
around
at
before
behind
below
beneath
beside
besides
between
beyond
but (meaning except)
by
concerning
down
during
except
for
from
in
inside
into
like
near
of
off
on
out
over
past
since
through
throughout
till
to
toward
under

underneath
until
up
upon

with
within
without

COMPOUND PREPOSTIONS

according to
as of
aside from
because of
by means of
in addition to
in front of

in place of
in spite of
instead of
on account of
out of
owing to
prior to

PRONOUNS
PERSONAL PRONOUNS

		Nominative Case	Objective Case	Possessive Case
Singular	First person	I	me	my, mine
	Second person	you	you	your, yours
	Third person	he, she, it	him, her, it	his, her, hers, its
Plural	First person	we	us	our, ours
	Second person	you	you	your, yours
	Third person	they	them	their, theirs

REFLEXIVE PRONOUNS
myself   ourselves
yourself   yourselves
himself, herself, itself   themselves

RELATIVE PRONOUNS
who   whom   whose   which   that

INTERROGATIVE PRONOUNS
  (used in questions)
who…?   whose…?   what…?   whom…?   which…?

DEMONSTRATIVE PRONOUNS
  (used to point out a specific person or thing)
this   that   these   those

INDEFINITE PRONOUNS
(not referring to a definite person or thing; frequently used without antecedents)

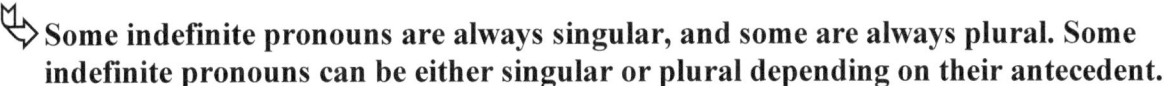Some indefinite pronouns are always singular, and some are always plural. Some indefinite pronouns can be either singular or plural depending on their antecedent.

Singular

anybody	neither
anyone	no one
anything	nobody
each	nothing
either	one
everybody	somebody
everyone	someone
everything	something

 NOTE: Singular indefinite pronouns can be remembered as the following: *each*, *either*, *neither*, and any word ending in *thing*, *one*, or *body*.

Plural
several   few   both   many

Either Singular or Plural
some   all   most   any   none

TRANSITIONS

CONCLUDE A POINT
as a result
consequently
finally
for this reason
in conclusion
in fact
since
so
therefore
thus

CONTRAST
although
but
however
in spite of
instead
nevertheless
on the contrary
on the other hand
otherwise
provided that
still
yet

INTRODUCE OR LINK IDEAS
also
besides
for example
for instance
from that point on
furthermore
in addition
in other words

SHOW IMPORTANCE
first
last
least
least important
mainly
more important
most important
then
to begin with

CHRONOLOGICAL ORDER
after
at last
at once
before
eventually
finally
first
later
meanwhile
next
now
then
thereafter
when

COMPARISON
also
and
another
moreover
similarly
too

ENGLISH PRACTICE TEST 1

THE PERFECT DOG

[1]

I can remember begging my parents to buy me a dog when I was a little girl. They never did because they thought it was too much responsibility for a <u>child, so when</u>[1] I graduated from college, found a job and moved into my own house, one of the first things I <u>did were start</u>[2] looking for a dog.

[2]

Because I had waited so long to have a pet, I wanted to have the "perfect" dog. After looking at the dogs in my neighborhood, I decided I wanted a large dog; my new neighbor had a Great Dane, and I fell in love with it. I found a breeder in my <u>area which raised</u>[3] Great Danes and made an appointment to visit his kennel. I arrived at the appointed <u>time, ready</u>[4] to select a puppy and take it home. <u>Great Danes can suffer from Hip Dysplasia which is a</u>[5]

[Question 5 text continued on next page]

1. A. NO CHANGE
    B. child; so when
    C. child; similarly, when
    D. child: so when

2. F. NO CHANGE
    G. did is start
    H. done was start
    J. did was start

3. A. NO CHANGE
    B. area who raised
    C. area they raised
    D. area whom raised

4. F. NO CHANGE
    G. time: ready
    H. time; ready
    J. time. ready

polygenetic hereditary disease that can cause pain and lameness even to the point of being crippling.
─────5─────

[3]

The breeder, Mr. Clarkson, asked me to have a seat in his living room while he went to get the puppies. As he left, four adult Great Danes bounded into the room, heading straight for me. Lily, Mason, Pete and Delilah crowded around me, sniffing and climbing all over me. Those dogs were so large and heavy that I couldn't get up from the couch or get them off me. They totally ignored my initially calm requests to get back; even when I began yelling and shoving them, they were oblivious. Before Mr. Clarkson even returned, I decided that I most certainly did not want a large dog. I fabricated some excuse for Mr. Clarkson and made my get-away. My quest for the "perfect" dog continued.

[4]

For an example of my disappointing
─────6─────
experience with large dogs, I decided I would think about small dogs. The family

5. A. NO CHANGE
   B. Hip Dysplasia can be very painful
   C. Great Danes are not in high demand because they can suffer from Hip Dysplasia.
   D. OMIT the underlined portion.

6. F. NO CHANGE
   G. To begin with,
   H. In spite of
   J. As a result of

that lived two doors down from me had a long-haired Chihuahua that was adorable. I found a site on the Internet that listed local Chihuahua breeders and made another appointment, confident that I was on the right track this time. Mrs. Anderson was enthusiastic about her Chihuahuas and proudly showing me the four new litters she had available. The puppies were as adorable as my neighbor's dog; but as I picked one up, I found myself becoming very nervous. What if I dropped it or stepped on it? It was so tiny that one wrong move on my part could be disastrous. Any dog that lived in my house needed to be more self-sufficient than this tiny animal. I regretfully apologized to Mrs. Anderson, put the charming puppy back in the basket with its brothers and sisters, and left, wondering if I would ever find the "perfect" dog for me.

[5]

At dinner with my friends later that evening, I complained about my fruitless search. Brian suggested that I try looking at

7. A. NO CHANGE
   B. proud, showed me
   C. proudly showed me
   D. proudly showed I

8. F. NO CHANGE
   G. dog, but
   H. dog, and
   J. dog; consequently,

9. A. NO CHANGE
   B. regretfully apologize
   C. regretfully apologized,
   D. regretfully have apologized

the Humane Society or local dog shelter. I had my doubts about the quality of mixed breed dogs, but both Brian and Stacey, another friend of mine, had adopted dogs from the Humane Society and adored them. After work the next day, I went to the local Humane Society and asked to view the dogs they had available. As I entered the kennel area, the dogs began to bark wildly; the noise[10] level almost deafened me. I walked slow down[11] the aisle between the cages of dogs, hoping to find the dog of my dreams. Although many of the animals were sweet, none of them gave me that feeling I was searching for. I was about to give up the search completely and forget about getting a pet when I saw a dog in the next to last cage that caught my eye.[12] It was sitting quietly at the door of its cage, looking straight at me with huge brown eyes. I asked the attendant about it; she said she knew that it was part Labrador Retriever, but she didn't know what else. Her name was Jessie.

10. F. NO CHANGE
　　G. wildly, the noise
　　H. wildly, but the noise
　　J. wildly: the noisy

11. A. NO CHANGE
　　B. walked slowly down
　　C. walks slowly down
　　D. walked, slowly, down

12. The best placement for the underlined portion would be
　　F. NO CHANGE
　　G. before *pet*.
　　H. before *dog*.
　　J. after *dog*.

[6]

I don't know what it was about Jessie that made my heart turn over, but I knew that she was the dog for me. Oddly enough, she seemed to know it, too. She sat calmly as the attendant got a leash and collar and opened her cage.

[7]

"She may be nervous about leaving," the attendant said, "so be careful and patient with her."

[8]

I carefully picked up the leash, and Jessie happily trotted out by my side.

Items 13-15 pose questions about the passage as a whole.

13. Which of the following sentences would be the best "clincher" sentence for this passage?

    A. Large dogs are preferable to small dogs.
    B. I wasn't sure that Jessie would be the perfect dog.
    C. I had found my "perfect" dog.
    D. Most people would prefer a purebred dog.

14. The author wants to insert the following information.
    Since Chihuahuas are small dogs, I knew I would never be overpowered by one of them.
    In which paragraph would this material be most effective?

    F. 2
    G. 3
    H. 4
    J. 5

15. Which of the following statements best expresses the main idea of this passage?
    A. Great Danes are exceptional dogs.
    B. Dogs from private breeders are superior to those from the Humane Society.
    C. Children can carry a grudge against their parents for years.
    D. The quest for perfection can lead to unexpected results.

This passage is adapted from information on the White House website, 2001.

FIRST LADY LAURA BUSH

[1]

As the nation's First Lady, Laura Bush is keenly aware of the opportunity she has to share her love of reading with Americans; especially young children. She will use her role as First Lady to encourage people to share the magic of reading and the love of the arts, to promote women's health care issues, to encourage Americans to pursue the honorable career of teaching and showcasing early childhood development initiatives that show results on behalf of children.

16. F. NO CHANGE
    G. Americans: especially
    H. Americans, especially
    J. Americans. Especially

17. A. NO CHANGE
    B. but showcasing
    C. and, to showcase
    D. and to showcase

[2]

[1] Mrs. Bush's passion for literary works was sparked at an early age. [2] As a child, Laura Bush dreamed of one day becoming a teacher. [3] Promoting her dream, Laura was introduced to books at her local library. [4] She was born in Midland, Texas. [5] She earned a bachelor's degree in education from Southern Methodist

18. F. NO CHANGE
    G. an earlier age.
    H. an early, young age.
    J. the early age.

19. A. NO CHANGE
    B. Laura's mother introduced her
    C. Lauras mother introduced she
    D. she was introduced by her mother

University and a Master's Degree in Library Science from the University of Texas at Austin. [6] She pursued a career as a public school teacher and librarian in the Houston, Dallas and Austin school systems. [20]

[3]

As First Lady of Texas, her love of the written word inspired her to share the magic of reading and education with others, especially children. Mrs. **Bush launches an**[21] early childhood development initiative in 1998 to help parents and caregivers prepare infants and young children for learning and reading when they enter **school the**[22] Texas initiative included a family literacy project, which was a collaborative effort with the Barbara Bush Foundation for Family Literacy. She helped organize the Texas Book Festival in 1996, an endeavor that has become an annual fundraiser for Texas public libraries. In four **years: the**[23] festival generated approximately $1 million for 325 public libraries.

20. Which of the sentences in paragraph 2 should be omitted for the sake of unity and coherence?
    F. 2
    G. 3
    H. 4
    J. 5

21. A. NO CHANGE
    B. Bush is launching a
    C. Bush launched an
    D. Bush will launch the

22. F. NO CHANGE
    G. school. The
    H. school—the
    J. school, the

23. A. NO CHANGE
    B. years; the
    C. years. The
    D. years, the

[4]

The First Lady's concern over women's health issues led her to highlight the importance of breast cancer awareness. In Texas, she worked with the Governor's Spouse Program of the National Governors Association to promote women's health issues. Working to establish Adopt-A-Caseworker programs and Rainbow Rooms throughout Texas. Rainbow rooms provide abused and neglected little kids with basic necessities such as clothing and diapers.

[5]

Mrs. Bush promotes and encourages the arts and enjoyed showcasing the works of Texas artists at the Governor's Mansion in Austin. After she and her husband take up residence in the White House, she hopes to find ways to spotlight artistic works in Washington, D.C.

24. F. NO CHANGE
    G. Working hard
    H. After working
    J. Mrs. Bush worked

25. A. NO CHANGE
    B. tykes
    C. children
    D. tots

26. F. NO CHANGE
    G. omit the underlined portion
    H. and participates in
    J. and advocates

27. A. NO CHANGE
    B. Until
    C. Provided that
    D. In other words, when

ENGLISH

Items 28-30 pose questions about the passage as a whole

28. The writer is contemplating dividing paragraph 2 into two paragraphs. To maintain the logic and coherence of the essay, the most appropriate action would be to

    F. leave the paragraph as it is.
    G. begin a new paragraph with sentence 5.
    H. Add a sentence explaining her background as an advocate for women's health
    J. begin a new paragraph with sentence 3.

29. Suppose the writer had been asked to write an essay about a person who had an impact in the field of education. Would this essay fulfill that requirement?

    A. Yes, because it discusses how she worked to improve literacy.
    B. Yes, because it encourages Americans to become teachers.
    C. No, because it discusses the activities of a First Lady.
    D. No, because the focus of the essay is her husband's achievement.

30. Assuming that all are true, which of the following sentences would add another example of Mrs. Bush's activities in a manner consistent with the main focus of the essay?

    F. Mrs. Bush is actively pursuing the acquisition of a bust of Winston Churchill as a model of great twentieth century leaders.
    G. Mrs. Bush has campaigned against removing reading programs from school curriculums.
    H. Mrs. Bush plans to continue her enthusiastic support of her husband's policies.
    J. Mrs. Bush seems to be uncomfortable in her role as a public advocate for the arts.

This passage is adapted from information on the U.S. Surgeon General's website, 2001.

CHILDREN'S MENTAL HEALTH

[1]

David Satcher, MD, PhD, Assistant Secretary for Health and Surgeon General, today released a National Action Agenda for Children's Mental Health, which outlines goals and strategies to improve the services for children and adolescents with mental health problems and <u>his families</u>. According to the report, the nation <u>are facing</u> a public crisis <u>for children and adolescents in mental health</u>.

[2]

In the United States, 1 in 10 children and adolescents suffer from mental illness severe enough to cause some level of impairment. Yet, in any given year, it is estimated that <u>less than</u> 1 in 5 of these children receives needed treatment. The long-term consequences of untreated childhood disorders are costly, in both human and fiscal terms.

31. A. NO CHANGE
    B. her families
    C. their families
    D. our families

32. F. NO CHANGE
    G. was facing
    H. is faced
    J. is facing

33. A. NO CHANGE
    B. for children and adolescents.
    C. in mental health for children and adolescents.
    D. for children and adolescents, in mental health.

34. F. NO CHANGE
    G. fewer than
    H. less then
    J. fewer then

[3]

The National Action Agenda identifies eight goals and multiple action steps, which include promoting public awareness of children's mental health issues, reduced the stigma associated with mental illness and improving the assessment and recognition of mental health needs in children.

35. A. NO CHANGE
    B. issues, by reducing
    C. issues, reducing
    D. issues; reducing

[4]

The Surgeon General's action steps encourage the wide adoption of science-based prevention and treatment services, as well as continued research. According to the report, in conclusion, bridging the gap between research and practice is not the only step. Connecting research and practice to policy is critical to ensuring access to quality mental health care for children and their families.

36. F. NO CHANGE
    G. Generals action
    H. Generals' action
    J. Generales action

37. The writer wishes to replace the underlined portion. Which of the following transitions would be most effective?

    A. NO CHANGE
    B. in addition
    C. however
    D. meanwhile

[5]

[1] The report calls for an increase in the coordination of mental health care services for families with mental health

needs. [2] At present, there exists no primary mental health care system for children.

[3] Because of the existence of mental health programs in many communities. [4] The nation lacks a basic mental health care infrastructure. [5] Insurance costs are astronomical and are beyond the reach of many families. [6] Mental health treatments and services are fragmented across many institutions; ranging from schools to primary care to child welfare and often the juvenile justice system. [7] Moreover, disparities in access exist across racial groups, ethnic groups and socioeconomic groups.

[6]

The National Action Agenda reflects the culmination of a series of activities over the past year, including the Surgeon General's Conference on Children's Mental Health in September 2000. The report includes proceedings from this conference and synthesizes recommendations from three major Federal agencies—the

38. F. NO CHANGE
G. Despite
H. In addition to,
J. As a result of,

39. A. NO CHANGE
B. communities; the
C. communities: the
D. communities, the

40. F. NO CHANGE
G. institutions: ranging
H. institutions. Ranging
J. institutions, ranging

41. A. NO CHANGE
B. racial, ethnic and socioeconomic groups.
C. a variety of racial groups, a cross-section of ethnic groups and a multitude of socioeconomic groups.
D. racial, ethnicity and socioeconomics

42. F. NO CHANGE
G. agencies. The
H. agencies; the
J. agencies, the

Department of Health and Human Services, the Department of Education and the Department of Justice—and a broad section of mental health stakeholders—youth and family members, professional organizations and associations, advocacy groups, faith-based practitioners, clinicians, educators, health care providers, and members of the scientific community and the health care industry.

Items 43-45 pose questions about the passage as a whole

---

43. Given that all of the following statements are true, which of them would be most effective when placed into paragraph 2?

    A. NO CHANGE
    B. Of the 4 children that do not receive necessary treatment, 2 will develop enduring psychological scars.
    C. The 1 child that receives treatment will become a productive citizen.
    D. That impairment can cause catastrophic damage.

44. In consideration of unity and coherence, which sentence should be removed from paragraph 5?

    F. NO CHANGE
    G. 5
    H. 6
    J. 7

45. Suppose the writer had been asked to submit an essay describing a potentially dangerous social issue. Would this essay fit that qualification?

    A. Yes, because the essay focuses on the public health crises in children's mental health.
    B. Yes, because the essay describes how children who suffer from mental health illness can be disruptive in the classroom.
    C. No, because the essay doesn't express immediate concern over the state of mental health facilities in the United States.
    D. No, because the writer believes services for the mentally ill are improving.

This passage is adapted from information on the White House website, 2001.

WINSTON CHURCHILL

[1]

I [George W. Bush] casually mentioned to the Ambassador [of Great Britain], right after my swearing-in that I lamented the fact that there was not a proper bust of Winston Churchill for me to put in the Oval Office. Churchill is a man of great action, because here sits a bust on loan from Her Majesty's government.

[2]

[1] People questioned my desire to have the bust of an Englishman in the Oval Office. [2] And the answer is because he was one of the great leaders in the 20th century. [3] He was an enormous personality. [4] Standing on principle. [5] Sir Churchill was a man of great courage. [6] He knew what he believed, and he really kind of went after it in a way that seemed like a Texan to me. [7] He wasn't afraid of public opinion polls: He didn't need focus

46. F. NO CHANGE
    G. right after my swearing-in,
    H. right after my swearing-in;
    J. right after my swearing-in:

47. A. NO CHANGE
    B. On the other hand, being that Her Majesty's government was kind, here sits a bust of Sir Winston Churchill.
    C. Consequently, Her Majesty's government was kind enough to loan a bust of Sir Winston, a man of great action.
    D. After all, he's a man of great action, because here sits a bust on loan from Her Majesty's government.

48. F. NO CHANGE
    G. The answer is
    H. And the reason is because
    J. And, because

49. A. NO CHANGE
    B. personality whom stood
    C. personality who stands
    D. personality. He stood

50. F. NO CHANGE
    G. sort of really went
    H. really went
    J. real kindly went

51. A. NO CHANGE
    B. polls; however, he
    C. polls, however, he
    D. polls and he

groups to tell him what was right. [8] He charged ahead, and the world's no better for it.

[3]

He also had a great sense of humor. There have been a lot of Churchill stories; some of which you can repeat on TV, some of which you can't, Mr. Ambassador. One that comes to mind was after he lost office in the election in 1945, King George VI offered him the Order of the Garter. He said he couldn't have accept the award because "his people have given me the order of the boot."

[4]

[1] Churchill reminds me of two things: one, we need more humor in the public arena. [2] He had a great wit. [3] Secondly, he reminds me of the importance of the relationship between Great Britain and America. [4] Both countries cooperate to make the world a better place. 56

52. F. NO CHANGE
    G. world's more better
    H. world is better
    J. worlds better

53. A. NO CHANGE
    B. stories—some
    C. stories; in fact, some
    D. stories—one

54. F. NO CHANGE
    G. couldn't hardly accept
    H. couldn't not accept
    J. couldn't accept

55. A. NO CHANGE
    B. among Great Britain and America.
    C. between Great Britain and America,
    D. among Great Britain/America:

56. Suppose the writer wanted to add the following sentence of support in paragraph 4.

    He had a fantastic way of making people smile and laugh.

    The best placement for the sentence would be
    F. before 1
    G. after 2
    H. after 3
    J. after 4

ENGLISH

Items 57-60 pose questions about the passage as a whole

57. Based on the predominant tone of the essay, President Bush's attitude toward Sir Churchill can best be described as

    A. jealous
    B. admiring
    C. suspicious
    D. insincere

58. Given that all of the following sentences are true, which best concludes the essay?

    F. And I have a lot of stress.
    G. Consequently, he is British, his advice can't be ignored.
    H. He is a constant reminder of a great leader.
    J. The Ambassador should be recognized for offering such a generous gift.

59. Suppose the writer wanted to add the following specific detail to paragraph 2.

    After World War II was over, Sir Winston Churchill was not re-elected to the office of Prime Minister.

    Which placement would be most unified and coherent?

    A. NO CHANGE
    B. After sentence 2
    C. After sentence 5
    D. After sentence 8

60. The writer wishes to add the following information in the essay.

    Because of this continued cooperation, our countries can look forward to a prosperous and mutually beneficial future.

    The new information best supports and would most logically be placed in paragraph

    F. 1
    G. 2
    H. 3
    J. 4

COFFEE

[1]

I knew I needed to improve my writing skills, but the writing class I was in was just not working. I wanted something tangible, a 4-step program, a checklist or a formula. Unfortunately, the instructor offered no such easy way out. She kept using all these "touchy, feely" words to describe writing, and I didn't feel no such affection. She talked about "finding my own voice," but my voice just wanted to scream, "Let me out of here!" To open the morning session, we always started with a freewrite. I didn't mind these too much. Because all I had to do was write some words on a page and nobody checked to see if they made sense. But, some participants would read their stories like they were a professional writer or act them out like they were reading a children's book. Then the instructor gave us the day's topic—coffee.

61. A. NO CHANGE
    B. skills and
    C. skillfully, and
    D. skills, nevertheless,

62. F. NO CHANGE
    G. tangible
    H. tangibly:
    J. tangible:

63. A. NO CHANGE
    B. felt no such
    C. didn't feel such no
    D. felt not any

64. F. NO CHANGE
    G. much because
    H. much, however,
    J. much: because

65. A. NO CHANGE
    B. However, I might share my writing sometime if the teacher would teach me how to write.
    C. Consequently, I always sit at the back of the room when I go to any class so I won't get called upon.
    D. Omit the underlined passage.

[2]

I almost immediately flew into a rage. What is a non-coffee drinker supposed to do with a topic like that? All the previous topics had had some potential—most embarrassing moments, most happy experience, or a proud accomplishment. But what could I possibly do with "coffee"? I don't like the stuff, I don't drink the stuff and I sure had nothing to say about coffee.

66. F. NO CHANGE
    G. were having
    H. hardly had
    J. had been

67. A. NO CHANGE
    B. potential. Most
    C. potential like
    D. potential for example

[3]

I knew anger was a sure way to stifle the writing process. Being mad at the topic was not going to get me anywhere and was certainly not going to help with my writing skills. I looked around for some sympathy, but it only enraged me farther to notice that everyone else was writing fast and furiously.

68. F. NO CHANGE
    G. me further to
    H. me completely to
    J. me to the largest extent possible

[4]

With a deep breath, I decided to put pen to paper and just write whatever words came to my mind. Remembering a writing tip about using my senses, I wrote down some words about the smell of coffee.

[5]

[1] Then it happened the smell of
coffee triggered a memory from my
childhood. [2] Suddenly, I visualized my
father standing in my room with a thermos
of coffee to wake me up for our long
awaited fishing trip to a local farm pond.
[3] He was an avid fisherman, but I rarely
had the time, interest or patience for the
sport. [4] But we had scheduled this time, and
he had promised that there was a big old
bass just waiting for me. [5] He drank his
coffee in the pick-up on the way to the pond,
all the time instructing me in the finer art of
catching the big bass. [6] My dad told me to
be very quiet walking across the field. [7] He
pointed out a large rock that jutted over the
pond next to a small tree. [8] He told me a
huge bass might just be under that rock. [9] I
quietly put a worm on the hook and slipped
the line into the water just where my dad
showed me and waiting for my fish. [10] To
my surprise

69. A. NO CHANGE
    B. happened. The
    C. happened; on the other hand, the
    D. happened, the

70. F. NO CHANGE
    G. and to wait for
    H. and waited for
    J. and began to wait for

the line and the float never stopped going down under the water. [11] I wondered what was wrong with the float that it was sinking under the water. [12] Then my dad yelled, "You've got one. Pull on the line." [71]

[6]

After what seemed like an epic battle, I finally reeled in the monster bass. My dad even said he'd never seen a largest bass in a farm pond. I was excited because we had our trophy bass to show the neighbors and to take pictures. And more important I had a moment with my father that I'll never forget. Not surprisingly, the rest of the morning I never had another bite.

[7]

"Let's write about coffee again," I angrily remarked to my teacher as I left class that day. [75]

71. Which of the following order of sentences will make paragraph 5 most logical?

   A. NO CHANGE
   B. 1, 2, 5, 3, 4
   C. 1, 5, 3, 2, 4
   D. 1, 4, 5, 3, 2

72. F. NO CHANGE
    G. largely a bass
    H. the largest bass
    J. a larger bass

73. A. NO CHANGE
    B. nevertheless,
    C. more than usual
    D. more importantly,

74. F. NO CHANGE
    G. smugly
    H. happy
    J. innocently

75. The writer is considering adding a final sentence to the last paragraph of the essay. Which of the following would best convey the author's attitude about her writing experience?

    A. "That's the best piece I've ever written."
    B. "I love my dad!"
    C. "Fishing could improve your relation with you father."
    D. "I think I might start drinking coffee now!"

ENGLISH PRACTICE TEST 2

THE WRONG HOUSE

[1]

My experience visiting a friend in a big city one summer turned out to be much different <u>then I planned</u>. <u>We'd</u> agreed to meet at his parent's house on a Sunday morning. I allowed myself plenty of time to get there knowing that my lack of experience driving in a large city might cause me to arrive later than I planned. <u>Fortunate to have</u> no problems arriving at the address I had been given. I was not surprised that his car was not in the driveway since I was several minutes early.

[2]

When I approached the front porch, I noticed that the inner front door was wide open, and through the screen door I could see and hear the television playing. <u>After repeatedly ringing</u> the doorbell, I was surprised that no one came to the door. Obviously, someone was home, and I knew they <u>was</u> expecting my arrival. I decided

1. A. NO CHANGE
   B. than I will plan.
   C. than I planned.
   D. then I would plan.

2. F. NO CHANGE
   G. We've
   H. We had
   J. We'll

3. A. NO CHANGE
   B. Fortunately, I had
   C. Fortunately I hadn't
   D. Fortunately not, I had

4. F. NO CHANGE
   G. repeated ringing of
   H. over and over ringing
   J. ringing over

5. A. NO CHANGE
   B. were
   C. aren't
   D. will be

they must be in the back yard since it appeared that someone must be home. I strolled around back, calling their names as I went through the gate to make sure I didn't sneak up upon someone and accidentally
                                              6
scare them. Again, I was shocked that no one was in the backyard either. I circled to the front of the house and sat on the porch to wait. Confident that someone would pull in
        7
the driveway or come to the door with an explanation at any minute.

[3]

After waiting patiently for several minutes, I began to feel more and more anxious and irritated at my friend for not arriving on time or at least arranging for his parents to be there. This was certainly not the warm welcome I had expected. My
                                              8
increasing anger, unfortunately, began to
              8
increase with the temperature. I decided that at least I would get out of the heat—obviously they had intended for me to come on in since the door was open and the television was playing. I entered, again

6. F. NO CHANGE
   G. surprise and alarm
   H. surprise
   J. surprisingly sneak up on

7. A. NO CHANGE
   B. wait, confident
   C. confidently wait
   D. wait; confident

8. F. NO CHANGE
   G. Increasingly, my anger,
   H. It was my anger, unfortunately
   J. My anger, unfortunately,

calling their names, looked for a note of explanation somewhere close to the door, and then decided to sit down, watch television, and wait.

[4]

Although I began to cool off, my anger was gradually replaced with a feeling of uneasiness as I sensed something was not right with this situation. I checked the address I had been given and rechecked the time, yet an overwhelming sensation of foreboding made me search for additional clues as to why no one was home.

[5]

Although I did not want to snoop, I began to look at the many photographs scattered about the room. On one wall I saw a picture of an American eagle surrounded by blue stars and red stripes and a reprint of the signing of the Declaration of Independence. The large grouping of family photos arranged on top of the stereo finally excited a moment of discovery, because none of the family pictures were of my

9. A. NO CHANGE
   B. The room was cheaply decorated with 1970's furniture in avocado, burnt orange and rust.
   C. The television was tuned to one of the Sunday morning news programs.
   D. Omit the underlined sentence.

10. F. NO CHANGE
    G. discovery, consequently,
    H. discovery:
    J. discovery; however,

friend or his family. I suddenly realized that I was sitting in the living room watching television in some stranger's house. In a panic I raced out the door, frantically searching for what explanation I could possibly have if the actual residents or the police arrived. As I drive off, my mind was racing as I was considering all the horrifying possibilities of what could have happened had I been discovered "breaking in" to someone's house. Soon I noticed that one block away there was another street with the exact same number.

11. A. NO CHANGE
    B. Driving off,
    C. As I drove
    D. As I drove off,

[6]

I spotted my friend's car and noticed he and his family were on the front porch waiting to welcome me. Through my tears of relief and humiliation, I breathlessly explained the cause of my delay. As I struggled to regain my dignity, they laughed hilariously at my blunder, never even apologizing for not mentioning there were two identically numbered streets.

12. Which transition would best connect the information in paragraph 5 with paragraph 6.

    F. Previously, I had spotted my friend's car
    G. At almost the same moment I spotted my friend's car,
    H. Consequently, I observed my friend's car
    J. Since I spotted my friend's car

Items 13-15 pose questions about the passage as a whole

13. The writer's description of the way this incident made her feel can best be described as

   A. scared.
   B. remorseful.
   C. insincere.
   D. insightful.

14. The writer of the passage wants to insert more information about the possible consequences of the mistake.

   "I imagined the homeowner's threatening me with a gun; I imagined trying to explain my presence to a disbelieving policeman."

   This new information would logically be inserted in paragraph

   F. 3
   G. 4
   H. 5
   J. 6

15. Suppose the writer is asked to submit an essay that describes embarrassing moments in her life. Would this essay be appropriate for the assignment?

   A. Yes, because it was embarrassing to have her friend and her family laughing about her experience.
   B. Yes, because it was embarrassing to be discovered breaking in to someone's house.
   C. No, because the writer is more concerned with the consequences of the homeowner owning a gun.
   D. No, because the writer is clearly terrified and angry, not embarrassed.

This passage is adapted from information on the National Oceanic Atmospheric Association website, 2001.

THE IRONCLAD

[1]

On July 16, 2001—for the first time in nearly 140 years, the engine of the shipwrecked Civil War Ironclad, *USS Monitor* broke the surface of the Atlantic Ocean in a recovery mission carried out by scientists from the National Oceanic Atmospheric Association (NOAA). The NOAA team, along with scores of U.S. Navy divers, worked without stopping around the clock for 28 days to free the ship's 30-ton steam engine from the "Graveyard of the Atlantic."

[2]

Designed by noted 19th-century engineer John Ericsson. *The Monitor* rests upside down on a sand-covered seafloor approximately 16 miles Southeast of Cape Hatteras, North Carolina, in the waters of NOAA's *Monitor* National Marine Sanctuary. A 400 ton crane aboard the

16. F. NO CHANGE
    G. 2001, because
    H. 2001; for
    J. 2001, for

17. A. NO CHANGE
    B. breaks
    C. has broken
    D. was broken

18. F. NO CHANGE
    G. around the clock for 28 days
    H. non-stop for 28 days and nights
    J. continual 28 days

19. NO CHANGE
    B. Ericsson; consequently, the
    C. Ericsson; the
    D. Ericsson, the

derrick barge *Wotan* hoisted the steam engine which had previously sunk from 240 feet below the ocean's surface to a waiting ferry barge. The engine is being transported to a 93,000 gallon steel tank at The Mariners' Museum in Newport News, Virginia, where conservators will begin the 10-year process to preserve the historic steam engine.

20. F. NO CHANGE
    G. which had previously sunk,
    H. which sunk
    J. OMIT the underlined portion

21. A. NO CHANGE
    B. (place after *Museum*)
    C. (place after *tank*)
    D. (place at the beginning of the sentence and capitalize *where*)

[3]

John Broadwater, manager of NOAA's *Monitor* National Marine Sanctuary, oversaw the archeological aspects of the mission. More than 150 divers from 17 commands logged more than 300 hours of bottom time on this mission. The Navy, through the Legacy Foundation, provided $4.9 million to save the famous warship. During this year's expedition, divers worked for four weeks to remove the lower hull plating and securing six lifting straps to key sections of the engine. They really got lucky after that. When that work was complete and the environmental

22. F. NO CHANGE
    G. to secure
    H. secured
    J. had secured

23. A. NO CHANGE
    B. There is a silver lining in every cloud.
    C. As everyone knows, the cloud is always darkest before the storm.
    D. OMIT the underlined portion.

conditions were right, Captain Murray and John Broadwater gave the order to raise the engine. More than 100 artifacts have been recovered this year alone, including a portion of what is believed to be Ericsson's forced-air ventilation system. A brass filigree wall sconce, several intact lantern chimneys, the engineers alarm bell and locating a completely intact engine room thermometer are among the other items retrieved.

[4]

In March 1862, the USS Monitor took part in the most famous naval exchange of the Civil War, a four-hour duel with the Confederate ironclad CSS Virginia, a converted Union ship the USS Merrimack, at Hampton Roads, Virginia. The Monitor was lost nine months later during a severe storm off Cape Hatteras. Efforts to raise the USS Monitor began more than a decade ago. NOAA scientists, concerned about the rapid deterioration of the ship, began plans to salvage the remainder of the ship before it

24. F. NO CHANGE
    G. engineer's alarm
    H. engineer's alarm's
    J. engineers's alarms

25. A. NO CHANGE
    B. location of
    C. finding the location of
    D. OMIT the underlined word

was lost forever. The Monitor 2001
Expedition continues as NOAA divers,
working alongside Navy salvage divers,
begin the recovery of the ship's innovative
revolving gun turret.
                         26

26. Suppose the writer wanted to improve the unity of this passage by moving this sentence to a different paragraph. Which paragraph provides the most logical location for the sentence?

   F. NO CHANGE
   G. 1
   H. 2
   J. 3

27. Suppose the writer decided that background information about the USS Monitor would be more effective if placed at the beginning of the essay. Which order of paragraphs would then be most effective?

   A. 1,2,3,4
   B. 4,1,2,3
   C. 2,3,4,1
   D. 4,3,2,1

28. The writer wants to add the following detail:

   Next, we hope the turn our attention to recovering the "soul" of the Monitor, her revolving gun turret.

   The sentence would most logically be placed in paragraph

   F. 1
   G. 2
   H. 3
   J. 4

29. Suppose the author had been asked to give his essay a new title. Which of the following would be the most appropriate title for the essay?

   A. Watery Grave
   B. Cape Hatteras
   C. NOAA Scientists
   D. John Ericsson

30. The writer's main purpose of this essay is

F. to campaign for more money to raise *The USS Monitor*.
G. to inform the audience about efforts to raise *The USS Monitor*.
H. to describe the watery grave of *The USS Monitor*.
J. to relate the history of an important Civil War battle.

This passage is adapted from information on the National Archives and Records Administration website, 2001.

EMANCIPATION PROCLAMATION

[1]

President Abraham Lincoln <u>issued</u>[31] the Emancipation Proclamation on January 1, 1863, as the nation approached <u>its</u>[32] third year of bloody civil war. The proclamation <u>declared; "that</u>[33] all persons held as slaves" within the rebellious states "are, and henceforward shall be free." <u>Moreover,</u>[34] the Emancipation Proclamation was limited in many ways. It applied only to states that had seceded from the <u>Union, and</u>[35] leaving slavery untouched in the loyal border states. It also expressly exempted parts of the Confederacy that had already come under Northern control. <u>Most important,</u>[36] the freedom it promised depended upon Union military victory.

[2]

Although the Emancipation Proclamation did not immediately free a single <u>slave,</u>[37] fundamentally transformed the character of the war. After January 1, 1863,

31. A. NO CHANGE
    B. issues
    C. has issued
    D. issued an set forth

32. F. NO CHANGE
    G. it's
    H. their
    J. it is

33. A. NO CHANGE
    B. declared; "That
    C. declared, "that
    D. declared. "That

34. F. NO CHANGE
    G. Despite this expansive wording,
    H. In addition to these words
    J. However the broad scope of

35. A. NO CHANGE
    B. Union, and by
    C. Union; leaving
    D. Union, leaving

36. F. NO CHANGE
    G. Most importantly,
    H. Conversely,
    J. In conclusion

37. A. NO CHANGE
    B. slave and transport them to freedom
    C. slave, it
    D. slave, like nothing else

every advance of federal troops expanded the domain of freedom. Moreover, the Proclamation announced the acceptance of black men into the Union Army and Navy, the liberated became liberators. 38 39

[3]

From the first days of the Civil War, slaves had acted to secure their own liberty and freedom. The Emancipation Proclamation confirmed their insistence that the war for the Union must become a war for freedom. It added moral force to the Union cause and strengthened the Union both militarily and politically. As a milestone along the road to slavery's final destruction, the Emancipation Proclamation has assumed a place among the great documents of human freedom.

[4]

[1] The original of the Emancipation Proclamation of January 1, 1863, is in the National Archives in Washington, DC. [2] With the text covering five pages the document was originally tied with narrow

38. F. NO CHANGE
G. Navy: the
H. Navy; however the
J. Navy, when the

39. Assuming all are true, which detail, if substituted for the last sentence in paragraph 2, would best support the writer's purpose?

A. After the end of the war, the Department of State transferred the document to the National Archives.
B. However, hundreds of escaped slaves had assisted the British during the War of Independence.
C. Parts of the seal on the document are still decipherable today.
D. By the end of the war, almost 200,000 black soldiers and sailors had fought for the Union and freedom.

40. F. NO CHANGE
G. liberty.
H. liberty and freedom from enfranchisement.
J. liberty and freedom:

41. A. NO CHANGE
B. both militarily and in politics.
C. both militarily and thus politically.
D. in the military and politically

42. F. NO CHANGE
G. The Emancipation Proclamation is a
H. Because the Emancipation Proclamation is a
J. Although the Emancipation Proclamation was a

red and blue ribbons, which were attached to the signature page by a wafered impression of the seal of the United States. [3] Most of the ribbon remains; parts of the seal are still decipherable, but other parts have worn off. [4] It's really too bad that you can't read all of the seal cause it would be great to know what it said. [5] The document was bound with other proclamations in a large volume preserved for many years by the Department of State. [6] When it was prepared for binding, it was reinforced with strips along the centerfolds and then mounted on a still larger sheet of heavy paper. [7] Written in red ink on the upper right-hand corner of this large sheet is the number of the Proclamation, 95, given to it by the Department of State long after it was signed.

Items 43-45 pose questions about the passage as a whole

43. The primary purpose of the last paragraph is to

   A. describe the actual document.
   B. give the history of the seal placed on the document.
   C. argue for the acceptance of the document by the state department.
   D. argue for better preservation of the document.

44. Which sentence in paragraph 4 should be eliminated in consideration of unity of style?

   F. NO CHANGE
   G. 2
   H. 3
   J. 4

45. Suppose an editor asked you to write a sentence which would summarize the passage. Which of the following would best serve that purpose?

   A. During the Civil War, thousands of African-American slaves joined their owners' fight for freedom.
   B. The participation of African-American slaves had a tremendous impact on the outcome of the Civil War.
   C. The Emancipation Proclamation has assumed a place among the great documents of human freedom.
   D. The Emancipation Proclamation was so limited in scope that it did not significantly impact the Civil War.

This passage is adapted from information on the U.S. Environmental Protection Agency website, 2001.

BEACHES

[1]

In summer Americans head to the beach, their favorite vacation choice. Thousands are headed for areas along the Gulf of Mexico. They'll soon be fishing, swimming, walking, beach combing, windsurfing, bird watching, scuba diving, and sunbathing. These activities are a fun-in-the-sun summer tradition which is loads of fun and are an important part of region's economy. In Texas alone, coastal tourism is a $7 billion industry, the fasting growing segment of which is nature tourism.

[2]

For scuba divers, favorite destinations in the Gulf are the Flower Gardens, the three northernly-most coral reefs in the nation. Perched atop underwater salt domes 70 miles southeast of Freeport and 100 miles from Galveston. The reefs were named by early fishermen who could see the colorful corals and sponges only

46. F. NO CHANGE
G. beach their
H. beach: their
J. beach: his

47 A. NO CHANGE
B. which is fun recreation
C. that is real fun
D. omit the underlined words

48 F. NO CHANGE
G. northern-most
H. most-northerly
J. mostly northern

49 A. NO CHANGE
B. Galveston; the
C. Galveston, the
D. Galveston, consequently the

50-60 feet below the water's surface. Many tourists can't figure out how the corals got their ridiculous names.
     50

[3]

Vacationers enjoying the Gulf will share its resources with an incredible array of fish, shellfish, aquatic plants, water birds and endangered species that also call the Gulf home. Many types of plants and sea grasses grow in the warm lagoons and
                    51
marshes of the Gulf beach ecosystem, making them important breeding areas for fish and shellfish. However, more than 365
                              52
species of birds have been found on the Texas coast, a larger number than in any other state. Millions of birds depend on the marshes for feeding, breeding or wintering habitat. Wading birds feed on small fish and shrimp in the marshes, and dune vegetation providing nesting areas for several kinds of
   53
birds and animals. Some 75 percent of migratory waterfowl use coastal beaches for refueling and rest stops. Marshes also protect against flooding by slowing and

50 F. NO CHANGE
    G. Many tourists are disturbed because all the corals are not given names.
    H. The names of the corals really don't fit the appearance.
    J. Omit the underlined sentence.

51 A. NO CHANGE
    B. grew
    C. growed
    D. have grown

52 F. NO CHANGE
    G. Consequently, more
    H. Increasingly, more
    J. More

53 A. NO CHANGE
    B. provides
    C. provided
    D. makes provisions for

dispersing runoff, and as a result, coastal vegetation filters silt, sewage and other pollution.

[4]

Since the Gulf Coast is a sensitive environment that supports life for a variety of important plants and animals, vacationers should be careful not to damage their beach playgrounds. Too much walking on dunes can erode and destroy vegetation. Trash dumped from boats can wash onto the beach and pose a threat to both marine life and humans. When boat sewage isn't disposed of properly, water quality is degraded. Americans love beaches, and they should, because beaches are fun and important to the economy and the environment.

54 F. NO CHANGE
G. runoff and
H. runoff;
J. runoff: and

55 A. NO CHANGE
B. should: Beaches
C. should, beaches
D. should, on the other hand, beaches

Items 56-60 pose questions about the passage as a whole

56 Suppose the writer wanted to add the following detail to the passage:

> Some 75 percent of migratory waterfowl use coastal beaches for refueling and rest stops.

Which paragraph would most logically include that information?

F. 2
G. 3
H. 4
J. 5

57 Which paragraph has a different purpose and tone than the other three?

A. 1
B. 2
C. 3
D. 4

58 What is the primary purpose of the essay?

F. to inform the public about southern beaches.
G. to compare popular beaches in the South.
H. to argue for increased federal funding to protect the beaches.
J. to discuss the wintering habits of migratory birds.

59 Suppose the writer wanted to add supporting detail about the biological diversity and breathtaking beauty of coral reefs. This information should most likely be placed in which paragraph?

A. 1
B. 2
C. 3
D. 4

60 Suppose the writer had been assigned an essay that detailed safety precautions for tourists traveling to beaches. Would this essay successfully fulfill that assignment?

F. Yes, because it provides details for avoiding dangerous plant and marine life.
G. Yes, because it describes safe locations for family vacations.
H. No, because the passage mainly informs the reader about what is available at America's southern beaches.
J. No, because the passage mainly provides an argument for stronger measures to prevent pollution of beaches.

CAREER CHOICE

[1]

The trouble all started when my college advisor Mr. Strickland asked me to declare a major. I had always imagined myself working in some sort of medical field, probably because both of my parents are doctors, but when the time came to choose a specific focus for my future. I was at a loss. Mr. Strickland recognized my indecision, uncertainty and indecisiveness and suggested that I take some time to think it over and return the next afternoon to discuss it with him.

[2]

[1] As I walked slowly across the tree-lined campus, I tried to imagine myself working in a job unrelated to the medical field. [2] Some careers were easy to eliminate. [3] Accounting didn't appeal to me, I didn't want to deal with numbers or do people's taxes. [4] Being a salesperson was out—I could not imagine trying to convince someone to buy something I knew they

61. A. NO CHANGE
    B. advisor—Mr. Strickland, asked
    C. advisor, Mr. Strickland asked
    D. advisor, Mr. Strickland, asked

62. F. NO CHANGE
    G. my future: I was
    H. my future; I was
    J. my future, I was

63. A. NO CHANGE
    B. my indecision and uncertainty and indecisiveness
    C. my indecision
    D. that I was very indecisive and uncertain

64. F. NO CHANGE
    G. me; I
    H. me and I
    J. me, on the other hand

65. A. NO CHANGE
    B. out, I
    C. out—she
    D. out. The reason was that I

didn't really need. [5] My roommate worked as a customer service clerk at a major department store, and I was constantly hearing horror stories about the angry and dissatisfied customers she had to deal with on a daily basis. [6] That didn't sound like something I would want to do for the rest of my life. [66]

[3]

I sat on a bench and opened a career catalog near the fountain in the center of campus that Mr. Strickland had given me before I left his office. As I pored over the listing of potential careers, one caught my eye: art historian ever since I was a young girl, I had always loved going to museums and exploring the background of the paintings, sculptures, and objects that appealed to me in some way. Could I really get paid to appreciate art? I decided to do some research in order to make the more informed decision I could.

66 The author is considering dividing paragraph 2 into two individual paragraphs. In consideration of logic and coherence, the best decision is to:
F. leave the paragraph as it is.
G. Begin a new paragraph with sentence 3.
H. Begin a new paragraph with sentence 4.
J. Begin a new paragraph with sentence 5.

67 A. NO CHANGE
B. [place after me]
C. [place after Mr. Strickland]
D. [place after bench]

68 F. NO CHANGE
G. historian, ever
H. historian. Ever
J. historian – obviously ever

69 A. NO CHANGE
B. the most informed
C. a more informed
D. the most informing

[4]

On the contrary, my best plan was to talk directly to an art historian to find out if the job would be compatible with my interests and abilities. My local museum should provide just the person I needed. The secretary I spoke with scheduled me an appointment the next day with Leland Smithers, the lead curator of our Modern Art Museum.

[5]

[1] Mr. Smithers shattered my image of a museum curator; I had pictured a musty, bent older man with thick glasses, but Mr. Smithers was none of that. [2] He was young, athletic-looking, and very personable. [3] He had actually worked in the Louvre in Paris before he had taken this job. [4] He welcomed me warmly into his office, offering me a comfortable, leather armchair. [5] After the introductions had been completed I came right to the point and asked him to explain exactly what his job entailed. [6] His eyes lit up with

70 F. NO CHANGE
    G. Obviously
    H. Eventually
    J. In addition

71 A. NO CHANGE
    B. completed, I
    C. completed: I
    D. completed. I

enthusiasm as he began to discuss his responsibilities at the museum. [7] After about an hour of talking with Mr. Smithers, I had made up my mind. [8] This was exactly the career I had been looking for. [9] What other job would allow me to travel the world collecting beautiful paintings, help restore priceless artifacts, and be a part of exposing young people to the world of fine art? [10] I couldn't believe someone would actually pay me to do those things. [72]

[6]

After thanking Mr. Smithers profusely, I raced over to my advisor's office, eager to let him know what major I had chosen. Mr. Strickland was almost <u>as pumped as</u> I was, and we enthusiastically
73
began planning my course selections.

72 Which of the sentences in paragraph 5 should be omitted for the sake of unity and coherence?

F. NO CHANGE
G. 1
H. 3
J. 5

73 A. NO CHANGE
B. as happy and thrilled as I told him
C. as terrified as
D. as excited as

Items 74-75 pose questions about the passage as a whole

74. The author wishes to add a final sentence to the end of paragraph 6.

    Which of the following statements is most effective?

    F. I knew my parents would be disappointed in my decision, but my brother could go to medical school instead of me.
    G. A huge burden had been lifted from my shoulders: I had chosen a major.
    H. I was so glad that Mr. Strickland was my advisor.
    J. I hoped that I would get to work for Mr. Smithers one day.

75. According to the passage, how does the young woman feel about choosing art history as her major?

    A. confused
    B. angry
    C. disappointed
    D. relieved

The ACT Assessment Writing Test

Preface
Don't take it. That's right, don't take it. This writing test is not designed to raise your score. No matter how great of a writer you think you are, I recommend you don't take this writing portion unless required. This section is more time, stress, and money, and most colleges don't even look at this score.

ACT has increased the time for this section from 30 minutes to 40 minutes. I took the sample 6 out of 6 essay ACT published and timed myself copying it. To simply re-write the essay in a somewhat legible form, it took me 24 ½ minutes. If it takes roughly 25 minutes to simply copy the essay, you need to be efficient in the other 15 minutes organizing your thoughts, editing, and re-writing.

What is it?
The ACT Assessment Writing Test is an optional writing assessment added to the ACT in 2004-2005. The test contains a writing prompt that will present a difficult issue then outline three different perspectives on the issue. The 40-minute test is designed to provide colleges and universities a "direct" writing sample produced in a timed, controlled setting. Paired with the information provided by the English test, the writing assessment scores provide postsecondary institutions with a measure of student skills with grammar, usage, mechanics, sentence skills, logic, organization, coherence, and style.

Who should take it?
1. If the college to which you are applying requires it.
2. If it is required by your state or school.

Good writing skills and writing well in a timed environment are important to earning a high score. If you have a hard time organizing your thoughts quickly or if you have to spend considerable time revising or editing, the writing test may be difficult. Look carefully at the criteria that will be used to evaluate essays. You might ask your English teacher or counselor to evaluate a practice writing sample.

How will it be evaluated?
Domain Scores: You will be given four domain scores from 2-12. This score is determined based on the following four areas of evaluation: ideas and analysis, development and support, organization, and language use and conventions.

ELA Score: An average of your English, reading, and writing scores.

Single-Subject Level Writing Score: Each domain is scored on a scale from 1-6. The subject-level score is the rounded average of the four domain scores. Two readers grade your essay. Your score is the sum of the two graders' scores. Your writing score will be from 2 to 12.

A complete breakdown of the domains and scoring rubric can be found on ACT's website. Visit podcast.chadcargill.com/41 to learn more.

6 Effective skills

    Unity
- Clear focus
- Focus consistent throughout
- Effective introduction and conclusion

    Development
- Specific detailed support
- Sufficient elaboration of ideas

    Coherence
- Logical sequence of support
- Clear organization
- Appropriate use of transitions

    Sentence skills
- Variety of sentence types
- Precise and varied word choice
- Few mechanical errors

5 Competent skills
4 Adequate skills
3 Developing skills
2 Inconsistent or weak skills
1 Little or no skills

How can I prepare?
1. Review the writing skills you already know so you are clear about expectations. Examine the criteria that the evaluators use to be sure you know what is expected of your writing. Review writing strategies that you have used in your English classes. Make sure you have a strategy for developing a thesis and getting started on your essay.

If you need additional practice with writing a thesis statement, consider the following formula for thesis development: TAP.

    T topic
    A attitude towards the topic
    P plan of attack to support the topic

Example: If you were given a writing prompt that asked you to take a stance on having a mandatory uniform policy at your high school, you can use the TAP strategy to formulate a thesis. Here is an example of the thought process you can use.

    T topic—mandatory uniform policy
    A attitude—don't want or need it
    P plan of attack—doesn't improve academics

inhibits freedom of expression
creates problems with enforcement

Using these ideas, you can come up with a thesis statement.

Thesis: A mandatory uniform policy is not needed at my high school because it would not improve academics, does not allow freedom of expression, and would create unneeded enforcement problems.

Remember that the subpoints in your plan of attack will become topic sentences for your support paragraphs. Practice the TAP strategy and write thesis statements for several of the writing prompt suggestions.

2. Review two "no-fail" introduction strategies. Remember that an introduction paragraph should grab your reader's attention and provide sufficient background on the topic for your reader to be able to understand your position. Here are 2 strategies that could work for almost any topic that you are given. Remember these strategies so you can quickly get started writing.

1. Begin with the big picture in mind—a broad general approach. Start by looking at the big picture and then narrow your topic to your thesis statement. In other words, situate the problem; provide a broad context for the issue. For example, if your topic was a mandatory uniform policy, you could begin your essay by describing the problems that exist in education that have caused authorities to propose the radical idea of mandatory uniforms for all students.

2. Introduce the opposite. Recognize the opposing arguments to a position you will support in your essay. Presenting the opposite situation in your introduction allows you the advantage of being able to write support paragraphs that argue your position as well as counter opposing arguments. For example, an essay opposing a mandatory uniform policy could begin with the arguments many schools have used to institute the policy.

3. Use timed-writing strategies.
- Go with the flow. Remember that in a timed writing it doesn't matter if the evaluators agree with your position. It is more important how you express yourself than what your opinion is. Take a stance your can best support on whatever issue is given, decide on what support you can provide, and go with it. Don't be distracted by arguing with the prompt or arguing with yourself about the issues.
- Don't flip flop. For a timed writing, don't try to cover more than one side of an issue. Select a position that you can best support and stick to that position.
- Start with the best. Present your best argument first in a timed writing. Your first support paragraph should be your best. You don't want to run out of time before you get to your strongest point, so start strong and save the ideas for which you have the weakest support for when you have the least time.
- End it quick. In a timed essay, don't write an entire conclusion paragraph. You don't want to use your allotted time and space restating ideas. Instead, write a one or two-sentence summary that is an original restatement of your thesis ideas. A summary sentence recapping

your thesis and main points will be all you have time for. End with a "clincher" if you have time. A clincher idea would be to answer the question, "So what?" In other words, if the ideas in your essay were carried out, "so what" would be the result? What is the big picture?

4. Practice outlining likely topics.
Since the topic must be something all high school students can write about, you can prepare by thinking through some of the more likely topics which the ACT might use. Look through the following list of prompts and practice outlining 4 or 5 paragraph essays you could write on the topics. Knowing how to organize your thoughts ahead will save you valuable time.

Sample Topic Ideas to Consider:
- Should high schools implement a mandatory uniform policy?
- If you could make changes in your school cafeteria, what would they be?
- Everyone has days that they will always remember as being very special. Think about a special day that you have had. Write an essay telling why it was so special.
- Rules are important. What are the most important rules at your school and why are they important?
- Why it is important to learn to read?
- We are learning all the time. Some of our learning takes place in school and some outside of school. Write about something you have learned recently and how it has affected you.
- Think of the ideal job for you when you graduate. Write an essay to explain why this is your ideal job.
- Think of a book that you have read and really enjoyed. Write an essay explaining why you really enjoyed that book.
- Imagine that time travel to the past is possible. Think of where and when you would like to go for a visit. Write an essay telling where and why you would go in the past and explain why you choose to go there.
- Imagine that you had no TV, computer, or video games for one week. Think of some activities that you can do instead to keep you busy and out of trouble. Write an essay to explain what you can do to keep occupied in a week of no technology.
- Think about your favorite year of school. Explain why it was your favorite year.
- Friends are important, but everyone has different opinions of what makes a good friend. Explain what makes a good friend.
- Some teachers are special. Explain why one teacher in your life was so special.
- Your principal has asked you to write your opinions about what needs to be changed in your school. What would you change?
- Write an essay describing the most admirable qualities of the person you most admire.
- Who are the three people you most want to emulate and why?
- All people must overcome obstacles in their lives. Explain an obstacle you have overcome and explain how you overcame it.
- What three personality characteristics do you feel you should improve to become a better and happier person?
- Some minor characters in novels can play major roles in the story. Identify a minor character in a novel you have read and discuss the important role he/she played in the novel.
- Physical education classes are necessary/ unnecessary for students.

- Commercials should/should not be banned on children's television programming.

5. Practice writing prompts and get feedback. Pick one of the above topics and practice timed writings. Strive to get at least a 5-paragraph essay in the 40-minute time period. Spend a few minutes creating your thesis and quickly outlining your support paragraphs. Then decide on a method of introduction and begin writing. Allow a few minutes to edit at the end. Be sure and add transitions within and between paragraphs for coherence if you did not include them as you wrote. You may want to review the lesson on transitions in this book. Ask someone familiar with the characteristics of effective writing to evaluate your writing. Maybe your English teacher would be willing to substitute a practice timed writing for a writing assignment you are currently working on in class.

Four Keys to a Successful ACT Writing Score:

1. Write in the five-paragraph essay format. Although there are many different ways to write persuasive essays, ACT graders appear to like the five-paragraph essay format. Include a short introduction with a good thesis sentence identifying your key points. Write a body paragraph for each point. Finish with a short conclusion paragraph.

2. Use a variety of sentence structure and convincing vocabulary. The essays with the highest scores include sentences with a variety of structure. For example, graders like the use of a colon where it sets off a summary sentence. Your vocabulary should be convincing and should show clear flow and focus on your position.

3. Write long paragraphs (about 8 sentences each). The paragraphs of the highest graded essays are long. Develop several thoughts to support each point.

4. Put your best point first. Make the first body paragraph the best paragraph you've ever written even at the slight expense of the rest of the essay. Convince the grader you're a great writer early. She'll skim the end. She's got hundreds more to grade.

Listen to podcast.chadcargill.com/41 for more information on the ACT writing test.

Episode 41: ACT Writing - When You Should Take It and How to Get a Great Score

CONCEPT: ADJECTIVE USE KEY
STUDENT PRACTICE PARAGRAPH (p. 13)

Adjectives are in bold type. Articles are included; you may wish to disregard them.

Because she was interested in **the tragic** history of World War II, Shelly decided to attend **a historical** lecture offered at **her local** university. **Several WWII** veterans were to discuss **their** experiences during **the** war and would answer questions following **the two-hour** program. As she entered **the chilly lecture** hall, she observed **a** group of men and women seated on **the** stage; they were dressed in uniforms from each of **the** branches of **the armed** forces. She made **her** way through **the crowded** room and found **a single**, **empty** seat toward **the** front. **An elderly**, **stooped** gentleman stepped to **the** podium and introduced himself as Nathan Gray, **an Air Force** pilot who had served from 1942 until January of 1945 when he was severely injured by **a hidden land** mine. Shelly was shocked to realize that **this stoic** stranger had sacrificed **his left** hand and most of **his left** leg in **the** service of **his** country. One by one, **the** people on **the** stage stepped forward to offer **their incredible** stories of **fierce** bravery, **intense** hardship and **unfaltering** courage. By **the** time **the mesmerizing** program was over, Shelly was convinced that **present-day** Americans truly owe **an enormous** debt of gratitude to what has been called **the <u>Greatest</u>** Generation.

CONCEPT: ADJECTIVE USE KEY
ACT TEST SAMPLE QUESTIONS (p. 13)

1. A. The verb *terrify* is incorrectly used as an adjective.
   B. The verb *terrifying* is incorrectly used as an adjective.
   C. Changing *my* to *the* does not change the incorrect use of *terrify*.
   D. **CORRECT: *terrified* is an adjective correctly describing *family*.**

2. A. Severely is an adverb used incorrectly as an adjective.
   B. **CORRECT: severe is an adjective modifying the noun damage.**
   C. Although using severe is correct, the relative pronoun *that* should only be used to refer to people not things.
   D. The damage is not advantageous.

3. A. The adverb *largely* is incorrectly used as an adjective.
   B. Use *the* when using the superlative form of an adjective (*largest*).
   C. CORRECT: the adjective *large* correctly modifies the noun *book*.
   D. Changing *a* to *the* does not change the incorrect use of the adverb *largely*.

4. A. *Pretty* and *attractive* is redundant.
   B. Separating the adjectives with semicolons is incorrect.
   C. Separating *pretty* and *adjective* with a dash is incorrect.
   D. CORRECT: removing *attractive* corrects the redundancy.

5. **A. CORRECT: *American* is an adjective correctly modifying the noun *citizen*.**
   B. The noun *America* is incorrectly used as an adjective.
   C. *The* is too limiting.
   D. *An* should be paired with a singular noun not the plural *citizens*.

CONCEPT: ADVERB USE KEY
STUDENT PRACTICE (p. 17)

1. A. Incorrect
   B. The adjective *certain* should be changed to the adverb *certainly*.

2. A. Correct
   B. The adverb *softly* correctly modifies the verb *spoke*.

3. A. Incorrect
   B. It is incorrect to pair *too* with the comparative form longer. To correctly use the comparative form, two items must be compared, but the sentence only speaks of one trip. Change *longer* to *long*.

4. A. Incorrect
   B. Change most to *more*. Use *more* with the comparative form.

5. A. Incorrect
   B. The adjective *swift* is incorrectly modifying the verb *run*. Change it to the adverb *swiftly*.

ACT TEST SAMPLE QUESTIONS (p. 17)

1. A. The adjective *quick* is being used incorrectly as an adverb.
   B. *Quick* and the comma are incorrect.
   C. CORRECT: the adjective is changed to an adverb *quickly*.
   D. *Quicker* is in the comparative form which is incorrect for this sentence.

2. A. The adjective *extreme* is incorrectly used as an adverb.
   B. CORRECT: the adjective is changed to an adverb *extremely*.
   C. The plural helping verb *have* does not agree with the singular subject.
   D. The use of the adjective *good* as an adverb is incorrect.

3. **A. CORRECT: the adverb *completely* correctly modifies the verb.**
   B. The adjective *complete* is incorrectly used as an adverb.
   C. The past tense helping verb *been* is incorrect for this sentence.
   D. The present tense of the verb *finish* is incorrect for this sentence.

4. A. The adjective *bad* is incorrectly used as an adverb.
   B. *Well* does not fulfill the contradiction expressed in the sentence.
   C. CORRECT: the adverb *badly* correctly modifies the verb.
   D. The plural verb *sing* does not agree with the singular subject.

5. A. The underlined portion contains a double negative: *never* and *nothing*.
   B. Changing the verb tense does not correct the double negative.
   C. CORRECT: changing *nothing* to *anything* corrects the double negative.
   D. Changing *never* to *not* does not correct the double negative.

CONCEPT: CONJUNCTION USE KEY
STUDENT PRACTICE (p. 20)
Answers may vary. Examples are given.

1. but
2. both; and
3. whenever
4. consequently
5. neither; nor
6. therefore
7. unless
8. or
9. not only; but also
10. hence

SENTENCE COMBINING (p. 21)
Answers will vary

ACT TEST SAMPLE QUESTIONS (p. 22)

1. A. *Accordingly* does not convey the intention of the sentence.
   B. Using a comma before a conjunctive adverb is incorrect. Using *accordingly* is also incorrect.
   C. CORRECT: *nevertheless* correctly signals the relationship between the two clauses.
   D. Separating *experiment* and *nevertheless* with a comma is incorrect.

2. **A. CORRECT: the subordinating conjunction *although* is used and punctuated correctly.**
   B. Placing a colon between *areas* and *although* is incorrect.
   C. Placing a semicolon between *areas* and *although* is incorrect.
   D. The subordinating conjunction *because* does not reflect the relationship between the two clauses.

3. A. A comma must be placed between *weekends* and *yet*.
   B. Semicolon use is incorrect.
   C. Colon use is incorrect.
   D. CORRECT: use a comma with a coordinating conjunction.

4. A. The subordinating conjunction *if* does not signal the relationship between the two sentences.
   B. Placing a comma after *if* is incorrect.
   C. CORRECT: the subordinating conjunction *As soon as* correctly signals the relationship between the sentences.
   D. Placing a comma after *as* is incorrect.

5. A. A comma must be used before the coordinating conjunction.
   B. CORRECT: An adverb dependant clause at the beginning of the sentence needs a comma.
   C. Using a semicolon is incorrect.
   D. The coordinating conjunction *and* does not signal the relationship between the clauses.

CONCEPT: VERB USE KEY
STUDENT PRACTICE (p. 25)

1. chosen
2. broke
3. driven
4. speaking
5. taken
6. flew
7. teach
8. talked
9. crying
10. seen

EXTENDED PRACTICE (p. 26)

1. followed
2. locked
3. CORRECT
4. slammed
5. turned
6. trapped
7. CORRECT
8. rescued
9. spent
10. said

CONCEPT: VERB USE KEY
ACT TEST SAMPLE QUESTIONS (p. 26)

1. A. The underlined portion has an unnecessary verb tense change.
   B. The verb tense is still incorrect.
   C. Using *have* with the verb incorrectly makes it a past participle; *have* is also plural and the subject is singular.
   D. **CORRECT: *races* is correctly changed to *raced*, making it consistent with the past tense established in the sentence.**

2. A. **CORRECT: the tense of *studied* is consistent with the past tense established in the sentence.**
   B. It is incorrect to use a comma after *that*.
   C. The tense of *studying* is not consistent with the past tense of the sentence.
   D. *Have* is plural, but the subject is singular.

3. A. The tense of *give* is not consistent with the tense of the rest of the sentence.
   B. The tense of *is giving* is not consistent with the tense of the rest of the sentence.
   C. **CORRECT: the past *gave* tense of agrees with the past tense of the sentence.**
   D. *Given* must be paired with a helping verb and is in the wrong tense.

4. A. *Land* is in the wrong tense.
   B. **CORRECT: the past tense of *landed* is consistent with the tense of the sentence.**
   C. The verb tense *landing* would make the sentence a run-on.
   D. *Lands* is in the wrong tense.

5. A. **CORRECT: *Ignored* is past tense and is consistent with the rest of the sentence.**
   B. *Ignores* is in the wrong tense.
   C. Separating *squirrel* and *ignored* with a comma is incorrect.
   D. *Has ignored* is a past participle not past tense.

CONCEPT: SUBJECT/VERB AGREEMENT KEY I
STUDENT PRACTICE (p. 29)
1. need
2. sisters
3. call
4. says
5. begin
6. boys
7. tries
8. swim
9. eats
10. producers

CONCEPT: SUBJECT VERB AGREEMENT KEY II
STUDENT PRACTICE (p. 31)
1. doesn't
2. disagrees
3. is
4. is
5. is
6. problem
7. don't
8. have
9. thinks
10. is

CONCEPT: SUBJECT VERB AGREEMENT KEY III
ACT TEST SAMPLE QUESTIONS (p. 32)

1. A. The singular verb *throws* does not agree with the plural subject *workers*.
   B. Changing *fields* to *field* does not correct the faulty subject verb agreement.
   C. Removing the comma does not correct the faulty subject verb agreement.
   D. CORRECT: the plural verb *throw* agrees with the plural subject *workers*.

2. **A. CORRECT: the number and tense of the subject and verb agree.**
   B. Placing a comma after the subject is incorrect.
   C. The plural helping verb *have* does not agree with the singular subject.
   D. The past tense of *became* does not agree with the tense established in the sentence.

3. A. The plural verb *want* does not agree with the singular subject caused by the pronoun *every*.
   B. CORRECT: the singular verb *wants* agrees with the subject.
   C. Placing a comma after *door* is incorrect.
   D. Changing *door* to *doors* does not correct the faulty subject verb agreement.

4. A. The plural verb *have* does not agree with the singular subject.
   B. Changing *dolls* to *doll* does not correct the faulty subject verb agreement.
   C. The article *A* indicates a singular noun; using *collectors* would be incorrect.
   D. CORRECT: the singular verb *has* agrees with the singular subject.

5. A. *Most* is plural because of its antecedent *attorneys*. The singular verb *believes* is incorrect.
   B. Using the singular *attorney* is incorrect.
   C. CORRECT: plural verb agrees with the plural subject.
   D. Wrong verb tense.

CONCEPT: PRONOUN USAGE KEY
STUDENT PRACTICE (p. 35)

1. He
2. them
3. mine
4. They
5. them
6. us
7. she
8. him
9. his
10. Their

ACT TEST SAMPLE QUESTIONS (p. 36)

1. A. Incorrect pronoun case
   B. *There* is an adverb not a pronoun
   C. CORRECT: the objective case should be used because the pronoun is the object of the preposition *of*.
   D. Incorrect pronoun case.

2. A. *It's* means *it is*.
   B. The plural *their* does not agree with the singular antecedent.
   C. *My* is first person and the pronoun should be in third person.
   D. CORRECT: *its* is a possessive pronoun.

3. A. The indirect object must be in the objective case not the nominative case.
   B. *She* is nominative case.
   C. CORRECT: *me* is in the objective case.
   D. *My* is a possessive pronoun.

4. **A. CORRECT: the direct object *me* is in the objective case.**
   B. *She* is in the nominative case.
   C. *We* is in the nominative case.
   D. Placing a common after *me* is incorrect.

5. **A. CORRECT:** ***They*** **is correct in person and in case.**
   B. *Them* is in the objective case; subjects should be in the nominative case.
   C. *There* is in the possessive case.
   D. *They're* means *They are* which is incorrect.

CONCEPT: PRONOUN AND ANTECEDENT AGREEMENT KEY
STUDENT PRACTICE (p. 38)
1. she
2. they
3. their
4. She
5. they
6. she
7. their
8. us
9. his or her
10. her

ACT TEST SAMPLE QUESTIONS (p. 39)

1. A. The singular pronoun *his* does not agree with the plural antecedent *neighbors*.
   B. CORRECT: the plural pronoun *their* agrees with the plural antecedents *neighbors*.
   C. The singular pronoun *her* does not agree with the plural antecedent *neighbors*.
   D. The possessive pronoun *my* does not agree with the antecedent *neighbors*.

2. A. The singular pronoun *it* does not agree with the plural antecedent *shirts*.
   B. CORRECT: the plural pronoun *them* agrees with the plural antecedent *shirts*.
   C. The singular pronoun *it* does not agree with the plural antecedent *shirts* and the semicolon is used incorrectly.
   D. The possessive pronoun *its* does not agree with the plural antecedent *shirts*.

3. A. The possessive pronoun *their* does not agree with the plural antecedent *Carlos and Jenni*
   B. The plural antecedent *Carlos and Jenni* takes a plural pronoun. *He* and *she* are singular pronouns.
   C. CORRECT: the plural pronoun *they* agrees with the plural antecedent *Carlos and Jenni.*
   D. The singular pronoun he does not agree with the plural antecedent *Carlos and Jenni*.

4. A. The masculine pronoun *his* does not agree with the feminine antecedent *Marci*.
   B. The plural pronoun *their* does not agree with the singular antecedent *Marci*.
   C. The feminine pronoun *her* agrees with the feminine antecedent *Marci*, but the plural verb *ask* does not agree with the singular subject *father*.
   D. CORRECT: the feminine pronoun *her* agrees with the feminine antecedent *Marci* and the past tense of the verb is appropriate.

CONCEPT: PRONOUNS (WHO AND WHOM) KEY
STUDENT PRACTICE (p. 40)

1. whom
2. who
3. who
4. whom
5. whom
6. who
7. Who
8. whom
9. whom
10. who

ACT TEST SAMPLE QUESTIONS (p. 40)

1. A. Use *which* to refer to things not people.
   B. CORRECT: the pronoun is the subject of the clause and should be in nominative case.
   C. *Whom* is not in nominative case.
   D. *Whose* is in possessive case.

2. A. The pronoun is the object of the preposition *for* and must be in objective case.
   B. CORRECT: the pronoun is in the objective case.
   C. *That* is illogical.
   D. *Him* is also illogical.

3. **A. CORRECT: the pronoun is the subject of the clause and is in nominative case**.
   B. *Whomever* is in objective case.
   C. The plural verb does not agree with the singular pronoun.
   D. *Who wishes* is illogical.

4. A. The use of *they* is illogical.
   B. The pronoun is the subject of the clause and should be in nominative case.
   C. CORRECT: the pronoun who is in nominative case.
   D. The plural verb does not agree with the singular pronoun.

5. A. The pronoun is the object of the preposition *to* and should be in the objective case.
   B. *Whose* is possessive.
   C. The plural noun does not agree with the singular pronoun (*his*) later in the sentence.
   D. CORRECT: *whom* is in the objective case.

CONCEPT: COMMA USAGE I KEY
STUDENT PRACTICE (p. 42)

1. Joe decided not to run, for the morning was icy cold.
2. I ran over some broken glass in the school parking lot, so I had to change the flat before work.
3. My friend loves to eat spaghetti, so I bought him a pasta maker for his birthday.
4. I desperately needed to finish my five-paragraph research paper, yet I couldn't make myself stay awake.
5. Two top athletes were given highest recognition at the banquet, for each had demonstrated excellence in sportsmanship and skill.
6. Monique may disagree strongly with the new student council guidelines for skirt length, for she likes to wear very short skirts.
7. Jack and Jill went up the hill to fetch a pail of water, but Jack refused to carry the bucket back down the hill for fear of falling.
8. Did you want to fight the crowds and heat to attend the U.S. Open, or did you want to stay and watch in the comfort of your own home?
9. John will explain to the policeman why he was speeding down the dirt road with incriminating evidence in the back of his pickup, or he will face the consequences of a fine and the wrath of his parents.
10. Debbie recently purchased a darling new Schnauzer puppy, and she will name him <u>Aspen</u> after her home in Colorado.

ACT TEST SAMPLE QUESTIONS - COMMA USAGE 1 (p. 43)
1. A. The sentence is a run-on without a comma to separate the independent clauses.
   B. CORRECT: The comma is needed between the independent clauses and before the nonessential phrase.
   C. The sentence is a run-on without a semicolon before *however*.
   D. A comma is needed after *frequently* to set off the nonessential phrase.

2. **A. CORRECT: *However* must be set off by commas, and the two independent clauses must be separated with a comma.**
   B. The semicolon is misplaced, and the sentence is a run-on without a comma after *effective*.
   C. A comma is needed before *however*.
   D. Commas are needed to set off *however* and the adverb use is incorrect.

3. A. The sentence is a run-on without a comma to separate the independent clauses.
   B. The transition is illogical and would require a comma.
   C. The transition is illogical.
   D. CORRECT: The independent clauses are separated by a comma.

4. **A. CORRECT: The independent clauses are separated by a comma.**
   B. The sentence is a run-on without a comma separating the independent clauses.
   C. The sentence is illogical without a conjunction.
   D. *Trip* must be followed by a semicolon if the conjunction is omitted.

5. A. The sentence is a run-on without a comma separating the independent clauses.
   B. *Irregardless* is nonstandard.
   C. No comma is needed after *for*.
   D. CORRECT: The independent clauses are separated by a comma.

CONCEPT: COMMA USAGE II KEY
STUDENT PRACTICE (p. 44)

1. I did mention that I keyed your new car on the way out of the gymnasium, didn't I?
2. Matt LeBlanc, who played Joey on Friends, is still one of my favorite comedians.
3. The Iliad and the Odyssey, epic poems attributed to the poet Homer, provide insight into the lives of the ancient Greeks, not actual history.
4. Astronomers have been fascinated by Saturn, the ringed planet.
5. His excellent work in accelerated classes, moreover, has enabled him to improve his class rank.
6. The poet Homer, not the cartoon character Homer Simpson, provides insight into the lives of the ancient Greeks.
7. Now is the time, my fellow citizens, to step up and do what is right for the cause.
8. The class lecture concerned Poe's definition of poetry, the rhythmical creation of beauty.
9. The book that I didn't read was on the test and Bean Trees, which I did read, was not.
10. Karen Carpenter, who many teenagers today would not recognize, was one of the first public figures known to have died from anorexia.

ACT TEST SAMPLE QUESTIONS—COMMA USAGE II (p. 45)
1. A. *I suppose* is a nonessential phrase that should be set off by commas.
   B. *I suppose* should be set off by commas.
   C. CORRECT: The nonessential phrase is set off by commas.
   D. The semicolon is used incorrectly.

ENGLISH – KEY

2. **A. CORRECT:** *Disdainful of drug tests* **should be set off by commas.**
   B. *Which* is the wrong pronoun to use to refer to people; *which are* is wordy.
   C. *Disdain* is the incorrect form.
   D. *As to the existence* is superfluous.

3. A. *Of course* is nonessential and should be set off by commas.
   B. CORRECT: The nonessential phrase is set off by commas.
   C. *Thus* is an illogical transition.
   D. *Since* have is illogical.

4. A. *To my chagrin* should is nonessential and should be set off by commas.
   B. *To my chagrin* should be set off by commas.
   C. *Chagrin* and *embarrassment* are redundant.
   D. CORRECT: The nonessential phrase is set off by commas.

5. **A. CORRECT: The nonessential phrase is set off by commas.**
   B. *Not Chevy* is nonessential and should be set off by commas.
   C. *Not only* is illogical.
   D. *However* is an illogical transition.

CONCEPT: COMMA USAGE III KEY
STUDENT PRACTICE (p. 46)
1. When I write, I try to pay attention to unity, support and coherence.
2. After having lived on the coast for several years, I have a new appreciation for life in the Midwest.
3. Furthermore, the information I gave you about computer programming may be obsolete by the time I install the new software.
4. With one hand on the steering wheel and the other on the radio dial, Jane made me nervous as we drove through rush-hour traffic.
5. Walking on the course before golfers arrive, I appreciate the tranquillity and beauty of unspoiled solitude.
6. Because lightening can be very dangerous, the golf professional sounds a siren to get everyone off the course in hazardous weather.
7. Swimming at a slow and steady pace, Jocelyn slowly overtook her competitors in the triathlon.
8. Frantically, Joseph waved at the oncoming traffic to get them to stop before the accident.
9. Shortly, you will be asked to clear off your desk and put away your notes to prepare for the test.
10. Even after a grueling 5-set match, professional tennis players have to face the media or risk a hefty fine.

ACT TEST SAMPLE QUESTIONS (p. 46)
1. A. A comma is needed after the transition word *nevertheless.*
   B. CORRECT: The transition word is correctly punctuated.
   C. The colon is used incorrectly.
   D. The semicolon is used incorrectly.

2. A. A comma is needed after *study*.
   B. This is a sentence fragment.
   C. **CORRECT: The introductory clause is punctuated correctly.**
   D. The semicolon is not correct.

3. A. **CORRECT: The introductory clause and the adverb need commas.**
   B. The introductory clause needs a comma.
   C. The semicolon is used incorrectly.
   D. *Amazing* is not the correct form.

4. A. **CORRECT: The introductory word *then* is correctly punctuated.**
   B. The transition is illogical.
   C. The transition is illogical.
   D. The transition is illogical.

5. A. The introductory phrase needs a comma.
   B. **CORRECT: The introductory clause is punctuated correctly.**
   C. *However* is illogical.
   D. *But* is illogical.

CONCEPT: COMMA USAGE IV KEY
STUDENT PRACTICE (p. 48)

1. A good fishing lure floats, bobs and wiggles in the water.
2. Excited, cheerful and boisterous, children at playgrounds often pay little attention to their surroundings.
3. The president had the rare combination of power, principle and commitment.
4. Joseppi could not decide which car to purchase, which finance arrangement was the best or which dealer offered the best service.
5. What to wear to school, what to eat for breakfast, and who to call for a ride are daily questions Chelsea has to consider.
6. Percy gave a quick, decisive answer to the professor's question.
7. Most visitors find the Holocaust Memorial to be a powerful, memorable experience.
8. Most children like watermelon because it is cold, sweet and juicy.
9. As a college-bound teenager I am faced with the issues of where I should go to school, how much money it will take to get my degree and what my major area of study will be.
10. Walking along the rushing, cascading stream, I slipped and fell into the cold, icy water.

ACT TEST SAMPLE QUESTIONS (p. 49)

1. A. **CORRECT: *Many successful* are unequal adjectives and can't be reversed so no comma is needed.**
   B, C, D. No punctuation is needed.

2. **A. CORRECT:** *Rushing* and *churning* **are adjectives of equal rank and can be reversed so the comma is needed.**
    B. No colon is needed after *churning*.
    C. No comma is needed after *churning*.
    D. *Which are rushing and churning* is wordy, not concise.

3. **A. CORRECT: ACT does not typically include a comma before the conjunction.**
    B. *24-hour* is redundant.
    C. A semicolon is incorrect.
    D. *Hourly* is not the correct form.

4. A, B, C. *Disastrous* and *tragic* are equal rank and redundant.
    D. CORRECT: *Tragic* **is the most concise choice.**

5. **A. CORRECT:** *Old* and *women* **cannot be reversed so they do not require a comma.**
    B. No comma is needed.
    C. *Elderly* is redundant.
    D. *Women* does not need a comma.

CONCEPT: SEMICOLON USE KEY
STUDENT PRACTICE (p. 50)

1. In her research paper on high school sports Mechelle cited Elliot Eisner, a leading educational researcher; Bobby Knight, a notoriously aggressive coach; and David Ledbetter, a golf instructor who works on the mental aspects of the game.

2. Oddly enough, Dennis subscribes to <u>Prevention,</u> a magazine about health; <u>Seventeen,</u> a trendy magazine for fashion-conscious teenagers; and <u>Sports Illustrated,</u> a sports magazine with great photographs.

3. Oklahoma City is unique among American cities; indeed, it is the site of a terrible terrorist act against Americans.

4. Politicians may initially refrain from negative campaigning; however, personal attacks seem to become more frequent as the election draws near.

5. Watching college basketball, football and other sports on television; renting action-packed, suspenseful movies; and eating junk food like chips, dip, buttered popcorn, chocolate candy bars and brownies are my favorite weekend activities.

6. The Best Picture award went to Casablanca in 1943; however, none of its legendary stars received any personal awards.

7. The Jenks High School football team has a long history of excellence; it will probably contend for the high school state title again this year.

8. In the playoffs the outstanding pitcher threw his fast ball, curve ball and slider; moreover, he threw them with more power and finesse than ever before.

9. Jerome brought leftovers from last night's steak dinner for his school lunch; he had to eat it with his fingers because he couldn't cut it with the plastic knives in the cafeteria.

10. Joan was excited about her improved ACT test score; indeed, her confidence grew on every test she took thereafter.

CONCEPT: SEMICOLON USE KEY
ACT TEST SAMPLE QUESTIONS—SEMICOLONS (p. 51)

1. **A. CORRECT: The semicolon is correctly placed.**
   B. This sentence would be a run-on without a semicolon or a conjunction.
   C. *However* is an illogical transition.
   D. *On the other hand* is an illogical transition.

2. A. *However* is a transition word that must be set off with commas.
   B. CORRECT: The transition word is set off by commas.
   C. The semicolon is incorrect.
   D. A comma is needed after *moreover*.

3. A. The semicolon is not used to introduce an appositive.
   B. *However* is illogical.
   C. The appositive must be set off by punctuation.
   D. CORRECT: The dash introduces the appositive that follows.

4. **A. CORRECT: The dash may be used to introduce a list.**
   B. The semicolon is not used to introduce a list.
   C. The semicolon is incorrect and *its* should have an apostrophe.
   D. *You now have* is not needed.

5. **A. CORRECT: The independent clauses should be separated by a semicolon and the conjunctive adverb needs a comma.**
   B. This sentence is a run-on with an illogical transition.
   C. This sentence is a run-on.
   D. This sentence is a run-on with an illogical transition.

CONCEPT: COLON USE 1 KEY
STUDENT PRACTICE (p. 52)

1. Her excuse for missing curfew was plausible**:** the 15-car pile up on the interstate took two hours to clear.

2. The doctor said I had nothing wrong with me at all**:** the aches were simply growing pains.

3. The Marilyn Manson concert was laced with violence**:** fourteen people were arrested and dozens were injured.

4. John's difficult academic load in his last semester had an unexpected reward**:** he enjoyed his summer break all the more.

5. Sue has eclectic taste in music**:** she likes Black Sabbath, Garth Brooks and N' Sync.

6. She found the main character in the movie to be much like her boyfriend**:** he was handsome, charming and incredibly arrogant.

7. Langston Hughes was a great poet of the Harlem Renaissance**:** two well-known poems are "Homecoming" and "Dream Deferred."

8. Some critics argue that part-time work helps teens**:** they learn discipline and respect for the value of a dollar.

9. Many educators vehemently oppose businesses who allow teens to work more than twenty hours per week**:** they decry the extra stress and time pressures.

10. Studies have shown the benefits of a summer reading program**:** students improve their reading scores and perform better academically.

ACT TEST SAMPLE QUESTIONS – COLON 1 (p. 53)

1. A. The second independent clause is a summary sentence so a colon would be a better choice.
   B. The adjective *sudden* is not correct.
   C. The comma and the transition are not correct.
   D. CORRECT: This sentence contains the correct use of a colon and the adverb form.

2. A. This sentence is a run-on.
   B. CORRECT: The colon introduces the summary sentence.
   C. The semicolon is not correctly used.
   D. *Although* is an illogical transition.

3. A. This sentence is a run-on.
   B. *Its* is a possessive, not a contraction.
   C. This is a run-on with the *its* problem.
   D. CORRECT: The summary sentence and the *its* is punctuated correctly.

4. A. This sentence is a run-on.
   B. The second clause is not a summary sentence.
   C. **CORRECT: The semicolon is the best choice for separating the two independent clauses.**
   D. *Consequently* is an illogical transition.

5. A. The colon is not correctly used.
   B. The transition is not logical.
   C. **CORRECT: The two independent clauses with a conjunctive adverb are correctly punctuated.**
   D. *As a result* is not logical.

CONCEPT: COLON USE II KEY
STUDENT PRACTICE (p. 54)

1. My summer plans include the following: rest, relaxation and recreation.

2. The school policy for appropriate dance behavior included the following regulation: no freak dancing.

3. Among the most scantily clad at the awards ceremony were several gorgeous young actresses: Jennifer Lopez, Wynona Ryder and Charlize Theron.

4. I find several restaurant cleanup chores to be absolutely the most repugnant: brushing the toilet, scrubbing the floors, scouring the sinks.

5. Teenagers cite the following as concerns about school: demanding teachers and administrators, too much homework, difficult tests.

6. The politician confidently began his speech: "The party in power has betrayed us. It has not only failed to keep its election promise but has sold out to the moneyed powers."

7. I finally decided on a career: paleontology.

8. "I had three chairs in my house: one for solitude, two for friendship, three for society." --Thoreau

9. The following students should report immediately to the main office: Michaela Green, Kim Evans, Heather Young.

10. My favorite Robert Frost poem is "Stopping By Woods on a Snowy Evening; my favorite passage goes as follows: "The woods are lovely, dark and deep./ But I have promises to keep,/ And miles to go before I sleep,/ And miles to go before I sleep."

CONCEPT: COLON USE II KEY
ACT TEST SAMPLE QUESTIONS - COLON II (p. 55)

1. A. The comma does not correctly introduce the quote.
   B. CORRECT: The colon introduces the quote.
   C. The comma is not correct, and capitalization is needed.
   D. *That followed* is redundant.

2. A. It is incorrect to use a semicolon after *especially*.
   B. CORRECT: no punctuation is needed after *especially*.
   C. The use of *however* is illogical.
   D. The use of *in other words* is illogical.

3. A. Using a comma after *said* is incorrect.
   B. Using a colon after *said* is incorrect.
   C. CORRECT: no punctuation is needed.
   D. Using a comma and quotation marks is incorrect.

4. **A. CORRECT: must have the comma because the sentence is compound and the dash because *lucky for me* is an interrupting phrase.**
   B. Missing the comma after *concert*.
   C. Using a colon after *concert* is incorrect.
   D. Using *however* is illogical.

5. A. Using a semicolon is incorrect because it does not connect two independent clauses.
   B. Placing a semicolon between *behavior* and *such as* is incorrect.
   C. Using *consequently* is illogical.
   D. CORRECT: use a colon to introduce a list of items.

CONCEPT: USING THE DASH KEY
STUDENT PRACTICE (p. 56)

1. Last Saturday night at the rave—have you ever seen so much skin?—I danced all evening long.
2. The May 3rd Oklahoma tornado struck early in the evening—to this day the survivors gasp as they retell the story.
3. The excessive slaughter in this war was caused by an enhancement of what we learned in the Civil War—the increased lethal power of explosives.
4. The cause of her debilitating illness—a strange virus affecting her nervous system—remains undiagnosed by her doctors.
5. Some of my friends—for example, Keith, Lakesta and Sorrell—waste too much time watching TV.
6. Modesty, honesty, loyalty, bravery, sincerity—these are the traits I admire in my heroes.
7. Even his Superbowl MVP trophy—his most prized possession—was lost in the fire.
8. Here's how to learn—study.

9. Documentary novels—two of the more successful are *An American Tragedy* and *In Cold Blood*—are fictionalized accounts of events based upon newspaper reports.
10. Some boisterous pranks—cow tipping, for example—don't seem much fun to me.

ACT TEST SAMPLE QUESTIONS – DASH (p. 57)

1. A. *Antics* must be followed by the second dash to set off the abrupt, interrupting phrase.
   B. *Antics* must be followed by a dash.
   C. CORRECT: The interrupting phrase is set off by dashes.
   D. *Which made him notorious* is redundant.

2. A. This sentence doesn't make sense.
   B. This sentence doesn't make sense.
   C. CORRECT: The introductory list is set off by a dash.
   D. The punctuation and transition are incorrect.

3. A. The abrupt, interruption of thought must be set off by dashes.
   B. CORRECT: The interrupting remark is set off by dashes.
   C. The interruption of thought must be set off by dashes.
   D. The interruption must be set off by dashes.

4. **A. CORRECT: The dash adds special drama to the obvious conclusion.**
   B. The semicolon is not used to introduce.
   C. *Its* should have an apostrophe.
   D. Strong punctuation is needed to set off *apathy*.

5. **A. CORRECT: The dash sets off the introductory list.**
   B. The semicolon does not introduce a list.
   C. The comma is not used correctly.
   D. *However* is not a logical transition.

CONCEPT: USING APOSTROPHES
STUDENT PRACTICE (p. 59)

1. she'd
2. Presley's album
3. Garth and Ted's paper
4. Mary's and Joe's friends
5. Hercules' labors
6. Hoss' and Pete's
7. anyone's books
8. Karlos' talking
9. Shakespeare's writing
10. won't

ACT TEST SAMPLE QUESTIONS (p. 59)

1. **A. CORRECT:** *People* **is plural so you add** *'s* **for the possessive.**
   B. A possessive is needed.
   C. The apostrophe should be before the *s* because *people* is plural.
   D. A possessive is needed.

2. **A. CORRECT:** *Villagers* **is plural so the apostrophe is after the** *s.*
   B. *Villagers* should be possessive.
   C. *Houses* is not possessive.
   D. A possessive is needed.

3. A. *Daily departure* is illogical.
   B. *Marks* should be possessive.
   C. CORRECT: The possessive is correct.
   D. *There* is not the right word.

4. **A. CORRECT: The possessive is correct.**
   B. The colon is incorrect.
   C. The possessive and the colon is incorrect.
   D. In *that they were* is too wordy and awkward.

5. **A. CORRECT: No possessive is needed.**
   B. *Writers* is not possessive.
   C. *Victorian* did not possess the writers.
   D. *Writers* is not possessive.

CONCEPT: DANGLING AND MISPLACED MODIFIERS KEY
STUDENT PRACTICE (p. 61)
Student's answers could vary. Examples are given.

1. Louie could not find his dictionary anywhere **on the top of the bookcase.**
2. Jesse always wants to be **under the table** to eat leftovers from my dinner.
3. CORRECT
4. CORRECT
5. The elderly neighbor **that lives three doors down** gave my son a new coloring book.
6. CORRECT
7. My husband, **who was angry that the flowers had been ruined**, yelled at the dog.
8. As the boy was **licking quickly**, the ice cream cone dripped on the sidewalk.
9. Home looked very inviting to the man, **having been in Europe for two months.**
10. **Hearing the children coming up the sidewalk**, we hurriedly stuffed the Christmas presents into the closet.

ACT TEST SAMPLE QUESTIONS (p. 62)

1. A. The adverb *completely* is misplaced.
   B. **CORRECT: *completely* is correctly placed before the word it modifies, *amazing*.**
   C. Separating *amazing* from *completely* with a comma is incorrect.
   D. *Completely* is misplaced; it should not modify *working*.

2. A. The phrase is dangling. It has no word to modify.
   B. The gifts were not working frantically.
   C. **CORRECT: *working frantically* correctly modifies the pronoun *I*.**
   D. The gifts were not working frantically and *wrapped* is in the wrong tense.

3. A. *Only* should not modify *I*.
   B. *Only* should not modify *fail*.
   C. *Only* should not modify *fail*.
   D. **CORRECT: the adverb *only* correctly modifies the adjective *another*, emphasizing that I was ONLY another statistic.**

4. A. The children were not floating in the air.
   B. **CORRECT: the bubbles were floating in the air.**
   C. The phrase would still incorrectly modify *children*.
   D. The phrase would still incorrectly modify *children*.

5. A. **CORRECT: *sweating profusely* correctly modifies *Ben*.**
   B. The phrase should not modify *sheet*.
   C. The phrase should be placed as closely to *Ben* as possible.
   D. The phrase would still incorrectly modify *sheet*.

CONCEPT: PARALLEL STRUCTURE KEY
ACT TEST SAMPLE QUESTIONS (p. 63)

1. A. The prepositional phrase *with a fighting spirit* is not parallel because d*etermination* and *strategy* are both nouns.
   B. **CORRECT: *fighting spirit* is a similar structure to *determination* and *strategy*. All three are nouns (two with adjectives).**
   C. The use of *however* is illogical because no contradiction is needed.
   D. The use of *thus* is illogical because *a fighting spirit* is not the result of the other two nouns.

2. A. The phrase *and because they like* destroys the parallelism.
   B. The use of the semicolon is incorrect and doesn't change the faulty parallelism.
   C. The use of *however* is illogical.
   D. **CORRECT: *lifestyle* and *money* are parallel; they are both nouns.**

ENGLISH – KEY

3. A. The phrase *people won't want to live there* is not parallel to *dangerous* and *dilapidated*.
   B. Adding *consequently* does not correct the faulty parallelism.
   C. *Dangerously run down* is repetitive; *dangerous* has been used previously.
   D. **CORRECT: Using *unlivable* creates parallelism among the three adjectives.**

4. A. The established pattern is a noun followed by a prepositional phrase. *Smelling gasoline* does not fit that pattern.
   B. The phrase does not fit the pattern.
   C. Inserting a comma does not correct the faulty parallelism.
   D. **CORRECT: *the smell of gasoline* fits the pattern of a noun followed by a prepositional phrase.**

5. A. The established pattern in the sentence is the use of gerund (phrase) followed by an adverb. *Clear expression* does not fit that pattern.
   B. Does not fit the pattern.
   C. **CORRECT: fits the pattern of gerund (phrase) followed by an adverb.**
   D. Although *writing* could be a gerund, it is not followed by an adverb.

CONCEPT: RHETORICAL SKILLS
TRANSITIONS
STUDENT PRACTICE (p. 65)

Watching the sinister Badley Mansion from the safety of the dirt road which curved in front of it, Michael and James were determined that this night would be the night they stayed in the haunted house until dawn. They had tried on three previous occasions, but had not yet been successful. This time, **however**, they had come prepared. **First,** they had carefully considered the equipment they would need: sleeping bags, water, food, cell phones and, **most importantly**, flashlights and extra batteries. They had **also** brought a camera and several rolls of film in order to document their stay. **Next**, they had researched the history of the Badley family so they would be prepared for any ghosts or haunts that still resided in the mansion. **Finally**, they had let their parents know exactly where they would be and had charged the batteries of their cell phones just in case they needed help. Taking a deep breath, Michael and James began the long, lonely walk to the front door. **In spite of** their fears, they were going to make it. They believed that until the front door swung open and an unseen, menacing voice whispered, "Welcome to my home." **As a result**, the boys never made it up the sidewalk or into the house. They were too busy racing for the car, frantically dialing their cell phones.

EXTENDED PRACTICE (p. 66)

     In the play *Antigone*, the pride of the main characters, Creon and Antigone, serves as the source of the main conflict while also giving meaning to the play. Each character believes in a different set of ethical standards, and the choices made <u>as a result</u> of these standards contribute to the conflict. Creon's decision to have his law preside over the laws of the gods reveals his pride. <u>Similarly</u>, Antigone's decision to bury her brother, Polyneices, according to her own personal ethics reflects a comparable stubbornness. <u>Moreover</u>, the meaning of the work lies at the heart of this conflict. Stubbornness and the inability to consider other's motives bring about tragic consequences to the principle characters and their loved ones. <u>For this reason</u>, the conflict reveals the true meaning of the play: Pride without restraint produces disastrous results. <u>Consequently</u>, both Antigone and Creon are punished for their arrogance by the loss of their families and, in Antigone's case, her life.

CONCEPT: RHETORICAL SKILLS
AMETHYST PASSAGES KEY

Paragraph A (p. 67)

First	2
Second	3
Third	7
Fourth	4
Fifth	8
Sixth	5
Seventh	1
Eighth	6

Paragraph B (p. 67)
The two sentences that do not belong are the following:
➢ They are mined in Sri Lanka, Uruguay and Madagascar.
➢ Diamonds are especially popular in marquis cuts.

Paragraph C (p. 67)
Redundancies: old and ancient; hair loss and baldness; stories and tales
Cliché: "beauty is only skin deep"
Substandard English: gross complexions; Irregardless; alot; nowdays

CONCEPT: RHETORICAL SKILLS
COMPUTER PASSAGE KEY
STUDENT PRACTICE (p. 68)

1. Sentence 1

2. Sentences 2, 8 and 15

3. Student answers will vary. Added sentences should give examples of the modern conveniences, flexible communication and enjoyable activities computers provide.

4. They'll; there're; haven't; can't

5. Sentences 16 and 17 are not consistent with the style and purpose of the passage for two reasons: 1) they discuss negative aspects of computer technology; the passage is focused on positive outcomes, and 2) the formal, sophisticated level of language is markedly different from the rest of the passage.

CONCEPT: RHETORICAL SKILLS
FRANKENSTEIN PASSAGE KEY
STUDENT PRACTICE (p. 70)

1. Student answers may vary. Example answer: Victor comes to realize that the monster is evil as well as very ugly and distorted.

2. Victor is horrified and disgusted by the monster he has created and is terrified of him. Student answers may vary. Example answers:
   - *horrible monster*
   - *creature is also evil*
   - *Victor doesn't accept the monster*
   - *the monster killed his wife and brother*
   - *Victor is deeply devastated over the destruction of his life.*

3. Sentence 2 contains the cliché *he nearly scares people to death*.
   Student rewrites may vary. Example answer: First, the horrible monster assembled by Frankenstein terrifies the people he encounters.

4. Sentences 9, 12, and 13. These sentences are too conversational in tone and/or do not fit with the rest of the passage.

5. Doesn't; wasn't; doesn't; he's

6. Student sentences will vary. Answers should focus on the destruction of Victor's life as a result of his tampering with nature.

7. Answers will vary. Examples: Furthermore; Obviously; As a result of his actions; In conclusion.

CONCEPT: RHETORICAL SKILLS
PRACTICAL JOKE PASSAGE KEY
STUDENT PRACTICE (p. 72)

1. Student answers will vary.

2. First; then; when; next; not surprisingly, fortunately; finally

3. Having previously been the victim of numerous practical jokes perpetrated by my college roommate, I decided the time had arrived to put an end to her pranks: I devised the ultimate practical joke to put an end to any doubt that I would be the victor of our unofficial competition.

4. Sentences 5 and 6 should be reversed.

5. Sentence 14

6. Student answers will vary. Could insert an additional sentence after sentence 18.

7. Sentence 7.

8. Details should be included in a preceding paragraph because the first sentence of the paragraph establishes that the author had been the victim of previous practical jokes.

9. Sentence 11. Redundant ideas: *"which made her look almost dead"* and *"girls in the dorm."*

10. This sentence would be inappropriate for this paragraph because it introduces a new idea. The paragraph is not about the serious consequences of the joke.

11. This paragraph would be appropriate to include because it relates a humorous college experience.

12. Suggested answers: What is on my feet? Why can't I move?

13. College roommate; my intended victim; my roomie; the victim; my prey; Sleeping Beauty; "the body".

14. Both A and D

CONCEPT: SUBSTANDARD ENGLISH KEY
ACT TEST SAMPLE QUESTIONS (p. 75)

1. **A. CORRECT**: *Than* **is used for comparisons.**
   B. *Like* is illogical.
   C. *Then* is used to express time not comparison.
   D. *As when* is also used to express time not a comparison.

2. A. This passage contains a double preposition and *up* is redundant.
   B. CORRECT: *From* **is the simplest and best choice.**
   C. This passage contains a double preposition.
   D. This passage contains a double preposition.

ENGLISH – KEY

3. A. *It's* is an incorrect contraction.
   B. CORRECT: The possessive form is needed.
   C. *His* is a vague pronoun reference.
   D. *Its'* is an incorrect contraction.

4. **A. CORRECT: This is the best expression of the point.**
   B. *A lot* is informal
   C. *Alot* is substandard.
   D. *A bunch* is informal.

5. A. Do not split an infinitive.
   B. CORRECT: This is the best expression.
   C. *Hopefully* is misplaced and redundant.
   D. *Hopeful* is an incorrect adjective form.

6. A. The contraction is informal.
   B. CORRECT: *Do not* is the most appropriate choice.
   C. *Dont'* is an incorrect contraction
   D. *Does* is an incorrect verb choice.

7. **A. CORRECT: *Further* indicates additional time.**
   B. *Farther* indicates distance and is illogical.
   C. *Further than* is illogical.
   D. *Farther* is illogical.

8. A. *Among* refers to three; *rival* is redundant.
   B. *Among* refers to three
   C. CORRECT: *Between* is the best choice.
   D. *Rival* is redundant.

9. A. *Of* should be have.
   B. *Could* is illogical.
   C. CORRECT: This is the best verb choice.
   D. *Couldn't of* is illogical.

10. A. *Fewer amounts of time* is illogical.
    B. *Fewer* is not used to refer to time.
    C. *Lesser time* is illogical and ungrammatical.
    D. CORRECT: This is the most concise and logical choice.

ENGLISH TEST ONE
KEYS

THE PERFECT DOG (p. 83)
1. A: correct comma use in a compound sentence
2. J: *was* is singular; *did* is in the correct tense
3. B: *who* is the correct pronoun
4. F: correct comma use with modifier
5. D: sentence interferes with the unity of the paragraph
6. J: *As a result of* is the most logical transition
7. C: the adverb *proudly* correctly modifies the past tense verb *showed*
8. G: correct comma use in a compound sentence; *but* is the most logical coordinating conjunction
9. A: the past tense verb *apologized* is correct
10. F: correct punctuation of a summary sentence
11. B: the past tense verb *walked* is correct
12. J: best placement of the modifier *that caught my eye*
13. C: captures the main idea of the passage
14. H: best choice in terms of paragraph unity
15. D: best expression of the main idea

LAURA BUSH (p. 88)
16. H: correct comma use with the modifier *especially young children*
17. D: parallel structure— *to encourage; to promote; to encourage* and *to showcase* are all infinitives
18. F: the adjective *early* correctly modifies the noun *age*
19. B: adding *Laura's mother introduced her* corrects the dangling modifier *Promoting her dream*
20. H: interferes with unity because it is irrelevant information
21. C: the past tense verb *launched* is correct
22. G: adding a period eliminates run-on sentence
23. D: correct comma use after an introductory phrase
24. J: adding the subject *Mrs. Bush* eliminates sentence fragment
25. C: *children* is a more appropriate level of language; the others are too informal
26. G: eliminates redundancy of *promote* and *encourage*
27. A: *After* is the most logical transition
28. F: leaving the paragraph as it is correct because no new information is introduced
29. A: the essay discusses how Mrs. Bush has encouraged the development of literacy.
30. G: it is a specific example of Mrs. Bush's activities consistent with the rest of the passage

CHILDREN'S MENTAL HEALTH (p. 92)
31. C: *their* is a plural pronoun
32. J: *is* is a singular helping verb which agrees with the singular subject *nation*
33. C: moving *in mental health* closer to *crisis* corrects the misplaced modifier
34. G: *fewer than* is correct because *children* can be counted individually
35. C: correct comma use between items in a series; the gerund *reducing* is parallel to the other gerunds in the sentence
36. F: the possessive of *General* is correct
37. C: *however* is the most logical transition
38. F: *At present* is the most logical choice
39. D: adding a comma correctly eliminates the sentence fragment
40. J: adding a comma correctly eliminates the sentence fragment
41. B: is the simplest expression because it eliminates the repetition of the word *groups*
42. F: the dash correctly introduces the items in a list
43. B: it is an example of the impairment that may result
44. G: the paragraph is not about insurance costs
45. A: correctly identifies the main idea of the passage

WINSTON CHURCHILL (p. 96)
46. G: it is the correct comma use after a nonessential phrase
47. C: provides an appropriate transition and the most logical arrangement of words
48. G: it eliminates the redundancy
49. D: the past tense verb *stood* is correct
50. H: eliminates the redundancy of *really kind of*
51. A: correct punctuation of a summary sentence
52. H: best expression of the author's purpose
53. B: the dash correctly sets off the remark directed to the Ambassador
54. J: *couldn't accept* is the correct verb tense
55. A: the expression is correct as it is
56. G: provides an example of his great wit
57. B: *admiring* best identifies the tone of the passage
58. H: provides the best summary of the passage
59. A: the detail would interfere with the unity of the paragraph
60. J: this paragraph is discussing the relationship between the two countries

COFFEE (p. 99)
61. A: comma is correctly used in a compound sentence
62. J: the colon correctly introduces the items in a list
63. B: eliminates the double negative *didn't feel no*
64. G: *much because* eliminates the sentence fragment
65. D: the sentence interferes with the unity of the paragraph
66. F: correct verb tense
67. A: the dash correctly introduces the list of essay topics
68. G: *further* correctly describes how angry she is
69. B: adding a period eliminates the run-on sentence
70. H: *waited* is parallel to the past tense verb *showed*
71. A: the paragraphs are most coherent the way they are currently arranged
72. J: *larger* is the correct comparative form of the adjective
73. D: *more importantly* is the correct adverb
74. G: *smugly* most correctly identifies the author's attitude
75. A: most correctly sums up the author's attitude toward her essay

ENGLISH TEST TWO
KEYS

WRONG HOUSE (p. 103)
1. C: the adverb *than* correctly identifies the comparison
2. H: eliminates the substandard use of the contraction
3. B: *Fortunately* is the correct adverb; needs a comma after the introductory adverb; adds the subject *I*
4. F: *After* is the correct adverb to use
5. B: *were* is a plural verb that agrees with the plural subject *they*
6. H: it is the simplest expression
7. B: adding a comma eliminates the sentence fragment
8. J: eliminates the redundancy
9. D: it is irrelevant information
10. H: the colon is the correct punctuation of a summary sentence
11. D: *drove* is the correct verb tense
12. G: has the most correct transition
13. A: correctly identifies the authors feelings about the incident
14. H: best supports the main idea of the paragraph
15. A: clearly describes her feelings

IRONCLAD (p. 108)
16. J: a comma is correct after an introductory phrase
17. A: *broke* is the correct past tense verb
18. G: the simplest expression
19. D: adding a comma eliminates the sentence fragment
20. J: the phrase is redundant
21. A: the phrase is correctly placed
22. G: *to secure* is parallel with the other infinitives in the sentence
23. D: eliminates the substandard phrase
24. G: correct possessive form of the noun *engineer*
25. D: eliminating *locating* makes the listing of items parallel
26. J: paragraph 3 discusses the raising of the ship
27. B: it is the most logical order of paragraphs
28. H: the detail most logically fits in paragraph 3
29. A: most appropriate title
30. G: best identifies the purpose of the essay

EMANCIPATION PROCLAMATION (p. 113)
31. A: correct verb tense
32. F: the possessive pronoun *its* is correct
33. C: correct punctuation to introduce the quotation
34. G: *Despite* is the most logical transition
35. D: use only a comma to set off a participial phrase
36. G: *Most importantly* is the most logical transition
37. C: correctly adds the subject *it*
38. G: the colon is the correct punctuation of a summary sentence
39. D: this detail elaborates on the participation of the black soldiers and sailors
40. G: simplest expression
41. A: the expression is parallel as it is
42. F: is the most logical expression
43. A: most correctly identifies the purpose of paragraph 4
44. J: eliminates the irrelevant information
45. C: the best summary of the passage

ENGLISH – KEY

BEACHES (p. 116)
46. F: correct punctuation of an appositive
47. D: eliminates the substandard phrase
48. G: *northern* is the correct adverb
49. C: adding the comma corrects the fragment
50. J: eliminates the irrelevant information
51. A: the past tense verb *grow* is correct
52. J: most logical expression
53. B: the present tense verb *provides* agrees with the subject *vegetation*
54. H: use a semicolon to connect clauses in a compound sentence
55. B: correct punctuation of a summary sentence
56. G: paragraph 5 is the most logical place for this detail
57. D: paragraph 4 tries to persuade tourists to care for the environment
58. F: correctly identifies the main purpose of the essay
59. B: because paragraph 2 describes the coral reefs
60. H: the main topic of the passage is not safety precautions

CAREER CHOICE (p. 120)
61. D: commas surround the appositive *Mr. Strickland*
62. J: comma connects the introductory clause with the main clause
63. C: eliminates the redundancy
64. G: semicolon correctly connects the clauses in a compound sentence
65. A: the dash is correctly used for dramatic effect
66. F: the examples in the paragraph are all about jobs she wouldn't like
67. D: the modifier should be located close to *bench*
68. H: adding the period corrects the run-on sentence
69. B: the superlative form of the adjective is correct
70. G: *Obviously* is the most logical transition
71. B: the comma is needed after the introductory adverb clause
72. H: the sentence is irrelevant
73. D: eliminates the substandard usage
74. H: correctly identifies the young girl's feelings about choosing a major
75. D: correctly identifies the girl's feelings

MATH – GENERAL TIPS AND STRATEGIES

60 Minutes	60 Questions

Area of Math Tested	Approx. % of Test	Approx. # of Questions
Algebra	50-55%	30-33
Geometry	35-40%	21-24
Trigonometry	5-8%	3-5

Algebra – The algebra questions on the ACT include what is typically covered in pre-algebra courses all the way through what is typically covered in most algebra II courses. It is absolutely imperative to have your algebra skills fine tuned for this test. Approximately 32 of the 60 math questions are algebra focused.

Geometry – This is probably the biggest killer of math scores. Most high school students take geometry when they are sophomores. Some advanced students will even take geometry as a freshman. If you are on any type of block scheduling (college-style scheduling where a class lasts a semester or trimester rather than a full year), then you are very likely to have taken geometry either your freshman or sophomore year. Probably the hardest thing about the math test is roughly 4 out of every 10 questions cover material many of you studied as a freshman or sophomore – geometry questions. If you are a senior, it has probably been some time since you used the midpoint or distance formulas.

You may be in an advanced math like trigonometry, math analysis, pre-calculus, or even an AP calculus course. This is great. But the bad news is there isn't any calculus on the ACT. I took AP calculus my senior year in high school, and one of the hardest things about the ACT math test was that 40% of the questions were over material I hadn't seen in 3 years, geometry.

Make sure you review the rules and formulas associated with geometry prior to taking the test. There is no worse feeling than walking into a test and not remembering the formula for the area of a circle because you haven't used it in a few years.

This book will provide you with ample review of the concepts you need to know for the ACT test. Study the concepts in this book and commit to memory the rules and formulas.

Trigonometry – As I work with students on the ACT, they always want to focus on the trigonometry problems on the math test. I constantly hear students talk about how there are so many trigonometry problems on the test. Then, those students follow by saying they haven't had trigonometry, so they can't score well in math.

Only about 5-8% of the math test is trigonometry. This means that out of the 60 questions, you will see 3-5 trigonometry questions. With a basic understanding of trigonometry, many students can get as many as 2 of the questions correct (even without taking trigonometry).

MATH – GENERAL TIPS AND STRATEGIES

When the average ACT math score nationwide is in the low 20s, there are many more algebra and geometry questions being missed than trigonometry questions. The few trigonometry questions simply are not making a huge impact on that average. For students with very high math scores, however, the trigonometry questions become very important. Each question is critical since very few are missed.

You are probably thinking that trigonometry is not that important based on what I said above, but trigonometry is very important. I did a statistical analysis of a large high school to determine what math classes are statistically significant to ACT scores. For college bound students, the math class offerings included the following courses: algebra I, geometry, algebra II, trigonometry, math analysis, pre-calculus, and AP calculus. College bound students were required to take four units of math. Therefore, the question was which four units should a student take to maximize ACT scores. All college bound students took algebra I, geometry, and algebra II, but the fourth unit was an option to the students. Some advanced students took algebra I in the eighth grade which opened two more classes after geometry and algebra II. Many students who had two units to take after geometry and algebra II chose pre-calculus and calculus to fill their requirements. Other students took trigonometry then pre-calculus. For the students who took algebra I, geometry, and algebra II, they had one choice for the 4th unit. About ½ of the students chose trigonometry and the other half chose pre-calculus.

After completing a statistical analysis using an analysis of variation study, we were able to determine with at least 95% confidence that trigonometry was statistically significant to an average increase of 3 points in math on the ACT at this high school. This increase in math scores is not because these students were probably able to get more of the 3-5 trigonometry questions correct; rather, it was because of this school's environment and curriculum. Trigonometry reinforced and expounded on the skills required in the geometry and intermediate algebra questions.

I know many of you will want to have a fun, easy senior year. You won't want to struggle doing advanced math homework every week. The easiest thing to do is not take that fourth or even fifth unit of math. Please reconsider taking it. The course is absolutely necessary for the ACT and for college. Many of you are considering taking college courses such as college algebra instead of another math such as trigonometry or calculus in high school. I encourage you to consider the pros and cons of staying at your high school and take the advanced math. Nothing will prepare you better for college than taking the high school advanced math class. In most cases, if you can be introduced to calculus in the high school environment, you will do much better than being introduced to it in college.

MATH – GENERAL TIPS AND STRATEGIES

1. The questions get harder as you take the test.

- Question 1 is the easiest and question 60 is the hardest.
- You do not have one minute per question.
- You can take the test backwards.

The problems get harder as you take the test. The first 20 questions will be much easier than the last 20 questions. You should expect to move quickly through the first several questions. Conversely, you should expect to move relatively slowly through the last several questions. The math test gets very difficult toward the end.

This test is 60 questions and 60 minutes, but this is one time 60 questions divided by 60 minutes is not one minute per question. Many students believe they have one minute to work each question and try to pace themselves to this rate. Maybe an overall average of one minute per question applies, but if you give yourself a minute per question, you will never finish. As mentioned above, the questions get progressively harder as you take the test. You should move through the problems much faster in the beginning than in the end.

One idea a good friend of mine used was to work the math test backwards. His philosophy was that since the latter problems are much more difficult, he wanted to do them when there was no pressure of the time ending. He started with number 60 and worked back to problem number one. He scored a perfect 36 on the math test using this method. Several students I have worked with use this method successfully, while others have tried it and do not like it. As with every section of the test and every method suggested, you must determine what works best for you. We all work differently. The key is to simply stay within the rules and get great results. I recommend you try this method to see if it works for you. You may find this section much less stressful working it backwards. If you go backwards, make sure you fill in the correct bubbles corresponding with the correct questions.

2. Don't waste too much time on any one question.

- If a problem is getting extremely long and difficult, you are approaching it the wrong way.
- You should stop working and decide whether to approach the problem another way or simply guess and go to the next problem.
- Try circling the problem and coming back to it at the end of the test if time remains.

No question on the ACT math test is designed to take you an extreme amount of time. As we discussed earlier, the math test gets progressively harder as you take it. The last several problems should take you longer than the first several problems, but no problem is designed to take 4 or 5 minutes.

Many times, you may approach a math problem the wrong way, and the problem takes you through an unending maze of equations and calculations. Try to recognize this situation as soon as possible. When this happens, stop working and decide whether to approach the problem a different way or simply guess and go to the next problem. A strategy I often used was to circle the problem and come back to it at the end of the test if time remained. Have you ever been working on a problem, and you just can't figure out how to solve it? Then, you walk away from it. When you return to the problem, the answer is obvious. This may be the case for you on the ACT math test. Try circling the problem in your test booklet and moving to the next problem. You can come back to your circled problems at the end if time remains. Just make sure you keep your bubble sheet in line with the problems you are working. Remember, if the test administrator is about to call time, at least guess. There is no penalty for guessing. If you leave it blank, it is definitely wrong.

3. **Don't overuse your calculator.**

- Become familiar with the functions and capabilities of your calculator.
- Graphing on your calculator should be limited, if any, during the test.
- Check the current rules on programming your calculator. Be able to quickly retrieve programmed formulas and solvers if allowed.

When ACT started allowing students to use calculators, students believed the test would become so much easier. The test has evolved into what some consider to be more difficult.

An interesting problem takes place during the math test now that didn't use to exist. You will do a very simple math calculation in your head, but because you have a calculator, you will also do the calculation on your calculator. Don't do this. Trust yourself.
5 + 5 = 10. You don't have to check this with your calculator.

Another example of overusing your calculator is graphs. There are several problems on the ACT where graphs are involved. Some of the problems can even be solved using a graphing calculator. Many students think because you have this expensive calculator that does graphs, you should try to make a graph on your calculator to get the answer.

The key is you do not need a graphing calculator to get a single question right on the ACT. Even if you do have one, you don't need to make a graph on your calculator to answer the questions. The people that make the ACT do not make a single question where you must make a graph on a calculator to find the correct answer. Why? Two key reasons:
1. Everyone can't afford to buy or has a school provided a graphing calculator.
2. This isn't a test to see who can make graphs on his or her calculator the fastest.

I encourage you to get very familiar with the functions and capabilities of your calculator. Know what your calculator will and will not do. You want to make sure you can quickly do exponents, square roots, and other algebraic functions. Another useful tool is the conversion between decimals and fractions. Using your calculator on the test is not a bad thing. Just make sure you understand its functions and programs. Don't overuse it.

Test administrators are to check to see if you are using a legal calculator. They are not told to clear the memory on your calculator. You need to check the updated list of legal calculators and the updated rules on programming your calculator. ACT's calculator rules are confusing. You are now required to clear all programs, documents, apps, and anything else that can solve algebraic equations from your calculator before you enter the testing center. At the time this book was published, ACT has exceptions to this rule allowing certain programs if they meet the following criteria: 25 lines or less of code, written in native language of calculator, not compiled, and only up to a single step operation solver. As currently written in the administrator's manual regarding calculators, administrators primary responsibility is to verify students are using a legal model calculator. The implied rule beyond the use of a legal model is students are to self-govern what they use as programs, solvers, equations, or apps. What a joke!

Commentary: At the time of this printing, ACT's calculator policy is completely uncontrolled and flawed. Most testing centers never check for programs or apps. Even if they did, most administrators don't know how to tell. ACT says it is the students' responsibility not to have certain programs or apps on the calculator and to delete them if so. Unless governed, students who know not to and want to obey the rules won't do it. Other students will continue to have an unfair advantage on the math section because ACT's failure to govern equally. ACT has a system that is out of control, and they know it. ACT should either ban all programmable calculators or allow all programs and apps. Until they do, I would govern to the best of your knowledge and load your calculator with every formula and solver, unless you know for sure it is illegal (which I have no idea how you would know). So, load them with formulas and solvers and use them.

4. Back solve using trial and error.

- See if the problem can be easily solved plugging in the choices.
- Start in the middle if the choices are in numerical sequence.
- Start at the bottom if the choices are NOT in numerical sequence.

Certain problems can be back solved easier than trying to figure out how to work through it. Back solving is the process of taking the choices and plugging them into the question. Let's look at an example

---

Solve the following equation for x if x > 0.

$x^2 = 16$

A. 1
B. 2
C. 3
D. 4
E. 5

Many of you know to take the square root of both sides to solve for *x*. But let's assume either you didn't know to do that, or you realized you could back solve quicker. To back solve this problem, just pick a choice and plug it in for *x*. For example, if you chose C, your calculation would be the following:
$3^2 = 9$ which is not equal to 16; therefore, we know the answer is not C. Then, you would continue to try each choice until you found the correct answer.

MATH – GENERAL TIPS AND STRATEGIES

When back solving, use the following quick strategies to save valuable time:

1. In the example above, the choices are in numerical sequence. You should start with choice C. If choice C is too low, move to D and E. If choice C is too high, try B and A.

2. If the choices are not in numerical sequence, I recommend you start at the bottom with choice E. The people that make the ACT know the problems that can easily be back solved. Typically, they will put the answer toward the bottom to penalize you the time of trying each choice. The reason for this is they are trying to test the concept, not whether you can back solve efficiently. If you back solve, they want to penalize you the time. Another approach is to quickly put the answers in numerical sequence before you start the back solve process.

This reasoning process is a valuable approach on all sections of the ACT. Reasoning means to not look for the right answer but to eliminate wrong answers. When you don't know how to do a math problem, don't panic. Just use reasoning. Try to eliminate wrong answers by back solving.

5. Don't show your work.

- There is no partial credit on the ACT.
- Break the rules you have been taught to use in the classroom concerning showing your work.
- Focus on speed – Just get the answer.

There are many good math students struggling on the ACT. One reason for this is attributed to students showing their work. In our high school math classes, we are typically taught to show every step. We even get partial credit for trying.

There is no partial credit on the ACT. The only thing that is viewed by the grader is a bubble sheet, and the grader is a machine. It doesn't matter if you write out one step or all the steps. You are either right or wrong based on your oval. Break the unwritten rule in your mind that you should show your work.

Don't show your work. There will be times where you will need to write out some steps, but don't waste your time on this test trying to show all your work. The key is to get the correct answer. That's it.

CONCEPT: ANGLES ADD TO 180°/ EQUILATERAL / ISOSCELES / AND RIGHT TRIANGLES

[See Page 230 for Example Problems]

The three interior angles of a triangle add to 180°. An interior angle is any angle inside the triangle. Angles *a, b, c* are interior angles.

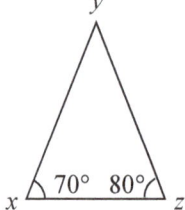

General equation $a + b + c = 180°$

↪ If we know two angles and need to solve for the third, just add the two known angles and subtract from 180°.

EXAMPLE #1: Given the following diagram, solve for ∠*y*.

First see that ∠*x* = 70° and ∠*z* = 80°. Then remember that the angles sum to 180°.

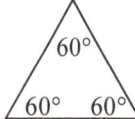

$$x + y + z = 180°$$
$$70° + y + 80° = 180°$$
$$150° + y = 180°$$
$$\underline{-150° \quad -150°}$$
$$y = 30°$$

Equilateral: All 3 interior angles in a triangle are equal. If they add to 180° then each angle is equal to $^{180°}/_3 = 60°$

$60° + 60° + 60° = 180°$

Isosceles: An isosceles triangle has two angles that are equal to each other. Since the sides of a triangle are proportional to the angle opposite the side, the two sides opposite the equal angles are equal.

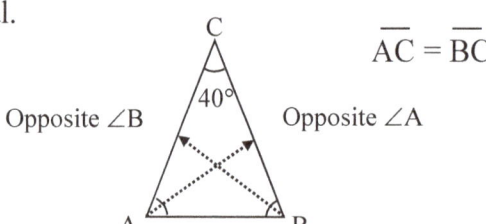

$\overline{AC} = \overline{BC}$

 TIP: If you place a dot at an angle, the side that doesn't touch the dot is the opposite side.

When the two angles that are equal to each other are 45°, the other angle is 90°.

$$45°+45°+90° = 180°$$

An angle equal to 90° is called a **right angle**. Therefore, if the 3 interior angles are 45°, 45° and 90° the triangle is called an isosceles right triangle.

Right Triangle: Any triangle with an angle equal to 90°

Scalene Triangle: Any triangle with no angles equal to each other

EXAMPLE #2: If isosceles ΔABC is drawn to scale and ∠ACB is 64°, what is the measure of ∠ABC?

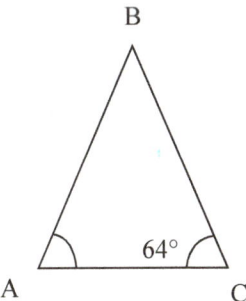

An isosceles triangle has two angles that are equal. In this case the equal angles are ∠BAC and ∠ACB. The sum of those two angles is 128°. The measure of ∠ABC must be 180°- 128° = 52°.

CONCEPT: AREA OF A TRIANGLE / TERMS ALTITUDE, MEDIAN, AND BASE

[See Page 233 for Example Problems]

⇨ The equation for the area of a triangle is **(Base · Height)/2** or **½(Base · Height)**

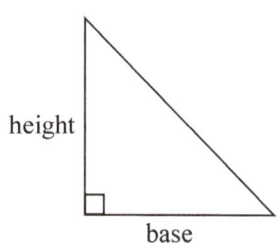

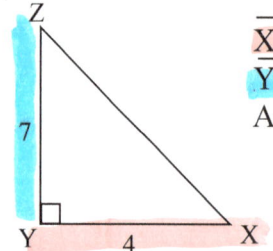

$\overline{XY}$=Base
$\overline{YZ}$=Height
$A = \frac{1}{2}(b \cdot h) = (4 \cdot 7)/2 = 28/2 = 14$

In a right triangle the base and height are easily identified. In other triangles we must drop an altitude or a median to determine the height. Consider the example below.

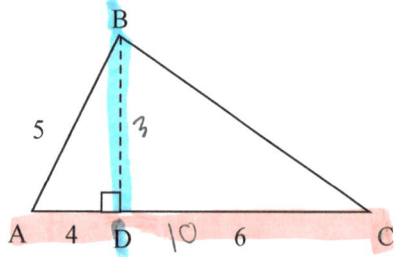

In ΔABC the base is $\overline{AC}$. The height is not as obvious. We must drop an altitude from point B to a new point D to establish the height.

⇨ An **altitude** is a vertical line from the highest point in the triangle forming a right angle with the base.

If $\overline{AD}$ = 4 and $\overline{AB}$=5, we can solve for $\overline{BD}$ using the Pythagorean theorem, $4^2 + (\overline{BD})^2 = 5^2$. Knowing the common right triangles, the length of $\overline{BD}$=3 (3-4-5). Therefore, the base=10 and the height = 3 giving the area:

$A = (b \cdot h)/2 = (10 \cdot 3)/2 = 30/2 = 15$

⇨ A **median** bisects the base. Bisects means equally divides.

⇨ In an isosceles right triangle, a **median** is an altitude that bisects the base if the median is dropped from the vertex.

EXAMPLE #1: Find the area of ΔABD.

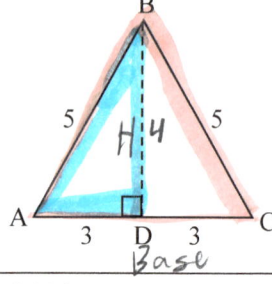

Using common right triangles, we have a 3-4-5. Set the median BD = 4. Therefore, the area of ΔABC
ΔABC = $(b \cdot h)/2 = (6 \cdot 4)/2 = 24/2 = 12$
ΔABD = $(b \cdot h)/2 = (3 \cdot 4)/2 = 12/2 = 6$

EXAMPLE #2: If the area of a triangle is 25ft² and its height is 5 feet, what is the base?

$A = (b \cdot h) \div 2 \qquad 25 = (b \cdot 5) \div 2 \rightarrow 50 = (b \cdot 5)$
$10 = b$

Set up the equation to show: area of Δ = ½ (b•h) = 25 = ½ (5•b). Solving for *b* produces *b* = 10.

EXAMPLE #3: The area of the square below is 40in². If ΔBCD has area of ¼ the area of ΔADE, what is the area of ΔBCD?

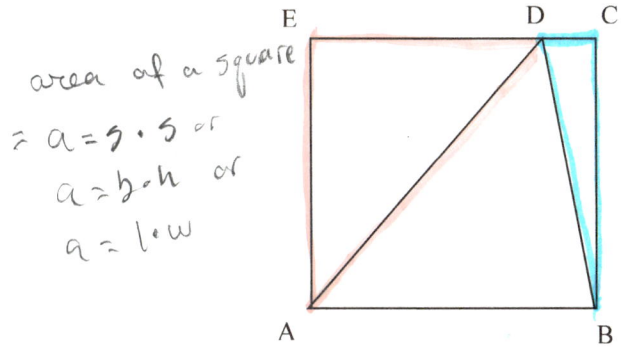

area of a square
= a = s · s or
a = b · h or
a = l · w

You must obtain the area of ΔBCD by subtraction and substitution.

First, note that the area of the whole square is *b•h*, (or *l•w*), and the area of ΔABD is ½*bh*. The rest of the square (or the sum of ΔADE and ΔBCD) must also be ½*bh*. This gives us ΔADE + ΔBCD = 20in².

Second, ΔADE is four times as large as ΔBCD, giving us 4•ΔBCD = ΔADE.

Last, substitute 4•ΔBCD for ΔADE in the first equation to get 4•ΔBCD + ΔBCD = 5•ΔBCD = 20in² and ΔBCD = ²⁰⁄₅ = 4in².

CONCEPT: AREA OF A CIRCLE / RADIUS / DIAMETER / CIRCUMFERENCE

[See Page 236 for Example Problems]

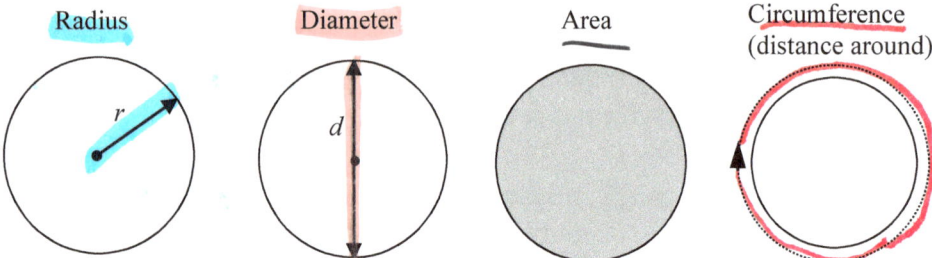

▷ The **diameter** is equal to twice the radius $2r = d$ or $d/2 = r$.
The **area** of a circle is πr^2.
The **circumference** of a circle is $2\pi r$ or πd.

EXAMPLE #1: If the diameter is 10, what is the radius?

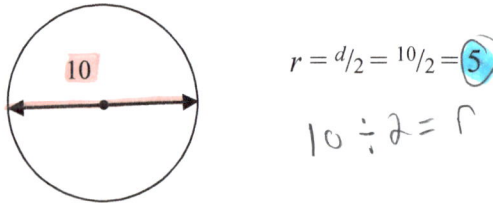

$r = d/2 = 10/2 = 5$

$10 \div 2 = r$

EXAMPLE #2: If the diameter is 10, what is the circumference?

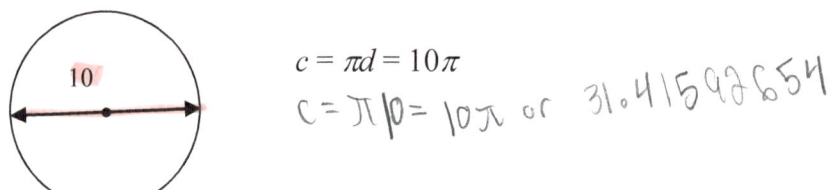

$c = \pi d = 10\pi$

$c = \pi \cdot 10 = 10\pi$ or 31.41592654

NOTE: Usually on the ACT, the answer will include the symbol π. If they want π converted to a number, the question will specify and tell you what to use (typically 3.14).

→ ACT is made to be able to be done without a calculator

EXAMPLE #3: If the radius is 5, what is the area?

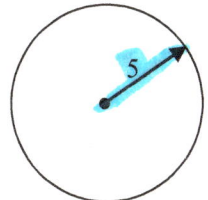

$a = \pi r^2 = \pi(5)^2 = 25\pi$

$a = \pi 5^2 = 25\pi$ or 78.53981634

👉 Sometimes the question will be asked backwards.

EXAMPLE #4: If the area is 25π, what is the diameter?

$a = \pi r^2 = 25\pi$ the π's cancel
$r^2 = 25$ taking the square root of both sides
$r = 5$

The answer is NOT 5! What did the question ask? The question asks for the diameter.

$d = 2r = 2(5) = 10$

 NOTE: Always make sure you answer the question that is asked. Just take a moment at the end of every problem to verify that your answer is what the question asked.

CONCEPT: MIDPOINT FORMULA

[See Page 239 for Example Problems]

Midpoint Formula $\left(\dfrac{x_1+x_2}{2}, \dfrac{y_1+y_2}{2}\right)$

The midpoint is the average of the *x* values and the average of the *y* values.

$\left(\dfrac{x_1+x_2}{2}\right)$ = midpoint (average) *x* coordinate

$\left(\dfrac{y_1+y_2}{2}\right)$ = midpoint (average) *y* coordinate

EXAMPLE #1: Find the midpoint of (-3,1) and (2,4)
Label the points (x_1, y_1) and (x_2, y_2)

$$\left(\dfrac{x_1+x_2}{2}, \dfrac{y_1+y_2}{2}\right) = \left(\dfrac{-3+2}{2}, \dfrac{1+4}{2}\right) = \left(\dfrac{-1}{2}, \dfrac{5}{2}\right)$$

↗ means backwards

EXAMPLE #2: The midpoint between two points is (2,4). If one of the two points is (3,-2), what is the second point?

Let (3,-2) be (x_1, y_1). The equation becomes $(2,4) = \left(\dfrac{3+x_2}{2}, \dfrac{-2+y_2}{2}\right)$. Consider separate equations for *x* and *y*: $\left(\dfrac{3+x_2}{2}\right) = 2$ and $\left(\dfrac{-2+y_2}{2}\right) = 4$.

For *x*, cross multiply and divide so that $3 + x_2 = 4$. Solve to find $x_2 = 1$
Similarly for *y* cross multiply and divide so that $-2 + y_2 = 8$, and $y_2 = 10$

The Second Point is (1,10)

EXAMPLE #3: Points A(-3, 2) and B(7, 4) determine line segment $\overline{AB}$ in the standard (x, y) coordinate plane. If the midpoint of $\overline{AB}$ is (*a*, 3), what is the value of *a*?

a is finding x value

Using the midpoint formula, we obtain

$$\left(\dfrac{x_1+x_2}{2}, \dfrac{y_1+y_2}{2}\right) = \left(\dfrac{-3+7}{2}, \dfrac{2+4}{2}\right) = (2,3), \text{ so } a = 2.$$

CONCEPT: PARALLEL LINES DIVIDED BY A TRANSVERSAL

[See Page 242 for Example Problems]

In the figure below, l_1 and l_2 are parallel and they are *transversed* (crossed) by l_3. Note $l_1 \parallel l_2$.

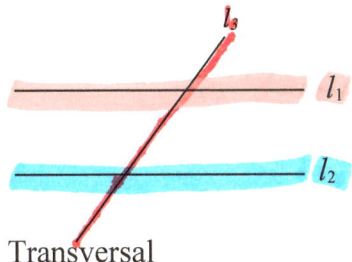

Transversal

NOTE: On the ACT you do not have to know all the fancy rules like: "Alternate interior angles are congruent." You simply must know which are equal.

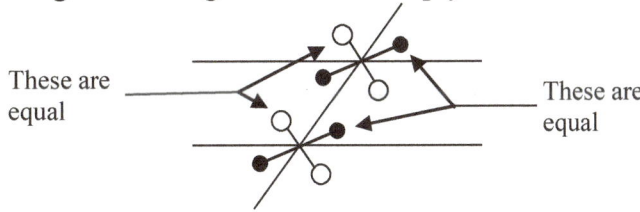

These are equal — These are equal

EXAMPLE #1: l_1 and l_2 are parallel. If $\angle ADB$ is 50°, find the measure of all the other angles.

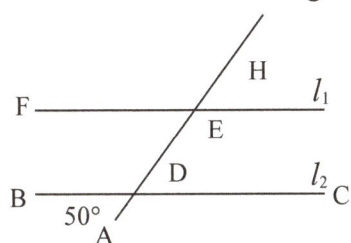

Notice that $\angle ADB$ & $\angle ADC$ are along a straight line and must add to 180°. (180°-50° = 130°).

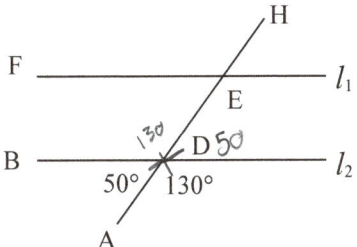

Now make the diagonal angles equal.

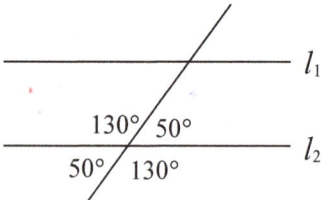

Because l_1 and l_2 are parallel, the angles created by l_1 and the transversal are the same as the angles created by l_2 and the transversal.

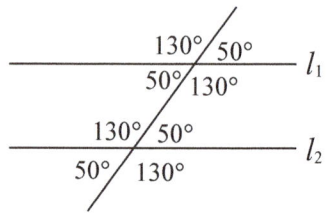

EXAMPLE #2: For ΔABC below, D and E are points on the sides of the triangle. If $\overline{AB}$ is parallel to $\overline{DE}$, what is the measure of ∠DEC?

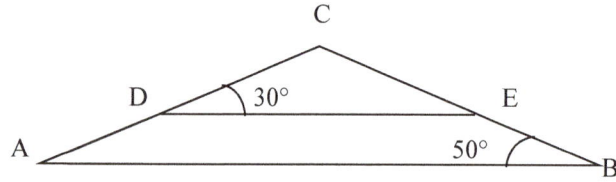

Because $\overline{AB}$ is parallel to $\overline{DE}$, ∠CED is equal to ∠ABC and is 50°.

EXAMPLE #3: In the parallelogram below, what is the measure of ∠BCD?

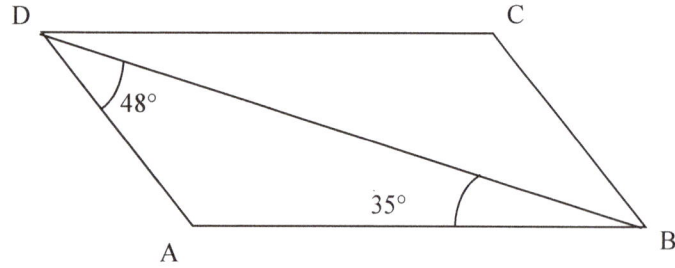

First note that ∠ADB = ∠CBD and ∠ABD = ∠BDC.
This means that ∠BCD = ∠BAD.
Which makes ∠BCD = 180° - (48° + 35°) = 180° - 83° = 97°

EXAMPLE #4: In the figure below, lines *a* and *b* are parallel, lines *c* and *d* are parallel, and two angles are shown. What is the measure of ∠*x*?

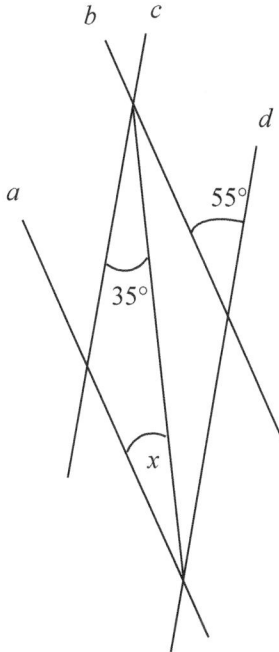

Because the given lines are parallel, ∠*x* = 55° - 35° = 20°. This is simple; don't let all the lines and labels intimidate you!

CONCEPT: INSCRIBED ANGLES \ CENTRAL ANGLES

[See Page 245 for Example Problems]

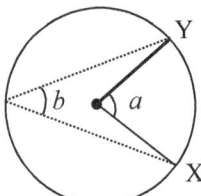

$\angle a$ is a central angle
$\angle b$ is an inscribed angle
$\angle b = \frac{1}{2} \angle a$

$\angle a$ is directly proportionate to the arc XY $\left(\dfrac{a}{360} = \dfrac{XY}{\text{circumference}} \right)$

EXAMPLE #1: If the circumference is 72m and arc XY is 6m, what is the measure of $\angle b$?

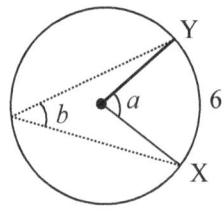

STEP 1: The arc is 6m out of a possible 72m; therefore, the first ratio is $^6/_{72}$. Notice that the top number (numerator) is the length of the arc from point X to point Y. The bottom number (denominator) is all the way around the circle.

STEP 2: If the central angle $\angle a$ is proportionate to the arc XY, then a is the numerator of the new fraction. Notice that $\angle a$ is $a°$ out of a possible 360°; therefore, the second ratio is $^a/_{360}$.

STEP 3: Establish the following proportion equation: $\dfrac{6}{72} = \dfrac{a}{360}$

STEP 4: Cross multiply and divide so that $72a = 6 \cdot 360$, and $a = \dfrac{6 \cdot 360}{72} = 30°$.

But remember, the question asks for the measure of $\angle b$ not $\angle a$! Use the relationship between a and b ($\angle b = \frac{1}{2} \angle a$) to get $\angle b = \frac{1}{2} (30) = 15°$

Make sure you always ask yourself, "What are we solving for?"

CONCEPT: PERCENTS

[See Page 248 for Example Problems]

A percent is a portion of a pie that has 100 pieces. For example, if 90% of your test answers are correct then 90 of 100, or $^{90}/_{100}$, of the answers are correct. The fraction applies even if you only answered 10 questions ($^{90}/_{100} = ^{9}/_{10}$).

▷ If the value is given as a percent, always move the decimal two spaces to the left to get the proportion or the decimal.

Like this: 12% = 12.0% = 0.12   8% = 8.0% = .08   0.1% = 0.1% = 0.001

▷ The standard form of a percent problem is, "What *number* is what *percent* of what *total*?" A question could ask you to solve for the number (call it *n*), the percent (it's the fraction $^{p}/_{100}$), or the total (*t*). Words in the question give clues to the operation needed to get the answer: When you see "is", think "=". When you see "of", think "multiply".

Therefore, the standard form could be written as the following: $n = {}^{p}/_{100} \cdot t$

EXAMPLE #1: 8 is what percent of 64?

$$8 = (^{p}/_{100}) \cdot 64$$
$$800 = 64p$$
$$x = 12.5$$

Note: Since we placed the *x* over 100, you do not need to move the decimal two places to the left.

EXAMPLE #2: What number is 5% of 200?

$$x = (^{5}/_{100}) \cdot 200$$
$$= {}^{1000}/_{100}$$
$$= 10$$

EXAMPLE #3: 7 is 10% of what number?

$7 = (^{10}/_{100}) \cdot t$, rearranges to become:
$$(^{10}/_{100}) \cdot t = 7$$
$$t = {}^{700}/_{10}$$
$$t = 70$$

NOTE: You should be able to quickly use your calculator to answer these questions. Make sure you are familiar with your calculator and don't use the % key unless you know how to use it correctly.

CONCEPTS: SQUARE ROOTS AND EXPONENTS

[See Page 251 for Example Problems]

Square Roots (radicals)

☞ The following are basic square root rules needed for the test:

$$\sqrt{x} = x^{\frac{1}{2}}$$

$$\sqrt{x} \bullet \sqrt{x} = x$$

$$\sqrt{a} + 2\sqrt{a} = (1+2)\sqrt{a} = 3\sqrt{a}$$

$$\sqrt{a} - 2\sqrt{a} = (1-2)\sqrt{a} = -\sqrt{a}$$

$$\sqrt{a} \bullet 2\sqrt{b} = (1 \bullet 2)\sqrt{a \bullet b} = 2\sqrt{ab}$$

$$\frac{\sqrt{a}}{2\sqrt{b}} = \frac{1}{2}\sqrt{\frac{a}{b}}$$

EXAMPLE #1: Given the following equation, find x.

$$\sqrt{3+x} = 2$$

Simply square both sides and remember $\sqrt{x} \bullet \sqrt{x} = x$

$$\left(\sqrt{3+x}\right)^2 = 2^2$$

Therefore,

$$\sqrt{3+x} \bullet \sqrt{3+x} = 2 \bullet 2$$
$$3 + x = 4$$
$$x = 1$$

Exponents

The following are basic exponent rules needed for the test:

☞ Add and subtract like terms. Like terms are those with the same values in the exponents and in the base. x^4 and $3x^4$ are like terms; x^4 and y^4 are not like terms; x^4 and x^3 are not like terms.

EXAMPLE #1A: $x^4 - 3x^4 = -2x^4$

EXAMPLE #1B: $x^a + 2x^a = (1+2)x^a = 3x^a$

EXAMPLE #1C: $x^a - 2x^a = (1-2)x^a = -x^a$

↪ When multiplying and dividing exponents, if the bases are the same add the values in the exponent.

EXAMPLE #2A: $x^4 \cdot x^2 = x^6$

EXAMPLE #2B: $x^a \cdot x^b = x^{a+b}$

↪ When dividing exponents, if the bases are the same subtract the values in the exponent.

EXAMPLE #3A: $\dfrac{x^6}{x^2} = x^4$

EXAMPLE #3B: $\dfrac{x^a}{x^b} = x^{a-b}$

↪ When raising an exponent to a power, multiply the exponents.

EXAMPLE #4A: $(x^4)^2 = x^8$

EXAMPLE #4B: $(x^a)^b = x^{a \cdot b}$

EXAMPLE #4C: $x^0 = 1$
(This is true if x is not equal to 0. Zero to the zero power is undefined.)

↪ Factoring involves pulling out pieces of terms that exist in all the terms. You must follow the simplification rules in reverse in order to factor.

EXAMPLE #5: $x^4 - 3x^4y = x^4(1-3y)$

CONCEPT: RATIONAL AND IRRATIONAL NUMBERS

[See Page 254 for Example Problems]

Rational numbers can be represented as a fraction
Irrational numbers are both non-repeating and non-terminating decimals

Determine if a number is irrational by asking yourself, "Is this number a non-repeating and non-terminating decimal?" If the answer is yes, the number is irrational; otherwise, the number is rational.

 NOTE: These numbers are irrational:

π, and square roots of 2, 3, 5, 6, 7, 8, 10, 11, 12, and 13

This concept is rarely used on the test. However, you should be familiar with this concept for those rare times when it is included.

EXAMPLE #1: Is $\dfrac{3}{\sqrt{49}}$ rational or irrational?

The fraction $3/7$ is a non-terminating, repeating decimal, so it is rational.

EXAMPLE #2: For what value of *x* is $\dfrac{1}{\sqrt{x}}$ irrational?

Look at the choices and eliminate common squares like 4, 9, 16, or 25. Use your calculator if you are still uncertain.

Factor a square root. A number is irrational if it has an irrational number as a factor.

EXAMPLE #3: Which of the following is a rational number?

A) $\sqrt{2}$
B) $\sqrt{3}$
C) $\sqrt{8}$
D) $\sqrt{27}$
E) $\sqrt{36}$

Of course, the answer is E, but if you needed to go through the list, you could remember that $\sqrt{2}$ and $\sqrt{3}$ are irrational. $\sqrt{8} = 2\sqrt{2}$ and $\sqrt{27} = 3\sqrt{3}$ and since $\sqrt{2}$ and $\sqrt{3}$ are factors, respectively, C and D are both irrational.

CONCEPT: SIMILAR TRIANGLES

[See Page 256 for Example Problems]

In similar triangles, the sides of the triangles are proportionate or ratios to each other.

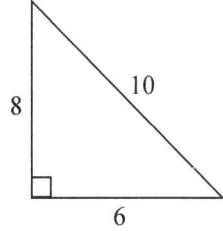 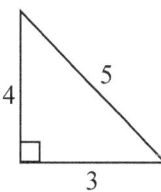

Since the triangles above are right triangles, these would be called similar right triangles. Notice that 3 is to 6 as 4 is to 8 as 5 is to 10.

EXAMPLE #1: △ABC is similar to △XYZ.

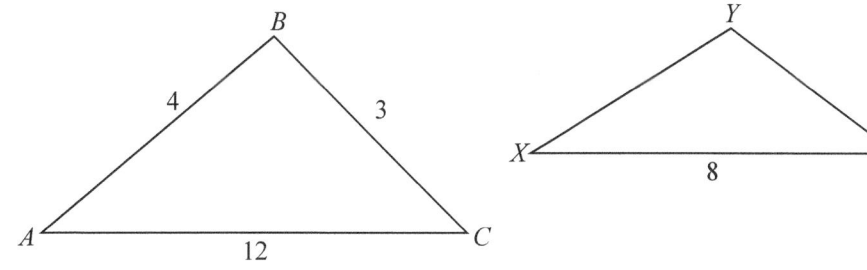

Find $\overline{XY}$ and $\overline{YZ}$.

8 is to 12 as $\overline{XY}$ is to 4 as $\overline{YZ}$ is to 3, or, $\dfrac{8}{12} = \dfrac{\overline{XY}}{4} = \dfrac{\overline{YZ}}{3}$

Cross Multiply and Divide

$\dfrac{8}{12} = \dfrac{\overline{XY}}{4}$ ⟶ $\dfrac{8}{12} \times \dfrac{\overline{XY}}{4}$ which yields $32 = 12\overline{XY}$ therefore $\overline{XY} = \dfrac{8}{3}$

$\dfrac{8}{12} = \dfrac{\overline{YZ}}{3}$ ⟶ $\dfrac{8}{12} \times \dfrac{\overline{YZ}}{3}$ which yields $24 = 12\overline{XY}$ therefore $\overline{YZ} = 2$

EXAMPLE #2: In the figure below, A lies on $\overline{XZ}$, B lies on $\overline{YZ}$, and $\overline{AB}$ is parallel to $\overline{XY}$. If $\overline{AB}$ is 12 units long, $\overline{BZ}$ is 16 units long, and $\overline{XY}$ is 15 units. How many units long is $\overline{BY}$?

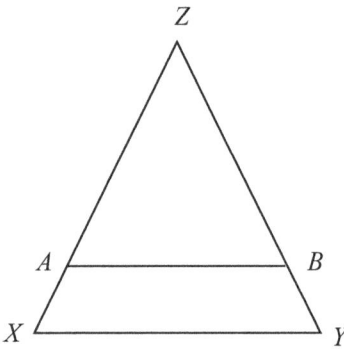

Use the ratio of the sides to obtain the length of $\overline{BY}$:

$$\frac{\overline{AB}}{\overline{BZ}} = \frac{\overline{XY}}{\overline{YZ}}, \text{ and } \frac{12}{16} = \frac{15}{\overline{YZ}}, \text{ so } \overline{YZ} = \frac{(16)(15)}{12} = 20,$$

therefore $\overline{BY} = 4$.

EXAMPLE #3: The lengths of sides of a right triangle are 5, 12, and 13. If the area of a similar triangle is 120 units, what is the hypotenuse of the second triangle?

The area of the given right triangle is ½ (5)(12) = 30 units². Equate the ratios to get

$$\frac{\sqrt{\Delta_1 \text{ area}}}{\sqrt{\Delta_2 \text{ area}}} = \frac{\Delta_1 \text{ hyp}}{\Delta_2 \text{ hyp}} = \frac{\sqrt{30}}{\sqrt{120}} = \frac{\sqrt{30}}{\sqrt{30 \cdot 4}} = \frac{1}{2} = \frac{13}{\Delta_2 \text{ hyp}},$$

so the hypotenuse of the second triangle must be 26.

CONCEPT: COMMON RIGHT TRIANGLES

[See Page 260 for Example Problems]

Common Right Triangles
The ACT math section usually has at least one problem containing a common right triangle. When given a right triangle and the lengths of only two of the three sides are known, we use the Pythagorean theorem to find the length of the third side. But if you recognize a common right triangle, you do not have to use the Pythagorean theorem.

The three common right triangles typically used are: 3-4-5, 6-8-10, 5-12-13

Verify that 5, 10, and 13 are the hypotenuses. The longest side of a right triangle is always the side opposite the right angle (the hypotenuse).

30° 60° Right Triangles
When faced with a 30° 60° right triangle there are four trig identities that are helpful. You need to remember the Pythagorean theorem and the following:

$$\sin(30°) = \frac{1}{2} = \cos(60°)$$

$$\sin(60°) = \frac{\sqrt{3}}{2} = \sin(30°)$$

You can also just remember the factors of each side rather than using trig if that's easier for you.

EXAMPLE #1: What is the length of x in the figure below?

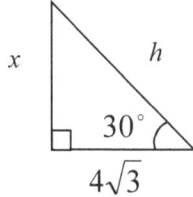

Since $\sin(60°) = \dfrac{4\sqrt{3}}{h} = \dfrac{\sqrt{3}}{2}$, cross-multiply and divide to show that the hypotenuse is 8. Use $\sin(30°) = \dfrac{1}{2} = \dfrac{x}{h}$. We know that $h = 8$, so $\dfrac{x}{8} = \dfrac{1}{2}$ therefore $x = 4$.

45° 45° Right triangles

The key to working with 45° 45° right triangles is to remember that the two sides (not the hypotenuse) have equal length. This means that the sines and cosines are also equal. The only place on the unit circle where the sin(x) = cos(x) is where they both equal $\sqrt{2}/2$.

👉 Remembering the factors of each side, rather than using trig, may be easier for you.

EXAMPLE #2: What is the length of x in the triangle below?

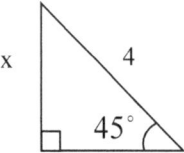

Since sin(45°) = $2\sqrt{2}$, we know that $\dfrac{x}{4} = 2\sqrt{2}$. Solve for *x* to find $x = 2\sqrt{2}$.

NOTE: If you learn the factors of each side and solve for *x*, the other sides can easily be determined.

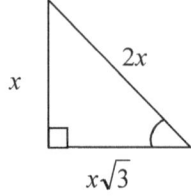 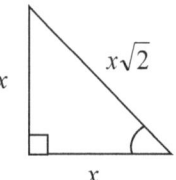

EXAMPLE #3: In the figure below, what is the value of $\overline{DE}$?

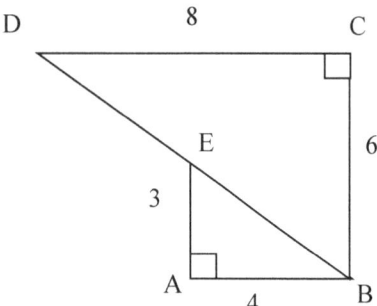

Noticing that there are two right triangles is critical. The larger is a 6, 8, 10 triangle. The second is a 3, 4, 5 triangle. $\overline{DE}$ must be the difference in the two hypotenuses, 10 - 5 = 5.

CONCEPT: WORD PROBLEMS GENERAL STRATEGY

[See Page 263 for Example Problems]

↪ 4 Step Plan to Answering Word Problems:
    STEP 1: What are they asking for?
    STEP 2: Pull Numbers/Make Equations
    STEP 3: Solve
    STEP 4: Sanity Check

1. **What are they asking for?**
Identify what the question asks and represent what is needed. For example, if the question asks for the radius, write "$r =$" or something similar. This is important especially on questions where you solve for the diameter, but they ask for the radius. If you identify what is asked, you will know what you choose answers the right question.

2. **Pull Numbers/Make Equations**
Read each sentence. Pull out any numbers and write them down in equation form. You may pull several numbers from different sentences before you are able to make equations. This should reduce the number of times you have to re-read a problem.

3. **Solve**
You may have to solve for something to use in another equation. If you first identified what the question asks, you will see that you must solve another equation to get the answers. As stated in the general ideas, there is no partial credit on this test. Don't show all your work. Solve quickly.

4. **Sanity Check**
You do not have time to check your answers on the math test. You need to develop enough confidence in your work that you can pick an answer and move on. However, on word problems a quick sanity check is appropriate. Just take a moment to see if your answer makes sense.

    EXAMPLE #1: Bennett had 8 pieces of candy on Monday. Three days later he had a fourth more than he had on Monday. How many pieces of candy did he have on Thursday?

    STEP 1: How many pieces of candy on Thursday?
    STEP 2: 8 pieces
             $1/4$ more than 8
    STEP 3: $8 + 8(1/4) = 8 + 8/4 = 8 + 2 = 10$
    STEP 4: We have more than 8, but not double or triple

EXAMPLE #2: At a home improvement store, Sheri and Tim purchase supplies to repair their kitchen plumbing. They purchase a faucet, regularly priced at $99, at a 15% discount, plus plumber's putty ($2), a plumbing wrench ($12.50), and 2 feet of PVC pipe, which costs (39 cents per foot). Estimate the total cost of the bill if tax is 10%.

STEP 1: total price

STEP 2: $99(1-.15)
$2
$12.50
2(.39)
all(.10)

STEP 3: [$99(.85) + $2 + $12.50 + 2(.39)] 1.10 = 109.37 an estimate would be even quicker: 85 + 2 + 12.5 + 1 = 100.5, then multiply by 1.1 and get 110.

STEP 4: Check percents (notice that .15 was given as the discount, but we multiplied by .85. Be sure to multiply the percents by the right number (.10 by the sum of the items). Make sure we added all that should be added and that the number is large enough but not too large.

CONCEPT: GEOMETRY-ACUTE, OBTUSE, RIGHT COMPLEMENTARY, AND SUPPLEMENTARY ANGLES

[See Page 269 for Example Problems]

Right, Complementary, and Supplementary Angles

Right angle = 90°
  Complementary: Two angles that add to 90°
  Supplementary: Two angles that add to 180°

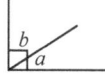   

Angles *a* and *b* are complementary.   Angles *x* and *y* are supplementary.

> NOTE: Angles less-than 90° are called **Acute**
> Angles greater-than 90° are called **Obtuse**
> Angles equal to 90° are called **Right**

EXAMPLE #1: In the figure below, if $b = 42°$, then $a = ?$

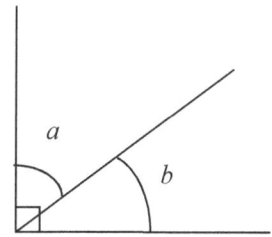

The sum of $\angle a$ and $\angle b$ is 90°, so $\angle a = 90 - 42 = 48°$.

EXAMPLE #2: In the figure below, the measure of $\angle b$ is 38°, what is the measure of its supplement?

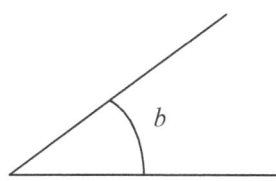

Remember supplemental angles add to 180°, so calculate the supplement of $\angle b$ (call it $\angle a$) as $\angle a = 180 - 38 = 142°$.

EXAMPLE #3: In the figure below points A, E, and D are on the same line. What is the measure of ∠BEC?

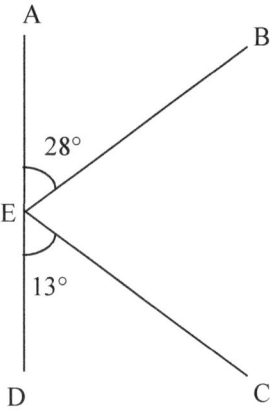

The sum of the three angles adds to 180°, so ∠BEC = 180 − 28 − 13 = 180 − 41 = 139°

CONCEPT: QUADRATIC EQUATION

[See Page 272 for Example Problems]

Three kinds of questions could be asked:

1. Find possible roots or the values of x for which the equation $ax^2 + bx + c$ equals zero.
   - Find roots by factoring
   - Find roots by using the quadratic equation
2. Simplify terms into quadratic equation
3. Solve for a, b, or c in quadratic equation

 NOTE: Most of the quadratic equations can be solved by factoring, and all the problems in this section can be solved by understanding how to solve for x, how to get the quadratic equation in $ax^2 + bx + c$ form, and by using basic algebra skills.

Finding Possible Roots

Factoring

Sometimes you can factor the equation so that the two terms multiply. Set each term equal to zero, and solve for x.

EXAMPLE #1: What are the possible roots of the expression $x^2 + 4x + 4$?

The equation factors to $(x+2)(x+2)$ so that the values of x for which the equation equals zero are $x = -2$ and $x = -2$.

Quadratic Equation

The quadratic equation gives the solutions for x when you plug the values of a, b, and c into $x = \dfrac{-b \pm \sqrt{b^2 - 4ac}}{2a}$.

Note that there are two solutions to the quadratic equation (one using the plus sign in the numerator and one using the minus sign in the numerator).

EXAMPLE #2: Find the roots of $x^2 + 4x + 4$ using the quadratic equation.

The values for the quadratic equation are $a = 1$, $b = 4$, and $c = 4$, so that the quadratic equation becomes

$$x = \frac{-4 \pm \sqrt{4^2 - (4)(1)(4)}}{(2)(1)} = -2.$$

Since we know that there are two roots to a quadratic equation, we say that both roots are -2.

Simplify Terms into the Quadratic Equation
You must simplify the equation by using FOIL (First, Outside, Inside, Last).

EXAMPLE #3: For all x, $(4x-3)(x+2) = ?$

Use FOIL to multiply the two terms and get: $4x^2 - 3x + 8x - 6$
Then combine like terms to get $4x^2 + 5x - 6$.

Solve for *a*, *b*, or *c* in Quadratic Equation
Some problems seem especially complicated, but just relax and use the equations and methods you know to find the answer.

EXAMPLE #4: If $(x+m)^2 = x^2 + 8x + n$ where m and n are integers, what is n?

Use foil to see the relationship between b and c. See that the FOIL process used on $(x+m)^2$ produces $x^2 + 2mx + m^2$. From this equation we see that $2m = 8$ and $n = m^2$. Solve the two equations and get $n = 16$.

CONCEPT: INEQUALITIES

[See Page 275 for Example Problems]

You should be familiar with the following aspects of inequalities:
1. The difference between equality and inequality on the number line
2. Inequalities in the (x, y) coordinate plane
3. Dividing or multiplying an inequality by a negative number reverses the direction of the inequality.

The Difference Between Equality and Inequality on the Number line

On a number line, a greater-than-or-equal-to ($\geq$) and less-than-or-equal-to ($\leq$) are indicated by a solid dot over the number to which it refers, like this number line showing ($x \geq 10$).

On a number line, a greater-than (>) and less-than (<) are indicated by a hollow dot over the number to which it refers, like this number line showing ($x > 10$).

 NOTE: ACT does not use interval notation using [ ] and ( ).

Inequalities in (x, y) coordinate plane

The graph below represents all the numbers where x is greater-than-or-equal-to 5.

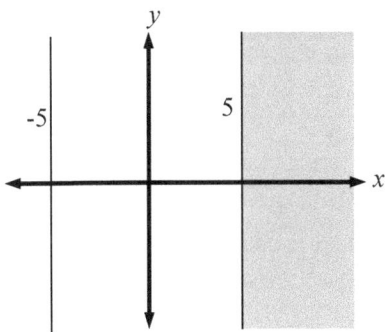

Multiplying or Dividing by a Negative Number

EXAMPLE #1: What is the largest value of x that satisfies the inequality $-3x \geq 6$?

Divide each side by 3, which produces $-x \geq 2$. To eliminate the minus sign, multiply each side by minus one, which reverses the direction of the sign resulting in the equation $x \leq -2$. We conclude that the largest value of x that satisfies the original inequality is -2.

EXAMPLE #2: Write the solution set for the inequality in the figure below.

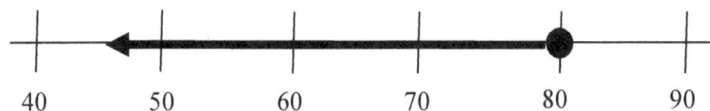

Notice the solid dot over the 80 mark. This means the answer will be "or-equal-to 80." Since the arrow points left, the answer will be less-than. The answer is $x \leq 80$.

EXAMPLE #3: Write the solution set for the inequality in the figure below.

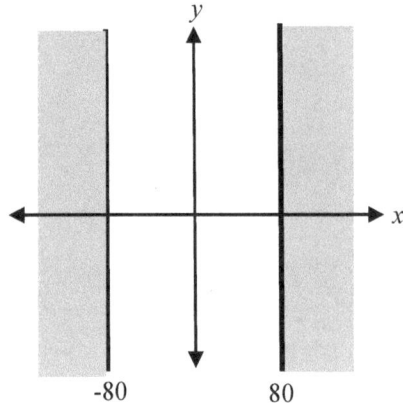

The inequality must include two areas: greater-than positive 80 and less-than negative 80. An absolute value sign works. The answer is: $|x| \geq 80$.

CONCEPT: LOGARITHMS

[See Page 280 for example problems]

A logarithm is the exponent (Y) to which the *base* (b) must be raised to produce a given number (X).

$$\text{Log}_b X = Y \quad \text{Converts to} \quad b^Y = X$$

Example #1: Given the following, find Y.

$\text{Log}_2 8 = Y \quad$ Converts to $2^Y = 8$

$2 \bullet 2 \bullet 2 = 8 \quad$ Therefore, $2^3 = 8$. $\quad Y = 3$

Example #2: Given the following, find X.

$\text{Log}_3 X = 4 \quad$ Converts to $3^4 = X$

$3 \bullet 3 \bullet 3 \bullet 3 = 81 \quad$ Therefore, $3^4 = 81$. $\quad X = 81$

Example #3: Given the following, find b.

$\text{Log}_b 125 = 3 \quad$ Converts to $b^3 = 125$

$5 \bullet 5 \bullet 5 = 125 \quad$ Therefore, $5^3 = 125$. $\quad b = 5$

CONCEPT: PYTHAGOREAN THEOREM

[See Page 282 for Example Problems]

Things to Know:
1. The theorem: $a^2 + b^2 = c^2$, where c is the hypotenuse and a and b are legs of a right triangle.
2. How to solve for either a, b, or c when given two of the values or one value and the area of a triangle

NOTE: a and b are always perpendicular to each other; c is always the hypotenuse (longest side).

EXAMPLE #1: The legs of a right triangle are 3 and 6 units. What is the length of the hypotenuse?

Solve by setting either a or b equal to 3 and the other equal to 6. The equation for this relationship is $3^2 + 6^2 = c^2$, or $c^2 = 9 + 36 = 45$. The length of the hypotenuse c equals $\sqrt{45}$, which simplifies to $3\sqrt{5}$.

EXAMPLE #2: The two longest sides of a right triangle are 11 and 8 inches. How long is the third side?

Be sure to notice that the hypotenuse length is given. You must solve for a leg. The equation is $8^2 + b^2 = 11^2$ Rearrange to get: $b = \sqrt{121 - 64} = \sqrt{57}$

CONCEPT: ABSOLUTE VALUES

[See Page 285 for Example Problems]

The **absolute value** is the number of spaces either direction from a given point on the number line.

EXAMPLE #1: $|2x-1| = 3$

Make two equations. For the *first* re-write the equation without the absolute value.

$2x-1 = 3$
$\quad 2x = 4$
$\quad\quad x = 2$

Obtain the *second* equation one of two ways. Some say to change the sign of everything inside the bars.

$-(2x-1) = 3$
$\quad -2x+1 = 3$
$\quad\quad -2x = 2$
$\quad\quad\quad x = -1$

Others say to change the sign of what is on the right. In this case, simplify the problem so that the absolute value is on one side and everything else is on the other.

$2x-1 = -3$
$\quad 2x = -2$
$\quad\quad x = -1$

Both answers 2 and –1 are correct. Although –1 may seem wrong since it is negative, remember we solved for *x* and not $|x|$. The value –1 satisfies the equation for *x*. Check:

$|2(-1)-1| = 3$
$\quad |-2-1| = 3$
$\quad\quad |-3| = 3$

EXAMPLE #2: If $|5x - 7| = 13$, what are the possible values of *x*?

First, solve without the absolute value sign to get:

$5x - 7 = 13$
$\quad 5x = 20$
$\quad\quad x = 4$

Second, change the sign of what is on the right (it seems easier in this case):
$5x - 7 = -13$
$\quad 5x = -6$
$\quad\quad x = -6/5$

So, the possible values of *x* are: $-6/5$ and 4.

You may also be asked to perform operations on absolute values.

EXAMPLE #3: $|2-7| - |7-5| = ?$

Solve each piece individually, then the whole:

$|2-7| - |7-5| = |-5| - |2| = 5 - 2 = 3$

EXAMPLE #4: $|6-12| \cdot |9-2| \cdot (-3) = ?$

$|-6| \cdot |7| \cdot (-3) = 6 \cdot 7 \cdot (-3) = -126$

Your answer may also include more than one answer for more than one variable.

EXAMPLE #5: For which values of x and y is $x|6-y| > 0$?

First, x must not be negative, so $x > 0$.

Second, $|6-y|$ must not be equal to 0, so $|6-y| \neq 0$.

Solve for $6 - y = 0$ and $-6 + y = 0$, to get $y \neq 6$.

The answer is $x > 0$ and $y \neq 6$.

CONCEPT: AVERAGES/TERMS: SUM, DIFFERENCE, PRODUCT, QUOTIENT, MEAN, MEDIAN, MODE

[See Page 288 for Example Problems]

To calculate an average, add the items you are averaging to get the sum. Divide the sum by the number of items you added.

EXAMPLE #1: Find the average of 4, 5, 6, and 7

$$\frac{4+5+6+7}{4} = 5.5$$

You may be able to answer from just looking at the problem. Remember, there is no partial credit, so don't spend time writing unless you need to.

Terms:
Sum-add
Difference-subtract
Product-multiply
Quotient-divide

Reverse average problem

EXAMPLE #2: Your final class average is 90. You made an 87, 93, and 82 on the first 3 tests. If the average is computed from 4 tests, what did you score on the 4th test?

STEP 1: Let x represent the 4th test:

$$\frac{87+93+82+x}{4} = 90$$

STEP 2: Cross-multiply and divide to get

$$(87 + 93 + 82 + x) = 90 \bullet 4$$
$$262 + x = 360$$
$$x = 98$$

You may also be asked to obtain an average from a table of numbers.

EXAMPLE #3: The scores for two basketball teams' three scorers are given in the table below. What is the average of the scorers for the Eagles?

Player	Team	Points
Ashley	Eagles	18
Campbell	Hawks	15
Jones	Hawks	15
James	Eagles	12
Garcia	Eagles	12
Graham	Hawks	6

The average is
$(18 + 12 + 12) / 3 = {}^{42}/_3 = 14.$

Terms:
- *Mean-* Average
- *Median-* Middle value or average of middle values if there is an even number of values
- *Mode-* Value that occurs the most
- *Range-* Difference in the highest value and the lowest value

EXAMPLE #4: Find the mean, median, and mode of the following series of numbers: 1,3,3,4,6,8,10,15.

Mean: (1+3+3+4+6+8+10+15)/8 = 50/8 = **6.25**
Median: The middle two numbers are 4 and 6.
The average of those two numbers is **5**.
Mode: The value that occurs the most is **3**.

CONCEPT: TRIGONOMETRY

[See Page 292 for Example Problems]

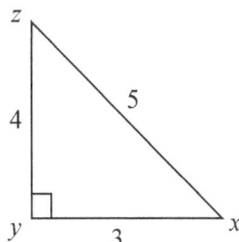 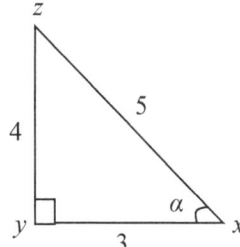

Example #1: Considering the figures above, solve for sin, cos, and tan of the angle that occurs at *x*. This problem could say solve for sin α, cos α, or tan α.

NOTE: The *x* in the three problems represents the angle that occurs at point *x*. This is usually identified with a curved symbol like in the triangle at the upper right. We use *x* for simplicity in this lesson. *Sin x* means the sine of the angle that occurs at *x*.

STEP 1: Place a dot at point *x*

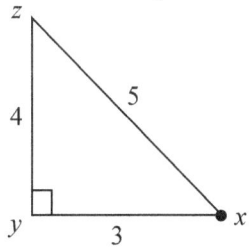

The side that **does not** touch the dot is the side opposite; therefore, $\overline{YZ}$ is opposite the angle of interest. Label it *o* for opposite.

STEP 2: The hypotenuse is the **longest** side. It is opposite the right angle. Label it *h* for hypotenuse.

STEP 3: There is only one side left. Label it *a* for adjacent. The side that is adjacent will always be next to the angle of interest. If you label *o* and *h* first, the only side remaining will always be the side adjacent.

The first thing you must memorize or have programmed in your calculator for trigonometry is the following:

$$\sin \angle x = \frac{\text{opposite}}{\text{hypotenuse}} = \frac{o}{h} \qquad \cos \angle x = \frac{\text{adjacent}}{\text{hypotenuse}} = \frac{a}{h} \qquad \tan \angle x = \frac{\text{opposite}}{\text{adjacent}} = \frac{o}{a}$$

Sin, cos, and tan are short for sine, cosine, and tangent, respectively.

↯ There are several tricks to learning these relationships.
- The most popular way is using the word

Soh~Cah~Toa

"S" stands for sin, "C" stands for cos, "T" stands for tan. Note that the first lower case letter is the numerator, and the second lower case letter is the denominator of the equation.

- Another way is through weird phrases like the following:
    Oscar **H**ad **A** **H**old **O**n **A**rthur.
    Oscar **H**ad **A** **H**eap **O**f **A**pples.
    Oh **H**eck **A**nother **H**eap **O**f **A**lgebra

- Another way that has all the letters is the following:
    Some **O**ld **H**ippie **C**aught **A**nother **H**ippie **T**urning **O**ld **A**lbums.

This phrase includes the S for sin, C for cosine, and T for tangent.

↯ Regardless of the method, you should be able to write or have programmed in your calculator Soh~Cah~Toa.

There are 3 other terms you must know. The inverses of sin, cos, and tan are cosecant, secant, and cotangent respectively. The abbreviations are the following:

cosecant = csc   secant = sec   cotangent = cot

To remember the sin, cos, and tan relationships read the "Soh~Cah~Toa" left to right. Soh~Cah~Toa. Since csc, sec, and cot are the inverses, we just read the word backwards: Soh~Cah~Toa. Therefore:

$$\csc \angle x = \frac{h}{o} \qquad \sec \angle x = \frac{h}{a} \qquad \cot \angle x = \frac{a}{o}$$

Consider the example again:

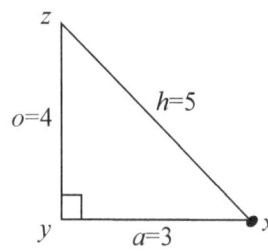

$\sin \angle x = \dfrac{o}{h} = \dfrac{4}{5}$ and $\csc \angle x = \dfrac{h}{o} = \dfrac{5}{4}$

$\cos \angle x = \dfrac{a}{h} = \dfrac{3}{5}$ and $\sec \angle x = \dfrac{h}{a} = \dfrac{5}{3}$

$\tan \angle x = \dfrac{o}{a} = \dfrac{4}{3}$ and $\cot \angle x = \dfrac{a}{o} = \dfrac{3}{4}$

NOTE: sin = $4/5$ and its inverse csc = $5/4$. They are reciprocals (inverse) of each other. This implies the following:

$1/\sin$ = csc and $1/\csc$ = sin $1/\cos$ = sec and $1/\sec$ = cos $1/\tan$ = cot and $1/\cot$ = tan

Finally, you must know the following two trig identities:

$\sin/\cos = \tan$

$\sin^2 + \cos^2 = 1$

When the Law of Sines or Law of Cosines is tested, it will typically be written out for you. A written explanation is also usually included.

EXAMPLE #2: Given that $\sin x = \dfrac{o}{8} = 0.75$, what is o?

   A) 2
   B) 3
   C) 4
   D) 5
   E) 6

Since we know that $\sin x = \dfrac{opposite}{hypotenuse}$ and $\sin x = 0.75$.

Solve for the opposite side by $0.75 \cdot 8 = 6$.

EXAMPLE #3: To what does the following expression reduce?

$(\sin x)(\sec x)(\tan x)(\cot x)(\csc x)$

   A) $\sec x$
   B) $\sin^2 x$
   C) $\cos x$
   D) $\tan x$
   E) $\tan^2 x$

Substitute to see that the expression equals $[(\sin x)(\sec x)(\tan x)(1/\tan x)(1/\sin x) = \sec x]$.

EXAMPLE #4: For the right triangle below, which of the following expressions is equal to $\cos\theta$?

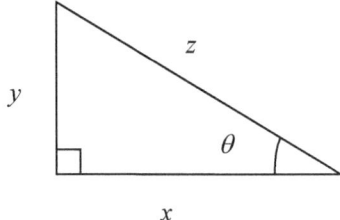

A) $\dfrac{x}{y}$

B) $\dfrac{y}{x}$

C) $\dfrac{x}{z}$

D) $\dfrac{z}{x}$

E) $\dfrac{y}{z}$

Since x is the adjacent side, z is the hypotenuse, and $\cos\theta = \dfrac{adjacent}{hypotenuse}$ find $\cos\theta = \dfrac{x}{z}$.

CONCEPT: ALGEBRA

[See Page 298 for Example Problems]

Algebra questions may involve many different concepts including, but not limited to, the following:

Substituting values into equations and solving
    EXAMPLE #1: If $y = -3$ and $x = 5$ what is the value of $x^2 + xy^4$?

$$\begin{aligned} ? &= x^2 + xy^4 \\ &= 5^2 + 5 \bullet (-3)^4 \\ &= 25 + 5 \bullet 81 \\ &= 25 + 405 \\ &= 430 \end{aligned}$$

Converting units (like converting from days to hours or vice versa)
    EXAMPLE #2: A yard is equal to three feet. If a piece of string is 4.5 yards, how many feet is it?

$$4.5 \text{ yards} \left(\frac{3 \text{ feet}}{1 \text{ yard}} \right) = 13.5 \text{ feet}$$

Building equations from word problems
    EXAMPLE #3: Mike had x cards in his basketball card collection three weeks ago. If he added 3 cards per week and continues adding for the next 7 weeks, how many cards will he have in 7 weeks from today?

10 weeks have passed from 3 weeks ago to 7 weeks from today
$x + 3(10) = x + 30$

CONCEPT: DISTANCE FORMULA

[See Page 301 for Example Problems]

Distance formula can be written two ways:
$$\text{Distance} = \sqrt{(x_2 - x_1)^2 + (y_2 - y_1)^2}$$
and
$$\text{Distance} = \sqrt{(x_1 - x_2)^2 + (y_1 - y_2)^2}$$

The key is to be consistent. If x_1 comes first, then y_1 must come first.

EXAMPLE #1: Find the distance between (-3,1) and (2,4).

Let (-3,1) be (x_1, y_1) and (2,4) be (x_2, y_2)

$$\begin{aligned}
\text{Distance} &= \sqrt{(x_2 - x_1)^2 + (y_2 - y_1)^2} \\
&= \sqrt{(2 - -3)^2 + (4 - 1)^2} \\
&= \sqrt{25 + 9} \\
&= \sqrt{34}
\end{aligned}$$

EXAMPLE #2: What is the distance between the two points shown below?

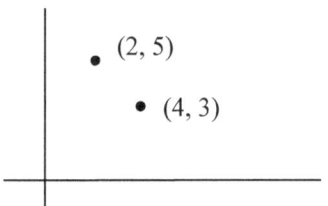

A) $\sqrt{5}$
B) 3
C) 5
D) 9
E) $2\sqrt{2}$

Set x_1 = (2, 5) and x_2 = (4, 3) so that the distance is

$$\begin{aligned}
d &= \sqrt{(x_2 - x_1)^2 + (y_2 - y_1)^2} \\
&= \sqrt{(4 - 2)^2 + (3 - 5)^2} \\
&= \sqrt{(2)^2 + (-2)^2} \\
&= \sqrt{4 + 4} \\
&= \sqrt{8} = 2\sqrt{2}
\end{aligned}$$

EXAMPLE #3: What is the x-coordinate of point B that is $\sqrt{29}$ away from A?

A • (3, 6)

B • (x_B, 1)

A) -2
B) -1
C) 1
D) 2
E) 3

Set $\sqrt{29}$ equal to the distance formula and solve for x_B:

$$\sqrt{29} = \sqrt{(x_A - x_B)^2 + (y_A - y_B)^2}$$
$$= \sqrt{(3 - x_B)^2 + (6-1)^2}$$
$$= \sqrt{(3 - x_B)^2 + 25}$$
$$29 = (3 - x_B)^2 + 25$$
$$4 = (3 - x_B)^2$$
$$2 = 3 - x_B$$
$$x_B = 1$$

CONCEPT: EQUATION OF A CIRCLE

[See Page 306 for Example Problems]

The general equation of a circle centered at the point (h, k) with a radius r is the following:

$$(x-h)^2 + (y-k)^2 = r^2$$

EXAMPLE #1: Write the equation for a circle whose diameter is 10 and is centered at the point (-2,3).

$d = 10$ therefore the radius = $^{10}/_2 = 5$

$(x- -2)^2 + (y-3)^2 = 25$

Answer: $(x+2)^2 + (y-3)^2 = 25$

EXAMPLE #2: Where is the center of the circle whose equation is $(x- 4)^2 + (y+7)^2 = 9$?

Answer: (4, -7) *not* (-4, 7)

EXAMPLE #3: What is the diameter of the circle whose equation is $(x- 4)^2 + (y+7)^2 = 9$?

$r = \sqrt{9} = 3$
$d = 2 \bullet 3 = 6$

Answer: 6

You need to be able to go from a picture to the equation and vice versa. For example, in the sketch below, we can see that the radius of the circle is 1 and that the coordinates of the center of the circle are (4, 3).

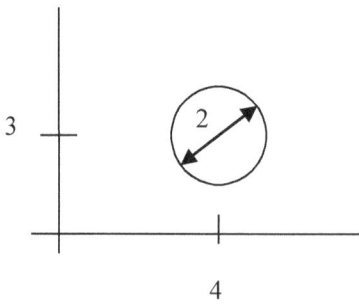

Therefore, the equation is: $(x-4)^2 + (y-3)^2 = 1$.

EXAMPLE #4: Which of the following graphs represents the circle with the equation $(x+8)^2 + (y-11)^2 = 4$?

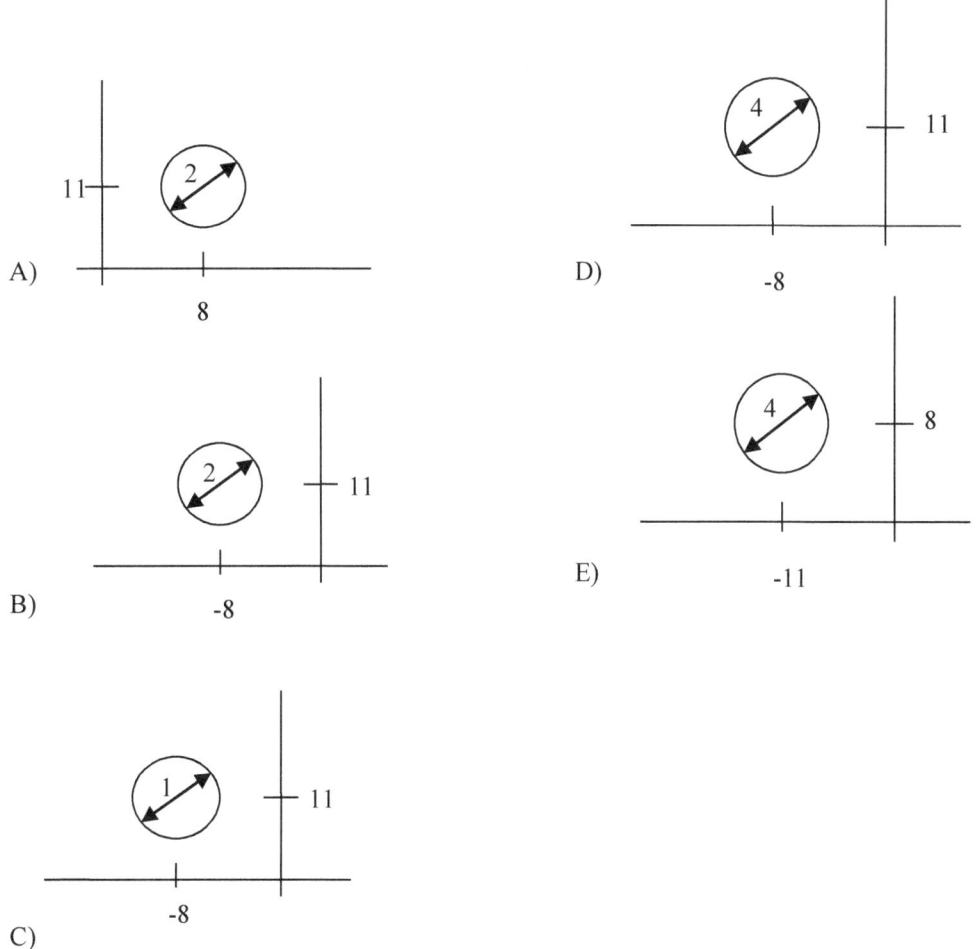

Immediately see the answer cannot be A because in that graph the center has *x* and *y* coordinates positive. Answer B has radius of 1, and our equation has a radius of 2. Likewise, C has a radius of 0.5. Both D and E have the correct radius, but the coordinates are different. Since our coordinates are (-8, 11), the answer must be D. Be careful with the radius and diameter. This can easily cause you to miss a question you really know how to do.

CONCEPT: FUNCTIONS / POLYNOMIALS

[See Page 311 for Example Problems]

Functions

Dealing with functions can be intimidating but remember that writing $f(x) = x - 3$ is a fancy way of writing $y = x - 3$. Using f(x) just displays the value of x that will be substituted into the function. For the equation above, $f(5) = 5 - 3 = 0$.

EXAMPLE #1: If $f(x) = 3x^2$ and $g(x) = 4$, what is $f(g(x))$?

$f(g(x)) = f(4) = 3(4)^2 = 48$

Notice that a factored function crosses the *x*-axis as many times as there is a unique *x* for $f(x) = 0$ (or when $y = 0$).

EXAMPLE #2: How many times does $f(x) = (x+4)(x-3)(x+2)(x-3)(x+3)$ cross the *x*-axis?

$f(x) = 0$ when $x = -4$, $x = 3$, $x = -2$, $x = 3$, and $x = -3$ (4 times)

Note that although $x = 3$ shows up twice, it can only cross the axis once, so we count it once.

 When working with graphed functions, remember you can build a table of *x* and *y* (or *x* and *f(x)*) values and sketch the graph.

Polynomials

Adding, multiplying, subtracting, and dividing polynomials usually means remembering your rules of factoring and/or simplification.

EXAMPLE #3: If $f(x) = 8$ and $g(x) = 2$, what is $\dfrac{f(x)}{g(x)}$?

This is simpler than it looks. The answer is simply: $^8/_2 = 4$.

Remember the factoring rules to solve more complex functions.

EXAMPLE #4: If $f(x) = (x - 5)(2x + 6)(x - 1)$ and $g(x) = (2x + 6)(x - 1)$, what is $\dfrac{f(x)}{g(x)}$?

Begin by plugging in the functions: $\dfrac{(x-5)(2x+6)(x-1)}{(2x+6)(x-1)}$. Cross out the common terms and simplify to get (*x*-5), which is the final answer.

CONCEPT: GREATEST COMMON FACTOR / LEAST COMMON MULTIPLE

[See Page 313 for Example Problems]

Greatest Common Factor
To get the greatest common factor for two numbers, determine what numbers will factor the smaller number. Then starting with the largest number, see if those factors will divide the second number.

> **EXAMPLE #1:** If x is a positive integer that evenly divides both 66 and 165, but does not evenly divide 6 or 11, what is the sum of the digits in x?

Factors for 66: 1, 2, 3, 6, 11, 22, 33, 66

Will these factor 165? 66? no; 33? yes.

The greatest common factor (x) of the two numbers is 33. But don't stop there, the final answer is the sum of the digits in x, which is 6.

Least Common Multiple
A fast way of finding least common multiples is to break down each of the numbers into a product of prime numbers. Eliminate numbers in one breakdown that are duplicated in the other. The product of the remaining numbers is the least common multiple.

> **EXAMPLE #2:** What is the least common multiple of 20 and 14?

$20 = 2 \bullet 2 \bullet 5$

$14 = 2 \bullet 7$ (eliminate 2 because it occurs in the breakdown of 20 and 14)

Least common multiple = $2 \bullet 2 \bullet 5 \bullet 7 = 140$

Remember that least common multiples can be asked in word problems such as the following:

> **EXAMPLE #3:** The tap of one drum sounds every 8 seconds. Another drum taps every 10 seconds. If they tap together at time = 0, how many seconds until they tap together again?

$8 = 2 \bullet 2 \bullet 2$

$10 = 2 \bullet 5$ (eliminate 2 because it occurs in the breakdown of 8)

Least common multiple = $2 \bullet 2 \bullet 2 \bullet 5 = 40$ seconds

CONCEPT: GENERAL EQUATION OF A LINE

[See Page 316 for Example Problems]

The equation for a line is $y = mx + b$ where m (slope) is rise / run = $(y_2-y_1) / (x_2-x_1)$ and $b = y$-intercept.

Finding the Slope

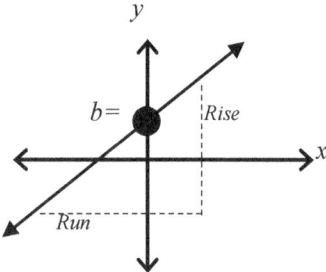

The slope of a line perpendicular is the *opposite reciprocal* of the slope of the first line.

To get the *opposite reciprocal*:
1. Take the opposite sign (make a positive negative or make a negative positive)
2. Take the inverse (flip the fraction over)

For example, if the slope of line X is ½, the slope of the line perpendicular is –2.

EXAMPLE #1: What is the slope of the line containing points (-5,2) and (2,-1)?

$$m = \frac{y_2 - y_1}{x_2 - x_1} = \frac{-1 - 2}{2 - -5} = \frac{-3}{7}$$

EXAMPLE #2: The scale on both axes of the standard (x, y) coordinate plane below are the same. What is the best estimate for the slope of $\overline{AB}$?

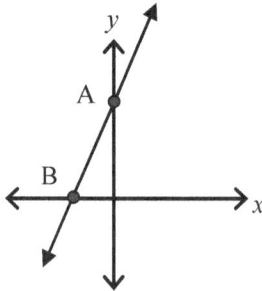

Since the distance from A to the origin is approximately twice the distance from B to the origin, the rise of $\overline{AB}$ is approximately twice the run. Also, note the slope will be positive. This means that a good estimate for the slope is +2; look for an answer that is close to +2.

Finding the Equation for a Line

The slope of the line is half the equation. Remember the equation is $y = mx + b$ where the slope is m. The other half of the equation is finding the y-intercept (b). The y-intercept is where the line crosses the y-axis. If a graph is drawn, identify the y-intercept from looking at the graph. If no graph is drawn, note that the y-intercept is the y value of the equation when the x value $= 0$ or $(0, b)$. You may also be able to manipulate the equation so that it is in the form $y = mx + b$ and identify b.

EXAMPLE #3: In the (x, y) coordinate plane, what is the y-intercept of the line $4x - y = 3$.

There are two ways to answer:

First, set $x = 0$ and solve for y. This is the y-intercept.

$$4(0) - y = 3$$
$$-y = 3$$
$$y = -3$$

The y-intercept is -3.

Second, try to manipulate the equation until it is in the standard form.

$$4x - y = 3$$
$$-y = 3 - 4x$$
$$y = 4x - 3$$

Again, the y-intercept is -3.

EXAMPLE #4: Given that $y = 4x + 6$ describes a line, where does the line cross the x-axis?

The line crosses the x-axis when $y = 0$. Substitute $y = 0$ in order to find the x-intercept:
$4x + 6 = 0$;
$\quad 4x = -6$
$\quad\ x = -6/4$
$\quad\ \ \ = -3/2$.

EXAMPLE #5: Which equation describes the line that goes through (3, 7) and has a slope = -2?

Since we already have the slope, we need only to find the *y*-intercept. Substitute the *x* and *y* values for the point and solve for *b*.

$y = -2x + b$;
$7 = -2(3) + b$;
$b = 7 + 6$
$ = 13$.

Our final answer is: $y = -2x + 13$.

EXAMPLE #6: Which equation describes the line that goes through (4, 7) and (-2, 6)?

You must obtain two pieces to determine the equation of the line: the slope and the intercept. Do these one at a time and eliminate answers as you go.

First, the slope: $m = \dfrac{\text{rise}}{\text{run}} = \dfrac{7-6}{4--2} = \dfrac{1}{6}$. Eliminate answers where $m \neq 1/6$.

Second, calculate the *y*-intercept using the slope, just as in Example 5. Start with $y = 1/6 x + b$ then substitute to get $7 = 1/6 (4) + b$. Rearrange to get $b = 7 - 4/6 = 38/6 = 19/3$. Note you get the same answer regardless of which point you substitute.

Our final answer is: $y = \dfrac{1}{6}x + \dfrac{19}{3}$.

EXAMPLE #7: Which of the following lines is perpendicular to the line described by $y = 1/6 x + 19/3$?

The line perpendicular will have a slope that is the opposite reciprocal (negative inverse). In this example, the line perpendicular to $y = 1/6 x + 19/3$ has slope = -6. Any answer without this slope cannot be correct.

EXAMPLE #8: Which of the following lines is parallel to the line described by $y = \dfrac{1}{6}x + \dfrac{19}{3}$?

The line parallel must have the same slope, $1/6$. Any answer without this slope cannot be correct.

CONCEPT: GRAPHING AND THE (X, Y) COORDINATE SYSTEM

[See Page 322 for Example Problems]

(x, y) Coordinate System

☞ Key things to remember about the standard (x, y) coordinate system are:
1. The (x,y) coordinate system is typically a grid where up and down is the ± y direction and right and left is the ± x direction. The axes should be labeled.
2. If part of a shape is moved on the grid, the whole shape must move as well.
3. Quadrant 1 has positive signs on both x and y coordinates; quadrant 2 has positive sign on y and negative sign on x; quadrant 3 has negative signs on both x and y; and quadrant 4 has positive sign on x and negative sign on y. ($Q_1 \Rightarrow (+, +)$, $Q_2 \Rightarrow (-, +)$, $Q_3 \Rightarrow (-, -)$, $Q_1 \Rightarrow (+, -)$)
4. Any shape on the (x, y) coordinate system is made up of points. Each point has an x value and a y value. Together these tell you the location of the point.

EXAMPLE #1: In the standard (x, y) coordinate plane, 3 corners of a rectangle are (-1, 2), (5, 2), and (5, -7). What is the location of the fourth corner?

You may need to sketch this in order to understand where the fourth point is.

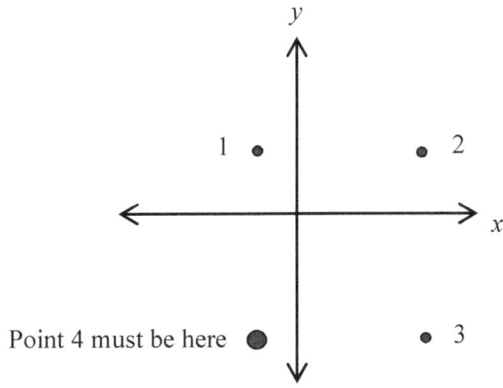

Even though the sketch may not be drawn to scale, we can tell that it must have the same y value as point 3 and the same x value as point 1. This means that the fourth point is (-1, -7). A quick check that the fourth point is in the 3rd quadrant and that both signs are negative is reassuring.

EXAMPLE #2: What is the location of the fourth corner, if the rectangle is shifted 2 units in the positive x direction and 1 unit in the negative y direction?

Since all four points will shift, we can add 2 to the x coordinate of the fourth point and subtract 1 from the y coordinate. This means that the new location of the fourth corner is (1, -8).

Graphing

If you are given an equation and asked about its shape on a graph, you can always make a short table of *x* and *y* values. Pick a few negative and a few positive values of *x* and solve for *y* to get the *y* values. A quick sketch will help you see its shape. Don't pick too many points, though, because that can take a long time.

If you are given a graph that you must read, it will likely be a parabola or a line. Refer to the **Equation of a Line** section for help on lines. Even if it is a chart with labels, if what is drawn is a straight line, you can use the equation of a line to answer questions.

Any question on parabolas should be answerable by building a table and/or solving for either *x* or *y* when the other value is determined.

EXAMPLE #3: The graph $y = 2x^2 - 2$ is in the standard (*x*, *y*) coordinate plane. Which of the following could be the *x*-intercept?

Remember that the *x*-intercept is where the graph crosses the *x*-axis. When the graph crosses the *x*-axis, the *y*-value is zero. Substituting 0 in for *y* produces

$$2x^2 - 2 = 0$$
$$2x^2 = 2$$
$$x = \pm 1$$

Note that there are two *x*-intercepts. Either +1 or −1 should be in the list of possible answers.

MATH - LESSONS

CONCEPT: PERIMETER

[See Page 326 for Example Problems]

Perimeter

☞ Perimeter is the distance around an object.

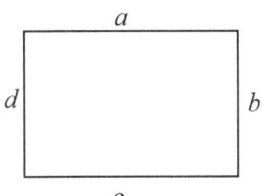

Perimeter = $a + b + c + d$

EXAMPLE #1: Given rectangle ABCD, what is the length of the perimeter?

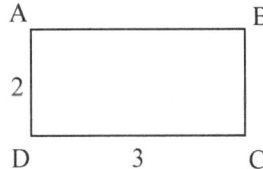

If $\overline{AD} = 2$, then $\overline{BC} = 2$
If $\overline{CD} = 3$, then $\overline{AB} = 3$

$2 + 2 + 3 + 3 = 10$

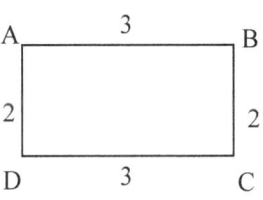

☞ For complex shapes, break the shape into pieces.

EXAMPLE #2: Given rectangle ABCD, what is the length of the perimeter?

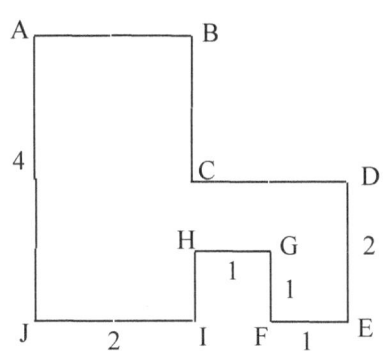
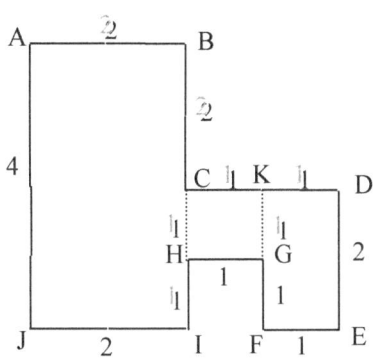

Break the shape into 3 pieces, connecting points H and C and points K and G. Determine the lengths of the unknown sides by recognizing the new shapes as rectangles. Opposite sides of a rectangle are equal. Shadowed numbers show the numbers determined by breaking up the shape. Add the individual segments to find the perimeter.

$$4 + 2 + 2 + 1 + 1 + 2 + 1 + 1 + 1 + 1 + 2 = 18$$

EXAMPLE #3: Given that the figure below has a perimeter of 13, what is the length of side a?

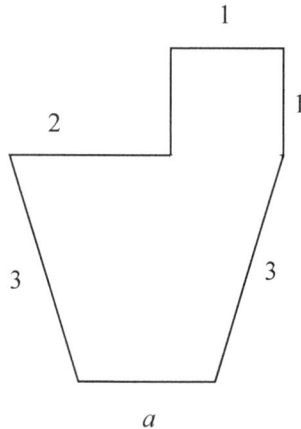

A) 1
B) 2
C) 3
D) 3
E) 5

Subtract all the known sides (don't forget to solve for sides not given) and obtain:

$13 - 3 - 1 - 1 - 1 - 2 - 3 = a = 2$

CONCEPT: AREA OF IRREGULAR SHAPES

[See Page 331 for Example Problems]

📎 Finding the area of an irregular shape is similar to finding the perimeter: Break the shape into sub-areas, calculate the area for each sub-area and add them together.

EXAMPLE #1: What is the area of the figure below if a half circle is added to the top of rectangle that is 8 units wide and 6 units high?

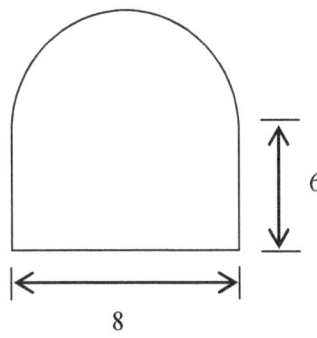

Break up the shape into a half circle and a rectangle. The area of the half circle is $\frac{1}{2}\pi r^2$ where r is half the length of the base of the rectangle, or 4. The area of the rectangle is bh, where the base $b = 8$ and the height $h = 6$. Therefore, the area of figure = area of half circle + area of rectangle =

$$\tfrac{1}{2}\pi \cdot 4^2 + 8\cdot 6 = 8\pi + 48$$

EXAMPLE #2: What is the area of the figure below?

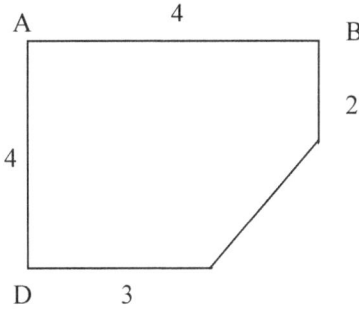

A) 14
B) 15
C) 16
D) 17
E) 18

Calculate the area of the large rectangle and subtract the area of the triangle. Note that the height of the triangle is 4-2 = 2 and the base is 4-3 = 1.
This gives: $4 \cdot 4 - \tfrac{1}{2} \cdot 2 \cdot 1 = 15$

EXAMPLE #3: Given that the area of the figure below is 12, what is the length of *a*?

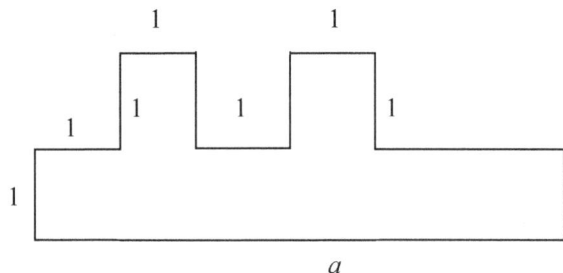

A) 5
B) 7
C) 8
D) 10
E) 12

Add the large rectangle (*a* • 1) and the two small squares (1 • 1 each).
This gives: $a \cdot 1 + 1 \cdot 1 + 1 \cdot 1 = 12$. Solving for *a* gives: $a = 12-2 = 10$

CONCEPT: AREA OF A TRAPEZOID

The area of a trapezoid as shown below is the following: $\frac{1}{2}(b_1+b_2)h$

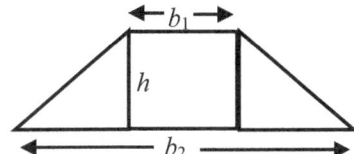

EXAMPLE #1: If one base is 4 and the other base is 10, what is the area of the trapezoid if the height is 8?

Area = $\frac{1}{2}(b_1+b_2)h$ Therefore $\frac{1}{2}(4+10)8 = \frac{1}{2}(14)8 = 56$.

EXAMPLE #2: If one base is 3 and the height is 4, what is the length of the other base if the area is 20?

Area = $\frac{1}{2}(b_1+b_2)h$ therefore

= $\frac{1}{2}(3+b_2)4 = 20$. Cross multiply to get

= $(3+b_2)4 = 40$. Divide and solve

= $(3+b_2) = 10$. Therefore $b_2 = 7$

CONCEPT: POLYGONS AND ANGLES

[See Page 336 for Example Problems]

A **polygon** is a shape with any number of sides. A rectangle is a polygon with 4 sides, and a octagon is a polygon with 8 sides. A **regular polygon** is one where the lengths of all the sides (and interior angles) are equal.

The sum of the interior angles of a polygon is the same whether the polygon is a regular polygon or not. For example, the sum of interior angles for the first two polygons (*a* and *b*) is the same even though one appears to be a regular pentagon and the other is far from it. The angles sum to the same number because they have the same number of sides and because they are both convex. The third pentagon (*c*) is not a convex polygon (note one of the angles is larger than 180°).

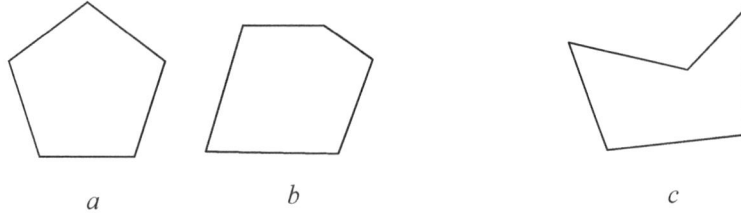

a   *b*   *c*

There are two types of questions that you may be asked:
1. How many sides are on a regular polygon given the measure of the interior angles?
2. Determine the measure of the interior angle given the number of sides.

The way to answer such questions is to treat the regular polygons like a pie that can be divided into equally sized pieces, like the hexagon and triangle below.

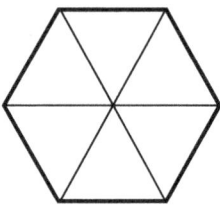   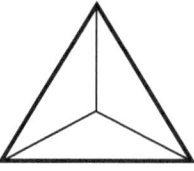

If you draw a circle around the center to make a round pie, you will get a circle/pie with equal sized pieces, all of which have the same center angle measurement. If we can get the center angle measurement, then we can determine the other two angle measurments. (Remember these are isosceles triangles.)

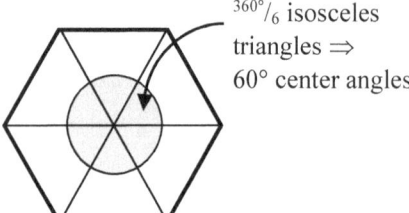   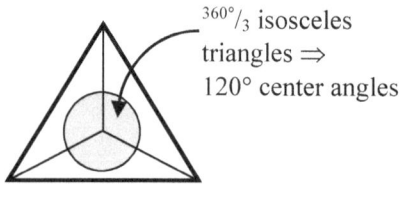

$360°/6$ isosceles triangles ⇒ 60° center angles $360°/3$ isosceles triangles ⇒ 120° center angles

Since a circle has 360°, we can divide 360 by the number of pieces in the pie to determine the angle at the center of the pie. The sum of the remaining angles in each isosceles triangle is 360° - center angle measurement. This value is equal to a single interior angle.

In general, we use the equation $x = 180° - {}^{360°}/n$ to solve for the measure of the interior angles, x, of an $n$gon. To get the number of sides, n, backsolve to get: $n = {}^{360°}/{180-x}$.

NOTE: If x denotes the measure of the interior angle of a polygon and n is the number of sides, then x and n are given by the equations

$$x = 180° - \frac{360°}{n} \quad \text{and} \quad n = \frac{360°}{180° - x}$$

EXAMPLE #1: If the measure of an interior angle for a regular polygon is 144° how many sides does it have?

First, without the equation: 180° - 144° = 36° is the measure of the center angles. There are n center angles in the 360° pie. 36°n = 360°, n = 10.
Using the second equation: x = 144°, so $n = {}^{360}/{180-144}$ = 10.

EXAMPLE #2: If a regular polygon has eight sides, what is the sum of the interior angles?

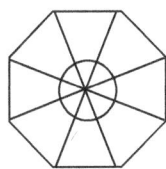

First, without the equation: Cut the 360° pie into 8 pieces. Each piece's angle at the center of the pie = ${}^{360°}/8$ = 45°. The remaining angles of each of the 8 pie pieces/triangles is 180° - 45° = 135°, so each interior angle is 135°. The sum of these 8 interior angles is 8•135° = 1080°.

Second, the equation for the measure of the interior angles is $x = 180° - {}^{360°}/n$. To get the sum of all n angles multiply by n to get $x = 180°n - 360° = (8)(180°) - 360° = 1080°$.

EXAMPLE #3: If a regular polygon has eight sides, what is the sum of the interior angles?

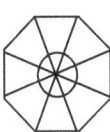

First, without the equation: Eight triangles times 180° minus the 360° in the circle: (8)(180°) − 360° = 1440° − 360° = 1080°. Divide the sum of the interior angles by the number of sides: ${}^{1080°}/8$ = 135°.

Second, the equation is $x = 180° - \dfrac{360°}{8} = 180° - 45° = 135°$

EXAMPLE #4: If the measure of the interior angle for a regular polygon is 144° how many sides does it have?

Using the second equation, we get: $n = \dfrac{360°}{180° - 144°} = \dfrac{360°}{36°} = 10$ sides.

MATH - LESSONS

CONCEPT: SIMPLIFICATION AND FACTORING

[See Page 339 for Example Problems]

As a continuation of exponents, let's look at how to factor and simplify terms. As always, try to eliminate 2 or 3 answers by looking for the right constant or exponent on a variable. For example, you may be able to immediately determine that x^4 is in the correct answer. Eliminate the answers with no x^4 and prevent yourself from working through those answers.

EXAMPLE #1: The product $x^4(2x^2 - 4)^2$ is equivalent to:

A) $4x^{16} - 12x^8 + 9x^6$
B) $4x^8 - 12x^6 + 9x^4$
C) $4x^8 - 16x^6 + 16x^4$
D) $4x^8 - 16x^6$
E) $4x^{16} + 16x^6$

Determine that x^8 will be in the answer because the $2x^2$ will be squared and multiplied by x^4. This eliminates A and E. You may be able to eliminate D because you know there will be three terms. Choose between B and C by simplifying. (Answer is C)

EXAMPLE #2: Which of the following is equivalent to $4x^5 + 12x^4 - 3x^3 - 9x^2$?

A) $(x^2 + 3)(x^3 - 3x^2)$
B) $(3x^2 - 3)(3^3 - 3x^2)$
C) $(4x^2 - 3)(x^3 + 3x^2)$
D) $(x^2 + 3)(4x^3 + x^2)$
E) $(5x^2 - 3)(x^3 - 3x^2)$

Notice that the first terms will not multiply to give $4x^5$ for answers A, B, or E. Eliminate those. The answer is C) $(4x^2 - 3)(x^3 + 3x^2)$.

EXAMPLE #3: Which of the following is a simplified equivalent of $\dfrac{15a^3c^4}{3ac^{11}}$?

A) $\dfrac{5a^3c^2}{a}$

B) $\dfrac{5a^2}{c^7}$

C) $5a^3c^2$

D) $\dfrac{a^2}{5c^2}$

E) $\dfrac{15ac^4}{c^2}$

Again, the constant must be a 5 so immediately eliminate D and E. Then look for the exponent on the *a*. It should be 2.

CONCEPT: SEQUENCES AND SERIES

[See Page 343 for Example Problems]

Finding patterns in sequences and series can be tricky. Sometimes you have to write out the sequence. Other times you maybe be able to see it without writing anything.

Start by asking yourself these questions:

▷ Are the numbers added (arithmetic series)? If so, continue to add until the answer reaches the correct term. You may have to use the first and last terms of the series to determine how much to add to get the answer.

EXAMPLE #1: If the first term in an arithmetic series is 7, the last term is 145, and the sum is 1824, what are the first 3 terms?

Use the three pieces of information given: the first term is 7, all the terms add to 1824, and the last term is 145.

STEP 1: Subtract the first term from the last term (145-7 = 138) to get the range of the series. The value to add to each term (say, x) and the number of terms in the sequence (say, y) must multiply to produce this range. ($xy = 138$).

STEP 2: Use the multiple choice answers to pick a *starting point* for x (say 3).

STEP 3: Use x to calculate a y value by dividing the range by x. If the range is 138 and $x = 3$, there are $^{138}/_3 = 45$ terms. This result *must* be an integer; if it's not go back to STEP 2 and choose another x.

STEP 4: Begin calculating the terms – *from the back end*. If the numbers are 3 digits apart, the next-to-last number in the series is 145 - 3 = 142, the 3rd-to-last number in the series is 142 - 3 = 139 and so on.

STEP 5: Evaluate the x by summing terms. Since the sum is too quickly approaching 1824, x must be greater-than 3. (Add three or four terms and see how large the sum is? There are still more-than 40 terms to go!) **Back to STEP 2.**

STEP 2: The previous x was way too small. Let's jump a bit and try $x = 6$.

STEP 3: This produces $^{138}/_6 = 23$ terms.

STEP 4: The terms would be 145, 139, 133, etc. This looks like it might work.

STEP 5: Rather than calculating and summing all the terms, quickly look at the other multiple-choice options and see if any of them might work. We'll find that the spacing of 6 is correct and the 1st, 2nd, and 3rd terms are: 7, 13, 19.

▷ Are the numbers multiplied (geometric series)? If so, continue to multiply until the answer reaches the correct term.

EXAMPLE #2: The first and second terms of a geometric sequence are g and gh, in that order. What is the 500th term of the sequence?

Since we have to go out so far, it helps to write out what the sequence looks like the following allowing us to establish a pattern.

Term number, n	term
1	$g^1 h^0 = g$
2	$g^1 h^1 = gh$
.	.
.	.
.	.
500	$g^1 h^{499}$

The key to answering this question is realizing that the term is $gh^{(n-1)}$ where n is the term number.

☞ Do the numbers involve powers? If so, it may help to build a table of relationships between the exponents and the term number.

EXAMPLE #3: If the ones digit of 3^2 is 9 and the ones digit of 3^3 is 7, what is the ones digit of 3^{28}?

Build a table and look for a relationship between the exponent and the ones digit.

Exponent, n	Value, 3^n	Ones digit
0	$3^0 = 1$	1
1	$3^1 = 3$	3
2	$3^2 = 9$	9
3	$3^3 = 27$	7
4	$3^4 = 81$	1
5	$3^5 = 243$	3

Since the table has begun to repeat ones digits, let's change it a bit to show only ones digits and extend the series.

Exponent, n	Ones digit
0, 4, 8	1
1, 5, 9	3
2, 6, 10	9
3, 7, 11	7

Which row will 28 fit into? We can see that 28 will fit nicely into row 1. In fact, if we continue to add 4 to the series in row 1 we will eventually hit 28. The answer is that the ones digit of 3^{28} is 1.

CONCEPT: PROBABILITY AND PROPORTIONS

[See Page 346 for Example Problems]

Most probability questions involve determining the probability of an event. An event could be drawing a green piece of candy out of a bowl or rolling a 4 on a pair of dice. There is an equation for determining probabilities, but you may be able to determine the answers with common sense.

 NOTE: The probability equation is $p = x/T$ where p is the probability, x is the number of ways the event can occur, and T is the total number of opportunities for the event to occur.

EXAMPLE #1: If a jar contains 3 red beads and 7 green beads, what is the probability that you will choose a green bead?

Since there are 7 ways to draw a green bead, and 10 total beads (3 red + 7 green), the equation looks like

$p = x/T = 7/10$

The probability is $7/10$ or 0.7.

↪ The question may involve drawing twice. If that's the case, you have to adjust your x and T for the new situation.

EXAMPLE #2: If a jar contained 3 red beads and 7 green beads and you just drew a red bead, what is the probability that you now will choose a green bead?

There are still 7 ways to draw a green bead, but only 9 total beads (2 red + 7 green), so the equation is $p = x/T = 7/9$.

The probability is $7/9$.

You could be given a table of probabilities or proportions and asked to compute a probability based on the table. These are easy if you remember which values to add.

For the following example, if the question asks for the probability of 3 or more flaws, add all the probabilities for 3 and above. If the question asks for the probability of less-than 2 flaws, add the probabilities for less-than two (not including two).

EXAMPLE #3: Inspection reveals that car doors manufactured in an automobile plant can have between 0 and 4 flaws. Their proportions are given in the table below. What is the probability that a car door will have more than 1 flaw?

Number of flaws	Probability
0	0.55
1	0.22
2	0.12
3	0.09
4	0.02

Add all the probabilities that have more than one flaw: $0.12 + 0.09 + 0.02 = 0.23$

➢ You may be asked to compute a ratio. A ratio is just a fraction showing the relationship between two events.

EXAMPLE #4: If a jar contains 3 red beads and 7 green beads, what is the ratio of red beads to green beads?

ratio = $3/7$

CONCEPT: EXPRESSIONS

[See Page 350 for Example Problems]

Expression problems ask you to provide an expression describing a relationship between two or more variables. Sometimes this expression will be in equation or graph form and is a more formal version of the relationship that the question describes in words. Other times, it is the other way around, and you need to put into normal language what is being shown in an equation. Here are some suggestions for solving expression problems.

4 Step Plan to Answering Word Problems:
    STEP 1: What are they asking for?
    STEP 2: Identify variables of interest
    STEP 3: Choose
    STEP 4: Sanity Check

1. What are they asking for?
Read through the whole question and get a feel for the general idea but focus specifically on the last sentence. This is usually where you will find what relationship should be defined. Make a note of this so that you can go back and make sure you are answering the right question. You can also get an idea of what they are asking for by looking at the multiple choices.

2. Identify variables of interest.
Look for variables; they may or may not be identified with a symbol. If not, look at the answers and use those symbols to help you get started. If you can quickly note relationships, then, go ahead.

3. Choose
Here you may be choosing an equation or graph that "rewrites" some portion of the question. You may also be choosing an interpretation of an equation that is given in the problem. As usual you should be able to quickly eliminate one or two possibilities. Mark those off then compare the remaining. Use the variables and relationships identified in STEP 2.

4. Sanity Check
You do not have time to check your answers on the math test. You need to develop enough confidence in your work that you can pick an answer and move on. You should, however, make sure that you have answered the appropriate question and take a moment to see if your answer makes sense.

 NOTE: Many times, you can make up numbers and plug into the choices. For example, if the problem says $a>0$, you could say $a=1$. If $a<b$, you could say $b=2$. Then plug in your numbers for the letters in the choices to quickly determine the correct answer. If a choice is $b>0$, you know it's the correct answer because $2>0$.

EXAMPLE #1: The diameter of the circle with equation $(x_1-h_1)^2 + (y_1-k_1)^2 = r_1^2$ is greater than the diameter of the circle with equation $(x_2-h_2)^2 + (y_2-k_2)^2 = r_2^2$. Which of the following statements is true about the relationship between r_1 and r_2?

- A. $r_1 > r_2$
- B. $r_1 < r_2$
- C. $r_1 \leq r_2$
- D. $r_1 \geq r_2$
- E. $r_1 > \sqrt{r_2}$

STEP 1: We need to find the *true* statement

STEP 2: What is the relationship between r_1 and r_2?

STEP 3: Where did the square root come from? We can eliminate that. We also know it cannot be C or D, because they are not equal to each other. Now choose between A and B – which one is "greater than"?

STEP 4: Quick check: true: A shows the first radius is greater than the second.

EXAMPLE #2: Abrianna is shopping for a new shirt. She searches on a half-off rack where all the clothes cost half of the original price. In addition, she plans on using an employee discount that allows her to take 10% off the final cost of any purchase. What proportion of the original price (x) will the final price be if the items are taken from this rack?

- A. 35%
- B. 45%
- C. 55%
- D. 65%
- E. 75%

STEP 1: Find the percent of the original price (not the percent off)

STEP 2: What is the relationship between x and the final price (let's call it y)? $y =$ (some percentage) times x, or even more formally our problem is: $y = px$; find p.

STEP 3: The first discount on x is 50%, so we have $0.5x$. But now we want to take off another 10%, so subtracting $0.1(0.5x)$ from $(0.5x)$ is:
$(0.5x) - 0.1(0.5x) = (1 - 0.10)0.5x = 0.9(0.5x) = 0.45x$
This is the same as 45% of x, which is B.

STEP 4: Quick check: we expect the new value to be less than 50% of the x because we are not looking at the amount of the discount but at what the cost is after the discount.

Angles add to 180°

1. What is the measure of ∠ABC in the triangle below?

   A) 50°
   B) 70°
   C) 80°
   D) 160°
   E) 180°

   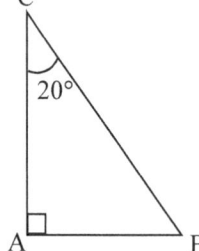

2. For △ABC below, D and E are points on the side of the triangle. If $\overline{AB}$ is parallel to $\overline{DE}$, what is the measure of ∠ACB?

   A) 70°
   B) 100°
   C) 110°
   D) 140°
   E) 170°

   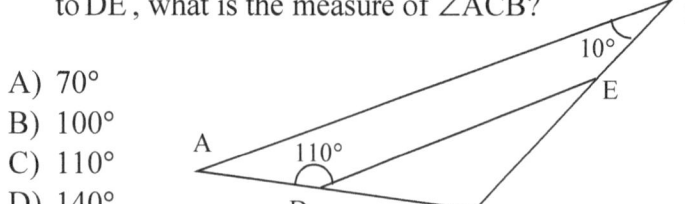

3. In right △ABD, point C lies on line $\overline{BD}$, and $\overline{AC}$ bisects ∠BAD. If ∠ACB is 115°, what is ∠CBA?

   A) 40°
   B) 60°
   C) 90°
   D) 110°
   E) 100°

   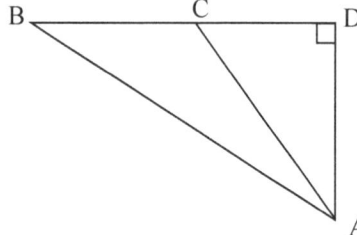

4. Consider the parallelogram ABCD. If ∠ABC = 120°, what is ∠CAB?

   A) 30°
   B) 40°
   C) 60°
   D) 85°
   E) 90°

   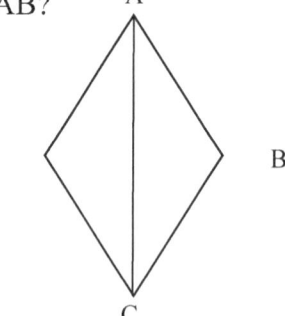

5. In the figure below, X is on $\overline{AY}$, ∠XYZ measures 20° and ∠AXZ measures 115°. What is the measure of ∠XZY?

A) 15°
B) 30°
C) 45°
D) 60°
E) 95°

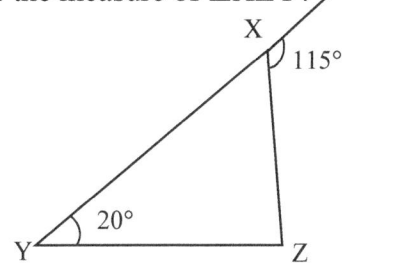

6. The measures of ∠'s in a △ are in the ratio of 2x:4x:6x as illustrated below. What is the measure of the smallest ∠ in the △?

A) 15°
B) 20°
C) 30°
D) 45°
E) 60°

7. The measures of ∠'s in a △ are in the ratio of 3x:3x:6x as illustrated below. What is the sum of the two smallest ∠s in the △?

A) 15°
B) 30°
C) 45°
D) 60°
E) 90°

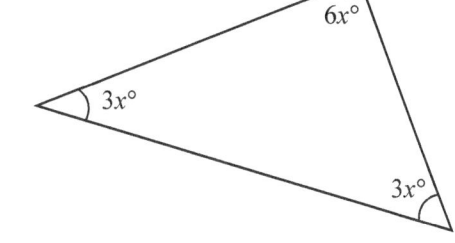

8. In △ABC below, ∠ABC = x+40, ∠BCA = 2x+40, and ∠CAB = 3x−20. What is the measure of ∠ABC?

A) 20°
B) 40°
C) 60°
D) 80°
E) 100°

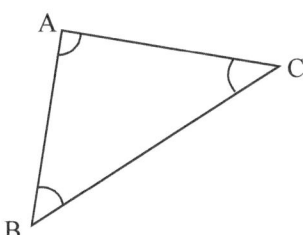

9. In △ABC below, ∠ABC = $3x+15$, ∠BCA = $2x+10$, and ∠CAB = $x-25$. What is the measure of the smallest ∠?

A) 5°
B) 25°
C) 30°
D) 60°
E) 70°

10. In △ABC below, ∠ABC is twice the measure of ∠ACB. If ∠BAC is 30°, what is the measure of ∠ABC?

A) 25°
B) 50°
C) 75°
D) 100°
E) 125°

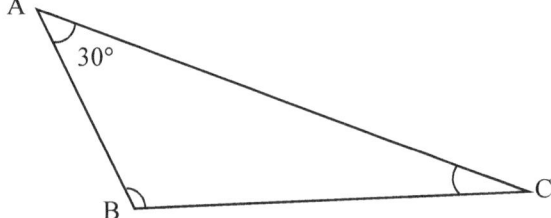

11. In △ABC below, ∠ABC is one-fourth the measure of ∠ACB. If ∠BAC is 30°, what is the measure of ∠ABC?

A) 30°
B) 60°
C) 90°
D) 120°
E) 150°

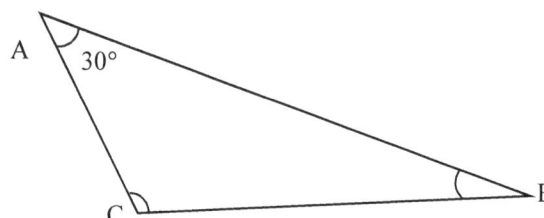

Area of a Triangle

1. What is the area, in square inches, of a right triangle with sides of length 9 inches, 12 inches, and 15 inches?

   A) 52
   B) 54
   C) 60
   D) 63
   E) 126

2. In the standard (*x,y*) plane, the triangle with vertices of (2,2) (2,*k*) and (4,*m*), where *m* is constant, changes shape as *k* changes. What happens to the triangle's area, expressed in square coordinate units, as *k* increases starting from 4?

   A) The area decreases as *k* increases.
   B) The area always equals *m*.
   C) The area increases as *k* increases.
   D) The area always equals 4.
   E) The area always equals 4*m*.

3. In the figure below, square ABCD has sides 14 inches long, and E is on side $\overline{AB}$. In square inches, what is the area of ΔDEC?

   A) 72
   B) 72.5
   C) 93
   D) 98
   E) 186

   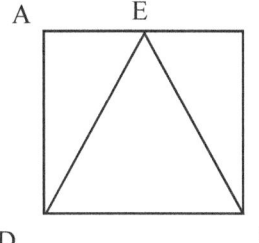

4. In the figure below, $\overline{AB}$ = 15 meters, $\overline{BD}$ = 12 meters, and $\overline{AD}$ = 9 meters. What is the area, in square meters, of △ABD?

A) 24
B) 27
C) 54
D) 81
E) 90

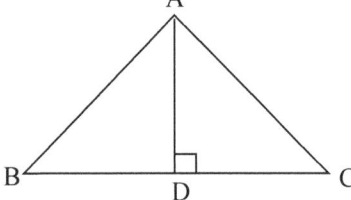

5. In the figure below, $\overline{WX}$ = 13 feet, $\overline{XY}$ = 10 feet, and $\overline{WZ}$ = 12 feet. What is the area, in square feet, of △WYZ if $\overline{WZ}$ bisects the $\overline{XY}$?

A) 60
B) 120
C) 30
D) 15
E) 15.5

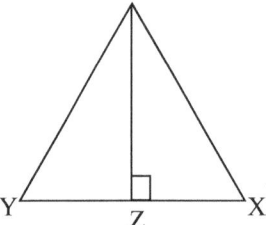

6. In the figure below, the triangle reaches ¾ of the way to the bottom edge from the top edge. What is the triangle's area in square centimeters?

A) 9
B) 12
C) 16
D) 18
E) 24

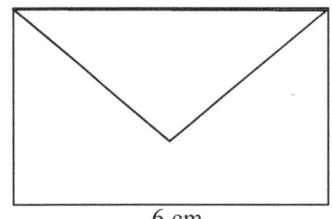

7. If the area of a triangle is 30 square feet and its base is 3 feet, what is its height?

A) 3 feet
B) 5 feet
C) 10 feet
D) 15 feet
E) 20 feet

8. What is the area of a right triangle with a height equal to $\sqrt{2}$ and hypotenuse equal to 2?

A) 1
B) $\sqrt{2}$
C) 2
D) $2\sqrt{2}$
E) 4

9. In the figure below square ABCD has sides 10 feet long and E is on side $\overline{BC}$. In square feet what is the area of $\triangle ADE$?

A) 10
B) 25
C) 30
D) 50
E) 100

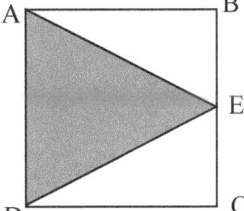

10. In the rectangle below, side $\overline{AB}$ is twice the length of $\overline{BC}$. If point E lies on side $\overline{BC}$ and $\overline{AB}$ is 12 inches, what is the area of $\triangle AED$ in square inches?

A) 144
B) 120
C) 96
D) 72
E) 36

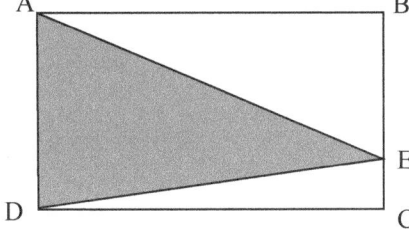

Area of a Circle

1. A circular coin has a radius of $5/8$ inch. When lying flat, how much area does the coin cover, in square inches?

   A) $5\pi/4$
   B) $5\pi/16$
   C) $10\pi/16$
   D) $25\pi/8$
   E) $25\pi/64$

2. What is the area, in square cm, of a circle with a diameter equal to 3 cm?

   A) $3\pi/4$
   B) $3\pi/2$
   C) $9\pi/4$
   D) 3π
   E) 9π

3. How many square feet of grass is watered by a sprinkler that spins, if it has a reach of 6 feet?

   A) 6π
   B) 9π
   C) 12π
   D) 18π
   E) 36π

   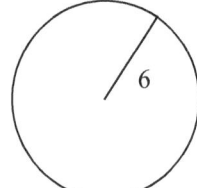

4. In the standard (x,y) coordinate plane, the graph of $(x-2)^2 + (y+4)^2 = 16$ is a circle. What is the area enclosed by the circle expressed in square coordinate units?

   A) 2π
   B) 4π
   C) 8π
   D) 12π
   E) 16π

5. In the standard (x,y) coordinate plane, the graph of $(x+6)^2 + (y-2)^2 = 4$ is a circle. What is the area enclosed by the circle expressed in square coordinate units?

A) 2π
B) 4π
C) 8π
D) 16π
E) 32π

6. A certain circle has an area of 9π square inches. How many inches long is its radius?

A) π
B) 3
C) 4.5
D) 9π
E) 10

7. A certain circle has an area of $^9/_{25}\pi$ square feet. How many feet long is its radius?

A) $^9/_{50}$
B) $^3/_{25}\pi$
C) $^3/_5$
D) $^6/_5\pi$
E) $^9/_5$

8. A certain circle has an area of 25π square inches. How many inches long is its radius?

A) 2.5
B) 5
C) 10
D) 25
E) 50

9. In the figure below a square is inscribed in a circle. The area of the square is 2, what is the area of the circle?

A) π
B) 2π
C) $2\sqrt{2}\pi$
D) $3\sqrt{2}\pi$
E) 8π

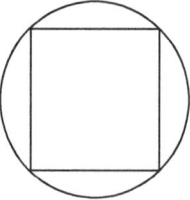

10. In the figure below a circle is inscribed in a square. The area of the square is 2, what is the area of the circle?

A) $\dfrac{\pi}{4}$
B) $\dfrac{\pi}{2}$
C) π
D) 2π
E) 4π

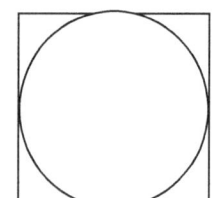

Midpoint Formula

1. Points A(-2,5) and B(8,3) determine line segment $\overline{AB}$ in the standard (x,y) coordinate plane. If the midpoint of $\overline{AB}$ is (a,4), what is the value of a?

    A) -5
    B) –3
    C) 2
    D) 3
    E) 5

2. What is the midpoint of the line segment with endpoints of (6,-4) and (4,8)?

    A) (4,-6)
    B) (4,2)
    C) (4,6)
    D) (5,0)
    E) (5,2)

3. Points A(-6,4) and B determine line segment $\overline{AB}$ in the standard (x,y) coordinate plane. If the midpoint of $\overline{AB}$ is (-2,6), what are the coordinates of point B?

    A) (-4,5)
    B) (-2,5)
    C) (2,5)
    D) (2,8)
    E) (4,8)

4. Points A(-5,3) and B(7,-1) determine line segment $\overline{AB}$ in the standard (x,y) coordinate plane. If the midpoint of $\overline{AB}$ is (a,1), what is the value of a?

    A. -6
    B. –1
    C. 1
    D. 3
    E. 6

5. What is the midpoint of the line segment with endpoints of (-3, 6) and (5, -4)?

A) (-1,-1)
B) (-1,1)
C) (1,1)
D) (1,2)
E) (4,5)

6. Points A(3,-4) and B determine line segment $\overline{AB}$ in the standard (x,y) coordinate plane. If the midpoint of $\overline{AB}$ is (-1,-2), what are the coordinates of point B?

A) (-5,0)
B) (-5,8)
C) (1,0)
D) (1,-3)
E) (3,0)

7. Points A(7, -2) and B(3, 3) determine line segment $\overline{AB}$ in the standard (x, y) coordinate plan. If the midpoint of $\overline{AB}$ is (5, b) what is the value of b?

A) ½
B) 1
C) ⁵/₂
D) 2
E) ⁷/₂

8. What is the midpoint of the line segment with endpoints of (2, 12) and (3, -6)?

A) (⁻¹/₂, 3)
B) (⁻¹/₂, 9)
C) (⁵/₂, 4)
D) (⁵/₂, 3)
E) (⁷/₂, 4)

9. Points A(7, 4) and B determine line segment $\overline{AB}$ in the standard (x, y) coordinate plane. If the midpoint of $\overline{AB}$ is (-2, -2), what are the coordinates of point B?

A) (8, -3)
B) (-8, -11)
C) (-11, -8)
D) (-3, 0)
E) (3, 0)

10. Points A(1, 4) and B(-3, -2) determine line segment $\overline{AB}$ in the standard (x, y) coordinate plane. If the midpoint of $\overline{AB}$ is (a, 1), what is the value of a?

A) -1
B) 0
C) ½
D) 1
E) 3/2

Parallel Lines Divided by Transversal

1. In the figure below, parallel lines *r* and *s* are intersected by line *t*. What is the measure of angle α?

   A) 60°
   B) 40°
   C) 160°
   D) 50°
   E) 140°

2. In parallelogram below, what is the measure of ∠DAC?

   A) 20°
   B) 40°
   C) 50°
   D) 55°
   E) 70°

   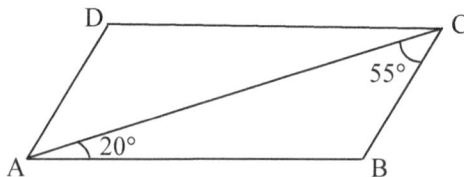

3. In parallelogram below, what is the measure of ∠DAC?

   A) 20°
   B) 40°
   C) 60°
   D) 70°
   E) 80°

   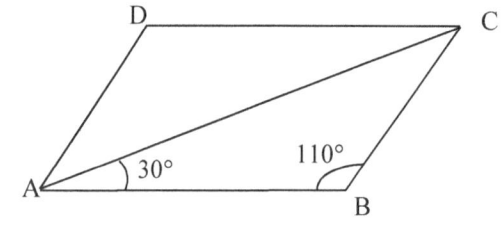

4. In the figure below, lines *j* and *k* are parallel, lines *m* and *n* are parallel and 2 angles are shown. What is the measure of ∠*x*?

   A) 20°
   B) 30°
   C) 40°
   D) 60°
   E) 80°

   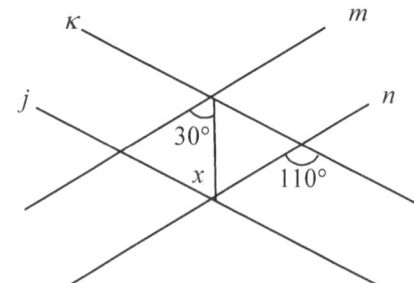

5. In the figure below, lines *j* and *k* are parallel, lines *m* and *n* are parallel and 2 angles are shown. What is the measure of ∠*x*?

A) 10°
B) 20°
C) 30°
D) 40°
E) 50°

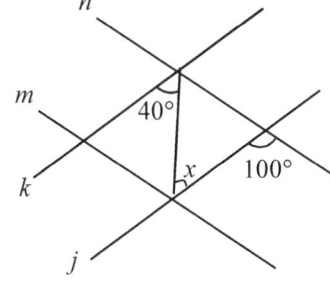

6. In the figure below, lines *j* and *k* are parallel. One ∠ is shown, what is the measure of *x*?

A) 85°
B) 95°
C) 105°
D) 115°
E) 125°

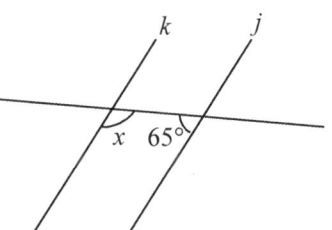

7. In the figure below, B is on $\overline{DE}$ and $\overline{DE}$ is parallel to $\overline{AC}$. Which of the following angle congruencies must hold?

A) ∠1 ≅ ∠2
B) ∠1 ≅ ∠4
C) ∠2 ≅ ∠3
D) ∠2 ≅ ∠4
E) ∠3 ≅ ∠4

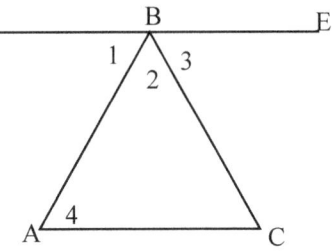

8. In the figure below, lines *j* and *k* are parallel and lines *m* and *n* are parallel. Which congruencies do not hold?

A) ∠1 ≅ ∠4
B) ∠1 ≅ ∠5
C) ∠2 ≅ ∠4
D) ∠2 ≅ ∠6
E) ∠3 ≅ ∠6

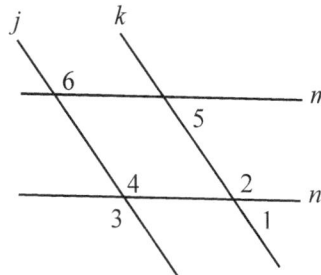

9. In the figure below, lines *j* and *k* are parallel and lines *m* and *n* are parallel. Which congruencies must hold?

A) $\angle 1 \cong \angle 6$
B) $\angle 2 \cong \angle 5$
C) $\angle 3 \cong \angle 6$
D) $\angle 3 \cong \angle 5$
E) $\angle 5 \cong \angle 6$

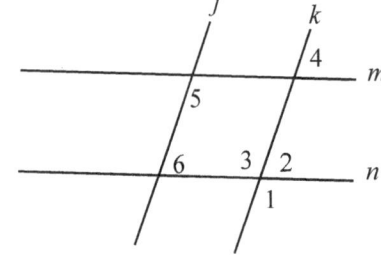

10. In the figure below, B is on $\overline{DE}$ and $\overline{DE}$ is parallel to $\overline{AC}$. What congruencies must hold?

A) $\angle 1+\angle 2 \cong \angle 5$
B) $\angle 1+\angle 5 \cong \angle 2$
C) $\angle 1+\angle 4 \cong \angle 5$
D) $\angle 1+\angle 2 \cong \angle 4$
E) $\angle 2+\angle 3 \cong \angle 5$

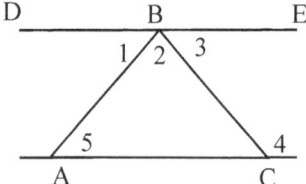

Inscribed Angles

1. The circumference of the circle below is 75 inches. If the length of arc AB is 15 inches, and $\overline{AO}$ and $\overline{BO}$ are both radii of the circle, what is the measure of the central angle *m*?

   A) 18
   B) 36
   C) 42
   D) 72
   E) 84

   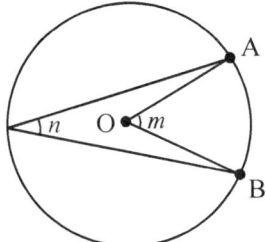

2. The circumference of the circle below is 75 inches. If the length of arc AB is 15 inches and $\overline{AO}$ and $\overline{BO}$ are both radii of the circle, what is the measure of the inscribed angle *n*?

   A) 18
   B) 36
   C) 42
   D) 72
   E) 84

   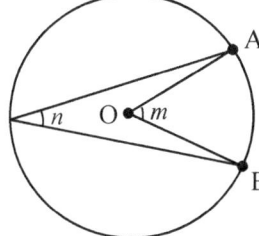

3. In the circle below, $\overline{OX}$ and $\overline{OY}$ are both radii of the circle with center O. What is the measure of the inscribed angle if the circumference is 15cm and arc XY is 5cm?

   A) 60°
   B) 80°
   C) 90°
   D) 100°
   E) 120°

   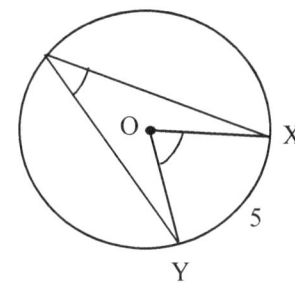

4. In the circle below, the central angle is 40° and the arc XY is 15 cm, what is the circumference of the circle?

A) 70 cm
B) 88 cm
C) 135 cm
D) 141 cm
E) 150 cm

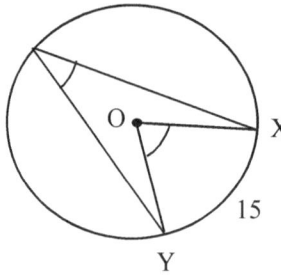

5. How many degrees does a minute hand on a clock sweep as it moves from 8:10 to 8:17?

A) 35°
B) 38°
C) 40°
D) 42°
E) 45°

6. The circumference of a circle below is 90 inches. If the length of arc AB is 12 inches and $\overline{OA}$ and $\overline{OB}$ are both radii of the circle, what is the measure of the inscribed angle j?

A) 20°
B) 24°
C) 28°
D) 32°
E) 35°

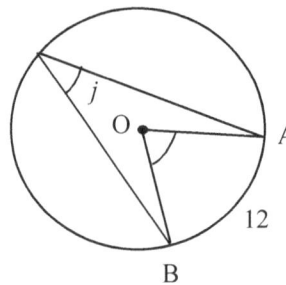

7. In the circle below, $\overline{OX}$ and $\overline{OY}$ are both radii of the circle with center O. What is the measure of the inscribed angle if the circumference is 9cm and arc XY is 2cm?

A) 30°
B) 35°
C) 40°
D) 45°
E) 50°

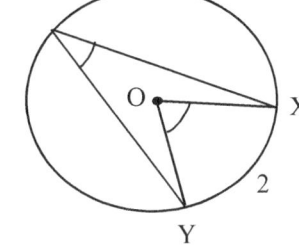

8. In the circle below, the central angle is 16° and the arc XY is 32 cm, what is the circumference of the circle?

A) 720 cm
B) 760 cm
C) 810 cm
D) 820 cm
E) 850 cm

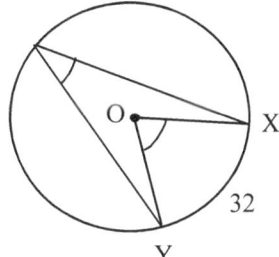

9. A minute hand on a clock moves 54°. How much time has passed?

A) 4 minutes
B) 9 minutes
C) 12 minutes
D) 17 minutes
E) 22 minutes

10. A tennis player's serve causes the tip of the racket to move in a 200° arc. If the tip of the racket traveled 5π feet, how long is the tennis player's arm and racket (the radius of the circle)?

A) 3 feet
B) 3.5 feet
C) 4 feet
D) 4.5 feet
E) 5 feet

Percents

1. Jessie's monthly salary is $650.00. If 15% is taken out for retirement, how much of Jessie's monthly salary is left?

   A) $420.00
   B) $455.00
   C) $463.50
   D) $520.00
   E) $552.50

2. If 30% of x equals 60, then x is?

   A) 16
   B) 18
   C) 30
   D) 200
   E) 2000

3. At a novelty shop, a charm for a bracelet is priced at $16.99. A sales tax of 7% of the $16.99 will be added (rounded to the nearest cent) to the price of the charm. You have 20 one-dollar bills; how much will you need in coins if you want to have exact change ready?

   A) $0.03
   B) $0.06
   C) $0.12
   D) $0.18
   E) $0.19

4. To the nearest hundredth, what is 7% of 18?

   A) 0.83
   B) 0.94
   C) 1.05
   D) 1.23
   E) 1.26

5. If 30% of *x* equals 83, then, rounded to the nearest hundredth, *x* is?

A) 263.84
B) 269.33
C) 276.67
D) 278.35
E) 281.02

6. A poll of 400 teenagers was conducted to gather information-covering views on taxes. Prior to the polling, it was believed that 20% of teenagers would be in favor of raising taxes. Results showed that the poll fell 10 responses short of this mark. How many of the teenagers polled responded in favor of raising taxes?

A) 55
B) 60
C) 65
D) 70
E) 90

7. Last year, 60% of the senior class at Cougar High played at least 2 sports. Of the remaining class members, 75% played 1 sport. What percent of the senior class played no sports?

A) 0%
B) 5%
C) 10%
D) 25%
E) 40%

8. A basketball player shot 30 free throws and made 18 of them. Then, the player missed 6 shots in a row. How many consecutive additional shots does the player need to make in order to bring his percentage back to at least what it was just before the 6 missed shots?

A) 3
B) 4
C) 6
D) 9
E) 15

9. In a group of 48 puppies, 18 are brown. What percentage of the group is brown?

A) 2.7%
B) 37.5%
C) 48%
D) 51.5%
E) 54%

10. In a room of people, 13 know how to swim. This number is exactly 20% of the total number of people in the room. How many people are in the room?

A) 42
B) 52
C) 65
D) 74
E) 85

11. A country expects a 5% increase in the current gross national product of 42,000 units. What would the new gross national product be if the country's expectations were met?

A) 42,005
B) 44,100
C) 46,300
D) 52,850
E) 63,000

Square Roots

1. If $\sqrt{2x-8} = -4$, then $x=$

   A) -18
   B) −8
   C) 8
   D) 9
   E) 12

2. If $\sqrt{2x-5} = 3$, then $x=$

   A) -18
   B) −6
   C) 4
   D) 7
   E) 32

3. $\sqrt{x-4}$ is a real number if and only if:

   A) $x \geq 0$
   B) $-4 < x < 4$
   C) $x \leq -4$
   D) $x < 4$
   E) $-4 < x < 0$

4. $\sqrt{x+3}$ is a real number if and only if:

   A) $x \geq -3$
   B) $0 < x < 3$
   C) $x \leq -3$
   D) $-3 < x < 0$
   E) $x=1$

5. Which of the following is equal to $\sqrt{40}$?

   A) $2\sqrt{5}$
   B) $2\sqrt{10}$
   C) $4\sqrt{10}$
   D) 20
   E) $20\sqrt{2}$

6. Which of the following is equal to $\sqrt{32}$?

A) $2\sqrt{2}$
B) $4\sqrt{2}$
C) $8\sqrt{2}$
D) 16
E) $16\sqrt{2}$

7. What integer most nearly approximates $\left(\sqrt{40}\right)\left(\sqrt{30}\right)$?

A) 11
B) 20
C) 35
D) 190
E) 219

8. What integer most nearly approximates $\left(\sqrt{50}\right)\left(\sqrt{40}\right)$?

A) 14
B) 45
C) 60
D) 283
E) 316

9. Which of the following is an equivalent form for $\dfrac{4x}{\sqrt{4x-z}}$?

A) $\dfrac{\sqrt{4x-z}}{x}$
B) $\dfrac{\sqrt{4x+z}}{x}$
C) $\dfrac{4x\sqrt{4x-z}}{16x^2-z}$
D) $\dfrac{4x\sqrt{4x+z}}{4x+z}$
E) $\dfrac{4x\sqrt{4x-z}}{4x-z}$

10. Which of the following is an equivalent form for $\dfrac{12a}{\sqrt{6a+c}}$?

A) $\dfrac{\sqrt{6a+c}}{2a}$

B) $\dfrac{12a\sqrt{6a+c}}{6a+c}$

C) $\dfrac{12a\sqrt{6a+c}}{36a^2+c^2}$

D) $\dfrac{\sqrt{6a+c}}{12a}$

E) $\dfrac{12a\sqrt{6a+c}}{6a-c}$

Irrational Numbers

1. Which of the following is an irrational number?

   A) 0.6
   B) $1/8$
   C) 0
   D) |-6.3|
   E) $\sqrt{13}$

2. Which of the following is an irrational number?

   A) 2^3
   B) $1/5$
   C) $\sqrt{6}$
   D) $\sqrt{16}$
   E) −0.3

3. Which of the following is an irrational number?

   A) 3^2
   B) π
   C) $1/7$
   D) $-\sqrt{9}$
   E) 10^{-4}

4. Which of the following is NOT an irrational number?

   A) $\dfrac{1}{\sqrt{2}}$
   B) π
   C) $\sqrt{3}$
   D) $33/7$
   E) $\sqrt{7}$

5. For what value of x is $\dfrac{2}{\sqrt{x}}$ irrational?

   A) 1
   B) 4
   C) 5
   D) 9
   E) 25

6. For what value of x is $\sqrt{x}$ rational?

   A) 2
   B) 3
   C) 4
   D) 5
   E) 6

7. Which of the following is NOT an irrational number?

   A) $\dfrac{1}{\sqrt{13}}$
   B) $\sqrt{3}$
   C) $\dfrac{7}{\sqrt{5}}$
   D) $\sqrt{8}$
   E) $\dfrac{5}{\sqrt{36}}$

8. For what value of x is $\dfrac{2}{\sqrt{x}}$ irrational?

   A) 8
   B) 9
   C) 16
   D) 25
   E) 36

Similar Triangles

1. The lengths of the sides of one triangle are 7, 9, and 14 inches, respectively. What is the perimeter, in inches, of a similar triangle whose longest side is 7 inches?

   A) 8
   B) 10
   C) 15
   D) 25
   E) 30

2. The lengths of the sides of one triangle are 3, 7, and 8 meters, respectively. If the perimeter of a similar triangle is 27 meters, what is the length of its longest side?

   A) 4
   B) 6
   C) 8
   D) 12
   E) 16

3. In the figure below, A lies on $\overline{CQ}$, P lies on $\overline{BQ}$ and $\overline{AP}$ is parallel to $\overline{BC}$. If $\overline{AP}$ is 7 units long, $\overline{PQ}$ is 9 units long, and $\overline{BC}$ is 14 units long, how many units long is $\overline{BP}$?

   A) 9
   B) 12
   C) 15
   D) 18
   E) 21

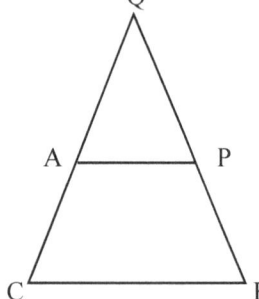

4. In the figure below, A lies on $\overline{CQ}$, P lies on $\overline{BQ}$ and $\overline{AP}$ is parallel to $\overline{BC}$. If $\overline{PQ}$ is 8 units long, $\overline{BQ}$ is 20 units long, and $\overline{AP}$ is 6 units long, how many units long is $\overline{BC}$?

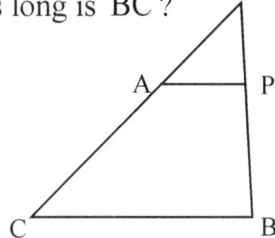

A) 9
B) 15
C) 18
D) 21
E) 24

5. The figure below shows 2 triangles where $\triangle ABC \sim \triangle A'B'C'$. In these similar triangles, $a=8$, $b=12$, $c=16$, and $a'=4$, with all dimensions given in feet. What is the value of b'?

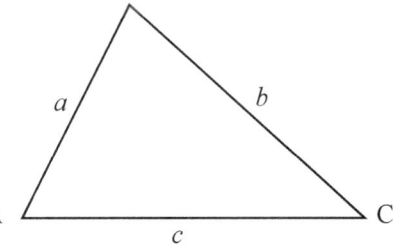
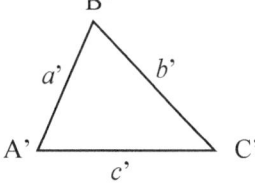

A) 2
B) 4
C) 6
D) 8
E) 10

6. A 12-foot pole cast a 20-foot long shadow. If at the same time a building casts a 30-foot long shadow, how tall, in feet, is the building?

A) 15
B) 18
C) 25
D) 45
E) 50

7. The figure below shows 2 triangles where ΔABC~ΔA'B'C'. In these similar triangles, a=9, b=15, and b'=20. If c'=28, what is c?

A) 7
B) 14
C) 15
D) 18
E) 21

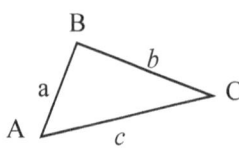
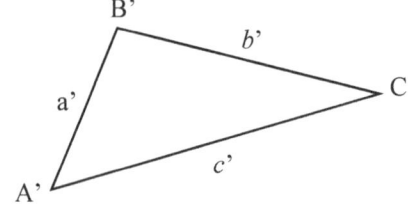

8. The lengths of the sides of a right triangle are 6, 8, and 10 feet, respectively. What is the area, in square feet, of a similar triangle whose longest side is 15 inches?

A) 48
B) 54
C) 60
D) 66
E) 96

9. The lengths of the sides of a right triangle are 3, 4, and 5 feet, respectively. If the area of a similar triangle is 24 square feet, what is the length of its shortest side?

A) 4
B) 4.5
C) 6
D) 7.5
E) 9

10. The lengths of the sides of a right triangle are 9, 12, and 15 feet, respectively. If the area of a similar triangle is 6 square feet, what is the length of its longest side?

A) 3
B) 4.5
C) 5
D) 12
E) 15

11. The figures below show 3 triangles where △ABC~△DEF~△GHI. In these similar triangles, the perimeter of △ABC is one-fifth the perimeter of △DEF, and the perimeter of △DEF is twice that of △GHI. If the sides of △ABC are 5, 8, and 12 units, respectively, what is the length of the shortest side of △GHI?

A) 0.5
B) 1
C) 2
D) 12.5
E) 25

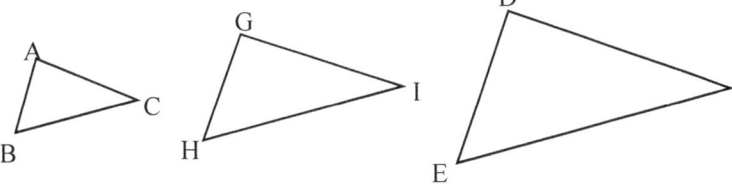

Common Right Triangles

1. What is the length of the hypotenuse of a right triangle whose legs are 3 units and 4 units?

    A) 5
    B) $3\sqrt{2}$
    C) 7
    D) $3\sqrt{5}$
    E) $4\sqrt{3}$

2. What is the length in inches of the hypotenuse of a right triangle whose legs are 6 inches and 8 inches?

    A) 9
    B) $5\sqrt{2}$
    C) 10
    D) $3\sqrt{7}$
    E) 14

3. What is the length, in meters, of the hypotenuse of a right triangle whose legs are 5 meters and 12 meters?

    A) 9
    B) $3\sqrt{5}$
    C) 10
    D) $3\sqrt{7}$
    E) 13

4. The route from Isaiah's house to Kim's home goes 3 miles north and 4 miles west around a field. If they cut through the field, how many miles will they save?

A) 2
B) 3
C) 3.5
D) 4.5
E) 5

5. Because of obstructions, it is impossible to measure the north wall of a rectangular room. If the diagonal of the wall is 13 feet and the west wall is 12 feet, how long, in feet, is the north wall?

A) 3
B) 4
C) 5
D) 8
E) 10

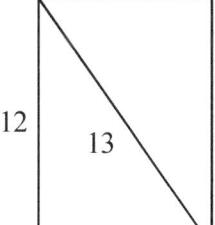

6. Ten feet of string are connected from a treetop to the ground. If the point where the string meets the ground is 6 feet from the base of the tree, how many feet tall is the tree?

A) $3\sqrt{2}$
B) 6
C) $3\sqrt{3}$
D) 8
E) 10

7. In the figure below, what is the value of *x*?

   A) $3\sqrt{5}$
   B) 9
   C) $5\sqrt{5}$
   D) 12
   E) 13

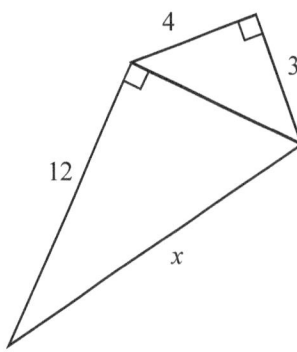

8. What is the altitude of an isosceles triangle with sides of 10 inches and base of 16 inches?

   A) 5
   B) 3
   C) $2\sqrt{13}$
   D) 6
   E) $2\sqrt{39}$

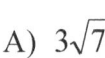

9. How many units long is a tunnel going straight through a mountain if the mountain's slopes have perfect lengths of 10 units long and the mountain is 8 units tall as shown in the diagram below?

   A) $3\sqrt{7}$
   B) $4\sqrt{2}$
   C) 6
   D) 12
   E) $2\sqrt{41}$

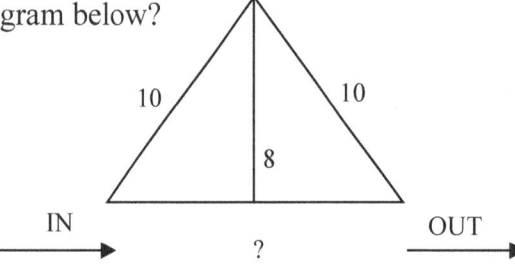

10. In the parallelogram shown below, find *y*.

    A) 3
    B) 5
    C) $3\sqrt{3}$
    D) 7
    E) $5\sqrt{3}$

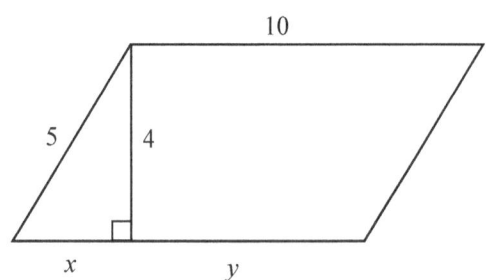

Word Problems

1. A sales woman receives $500 per month plus $25 for each sale she makes. If the saleswoman makes x sales per month, which of the following expressions represents the total monthly pay of the saleswoman?

   A) $25 + 500x$
   B) x + $500
   C) $500 - 25x$
   D) $500 + $25/x$
   E) $500 + 25x$

2. A home purchased 5 years ago for $95,000 is now worth 15% more. Which of the following calculations gives the current value, in dollars, of the house?

   A) 95,000 – 95,000(0.15)
   B) 95,000 + 95,000(0.15)
   C) 95,000 + 95,000(0.015)
   D) 95,000(0.015)
   E) 95,000(0.15)

3. What is the largest possible product for 2 even integers whose sum is 42?

   A) 185
   B) 272
   C) 320
   D) 440
   E) 441

4. In a laboratory experiment, bacteria A lives 7 hours longer than bacteria B, and bacteria B lives 3 times as long as bacteria C. If n is the lifespan of bacteria C in hours, what is the lifespan of bacteria A in terms of n?

A) 3n + 7
B) 3n – 7
C) 5n + 3
D) 7n + 3
E) 7n

5. A long distance phone company charges ($4x + 0.15y$) dollars where x is the number of installed phone lines and y is the number of long distance minutes. What is the bill for a home with two phone lines and 432 minutes?

A) $64.80
B) $68.80
C) $72.80
D) $74.60
E) $82.80

6. Selena purchased 3 pair of tights and one bodysuit. The bodysuit was regularly $30, but was on sale for 20% off. The tights, regularly $10 each were 15% off. What was the total price of Selena's purchase (assuming no sales tax)?

A) $10.50
B) $27.50
C) $32.50
D) $41.00
E) $49.50

7. The specific gravity of a substance is the ratio of the weight of the substance to the weight of an equal volume of water. If 1 cubic foot of water weighs 62.5 pounds, what is the specific gravity of a liquid that weighs 31.25 pounds per cubic foot?

A) 0.25
B) 0.5
C) 1.0
D) 1.25
E) 1.75

8. Your heart rate in beats per minute (bpm) is estimated by counting the number of heart beats in one minute. If you count 18 beats in 15 seconds, what is the bpm?

A) 68
B) 72
C) 94
D) 108
E) 270

9. What is the total cost of 2.6 pounds of apples at $0.99 per pound, 0.5 pounds of garlic at $1.25 per pound, and 3 pounds of tomatoes at $1.98 per pound?

A) $4.54
B) $7.27
C) $8.14
D) $9.14
E) $11.63

10. Starting at the stop sign, Tasha skated at 3 meters per second for 10 seconds. She skated back at 3 meters per second and stopped at the stop sign after 10 more seconds. Which of the following would resemble the graph of Tasha's distance from the stop sign as a function of time (t)?

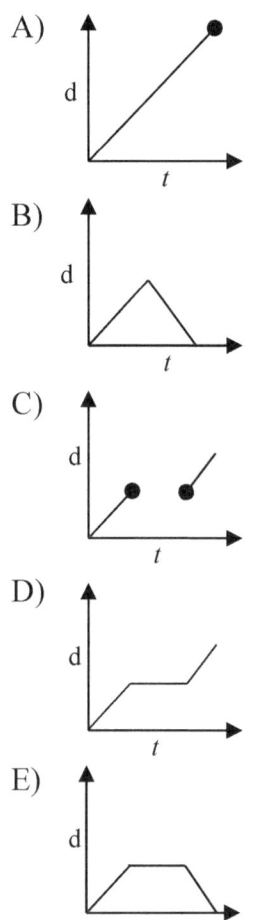

11. The height of a rose bush grew by a factor of five during the growing season after which it was cut back 35 inches to be only 10 inches tall. How tall, in inches, was the rosebush at the beginning of the growing season?

A) 6
B) 7
C) 8
D) 9
E) 10

12. The cost of getting a babysitter for one evening is a fixed rate of $5 per child plus $3 per hour per child. Which of the following expressions describes the total cost for x hours and y children?

A) $5 + 3x/y$
B) $5/x + 3/y$
C) $5x + 3y$
D) $5y + 3xy$
E) $5x + 3xy$

13. The mail sorter can sort 12 pieces of mail in 1 minute. A helper sorts 6 pieces of mail in 1 minute, but causes the first mail sorter to be a bit slower, decreasing to only 10 pieces of mail per minute. How many more pieces of mail per hour can the pair sort when compared to the first mail sorter working alone?

A) 200
B) 240
C) 360
D) 480
E) 520

14. Consider the following two logical statements:

-If the length of $\overline{AB}$ is 9, then the length of $\overline{BC}$ is 6.
-The length of $\overline{BC}$ is NOT 6.

If these statements are both true, then it follows that the length of

A) $\overline{AB}$ is 9
B) $\overline{BC}$ is 6
C) $\overline{BC}$ is 9
D) $\overline{BC}$ is NOT 9
E) $\overline{BC}$ is not able to be determined by this information.

15. Dave, Monica, Harris, Kaden, and Eddie are friends. Monica is shorter than Eddie, but taller than Harris. Dave is shorter than Harris, but taller than Kaden. Which of the friends is the tallest?

A) Dave
B) Monica
C) Harris
D) Kaden
E) Eddie

Geometry

1. In the figure below if *b* = 65°, then *a* =

   A) 35°
   B) 25°
   C) 115°
   D) 45°
   E) 145°

   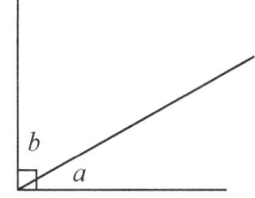

2. In the figure below if *b*=25°, then *a* is:

   A) 25°
   B) 175°
   C) 125°
   D) 155°
   E) 140°

   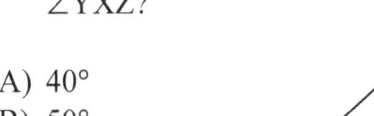

3. In the figure below, *x* is on AY and ∠AXZ measures 140°. What is the measure of ∠YXZ?

   A) 40°
   B) 50°
   C) 60°
   D) 70°
   E) 80°

   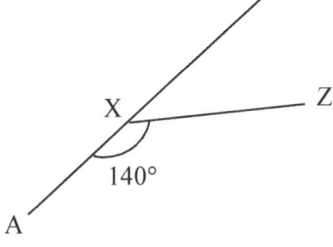

4. In the figure below, points A, E, and D are on the same line. What is the measure of ∠CED?

   A) 60°
   B) 70°
   C) 80°
   D) 100°
   E) 110°

   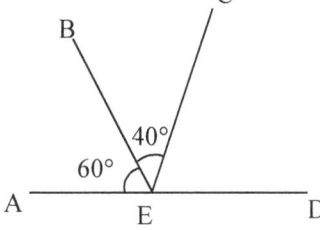

5. In the figure below points A, E, and D are on the same line. What is the measure of ∠BEC?

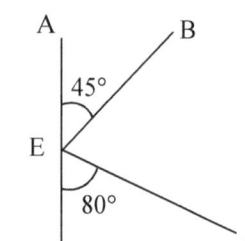

A) 35°
B) 45°
C) 55°
D) 65°
E) 85°

6. In the figure below, ∠AED is a right angle. What is the measure of ∠AEB?

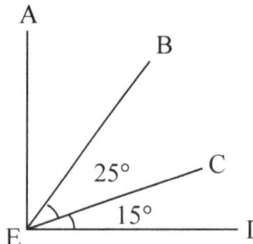

A) 45°
B) 50°
C) 55°
D) 60°
E) 65°

7. In the figure below, the measure of ∠a is 70°. What is the complement of ∠a?

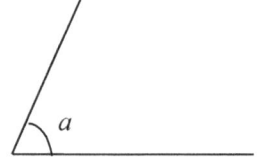

A) 10°
B) 20°
C) 80°
D) 110°
E) 130°

8. In the figure below, the measure of ∠a is 85°. What is the supplement of ∠a?

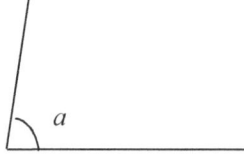

A) 5°
B) 15°
C) 65°
D) 95°
E) 115°

9. An analog clock shows 5 minutes after the hour. How many degrees must the minute sweep until it reaches 15 minutes after the hour?

A) 30°
B) 45°
C) 60°
D) 70°
E) 85°

10. In the figure below, if $x = 80°$ then y is:

A) 5°
B) 10°
C) 20°
D) 25°
E) 30°

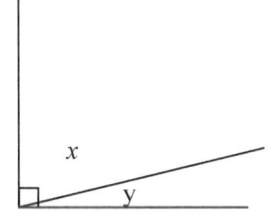

Quadratic Equations

1. Which of the following is a possible root of
   $x^2 - 2x + 5 = 8$?

   A) -5
   B) 1
   C) –3
   D) 2
   E) –1

2. Solve for x: $x^2 + x - 2 = 0$

   A) $x=1, x=-1$
   B) $x=-2, x=2$
   C) $x=-2, x=1$
   D) $x=3, x=-3$
   E) $x=1, x=3$

3. If $(x+m)^2 = x^2 + 16x + n$ where m and n are integers. What is n?

   A) 20
   B) 36
   C) 64
   D) 16
   E) 56

4. If $2x^2 + 6x - 8 = 0$, then what can $x/4$ equal?

   A) ¼
   B) –1/4
   C) 4
   D) –1/2
   E) 2

5. For all x, $(2x-4)(x+6)$:

   A) $x^2+8x+24$
   B) $2(x^2-x-12)$
   C) $2(x^2+x-12)$
   D) $2(x^2+4x-12)$
   E) $2(x^2-4x+12)$

6. For all x, $3x^2-7x-6$:

A) $(x-1)(x-6)$
B) $(x-2)(x+4)$
C) $(3x+2)(x-3)$
D) $(3x-2)(x+3)$
E) $(3x-1)(x+6)$

7. For all $x > 0$, $\dfrac{3x^2 + 6x - 24}{x + 4}$ simplifies to:

A) $x+4$
B) $x-2$
C) $3(x+4)$
D) $3(x+4)(x-2)$
E) $3(x-2)$

8. For all $x > 0$, $\dfrac{x^2 + 3x - 10}{x + 5}$ simplifies to:

A) $2(x+2)$
B) $x-2$
C) $x-5$
D) $2(x-5)$
E) $(x-2)(x-5)$

9. If the expression $x^2 - kx - 12$ is equal to zero when $x = 3$, what is the value of k?

A) 4
B) 3
C) 0
D) −1
E) −4

10. f the expression $x^2 - kx + 4$ is equal to 0 when $x = 4$, what is the value of k?

A) 5
B) 3
C) –1
D) –5
E) –7

11. What is the product of the 2 real solutions to $2x^2 + 5x - 3$?

A) 2 ½
B) 3/2
C) –2 ½
D) –3/2
E) –3 ½

12. What is the sum of the two real solutions to $x = x^2 - 20$?

A) 5
B) 4
C) 1
D) –1
E) –4

13. If $x < 0$ and $x^2 + x - 12 = 0$, then x is?

A) -1
B) –3
C) –4
D) –6
E) –12

14. If the equation $x^2 - 8x + 16$ has only one solution for x, what is $4x + 16$?

A) 0
B) 4
C) 8
D) 16
E) 32

Inequalities

1. Which of the following shows the solution set for the inequality, $8x - 18 \geq 6$?

A)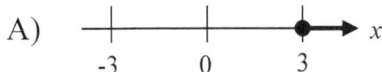

B)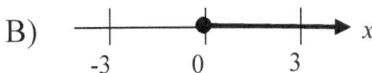

C)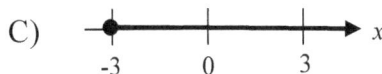

D)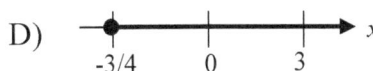

E)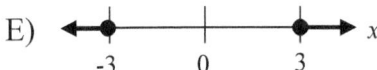

2. Which of the following, shaded regions is the graph in the standard (x,y) coordinate plane of the points that satisfy the inequality $|x| \leq 6$?

A)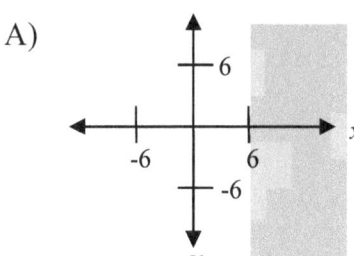

B)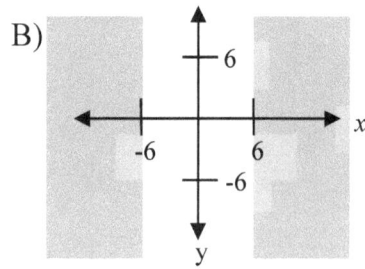

C)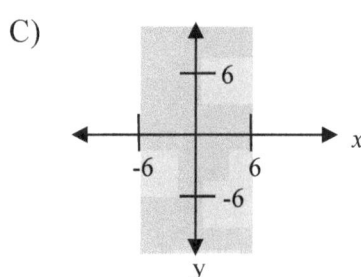

D)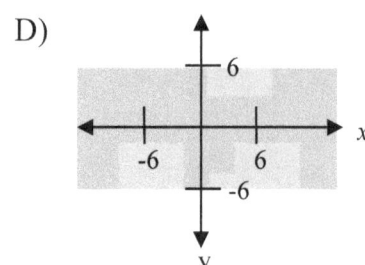

E)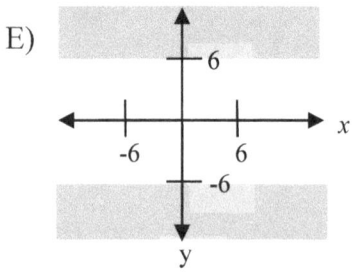

3. What is the smallest positive integer y such that $|4-y| \geq 8$?

A) 4
B) 6
C) 8
D) 12
E) 16

4. Which of the following is the graph of the solution set for $x^3 > 8$?

A)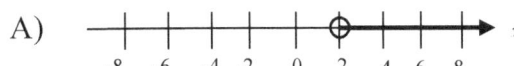

B)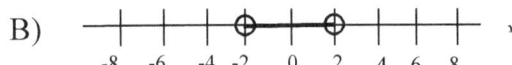

C)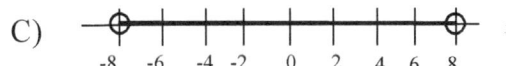

D)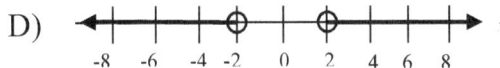

E)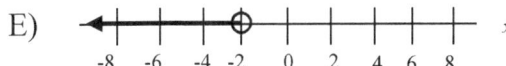

5. Which of the following is the graph of the solution set of $x-1 > 5$?

A)

B)

C)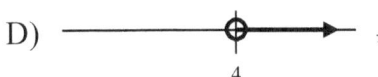

D)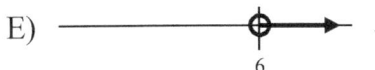

E>

6. How many different integer values of *n* satisfy the inequality $2/11 > 4/n > 2/13$?

A) 1
B) 2
C) 3
D) 4
E) 5

7. Which of the following is the graph of the solution set of $-3x < 6$?

A) ◦————+————◦ *x*
    -2   0   2

B) ◦————+————+→ *x*
    -2   0   2

C) ←◦————+————◦→ *x*
    -2   0   2

D) ←◦————+————+ *x*
    -2   0   2

E) ←————+————◦ *x*
    -2   0   2

8. When 6 times *x* is increased by 4, the result is less than 22. Which of the following is a graph of the real numbers *x* that satisfy this relationship?

A) ————◦————+————→
       -3   0

B) ————+————◦————→
       0   3

C) ←————+————◦————
       0   3

D) ←————+————◦
       0   6

E) ————+————•————→
       0   3

9. If a and b are real numbers, and $a<b$ and $a>0$, then which of the following inequalities must be true?

A) $b<0$
B) $b>0$
C) $a^2>b^2$
D) $ab<0$
E) $b^2<0$

Logarithms

1. Find X if $\log_8 X = 2$

   A) 2
   B) 3
   C) 4
   D) 16
   E) 64

2. Find b if $\log_b 81 = 4$

   A) 5
   B) 4
   C) 3
   D) 2
   E) 1

3. Find Y if $\log_5 625 = Y$

   A) 1
   B) 2
   C) 3
   D) 4
   E) 5

4. Find X if $\log_4 X = 3$

   A) 2
   B) 3
   C) 4
   D) 16
   E) 64

5. Find b if $\log_b 216 = 3$

   A) 2
   B) 4
   C) 5
   D) 6
   E) 8

6. Find b if $\log_b 243 = 5$

A) 2
B) 3
C) 4
D) 6
E) 7

7. Find Y if $\log_5 125 = Y$

A) 2
B) 3
C) 4
D) 5
E) 6

8. Find X if $\log_8 X = 3$

A) 2
B) 4
C) 8
D) 64
E) 512

9. Find Y if $\log_{1.5} 2.25 = Y$

A) 1.5
B) 2
C) $5/3$
D) 3
E) 3.5

10. Find b if $\log_b 81/16 = 4$

A) $81/16$
B) 4
C) 3
D) 2
E) $3/2$

Pythagorean Theorem

1. The lengths on the figure below are in centimeters. How many centimeters long is $\overline{AB}$?

    A) 3
    B) $\sqrt{13}$
    C) 4
    D) 5
    E) $\sqrt{15}$

    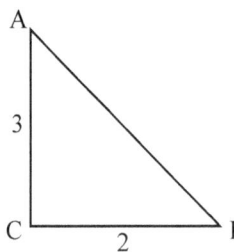

2. The lengths on the figure below are in feet. How many feet long is $\overline{AC}$?

    A) 10
    B) 13
    C) 14
    D) $\sqrt{983}$
    E) 576

    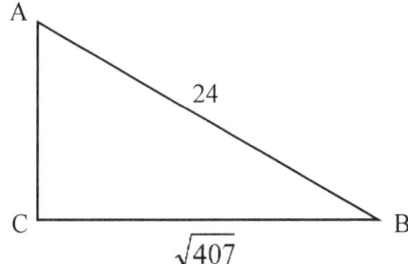

3. The path from the drugstore to the supermarket goes 5 miles east then 2 miles south. How many miles could be saved if a direct path were taken?

    A) $\sqrt{7}$
    B) $\sqrt{29}$
    C) $7 - \sqrt{7}$
    D) $7 - \sqrt{29}$
    E) $7 + \sqrt{29}$

    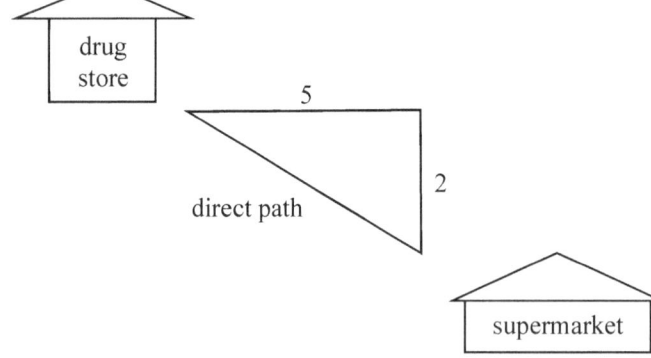

4. In the figure below $\overline{CD}$ is an altitude of equilateral triangle ΔABC. If $\overline{CD}$ is $4\sqrt{3}$ units long, how many units long is $\overline{AC}$?

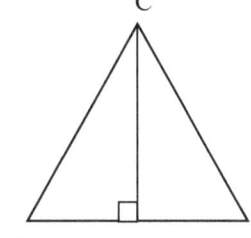

A) $3\sqrt{2}$
B) 4
C) 8
D) $8\sqrt{3}$
E) 12

5. What is the length, in centimeters, of the hypotenuse of a right triangle with legs measuring $\sqrt{2}$ cm and 3 cm?

A) 3
B) $\sqrt{11}$
C) $\sqrt{13}$
D) $3\sqrt{10}$
E) 10

6. Square ABCD below has a perimeter of 36 inches. How many inches long is diagonal $\overline{AC}$?

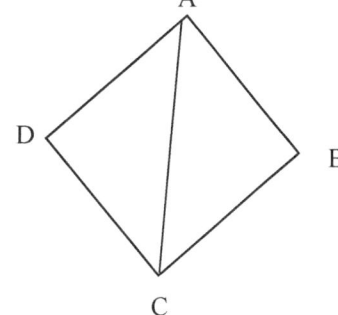

A) 6
B) $3\sqrt{6}$
C) 9
D) $9\sqrt{3}$
E) $9\sqrt{2}$

7. Rectangle ABCD below has sides with lengths of 7 meters and 13 meters. How many meters long is diagonal $\overline{AC}$?

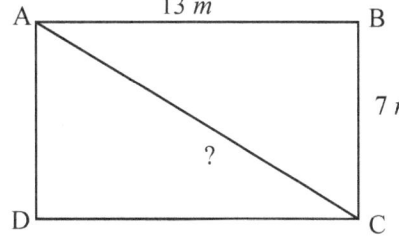

A) $3\sqrt{5}$
B) 8
C) $5\sqrt{3}$
D) $\sqrt{218}$
E) 15

8. Two archers shoot their arrows at a target. Arrow #1 hits 3 inches above and 2 inches to the right of the target. Arrow #2 hits 4 inches below and 1 inch to the left. If d_1 is the distance arrow #1 is from the target and d_2 is the distance arrow #2 is from the target, what is the difference in d_1 and d_2?

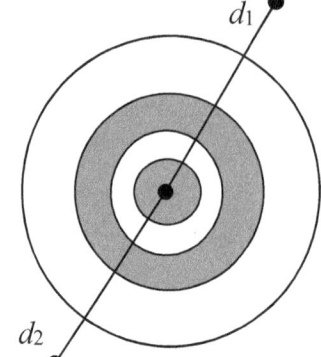

A) $\sqrt{13}$
B) $\sqrt{13} - \sqrt{17}$
C) $\sqrt{5} - \sqrt{15}$
D) $\sqrt{5} + \sqrt{17}$
E) $\sqrt{13} + \sqrt{16}$

9. In the figure below, what is the value of x?

A) $\sqrt{5}$
B) $\sqrt{21}$
C) 5
D) $\sqrt{37}$
E) 7

10. What is the length, in inches, of the hypotenuse of a right triangle with legs measuring $\sqrt{7}$ inches and 4 inches?

A) 3
B) $\sqrt{11}$
C) $\sqrt{13}$
D) $\sqrt{23}$
E) 5

Absolute Values

1. $|-5| \cdot |2| =$

   A) -10
   B) -7
   C) -3
   D) 0
   E) 10

2. $-|-5| - (-5) =$

   A) -25
   B) -10
   C) 0
   D) 10
   E) 25

3. What are the values of a and b, if any, where $a|b-5| < 0$?

   A) $a<0$ and $b \neq 5$
   B) $a<0$ and $b=5$
   C) $a \neq 0$ and $b>2$
   D) $a>0$ and $b<2$
   E) There are no such values of a and b.

4. $|2-5| - |3-8| =$

   A) -15
   B) -2
   C) 2
   D) 8
   E) 15

5. $-|2-4| - |3-1| =$

   A) -8
   B) -4
   C) 0
   D) 4
   E) 8

6. $|3-5| \bullet |8-4| =$

A) -8
B) –6
C) 0
D) 6
E) 8

7. $-|9| \div |-3| =$

A) -27
B) –6
C) –3
D) 3
E) 6

8. $-|11-5| \div |5-8| =$

A) -18
B) –2
C) 2
D) 3
E) 18

9. $|-3| \bullet |2| =$

A) -7
B) –6
C) –1
D) 6
E) 8

10. For which values of a and b is $a|3-b|>0$?

A) $a>0$ and $b \neq 3$
B) $a \neq 0$ and $b>3$
C) $a<0$ and $b>3$
D) $a \neq 0$ and $b \neq 0$
E) $a<0$ and $b<3$

11. If $|6x-7| = 3$, what are the possible values of x?

A) -3 and +3
B) $5/3$ and $2/3$
C) $-5/3$ and $-2/3$
D) $5/7$ and $7/3$
E) 7 and 3

12. If $|4x+3| = 5$, what are the possible values of x?

A) -2 and -4
B) 2 and 4
C) $5/3$ and $-3/5$
D) $-1/2$ and 2
E) $1/2$ and -2

13. For which values of x and y is $x|7+y|>0$?

A) $x<0$ and $y=7$
B) $x\neq 0$ and $y>-7$
C) $x>0$ and $y\neq -7$
D) $x\neq 0$ and $y\neq 0$
E) $x<0$ and $y<7$

14. If $|3a+4| = 8$, what are the possible values of a?

A) $4/3$ and -4
B) $-4/3$ and -4
C) $-4/3$ and 4
D) $-3/4$ and 2
E) $3/4$ and -2

15. If $|2a-7| = 3$, what are the possible values of a?

A) -2 and 2
B) -3 and 3
C) 3 and 3
D) 5 and 2
E) 5 and -2

Averages

1. Frederick went to an arcade several times last year. He recorded the number of quarters he spent each time in a table, as shown below. What was the mean number of quarters he spent per arcade visit?

Visit	1	2	3	4	5
Quarters spent	36	18	22	24	20

A) 12
B) 16
C) 24
D) 26
E) 30

2. Find the median of the quarters listed in problem #1.

A) 18
B) 20
C) 22
D) 24
E) 36

3. What is the average of 4, 4, and 5?

A) 4
B) $4 \frac{1}{3}$
C) $4 \frac{1}{2}$
D) $4 \frac{2}{3}$
E) 5

4. What is the average of $^{11}/_{16}$ and .125?

A) .07325
B) .40625
C) .73250
D) .81250
E) .92325

5. The average of 8 numbers is 6.75. If each of the numbers is decreased by 2, what is the average of the 8 new numbers?

A) 3
B) 4
C) 4.75
D) 6.75
E) 8

6. Contributions to a scholarship fund are made by 4 companies as indicated in the table below. What is the average of the contributions made by the 4 companies?

Company	1	2	3	4
Contributions in dollars	325	250	400	225

A) $275.00
B) $300.00
C) $375.00
D) $450.00
E) $462.50

7. Find the median contribution as given in problem #5 above.

A) $225.00
B) $250.00
C) $275.00
D) $287.50
E) $325.00

8. The average of a set of four integers is 13. When a fifth number is included in the set, the average of the set increases to 15. What is the fifth number?

A) 11
B) 15
C) 18
D) 23
E) 25

9. A group of judges scored a performance on a 3-point scale. A score of 1 was given by 20% of the judges; a score of 2 was given by 45%, and a score of 3 was given by 35%. To the nearest tenth, what was the average of the score?

A) 1.8
B) 1.9
C) 2.0
D) 2.2
E) 2.5

10. What is the average of $^{11}/_8$ and 0.645?

A) 1.01
B) 1.40
C) 1.62
D) 1.65
E) 2.02

11. Bernard went on 3 field trips last school year. He recorded the amount of money he spent each trip in a table, as shown below. What was the mean amount of money he spent per trip, to the nearest hundredth?

Trip	1	2	3
Money spent	$6	$3	$4

A) $3.75
B) $4.00
C) $4.33
D) $4.50
E) $5.33

12. The average of 9 numbers is 8.25. If each of the numbers is increased by 8, what is the average of the 9 new numbers?

A) 8
B) 8.25
C) 10.25
D) 12.75
E) 16.25

13. The number of questions missed on a recent trigonometry exam for a class of 15 students is: 0, 0, 1, 1, 2, 2, 2, 4, 4, 5, 5, 6, 7, 7, 8. What is the mode of these numbers?

A) 2
B) 3.5
C) 4
D) 4.5
E) 7

Trigonometry

1. In right △ below if the tangent of ∠C is 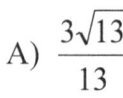, what is the length of $\overline{AB}$?

A) $\dfrac{3\sqrt{13}}{13}$

B) $\sqrt{13}$

C) 2

D) 3

E) 13

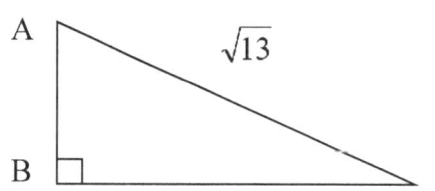

2. In △ABC, if ∠A and ∠B are acute angles, and sin A = ⁴/₅, what is the value of cos A?

A) ⁴/₂₅
B) ⁹/₂₅
C) ²/₅
D) ³/₅
E) ¹⁶/₂₅

3. In the right triangle △ABC below, what is the sin of ∠A?

A) $\dfrac{7\sqrt{218}}{218}$

B) $\dfrac{13\sqrt{218}}{218}$

C) $\dfrac{7}{13}$

D) $\dfrac{13}{7}$

E) $\dfrac{\sqrt{218}}{7}$

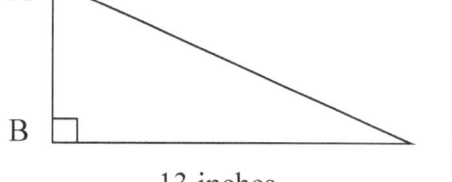

4. For the right triangle below, which of the following expressions is equal to $\cos\theta$?

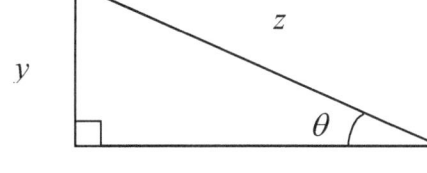

A) $\dfrac{y}{z}$

B) $\dfrac{z}{x}$

C) $\dfrac{x}{z}$

D) $\dfrac{x}{y}$

E) $\dfrac{y}{x}$

5. For the right triangle below, which of the following expressions is equal to $\sin\theta$?

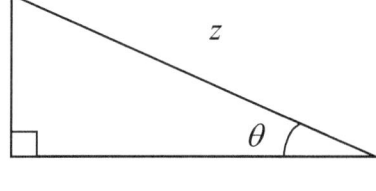

A) $\dfrac{y}{z}$

B) $\dfrac{z}{x}$

C) $\dfrac{x}{z}$

D) $\dfrac{x}{y}$

E) $\dfrac{y}{x}$

6. If in the right triangle below, ∠C has sine of $\dfrac{7}{\sqrt{113}}$, cosine of $\dfrac{8}{\sqrt{113}}$, and tangent of $\dfrac{7}{8}$, all in inches, how many inches long is $\overline{AB}$?

A) 14
B) 7
C) $\dfrac{\sqrt{113}}{2}$
D) 113
E) $\dfrac{15\sqrt{113}}{113}$

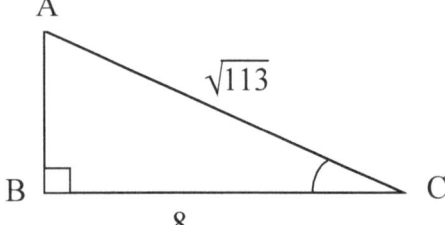

7. An object six feet tall casts a 2 feet shadow when the angle of elevation of the sun is θ. What is tan θ?

A) ¼
B) ⅓
C) 3
D) 4
E) 12

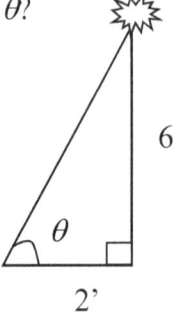

8. What is the cosine of angle A in triangle ABC below?

A) $\dfrac{7}{\sqrt{22}}$
B) $\dfrac{6\sqrt{2}}{11}$
C) $\dfrac{11}{7}$
D) $\dfrac{7}{\sqrt{11}}$
E) $\dfrac{7}{6\sqrt{2}}$

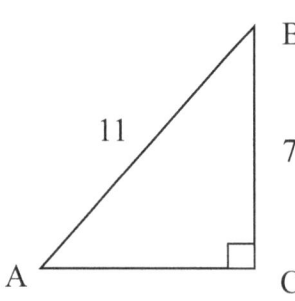

9. What is the sine of angle A in triangle ABC below?

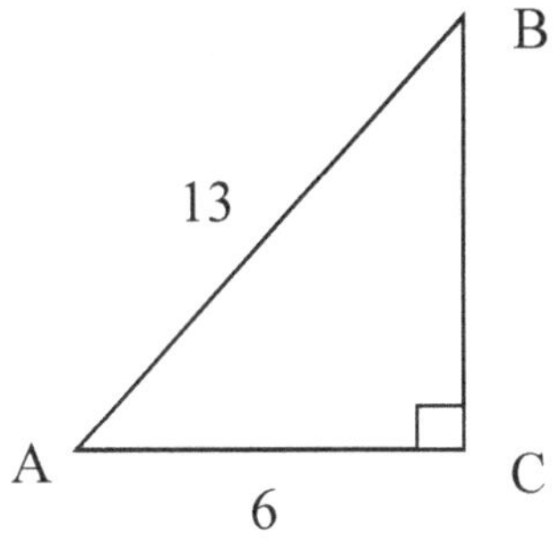

A) $\dfrac{6}{13}$

B) $\dfrac{\sqrt{133}}{13}$

C) $\dfrac{13}{6}$

D) $\sqrt{133}$

E) $6\sqrt{133}$

10. Given that $\tan x = \dfrac{o}{10} = 0.4$, what is o?

A) 2
B) 3
C) 4
D) 5
E) 6

11. Given that $\cos x = \dfrac{1}{h} = 0.2$, what is h?

A) 2
B) 3
C) 4
D) 5
E) 6

12. Given that $\tan x = \dfrac{2}{a} = 0.5$, what is $\sec x$?

A) $4\sqrt{5}$

B) 5

C) $\dfrac{4\sqrt{5}}{2}$

D) $\dfrac{\sqrt{5}}{2}$

E) $\dfrac{2\sqrt{5}}{5}$

13. Given that $\cos x = \dfrac{a}{8} = 0.375$, what is a?

A) 0.125
B) 0.5
C) 3
D) 4
E) 6

14. To what does the following expression reduce?

$(\sin x)(\tan x)(\cos x) + (\cos x)(\cot x)(\sin x)$

A) 1
B) 2
C) $\sin^2 x$
D) $\sin x + \cos x$
E) 1 sin x

15. To what does the following expression reduce?

$(\sin x)(\cot x)(\cos x) + (\cos x)(\tan x)(\sin x)$

A) 1
B) $2\sin^2 x$
C) $\sin^2 x$
D) $\cos x + \sin x$
E) $2\cos x$

16. To what does the following expression reduce?

$(\cos x)(\csc x)(\tan x) + (\sin x)(\sec x)(\cot x)$

A) 1
B) 2
C) $\sin^2 x$
D) $\cos x + \sin x$
E) $1 + \tan^2 x$

17. To what does the following expression reduce?

$(\cos x)(\csc x)(\tan x) + (\sin x)(\sec x)(\tan x)$

A) 1
B) 2
C) $\sin^2 x$
D) $\cos x + \sin x$
E) $1 + \tan^2 x$

Algebra

1. If $x = 2$ and $y = 4$ what is $x^5 - 9y$?

   A) -32
   B) -20
   C) -4
   D) 4
   E) 20

2. A foot contains 12 inches. If a piece of rope is 3.5 feet, how many inches is it?

   A) 6
   B) 30
   C) 36
   D) 40
   E) 42

3. What is the remainder of 17 divided by 5?

   A) 0
   B) 1
   C) 2
   D) 3
   E) 4

4. Joe has c books to read for a class when his teacher assigns an additional 3 books. How many books does Joe need to read after he has read one fifth of those assigned?

   A) $(c/5 + 3)$
   B) $(c/5 - 3)$
   C) $(c/3 + 5)$
   D) $\frac{1}{5}(c + 3)$
   E) $\frac{4}{5}(c + 3)$

5. If $a = 4$, $b = 2$ and $c = 1$ what is $2a^2 - 2ab + c^2$?

A) 0
B) 1
C) 15
D) 16
E) 17

6. A gallon contains 4 quarts, a quart contains 2 pints, a pint contains 2 cups, and a cup contains 8 ounces. How many ounces are in $^3/_4$ of a gallon?

A) 24
B) 32
C) 48
D) 96
E) 192

7. What is the remainder of 47 divided by 7?

A) 0
B) 2
C) 3
D) 5
E) 6

8. A room with x full rows of chairs has every chair filled with a person. If there are y people standing without a chair and z chairs in a row, how many people are in the room?

A) $xz + y$
B) $xy + z$
C) $(x + y)z$
D) $(x + z)y$
E) xz

9. If $x = 2$, $y = 0$ and $z = 7$ what is $2x^y - xyz + xz$?

A) -12
B) 2
C) 12
D) 16
E) 30

10. A dut contains 4 dats and a din contains 3 duts. How many dats are in 5 dins?

A) 12
B) 15
C) 20
D) 60
E) 120

11. What is the remainder of 66 divided by 12?

A) 0
B) 2
C) 5
D) 6
E) 8

12. A jar filled with y beads falls over and exactly half roll out. Someone quickly adds 75 beads back to the jar. If this event happened the same way twice, how many beads would the jar contain after the second set of 75 were added to the jar?

A) $\dfrac{y}{2} + 75$

B) $\dfrac{y}{4} + 75$

C) $\dfrac{y + 450}{4}$

D) $\dfrac{y + 500}{4}$

E) $\dfrac{y + 225}{4}$

Distance Formula

1. What is the distance between the two points shown below?

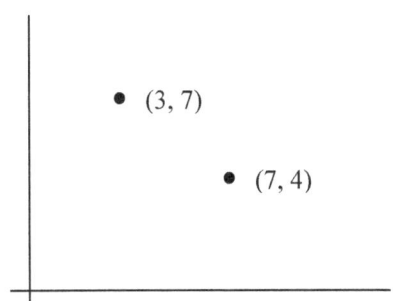

A) 3
B) $\sqrt{19}$
C) 5
D) 7
E) $\sqrt{109}$

2. What is the distance between the two points shown below?

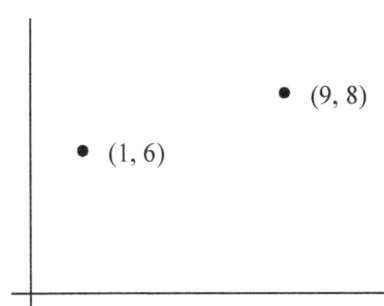

A) $\sqrt{5}$
B) 8
C) $2\sqrt{17}$
D) 10
E) $2\sqrt{29}$

3. What is the distance between the two points shown below?

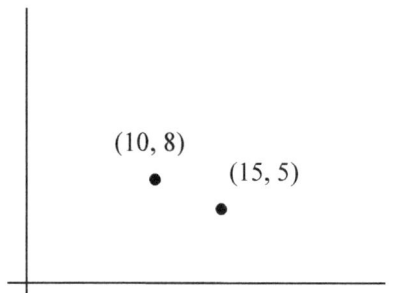

A) $\sqrt{5}$
B) 4
C) 5
D) $\sqrt{34}$
E) 6

4. What is the *x*-coordinate of point A that is $\sqrt{52}$ units away from B?

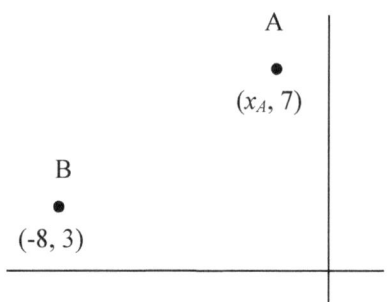

A) -2
B) -1
C) 4
D) 10
E) 14

5. What is the *x*-coordinate of point B that is $\sqrt{58}$ units away from A?

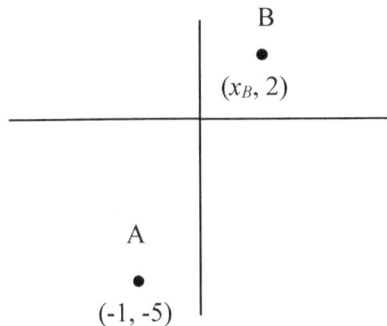

A) -2
B) 2
C) 4
D) 10
E) 12

6. What is the *y*-coordinate of point A that is 5 units away from A?

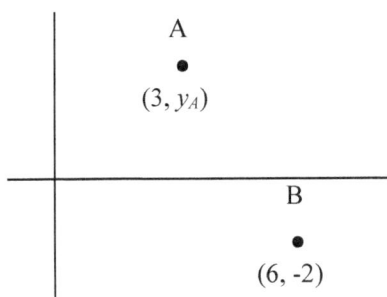

A) -2
B) 2
C) 6
D) 10
E) 12

7. What is the *y*-coordinate of point A that is $\sqrt{97}$ units away from A?

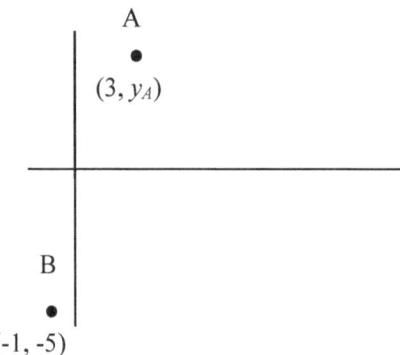

A) 0
B) 4
C) 10
D) 14
E) 16

8. What is the distance between the two points shown below?

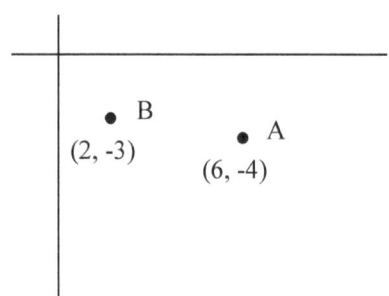

A) $\sqrt{17}$
B) 7
C) $\sqrt{65}$
D) $\sqrt{103}$
E) $\sqrt{113}$

9. What is the distance between the two points shown below?

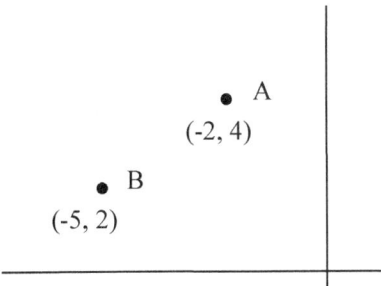

A) 2
B) $\sqrt{8}$
C) $\sqrt{13}$
D) 5
E) $\sqrt{113}$

10. Which of the following sets of points is not $\sqrt{20}$ distance apart?

A) (5, -1) and (7, 3)
B) (5, -1) and (3, 3)
C) (0, -6) and (2, -2)
D) (9, -8) and (7, 4)
E) (9, -8) and (7, -4)

Equation of a Circle

1. What is the equation of a circle whose diameter is 6 and is centered at the point (4, -1)?

   A) $(x - 4)^2 + (y - 1)^2 = 6$
   B) $(x + 4)^2 + (y - 1)^2 = 36$
   C) $(x - 4)^2 + (y + 1)^2 = 36$
   D) $(x - 4)^2 + (y - 1)^2 = 9$
   E) $(x - 4)^2 + (y + 1)^2 = 9$

2. What is the center of the circle defined by the equation: $(x + 4)^2 + (y - 2)^2 = 8$

   A) (-4, 2)
   B) (-4, -2)
   C) (4, -2)
   D) 64
   E) $\sqrt{8}$

3. What is the equation of a circle whose radius is 9 and is centered at the point (-7, -1)?

   A) $(x - 1)^2 + (y - 7)^2 = 3$
   B) $(x + 1)^2 + (y + 7)^2 = 3$
   C) $(x + 7)^2 + (y + 1)^2 = 9$
   D) $(x + 7)^2 + (y + 1)^2 = 81$
   E) $(x + 1)^2 + (y + 7)^2 = 81$

4. What is the radius of the circle defined by the equation: $(x + 4)^2 + (y - 2)^2 = 8$

   A) (-4, 2)
   B) (-4, -2)
   C) (4, -2)
   D) 64
   E) $\sqrt{8}$

5. Which of the following graphs represents the circle with the equation $(x-7)^2 + (y-5)^2 = 9$?

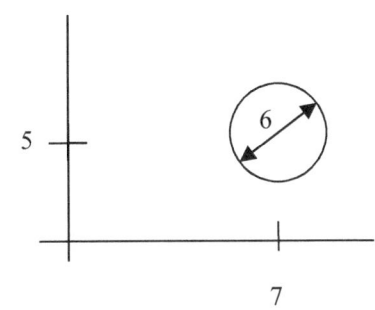

A)

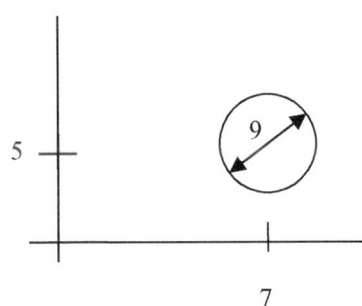

B)

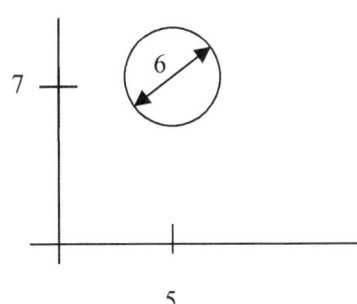

C)

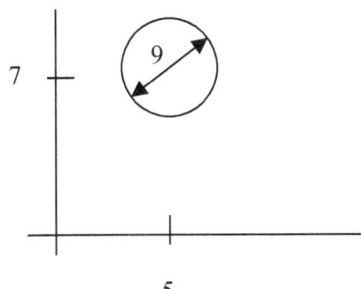

D)

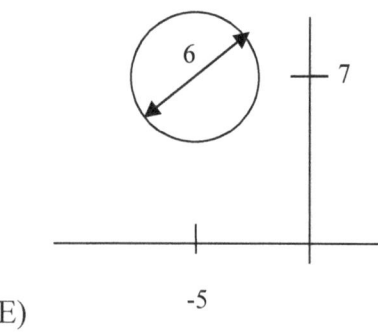

E)

6. What is the equation of a circle whose radius is 16 and is centered at the point (-3, 6)?

A) $(x - 6)^2 + (y - 3)^2 = 4$
B) $(x + 3) + (y - 6) = 16^2$
C) $(x + 3)^2 + (y - 6)^2 = 4$
D) $(x + 3)^2 + (y - 6)^2 = 16$
E) $(x + 3)^2 + (y - 6)^2 = 16^2$

7. Which of the following equations represents the circle shown below?

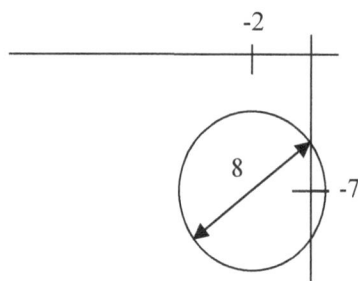

A) $(x - 2)^2 + (y - 7)^2 = 16$
B) $(x + 2) + (y + 7) = 16$
C) $(x - 2)^2 + (y + 7)^2 = 4$
D) $(x + 2)^2 + (y + 7)^2 = 16$
E) $(x + 2)^2 + (y + 7)^2 = 64$

8. Which of the following graphs represents the circle with the equation $(x-8)^2 + (y+5)^2 = 9$?

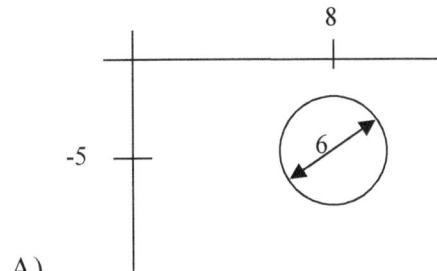
A)

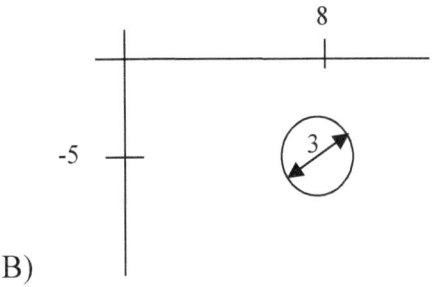
B)

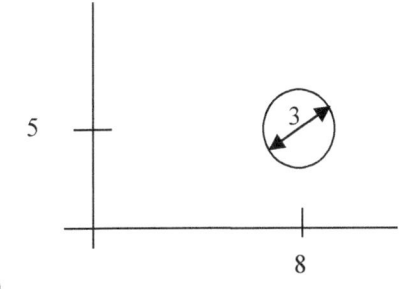
C)

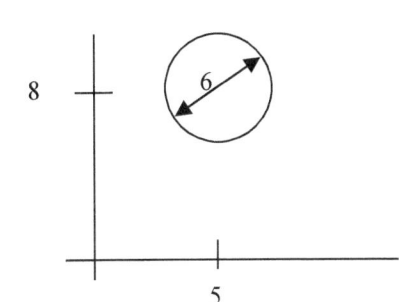
D)

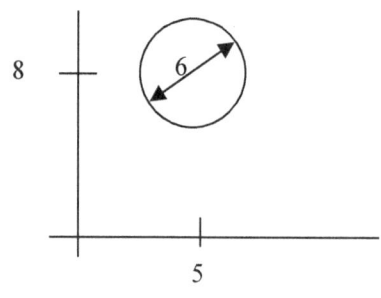

E)

9. What is the equation of a circle whose radius is 5 and is centered at the point (6, 2)?

A) $(x - 6)^2 + (y + 2)^2 = 25$
B) $(x - 6)^2 + (y - 2)^2 = 25$
C) $(x + 6) + (y + 2) = 25$
D) $(x + 2)^2 + (y + 6)^2 = 5$
E) $(x - 2)^2 + (y - 6)^2 = \sqrt{5}$

10. Which of the following equations represents the circle shown below?

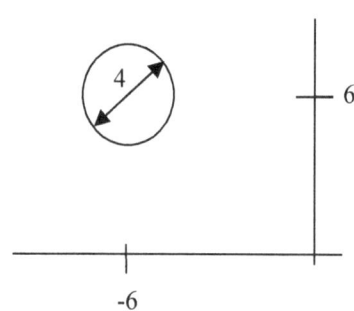

A) $(x + 6)^2 + (y - 4)^2 = 16$
B) $(x - 4) + (y + 4) = 4$
C) $(x - 6)^2 + (y + 6)^2 = 4$
D) $(x + 6) + (y - 6) = 4$
E) $(x + 6)^2 + (y - 6)^2 = 4$

Functions & Polynomials

1. If $f(x) = 0.5x^4$ and $g(x) = 3$, what is $f(g(x))$?

   A) 4.5
   B) 9.5
   C) 13.5
   D) 20.5
   E) 40.5

2. How many times does $f(x) = (x - 6)(x + 3)(x - 7)(x + 4)$ cross the x-axis?

   A) 0
   B) 3
   C) 4
   D) 6
   E) 7

3. If $f(x) = (x - 2)(x + 4)(x - 2)(x + 5)$ and $g(x) = (x + 4)(x - 2)$, what is $\dfrac{f(x)}{g(x)}$?

   A) 0
   B) $(x - 2)(x + 5)$
   C) $(x - 2)(x + 4)$
   D) $(x - 2)$
   E) $(x + 5)$

4. If $f(x) = (x - 5)(x + 1)$ and $g(x) = (x + 1)(x + 3)$, what is $f(x) - g(x)$?

   A) $(x - 5)(x + 3)$
   B) $x^2 - 2x - 15$
   C) -8
   D) $8(x - 1)$
   E) $-8(x + 1)$

5. If $f(x) = 2x^3 - 3x$ and $g(x) = 3x$, what is $f(g(x))$?

   A) 45
   B) 54
   C) $27x^3 - 3x$
   D) $54x^3 - 9x$
   E) $36x^3 - 9$

6. How many times does $f(x) = x^2(x + 3)(x + 1)$ cross the x-axis?

A) 3
B) 4
C) 5
D) 6
E) 7

7. If $f(x) = x^5(x + 7)$ and $g(x) = x^{-5}(x + 4)$, what is $f(x) \cdot g(x)$?

A) $(x + 7)(x + 4)$
B) $x^2 + 3x + 28$
C) $28x^{25} + x^2 + 3x$
D) 3
E) 28

8. If $f(x) = (x - 2)(x^2 - 1)$ and $g(x) = (x + 3)(x + 2)$, what is $f(x) + g(x)$?

A) $x^3 - 3x^2 - 6x - 4$
B) $-7x^2 - 6x + 6$
C) $x^3 - x^2 + 4x + 8$
D) $2x^2 + 5x + 5$
E) $8x - 8$

9. How many times does $f(x) = x(x + 2)(x + 3)(x - 2)(x + 3)(x - 1)(x + 1)$ cross the x-axis?

A) 3
B) 4
C) 5
D) 6
E) 7

10. If $f(x) = x^4 + 1$, $g(x) = x/2$, and $h(x) = 4$, what is $f(g(h(x)))$?

A) 17
B) 18
C) 64
D) 256
E) 257

Greatest Common Factor / Least Common Multiple

1. If x is a positive integer that divides both 98 and 42, but divides neither 7 nor 10, what is the sum of digits in x?

   A) 3
   B) 4
   C) 5
   D) 7
   E) 10

2. What is the least common multiple of 10 and 12?

   A) 2
   B) 4
   C) 60
   D) 90
   E) 120

3. What is the greatest common factor of 105 and 135?

   A) 15
   B) 18
   C) 20
   D) 30
   E) 35

4. A pendulum swings back and forth every 6 seconds. A second pendulum takes 14 seconds to swing back and forth. If they start at the back position together at time = 0, how many seconds until they both arrive at the back position again?

   A) 2
   B) 6
   C) 21
   D) 28
   E) 42

5. If *x* is a positive integer that divides both 225 and 100, but doesn't divide 20, what is the sum of digits in *x*?

A) 3
B) 4
C) 5
D) 7
E) 10

6. What is the least common multiple of 15 and 18?

A) 90
B) 120
C) 135
D) 150
E) 180

7. Two planets orbit a sun. The first planet takes 8 earth months to orbit the sun and the second planet takes 12 earth months to orbit the sun. If they are aligned beside each other at time month = 0, how many months until they are again aligned beside each other at that same point?

A) 24
B) 32
C) 40
D) 48
E) 56

8. If *x* is a positive integer that divides both 112 and 144, but doesn't divide 8, what is the sum of digits in *x*?

A) 3
B) 4
C) 5
D) 7
E) 10

9. What is the least common multiple of 7 and 15?

A) 30
B) 35
C) 70
D) 105
E) 135

10. What is the greatest common factor of 112 and 56?

A) 7
B) 28
C) 32
D) 36
E) 56

11. Jake and his son Stephen walk beside each other. Jake can walk 6 yards in 6 steps. Stephen takes 15 steps to walk 6 yards. If they both start at the same point with their right foot, how many yards until they are both walking with their right foot at exactly the same time again?

A) 2
B) 6
C) 12
D) 24
E) 30

12. If x is a positive integer that divides both 140 and 105, but doesn't divide 5, or 7 what is the sum of digits in x?

A) 5
B) 6
C) 7
D) 8
E) 10

General Equation of a Line

1. What is the slope of a line containing points (-3, 7) and (4, 8)?

   A) -7
   B) -1
   C) $-1/7$
   D) $1/7$
   E) 7

2. The scale on both axes of the standard (x, y) coordinate plane below is the same. What is the best estimate for the slope of $\overline{AB}$?

   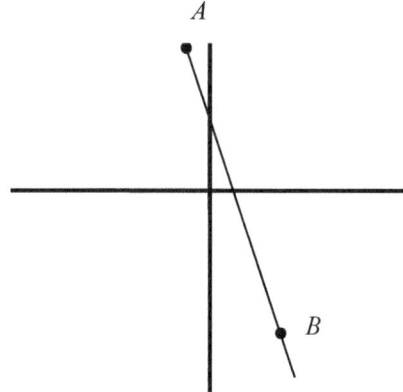

   A) -1000
   B) -2
   C) $-1/2$
   D) $1/2$
   E) 2

3. In the (x, y) coordinate plane, what is the y-intercept of the line $6x - 7y = 3$?

   A) $-7/3$
   B) $-6/7$
   C) $-3/7$
   D) $3/7$
   E) $6/7$

4. Given that $y = \frac{5}{9}x + 7$ describes a line, where does the line cross the *x*-axis?

A) $\frac{-63}{5}$

B) -9

C) $\frac{-35}{9}$

D) $\frac{35}{9}$

E) $\frac{63}{5}$

5. Which equation describes the line that goes through (1, 4) and has slope = -4?

A) $y = -4x - 8$
B) $y = -4x + 8$
C) $y = -4x + 2$
D) $y = 6x$
E) $y = -6x$

6. Which equation describes the line that goes through (9, 1) and (3, -6)?

A) $y = x - 1$

B) $y = \frac{7}{6}x - 10$

C) $y = \frac{6}{7}x - \frac{19}{2}$

D) $y = -\frac{7}{6}x - \frac{19}{2}$

E) $y = \frac{7}{6}x - \frac{19}{2}$

7. Which of the following lines is perpendicular to the line described by $y = -8x + 27$?

A) $y = -8x - \dfrac{1}{27}$

B) $y = 8x + 27$

C) $y = -\dfrac{1}{8}x + 27$

D) $y = 8x - 27$

E) $y = \dfrac{1}{8}x + 27$

8. Which of the following lines is parallel to the line described by $y = -8x + 27$?

A) $y = -8x - \dfrac{1}{27}$

B) $y = 6x + 27$

C) $y = -\dfrac{1}{8}x + 27$

D) $y = -6x - 27$

E) $y = \dfrac{1}{8}x + 27$

9. What is the slope of a line containing points (2, 4) and (0, 0)?

A) -4
B) -2
C) 0
D) 2
E) 4

10. The scale on both axes of the standard (x, y) coordinate plane below is the same. What is the best estimate for the slope of $\overline{AB}$?

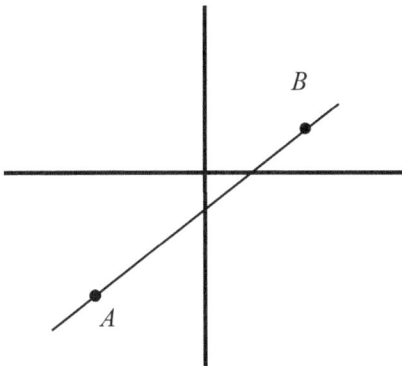

A) -2
B) -1
C) 0
D) $1/10$
E) 1

11. In the (x, y) coordinate plane, what is the y-intercept of the line $2x + 3y = -4$?

A) $-4/3$
B) -1
C) $-2/3$
D) $2/3$
E) $4/3$

12. Given that $7x - 5y = 1$ describes a line, what is the x-intercept?

A) -7
B) $-1/5$
C) $1/7$
D) 5
E) 7

13. Which equation describes the line that goes through (3, 8) and has slope = $-1/2$?

A) $x + 2y = 19$
B) $x - 2y = 19$
C) $2x + y = 19$
D) $2x - y = 19$
E) $x + 2y = -19$

14. Which equation describes the line that goes through (6, -4) and (0, 2)?

A) $x + y = 2$
B) $x - y = 2$
C) $2x + 2y = 2$
D) $3x + 3y = 2$
E) $x + y = 1$

15. Which of the following lines is perpendicular to the line described by $8x + 2y = 27$?

A) $x - 4y = 24$
B) $x + 4y = 24$
C) $4x + 4y = -6$
D) $4x + 4y = 6$
E) $4x + 2y = -6$

16. Which of the following lines is parallel to the line described by $8x + 4y = 27$?

A) $6x - 4y = 24$
B) $6x + 4y = 24$
C) $6x + 4y = -6$
D) $4x + 2y = 6$
E) $4x - 2y = -6$

17. When graphed in the standard (x, y) coordinate plane, the lines $x = 4$ and $y = 2x-6$ intersect at what point?

A) $(2, 4)$
B) $(4, 2)$
C) $(4, 4)$
D) $(4, 6)$
E) $(6, 4)$

18. Given that $9x + 4y = 3$ is a line, where does it cross the x-axis?

A) $x = -4/9$
B) $x = 1/3$
C) $x = -3/4$
D) $x = 4$
E) $x = 9$

19. Given that $y = 3x + 27$ is a line, where does it cross the x-axis?

A) $x = 4/9$
B) $x = -1/3$
C) $x = 3/4$
D) $x = 4$
E) $x = -9$

20. Given that a line passes through $(3, 1)$ and $(-2, 4)$, where does it cross the x-axis?

A) $x = 3/5$
B) $x = 14/5$
C) $x = 3/4$
D) $x = 9/5$
E) $x = 14/3$

Graphing and the (x, y) Coordinate System

1. In the standard (x, y) coordinate plane, 3 corners of a rectangle are (-7, 2), (6, 2), and (6, -5). What is the location of the fourth corner?

   A) (-7, 5)
   B) (-7, -5)
   C) (7, -5)
   D) (2, 6)
   E) (2, -6)

2. In the standard (x, y) coordinate plane, three corners of a rectangle are (-7, 2), (6, 2), and (6, -5). What is the location of the fourth corner of a rectangle if the rectangle is shifted 3 units in the positive x direction and 3 units in the negative y direction?

   A) (-10, 8)
   B) (-7, -5)
   C) (-10, -2)
   D) (-4, -8)
   E) (-4, -2)

3. The graph $y = 4x^2 - 1$ is in the standard (x, y) coordinate plane. What is its shape?

   A) straight line with a negative slope
   B) straight line with a positive slope
   C) horizontal line
   D) parabola, upright U-shaped
   E) parabola, upside-down U

4. The graph $y = 4x^2 - 1$ is in the standard (x, y) coordinate plane. Which of the following could be the x-intercept?

A) -2
B) 0
C) ½
D) 1
E) 2

5. In the standard (x, y) coordinate plane, 2 corners of a right triangle are (-3, 1) and (-3, -10). If the base of the triangle is parallel with the x-axis, which of the following could be the location of the third corner?

A) (14, -3)
B) (-3, 14)
C) (-3, 14)
D) (14, -10)
E) (-3, 1)

6. In the standard (x, y) coordinate plane, 2 corners of a right triangle are (-7, 6) and (-2, 8). The base of the triangle is parallel with the x-axis. Which of the following could be the location of the third corner of the triangle after the triangle is shifted 1 unit in the negative x direction and 2 units in the negative y direction?

A) (-2, 6)
B) (-7, 8)
C) (-3, 4)
D) (-9, 7)
E) (-4, 5)

7. The graph $y = 18x - 9$ is in the standard (x, y) coordinate plane. What is its shape?

A) straight line with a negative slope
B) straight line with a positive slope
C) horizontal line
D) parabola, U-shaped
E) parabola, upside-down U

8. The graph $y = \sqrt{x} - 5$ is in the standard (x, y) coordinate plane. Which of the following could be the x-intercept?

A) -25
B) -5
C) 0
D) 5
E) 25

9. In the standard (x, y) coordinate plane, the center of a circle is at (5, -3). If the radius of the circle is 7, which of the following points could lie on the circle?

A) (12, -3)
B) (-3, 12)
C) (7, 0)
D) (0, 7)
E) (5, 12)

10. In the standard (x, y) coordinate plane, the center of a circle is at $(5, -3)$. If the radius of the circle is 4, and the circle is moved 2 units in the positive x-direction and 6 units in the negative y-direction, which of the following points could lie on the circle?

A) $(7, -5)$
B) $(-7, -5)$
C) $(9, 3)$
D) $(1, 3)$
E) $(7, -9)$

11. The graph $y^2 = -x^2 + 3$ is in the standard (x, y) coordinate plane. What is its shape?

A) hyperbola
B) circle
C) horizontal line
D) parabola, upright U-shaped
E) parabola, upside-down U

12. The graph $y^2 = -x^2 + 3$ is in the standard (x, y) coordinate plane. Which of the following could be the y-intercept?

A) -3
B) -1
C) 0
D) 1
E) $\sqrt{3}$

Perimeter

1. Given rectangle ABCD, what is the length of the perimeter?

   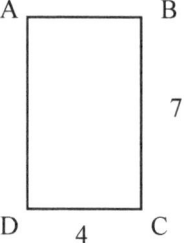

   A) 11
   B) 15
   C) 18
   D) 22
   E) 28

2. Given that rectangle ABCD has a perimeter of 14, what is the length of side AD?

   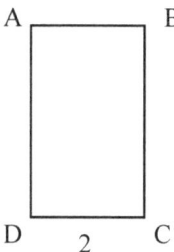

   A) 2
   B) 5
   C) 6
   D) 7
   E) 9

3. Given square ABCD, what is the length of the perimeter?

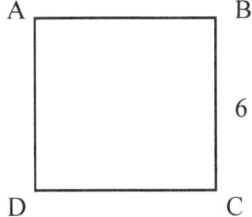

A) 12
B) 24
C) 28
D) 30
E) 36

4. Given the figure below, what is the length of the perimeter?

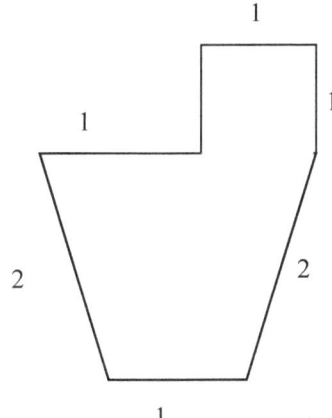

A) 8
B) 9
C) 10
D) 11
E) 13

5. Given the figure below, which has all right angles, what is the length of the perimeter?

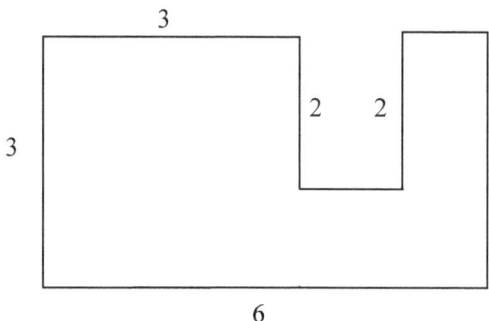

A) 16
B) 18
C) 22
D) 31
E) 36

6. Given that the figure below has perimeter equal to 26, what is the length of *a*?

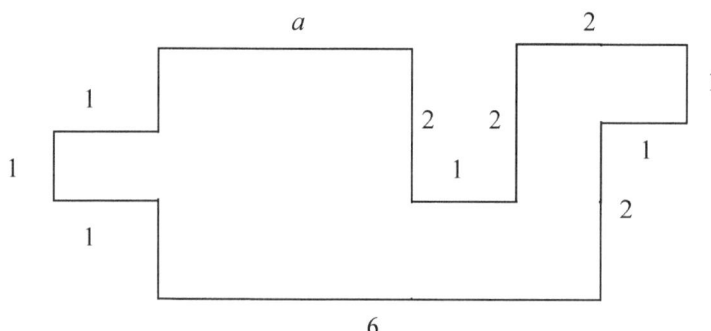

A) 4
B) 5
C) 6
D) 7
E) 8

7. What is the length of the perimeter of the figure below?

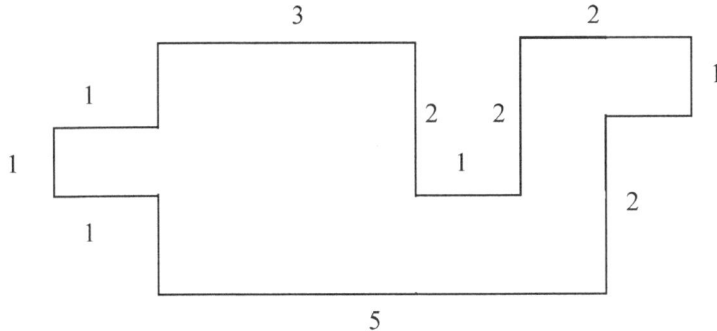

A) 16
B) 18
C) 20
D) 22
E) 24

8. Given that the figure below has perimeter equal to 24, what is the sum of *a* and *b*?

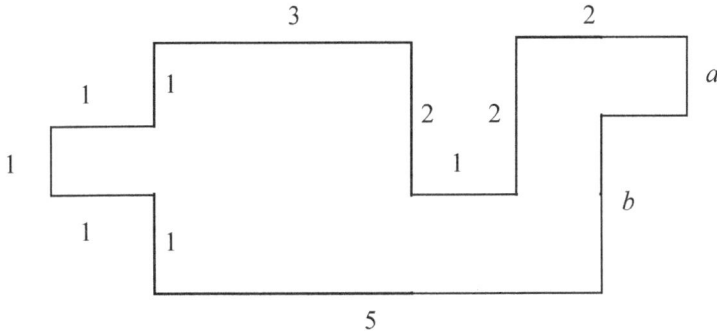

A) 1
B) 3
C) 4
D) 5
E) 6

9. Given the figure below, what is the length of the perimeter?

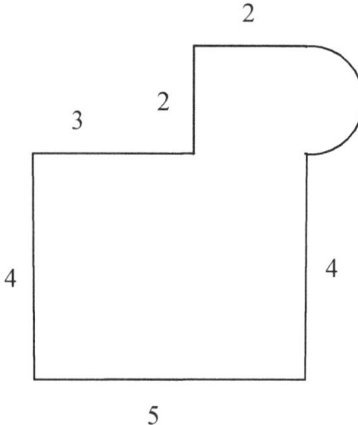

A) 16
B) 16+2π
C) 20
D) 20+π
E) 20+2π

10. What is the perimeter of the figure below if a half circle is added to the side of the larger rectangle as shown in the figure below?

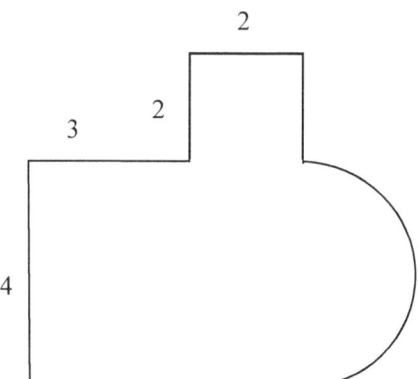

A) 13
B) 13+2π
C) 15+π
D) 16+2π
E) 18+2π

Area

1. Given rectangle ABCD, what is the area?

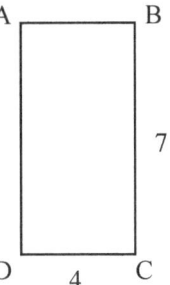

   A) 11
   B) 14
   C) 18
   D) 22
   E) 28

2. Given that rectangle ABCD has a perimeter of 14 and one side is length 2, what is the area?

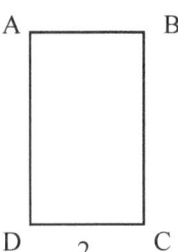

   A) 7
   B) 10
   C) 14
   D) 22
   E) 28

3. Given that a triangle, with a base half the length of a side of square ABCD and a height of 3, is added to square ABCD, what is the area of the new figure?

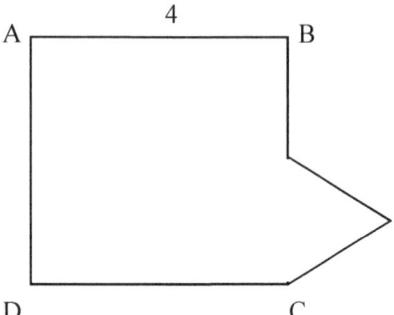

A) 16
B) 19
C) 20
D) 22
E) 30

4. Given the figure below, what is the area?

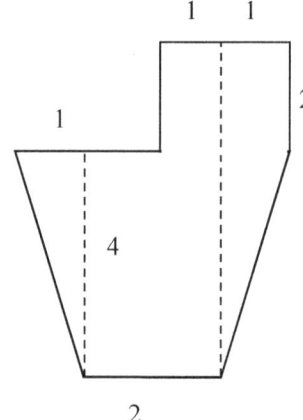

A) 8
B) 10
C) 12
D) 14
E) 16

5. Given that the figure below has an area of 13 and that the trapezoid has an area of 9, what is the length of side a?

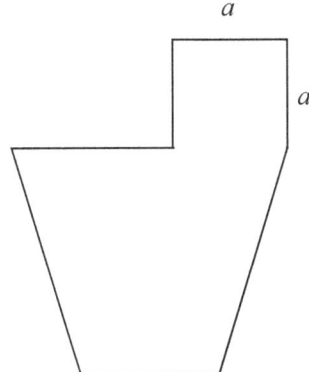

A) 2
B) 3
C) 4
D) 5
E) 9

6. Given the figure below, which has all right angles, what is the area?

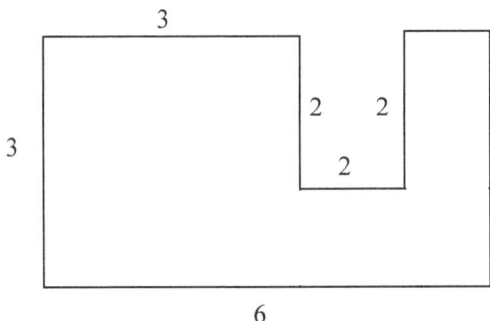

A) 9
B) 10
C) 12
D) 14
E) 18

7. Given that the figure below has area equal to 17, what is the length of *a*?

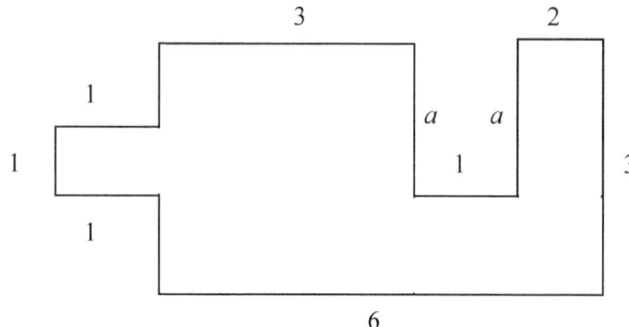

A) 1
B) 2
C) 5
D) 6
E) 7

8. Given the figure below what is the area?

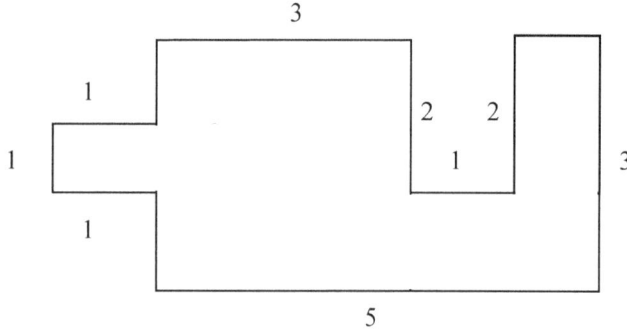

A) 8
B) 9
C) 11
D) 13
E) 14

9. What is the area of the figure if a half circle is added to the side of the smaller square as shown below?

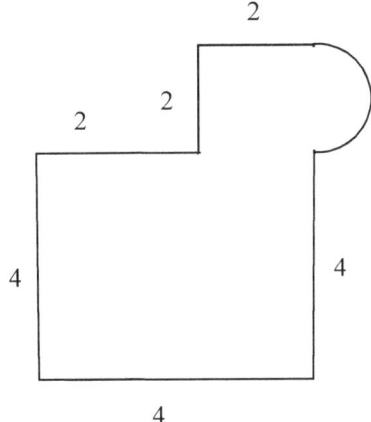

A) 16
B) $16+\pi$
C) $20+\pi/2$
D) $20+\pi$
E) $22+\pi/2$

10. What is the area of the figure if a half circle is added to the side of the larger rectangle as shown below?

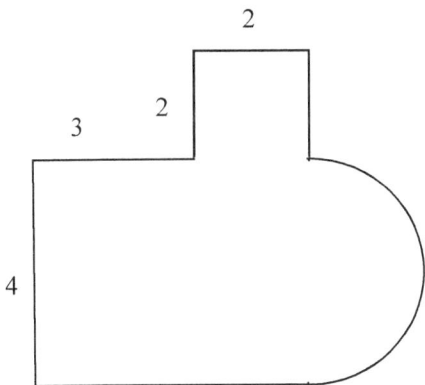

A) 16
B) $16+\pi$
C) $16+2\pi$
D) 24
E) $24+2\pi$

Polygons and Angles

1. If a regular polygon has interior angles with a measure of 120°, how many sides does the polygon have?

   A) 3
   B) 4
   C) 5
   D) 6
   E) 7

2. If a regular polygon has interior angles that sum to 180°, how many sides does the polygon have?

   A) 3
   B) 4
   C) 5
   D) 6
   E) 7

3. If a regular polygon has interior angles with a measure of 108°, how many sides does the polygon have?

   A) 3
   B) 4
   C) 5
   D) 6
   E) 7

4. If a regular polygon has interior angles with a measure of 140°, how many sides does the polygon have?

   A) 8
   B) 9
   C) 10
   D) 11
   E) 12

5. If a regular polygon has interior angles with a measure of 150°, how many sides does the polygon have?

A) 8
B) 9
C) 10
D) 11
E) 12

6. What is the measure of its interior angle if a regular polygon has 5 sides?

A) 90°
B) 108°
C) 120°
D) 144°
E) 180°

7. What is the measure of its interior angle if a regular polygon has 10 sides?

A) 72°
B) 80°
C) 90°
D) 120°
E) 144°

8. What is the measure of its interior angle if a regular polygon has 9 sides?

A) 72°
B) 80°
C) 90°
D) 140°
E) 144°

9. What is the measure of its interior angle if a regular polygon has 3 sides?

A) 52°
B) 60°
C) 108°
D) 120°
E) 144°

10. What is the measure of the angle between two sides if a regular polygon has 6 sides?

A) 90°
B) 100°
C) 120°
D) 135°
E) 144°

11. The geometric figures below are examples of convex hexagons. Which of the following conclusions can be drawn about the sums of the measures of the interior angles of each hexagon and for any two hexagons?

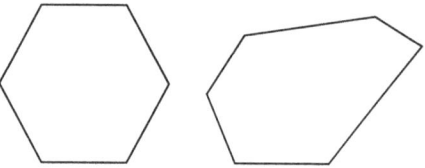

A) The sums are always different.
B) The sums are the same only when the octagons are congruent.
C) The sums are the same if and only if the octagons are similar.
D) The sums are the same but cannot be determined from the given information.
E) The sums are always the same: 1080°

Simplification and Factoring

1. Which of the following is equivalent to the expression $x^5 - 9x$?

   A) $(x^2 - 3)(x^3 + 3x)$
   B) $(3x^3 - 3)(3^2 - 3x)$
   C) $(x^2 + 3)(x^3 + 3x)$
   D) $(3x^2 + 3)(3x^3 + x^2)$
   E) $(x^2 - 3)(x^3 - 3x^2)$

2. Which of the following is equivalent to the expression $x^2 + 3x - 18$?

   A) $(x - 2)(x + 9)$
   B) $(x + 2)(x - 9)$
   C) $(x - 6)(x + 3)$
   D) $(x + 3)(x - 6)$
   E) $(x - 3)(x + 6)$

3. Which of the following is equivalent to the product $(x + 3)(x^2 - 5)(x - x^2)$?

   A) $x^5 + 2x^4 - 5x^3 - 13x^2 + 15x$
   B) $-x^5 + 2x^4 - 8x^3 - 10x^2 + 15x$
   C) $-x^5 - 2x^4 + 8x^3 + 10x^2 - 15x$
   D) $x^5 + 2x^4 - 8x^3 - 10x^2 + 15x$
   E) $x^4 + 2x^3 - 5x^2 - 13x + 15$

4. Which of the following is equivalent to the product $x^6 (2x - 4)^2$?

   A) $4x^8 - 16x^7 + 16x^6$
   B) $4x^2 - 16x + 16x$
   C) $4x^2 + 16x - 16x$
   D) $4x^8 - 16x^6$
   E) $4x^8 + 16x^6$

5. For all nonzero a and c, $\dfrac{5a^3c^4}{ac^6}=?$

A) $\dfrac{5a^3c^2}{a}$

B) $\dfrac{5a^2}{c^2}$

C) $5ac^2$

D) $\dfrac{a^2}{5c^2}$

E) $\dfrac{5ac^4}{c^2}$

6. Which of the following is a simplified equivalent of $\dfrac{15a^3c^4}{3ac^6}$?

A) $\dfrac{5a^3c^2}{a}$

B) $\dfrac{5a^2}{c^2}$

C) $5ac^2$

D) $\dfrac{a^2}{5c^2}$

E) $\dfrac{5ac^4}{c^2}$

7. Which of the following is a simplified equivalent of $\dfrac{(6x^2 y)^3}{3xy^2}$?

A) $\dfrac{6x^5 y^3}{3xy^2}$

B) $2x^4 y$

C) $72x^5 y$

D) $\dfrac{72x^4 y}{3xy}$

E) $24x^5 y$

8. Which of the following is equivalent to $\dfrac{5x^3}{9y}$?

A) $\dfrac{5(x^5 y^3)^2}{3xy^2}$

B) $\dfrac{(5x^5 y^3)^2}{3xy^2}$

C) $\dfrac{5x^5(y^3)^2}{3xy^2}$

D) $\left(\dfrac{5x^5 y^3}{3xy^2}\right)^2$

E) $\dfrac{5x^5 y^3}{(3xy^2)^2}$

9. Which of the following is equivalent to
   $2x^4y^{-2}$?

A) $\dfrac{4(x^5y^3)^2}{2xy^8}$

B) $\dfrac{(4x^5y^3)^2}{2xy^8}$

C) $\dfrac{4x^5(y^3)^2}{2xy^8}$

D) $\left(\dfrac{4x^5y^3}{2xy^8}\right)^2$

E) $\dfrac{4x^5y^3}{(2xy^4)^2}$

10. Which of the following is equivalent to
    $4x^8y^{-10}$?

A) $\dfrac{4(x^5y^3)^2}{2xy^8}$

B) $\dfrac{(4x^5y^3)^2}{2xy^8}$

C) $\dfrac{4x^5(y^3)^2}{2xy^8}$

D) $\left(\dfrac{4x^5y^3}{2xy^8}\right)^2$

E) $\dfrac{4x^5y^3}{(2xy^4)^2}$

Sequences and Series

1. If the first term in an arithmetic series is 3, the last term is 99, and the sum is 1275, what are the first three terms?

   A) 3, 7, 11
   B) 3, 6, 9
   C) 3, 9, 15
   D) 3, 11, 19
   E) 3, 8, 13

2. The first, second, and third terms of a geometric sequence are gh^2, g^4h^4, and g^9h^6 in that order. What is the 10th term of the sequence?

   A) g^5h^{100}
   B) $g^{10}h^{10}$
   C) $g^{10}h^{100}$
   D) $g^{50}h^{100}$
   E) $g^{100}h^{20}$

3. If the ones digit of 7^2 is 9 and the ones digit of 7^3 is 3, what is the ones digit of 7^{17}?

   A) 0
   B) 1
   C) 3
   D) 7
   E) 9

4. If the first term in an arithmetic series is 2, the last term is 212, and the sum is 1605, what are the first three terms?

   A) 2, 11, 20
   B) 190, 201, 212
   C) 2, 9, 16
   D) 182, 197, 212
   E) 2, 17, 32

5. The first and second terms of a geometric sequence are $b^2\sqrt{a}$ and ab^3 in that order. What is the 100th term of the sequence?

A) $\dfrac{a^{51}b^{100}}{\sqrt{a}}$

B) $a^{50}b^{102}$

C) $a^{50}b^{101}$

D) $\dfrac{a^{51}b^{100}}{\sqrt{ab}}$

E) $\dfrac{a^{50}b^{100}}{\sqrt{a}}$

6. If the hundreds digit of 5^3 is 1 and the hundreds digit of 5^4 is 6, what is the hundreds digit of 5^{50}?

A) 1
B) 2
C) 5
D) 6
E) 9

7. If the first term in an arithmetic series is 4, the last term is 172, and the sum is 2200, what are the last three terms?

A) 4, 11, 18
B) 158, 165, 172
C) 4, 9, 14
D) 166, 169, 172
E) 150, 161, 172

8. The first and second terms of a geometric sequence are $\dfrac{y^3}{x}$ and y^6 in that order. What is the 99th term of the sequence?

A) $x^{99}y^{300}$

B) $x^{97}y^{297}$

C) $\dfrac{y^{300}}{x^{300}}$

D) $\dfrac{y^{297}}{x^{305}}$

E) $x^{-97}y^{297}$

9. The first five terms in a series are 0, 2, 6, 12, and 20. If the series contains both arithmetic and geometric components, what are the next three terms?

A) 30, 42, 56
B) 30, 45, 60
C) 22, 28, 40
D) 20, 22, 28
E) 15, 21, 28

10. The first five terms in a series are 0, 3, 9, 18, and 30. If the series contains both arithmetic and geometric components, what are the next three terms?

A) 30, 33, 42
B) 33, 42, 60
C) 45, 63, 84
D) 57, 138, 411
E) 81, 273, 419

Probability and Proportions

1. If a box contains 12 red balls, 8 green balls, and 10 yellow balls, what is the probability that you will blindly choose a green ball?

   A) 8/30
   B) 10/30
   C) 12/30
   D) 8/20
   E) 12/20

2. A box contained 12 red balls, 8 green balls, and 10 yellow balls. Given that you just removed a red ball, what is the probability that you will blindly choose a green ball?

   A) 8/29
   B) 10/29
   C) 12/29
   D) 8/19
   E) 12/19

3. Using the table of probabilities below, what is the probability that $x > 3$?

x	p
0	0.05
1	0.35
2	0.15
3	0.10
4	0.05
5	0.30

   A) 0.10
   B) 0.35
   C) 0.40
   D) 0.45
   E) 0.55

4. A ball player's historical performance is given below. For example, 20% of the time our player strikes out. Using history to obtain probabilities, what is the probability that the player will get a hit?

Result of At Bat	p
Strike out	0.20
Safe on First	0.20
Safe on Second	0.15
Safe on Third	0.10
Home Run	0.05
Out or Fielder's Choice	0.30

A) 0.10
B) 0.15
C) 0.20
D) 0.50
E) 0.80

5. A soccer team needs 3 goalies. Given that 6 goalies try out in addition to Jessie, what is the probability that Jessie will make the team?

A) $1/7$
B) $1/6$
C) $1/3$
D) $3/7$
E) $3/6$

6. A standard card deck contains 4 each of 13 different cards, totaling 52 cards. During a card game, Tom shows his cards and he has a seven and an eight. Camryn has a seven and a nine. What is the probability of Camryn winning by drawing a seven or a nine?

A) $2/52$
B) $2/48$
C) $4/48$
D) $5/52$
E) $5/48$

7. The following table gives the number of prizes that will be given away in a lottery. If 100,000 people enter the lottery, what is the probability that you will win more than $100?

Prize	Number Given Away
$10	100
$100	50
$250	10
$500	5
$1000	2
$50,000	1

A) $17/100,000$
B) $18/100,000$
C) $67/100,000$
D) $68/100,000$
E) $168/100,000$

8. A mini roulette wheel contains 30 pie pieces, half black and half red, each numbered with a unique number from 1 to 30. The game is played by spinning the wheel and dropping a marble on the wheel. When the wheel stops, if the marble lands on the pie piece(s) on which you bet, you win. You can bet on a specific number, on black or red, or on odd or even numbers. If seven of the black pie pieces are odd, what is the probability that the marble lands on a red, odd pie piece?

A) $1/8$
B) $1/7$
C) $1/5$
D) $7/30$
E) $8/30$

9. A jar contains 5 red marbles, 5 clear marbles, and 5 blue marbles. You can grab 2 at a time, what is the probability that you will grab at least one red marble in your first grab?

A) $75/225$
B) $100/225$
C) $125/225$
D) $10/15$
E) $200/225$

10. Historical performance for a store's semi-annual clearance sale is given below. For example, 50% of the people who come in the store ask questions, but only 35 of those 50 actually make a purchase. Using history to obtain probabilities, given that a customer doesn't ask questions, what is the probability that he will make a purchase?

	Buy	No Buy	Total
Asks Questions	35	15	50
No Questions	10	40	50
Total	45	55	100

A) 0.10
B) 0.15
C) 0.20
D) 0.40
E) 0.50

11. If the probability Terrance will make a free throw is 0.8, what is the probability that he will NOT make the free throw?

A) 0.0
B) 0.1
C) 0.2
D) 0.8
E) 1.8

Expressions

1. The area of a triangle is given by $A=\frac{1}{2}bh$. If the base b increases by a factor of 10 so that $b_{new} = 10b$, which of the following is true about the new area?

    A) It is unchanged
    B) It is one tenth as large
    C) It is 10 units larger
    D) It is five times larger
    E) It is ten times larger

2. If $3x + 4 \leq 7$ is true, which of the following is true about x?

    A) Less than 1
    B) Less than -1
    C) Less than or equal to 1
    D) Less than or equal to -1
    E) Greater than or equal to 1

3. If x is increased by 4 and the resulting number is then multiplied by 20 what expression defines the final number?

    A) (x + 4 + 20)
    B) (x + 4) + 20
    C) (x + 4)/20
    D) 20(x + 4)
    E) x(20 + 4)

4. Timmy has five dollars to spend at the corner store. How many candy bars can he buy if they cost x dollars each?

    A) $x/5$
    B) $5/x$
    C) $5x$
    D) $x - 5$
    E) $5 - x$

5. Kayla shopped for groceries with costs in mind. She buys 5 boxes of cereal at x dollars per box, 2 gallons of milk at y dollars per gallon, and 3 loaves of bread at z dollars per loaf. If there is a 1% tax on the sum of her purchases, what expression defines the tax on her final bill?

A) $5x + 2y + 3z$
B) $0.10(5x + 2y + 3z)$
C) $0.01(5x + 2y + 3z)$
D) $0.90(5x + 2y + 3z)$
E) $0.99(5x + 2y + 3z)$

6. Jeff worries about maintaining a B average (at least 80%) in his Algebra class. His scores are 75%, 82%, and 80%. He gets to choose how many more assignments he turns in (n). If all the scores have equal weight which equation will allow him to correctly calculate how many x% scores are needed to get that 80% B-average?

A) $\dfrac{(75 + 82 + 80 + nx)}{n - 3} = 80$

B) $\dfrac{(75 + 82 + 80 + nx)}{n} = 80$

C) $\dfrac{(75 + 82 + 80 + 80n)}{n + 3} = 80$

D) $\dfrac{(75 + 82 + 80 + nx)}{n + 3} = 80$

E) $\dfrac{(75 + 82 + 80 + 80x)}{n - 3} = 80$

7. Two numbers are *reciprocals* if their product is equal to 1. If x and y are reciprocals and x is at least 2, then which of the following is not always true about y?

A) $y < 1/2$.
B) $y < 1$
C) $y < 2$
D) $y > 0$.
E) $0 < y \leq 1/2$

8. All of the following graphs have equal scales on the axes. Which graph identifies a point where the y-coordinate is half of the x-coordinate?

A)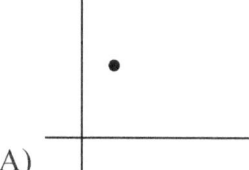

B)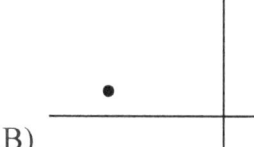

C)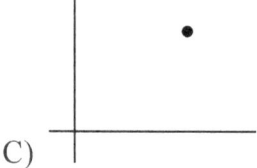

D)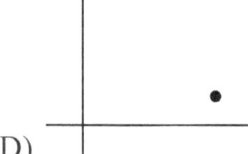

E)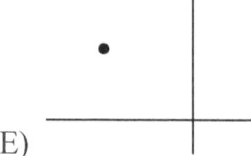

9. Which of the following is true for all negative consecutive integers a and b such that $a > b$?

A) $a + b$ is even
B) $b^2 - a^2$ is odd
C) $a^2 + b^2$ is even
D) a is odd
E) b is odd

10. Brolin keeps a money jar for allowance. When the money jar is empty he can get a loan from his parents; this equates to having negative money in his jar. Which of the following graphs correctly depicts the amount of money Brolin has at the end of each day of the week if he starts Monday with $10, spends $4 on snacks on Tuesday, spends $5 on gas on Thursday, borrows $10 for the movies on Friday, and gets his $15 allowance on Saturday.

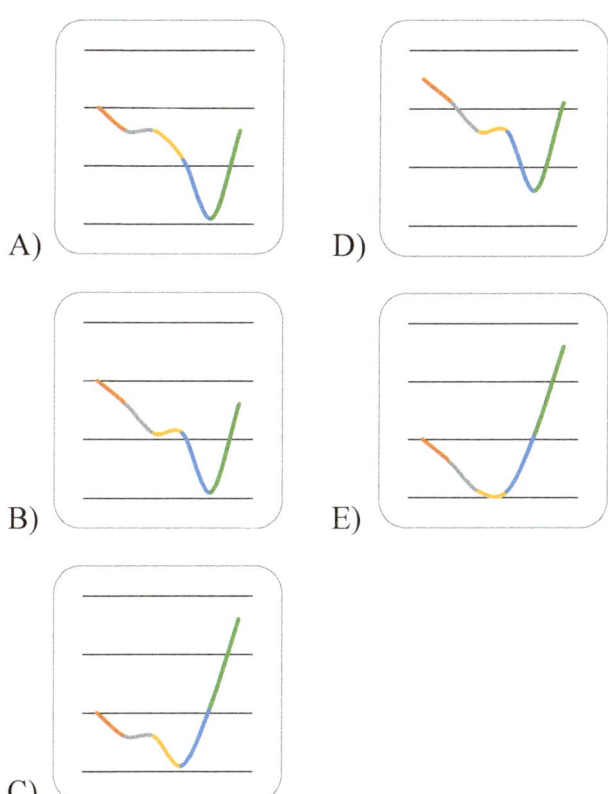

1. In the figure below, if ∠y = 155°, then ∠x is:

   A) 15°
   B) 25°
   C) 35°
   D) 45°
   E) 65°

   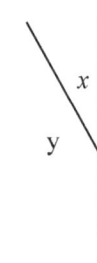

2. In the figure below point F lies on $\overline{AE}$. What is the measure of ∠CFD?

   F) 25°
   G) 30°
   H) 40°
   J) 45°
   K) 50°

   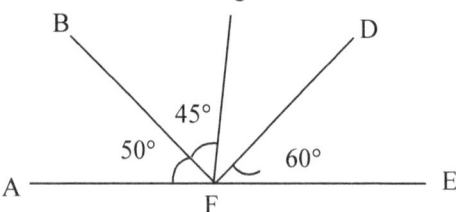

3. △ABC is one eighth of an octagon with equal sides. If ∠CAB = $^{360°}/_8$ = 45°, what are the measures of the other two angles in △ABC?

   A) 22.5° and 45°
   B) 45° each
   C) 67.5° each
   D) 90° and 45°
   E) 120° and 15°

   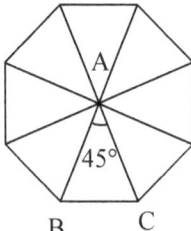

4. On a Friday night, a restaurant has four chefs making pizzas as indicated in the table below. What is the average number of pizzas made by the four chefs?

Chef	1	2	3	4
Number of pizzas made	12	2	0	15

   F) 6
   G) 7.25
   H) 8.50
   J) 11.25
   K) 13

5. Shoes that normally sell for $39.99 are on sale for 20% off. How much do they cost during the sale, to the nearest dollar?

A) $8
B) $10
C) $9
D) $30
E) $32

6. In the figure below, ΔABC is an equilateral triangle and $\overline{BC}$ is 8 units long. How many units is the perimeter of ΔABC?

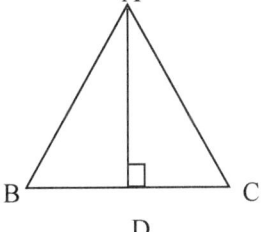

F) 13.5
G) 18
H) $13\sqrt{2}$
J) 32
K) 24

7. A three-man comedy troupe gets 30% of the money from sales of tickets to their shows. That 30% is split equally among the troupe members. If ticket sales generate $800,000, how much does one troupe member receive?

A) $8,000
B) $80,000
C) $83,333.33
D) $240,000
E) $300,000

8. If a round swimming pool has a radius of 15 feet, what is the area, in square feet, of the circular piece of vinyl required to cover it?

F) 30π
G) $225\pi/4$
H) 75π
J) 225π
K) 900π

9. When graphed on the (x,y) coordinate plane, 2 points from among (-6,4), (-2,-3), (3,-2), and (3,4) are in the first and second quadrants. Which two points are they?

A) (-6,4), (-2,-3)
B) (-6,4), (3,-2)
C) (-6,4), (3,4)
D) (-2,-3), (3,-2)
E) (-2,-3), (3,4)

10. A yard is a unit of length equal to three feet. Consider a path that is 97.5 feet. To the nearest tenth yard, how long is the path?

F) 17.6
G) 29.1
H) 32.5
J) 41.6
K) 44.8

11. If $a+b = 3$, then in terms of b, $a^2 =$

A) $b^2 + 6$
B) $b^2 + 6b - 9$
C) $b^2 + 9$
D) $b^2 - 6b + 9$
E) $9 - b^2$

12. A map is drawn to scale so that 2.3 centimeters represents 50 meters. How many meters does 3.1 centimeters represents?

F) 44
G) 56.8
H) 67.4
J) 74.2
K) 86

13. In the figure below point F lies on $\overline{AE}$. What is the measure of ∠DFE?

A) 10°
B) 20°
C) 25°
D) 40°
E) 150°

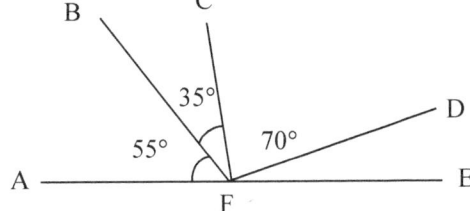

14. To keep up with raising expenses, a car manufacturer needs to raise the $11,000 price of a car by 7.5%. What will be the new total price?

F) $11,007.50
G) $11,075.00
H) $11,750.00
J) $11,825.00
K) $19,250.00

15. A radio station conducts a telephone poll to determine listeners' reactions to a music format change. Of the 900 people who answered, 350 liked the new format, 325 disliked it, and the rest were undecided. What percent of those who answered were undecided about the new format?

A) 18.5%
B) 20%
C) 25%
D) 42.5%
E) 120%

16. In the standard (x,y) coordinate plane, 2 corners of a square are (-6,3) and (-6,0). Which of the following can be the other two corners?

F) (6,0), (-3,0)
G) (3,6), (6,3)
H) (6,0), (6,3)
J) (3,0), (3,0)
K) (-3,0), (-3,3)

17. Among the points on the number line below, which is closest to 6.34?

A) A
B) B
C) C
D) D
E) E

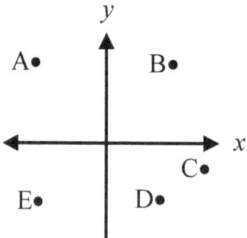

6.0 A   B C   D E   7.0

18. Which of the points on the (x,y) coordinates plane could be (-3,6)?

F) A
G) B
H) C
J) D
K) E

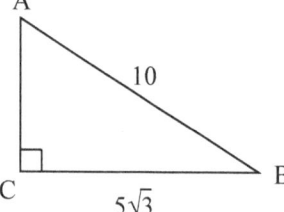

19. How long is $\overline{AC}$ in triangle ABC?

A) 3
B) 5
C) $3\sqrt{5}$
D) 7
E) $3\sqrt{7}$

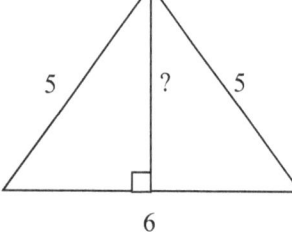

20. The base of a tent is 6 feet; the sides of the tent are 5 feet long. How many feet long should the pole be to hold up the peak of the tent?

F) 3
G) 4
H) $\sqrt{7}$
J) 7
K) $\sqrt{11}$

21. In the figure below, B is on $\overline{DE}$ and $\overline{DE}$ is parallel to $\overline{AC}$. What congruencies must hold?

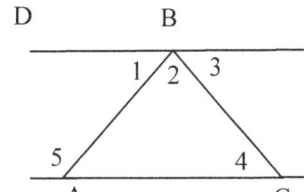

A) ∠1 + ∠3 ≅ ∠5
B) ∠1 + ∠2 ≅ ∠4
C) ∠1 + ∠4 ≅ ∠5
D) ∠2 + ∠3 ≅ ∠4
E) ∠2 + ∠3 ≅ ∠5

22. An English teacher grades 100 papers and finds results listed in the table below. If one paper is selected at random, what is the probability that it contains 2 or more errors?

Number of Errors	Proportion of Papers
0	0.30
1	0.25
2	0.20
3	0.15
4 or more	0.10

F) 0.10
G) 0.20
H) 0.25
J) 0.45
K) 0.70

23. Which of the following is an irrational number?

A) $|-3.4|$
B) 0
C) 1.52
D) $\sqrt{13}$
E) 8^3

24. The circumference of the circle below is 108 meters. If the inscribed angle *n* is 30° and $\overline{AO}$ and $\overline{BO}$ are both radii of the circle, what is the length in meters of arc AB?

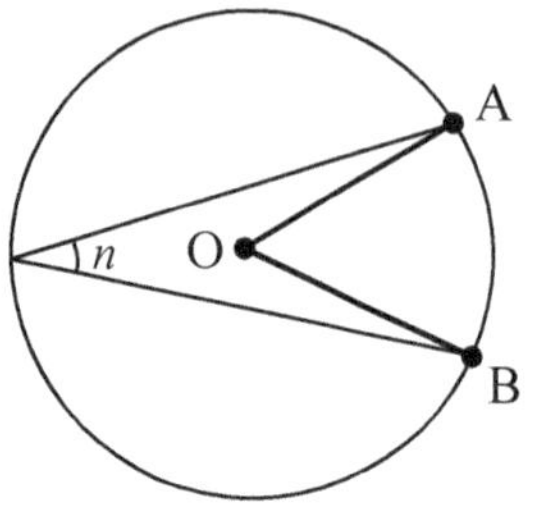

F) 5
G) 9
H) 11
J) 12
K) 18

25. In the standard (*x,y*) coordinate plane, the graph of $(x-7)^2 + (y+1)^2 = 25$ is a circle. What is the area enclosed by the circle?

A) 5π
B) 10π
C) 25π
D) 125π
E) 625π

26. Triangle ABC has vertices (2,4), (3,-1), and (-1,-2) in the standard (*x,y*) coordinate plane. Suppose ABC is translated 3 units to the right and 2 unit down, forming A'B'C'. Which of the following shows the coordinates of A'B'C'?

F) (0,7), (1,2), (-3,1)
G) (5,6), (6,1), (2,0)
H) (4,7), (5,2), (1,1)
J) (0,1), (1,-4), (-3,-5)
K) (5,2), (6,-3), (2,-4)

27. If in the (*x,y*) coordinates plane the point (-1,3) is on the graph $y = ax^2$, what is the value of *a*?

A) -3
B) $-1/3$
C) 0
D) $1/3$
E) 3

28. The graph below plots the per season number of games won for a local baseball team plotted against the number of fielding errors. How many games were won if no errors were committed?

F) 0
G) 5
H) 10
J) 15
K) 20

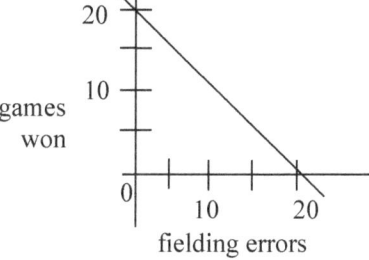

29. The size of a computer monitor is usually given as the length of its diagonal. What is the size of a monitor, in inches, whose sides are 13 inches and 10.95 (or $2\sqrt{30}$) inches?

A) 15
B) 17
C) 19
D) 21
E) 22

30. What is the hypotenuse in meters of a right ΔABC if its legs are 6 meters and 8 meters long?

F) $2\sqrt{3}$
G) 8
H) 9
J) 10
K) $5\sqrt{3}$

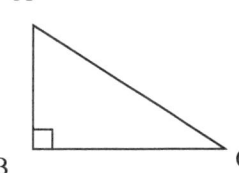

31. A donut recipe calls for 3 cups of flour to make two dozen donuts. According to this recipe how many cups of flour are required to make 80 donuts?

A) 10
B) 12
C) 13
D) 14
E) 16

32. The first and second terms of a geometric sequence are y/x^4 and $(y^2z)/x^3$, in that order. What is the next term of the sequence?

F) $(y^2z^2)/x^2$
G) $(y^2z)/x^2$
H) $(y^3z^2)/x^2$
J) $(yz^2)/x^4$
K) $(yz^2)/x^2$

33. Two chefs in a restaurant work separately to prepare meals for customers. If one chef can prepare an average of 3 meals in 12 minutes and another can prepare an average of 7 meals in 20 minutes, how many meals can the kitchen prepare in a 4-hour dinner shift?

A) 36
B) 72
C) 144
D) 226
E) 600

34. The area of a tabletop is 2400 square inches. If the length is 50% larger than the width, which of the following measurements for tablecloths will exactly cover the surface of the table?

F) 30×40
G) 30×70
H) 40×40
J) 40×60
K) 50×70

35. The diagonal of a square has length of 8. What is the length of one side?

A) 4
B) $4\sqrt{2}$
C) $5\sqrt{3}$
D) $5\sqrt{5}$
E) 12

36. The lengths on the figure below are given in inches. How many inches long is $\overline{AB}$?

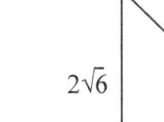

F) 3
G) $3\sqrt{2}$
H) 5
J) $2\sqrt{5}$
K) 7

37. If $x^2-kx+25 = 0$ and only one real solution for x exists, what is the value of k?

A) 0
B) 5
C) 8
D) 10
E) 20

38. In the figure below, lines j and k are parallel, lines m and n are parallel and 2 angles are shown. What is the measure of $\angle x$?

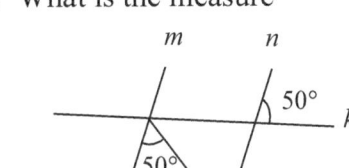

F) 60°
G) 80°
H) 100°
J) 120°
K) 140°

39. What is the largest possible product for 2 even integers whose sum is 42?

A) 185
B) 272
C) 320
D) 440
E) 441

40. Three similar triangles have the relationship $\triangle ABC \sim \triangle DEF \sim \triangle GHI$. The perimeter of $\triangle ABC$ is one-third the perimeter of $\triangle DEF$, and the perimeter of $\triangle DEF$ is 4 times that of $\triangle GHI$. If the sides of $\triangle ABC$ are 2, 7, and 5, what is the length of the shortest side of $\triangle GHI$?

F) 1
G) 1.5
H) 2
J) 4
K) 6

41. Which of the following is the graph of the solution set for $2(2+x) < 6$?

A)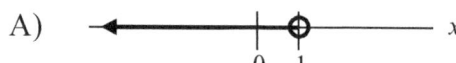

B)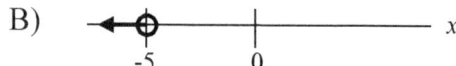

C)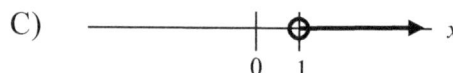

D)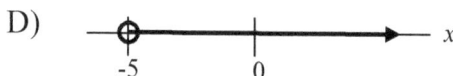

E)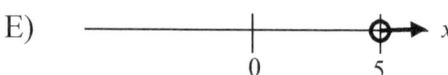

42. If a and b are real numbers, and $a < b$ and $b > 0$, then which of the following inequalities must always be true?

F) $a > 0$
G) $a < 0$
H) $a^2 > b^2$
J) $a^2 < b^2$
K) $a^2 \geq 0$

43. |6-3| - |3-5| =

A) -5
B) −1
C) 0
D) 1
E) 2

44. Points A (1,4) and B determine line segment $\overline{AB}$ in the standard (x,y) coordinate plane. If the midpoint of $\overline{AB}$ is (-3,2), what are the coordinates of point B?

F) (-7,-3)
G) (-7,0)
H) (-1,-3)
J) (-1,0)
K) (7,0)

45. If sin x = 3/5, what is cos x?

A) 4/5
B) 5/3
C) 3/4
D) 4/3
E) 3/5

46. What is the measure of the diameter of a circle with an area of 36π units?

F) 8
G) 6
H) 12
J) 16
K) 4

47. If f(x) = $4x^3 - 2x^2 - 4x + 3$, what is f(-2)?

A) -29
B) −7
C) 27
D) 35
E) 43

48. The lengths in parallelogram ABCD below are shown in inches. How long is $\overline{EC}$?

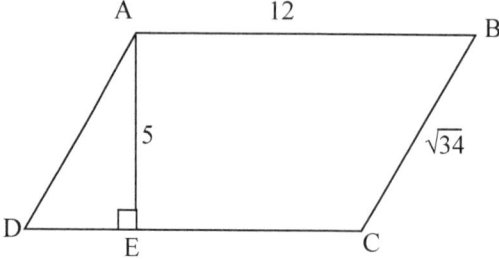

F) 3
G) 5
H) 7
J) 9
K) 10

49. Which of the following is equivalent to $\dfrac{3x}{\sqrt{6x-2}}$?

A) $\dfrac{x\sqrt{6x-2}}{2x-2}$

B) $\dfrac{3x\sqrt{6x-2}}{6x-2}$

C) $\dfrac{\sqrt{6x-2}}{2}$

D) $\dfrac{9x^2}{6x-2}$

E) $\dfrac{18x^2-6x}{6x-2}$

50. If the angles ∠X and ∠Y each measure between 0° and 90° and if sin X = cos Y, what is the sum of the measures of the angles ∠X and ∠Y?

F) 30°
G) 45°
H) 60°
J) 90°
K) 135°

51. Two gears have hands that rotate at different speeds. The larger gear rotates at 8 minutes per rotation and the smaller gear rotates at 12 minutes per rotation. How many rotations will the large gear make before both gears return to their original position at the same time?

A) 1
B) 2
C) 3
D) 16
E) 24

52. What is the smallest number greater than 1 that, when divided by 3, 4, 5, or 6 leaves a remainder of 2 in each case?

F) 14
G) 44
H) 292
J) 362
K) 722

53. If all the angles in a baseball diamond are right angles, how many degrees will a fielder on 2nd base have to sweep as he receives a throw from the catcher at home plate to tag out a sliding runner between 1st base and 2nd base?

A) 30°
B) 45°
C) 60°
D) 75°
E) 90°

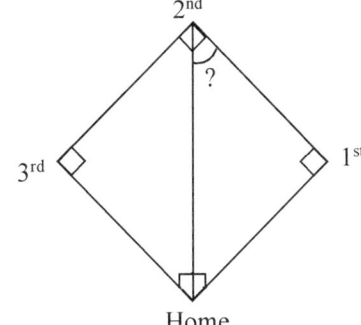

54. When $x = y$ and $m = n$, then which of the following equations is NOT true?

F) $y/m = x/n$
G) $y+n = x+m$
H) $y-n = x-m$
J) $y+m = x+n$
K) $y+x = m+n$

55. What is the next term in the series 4, 7, 16,…?

A) 34
B) 43
C) 54
D) 69
E) 82

56. When 5 times x is increased by 2 the result is no greater than 12. Which of the following is the graph of the real numbers x that satisfy this relationship?

F)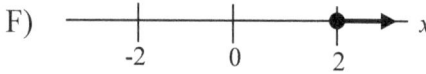

G)

H)

J)

K)

57. In the figure below a square is inscribed in a circle. If the area of the square is 16, what is the area of the circle?

A) 2π
B) 4π
C) 8π
D) 16π
E) 32π

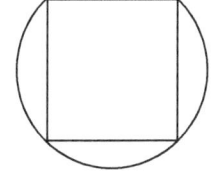

58. The two lines $y = ax+b$ and $y = cx+d$ cross the y-axis at the same place. Which of the following must be true?

  I. $a = c$
  II. $y = x$
  III. $b = d$

F) I only
G) II only
H) III only
J) I and II only
K) II and III only

59. In trigonometric terms, how long in feet would a woman's shadow be if she is 6 feet tall and the sun is at a 45° angle with the earth under her?

A) $\dfrac{\tan 45°}{6}$

B) $\dfrac{6}{\tan 45°}$

C) $\tan 45°$
D) $\cot 45°$
E) $\sin 45°$

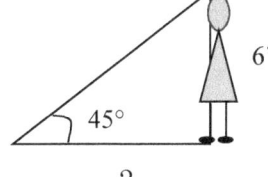

60. If cosecant $\angle A$ is 1.74, what is sin $\angle A$?

F) 0.50
G) 0.57
H) 0.71
J) 1.00
K) 2.92

1. The temperature outside increases from -4° to 7°. By how many degrees has it heated up?

   A) -4°
   B) -3°
   C) 3°
   D) 11°
   E) 15°

2. In the figure below, if $x = 50°$ the y is:

   F) 40°
   G) 90°
   H) 120°
   J) 130°
   K) 140°

   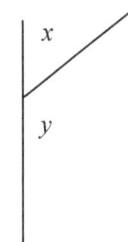

3. If right △ABC has one angle equal to 40° and a second angle equal to 90°, what is the third angle?

   A) 50°
   B) 60°
   C) 65°
   D) 70°
   E) 80°

   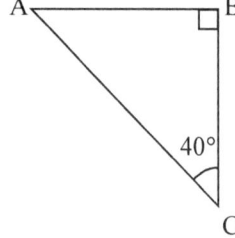

4. At a restaurant, a meal costs $11.99. Senior citizens get a discount of 15% off. How much would a senior citizen pay for this meal to the nearest dollar?

   F) $2
   G) $3
   H) $9
   J) $10
   K) $11

5. What is the area, in square meters, of a right triangle with sides of length 7 meters, 13 meters, and 14.765 meters?

A) 39
B) 45.5
C) 51.7
D) 60
E) 64.5

6. The lengths in the figure below are given in inches. How many inches long is $\overline{AB}$?

F) 6
G) 8
H) $5\sqrt{3}$
J) $2\sqrt{34}$
K) 16

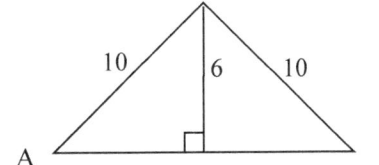

7. What is the smallest nonzero whole number that evenly divides both 42 and 87?

A) 2
B) 3
C) 4
D) 6
E) 14

8. Which of the following equations represents the circle shown below?

F) $(x - 6)^2 + (y - 5)^2 = 25$
G) $(x + 6)^2 + (y + 5)^2 = 25$
H) $(x - 5)^2 + (y - 6)^2 = 100$
I) $(x + 5)^2 + (y + 6)^2 = 100$
J) $(x + 5)^2 + (y + 6)^2 = 25$

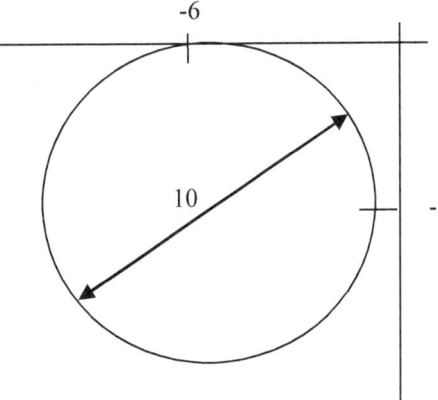

9. To match expenses, an airline must raise the $230 price of a ticket by 14%. What will be the new price?

A) $244.00
B) $262.20
C) $281.30
D) $292.20
E) $427.80

10. How far away in miles is an object that is 5 miles north and 12 miles east?

F) $\sqrt{72}$
G) 9
H) $\sqrt{119}$
J) 13
K) $7\sqrt{7}$

11. What is the midpoint of the line segment with the endpoints of (-3,2) and (-9,6)?

A) (-12,8)
B) (-6,2)
C) (-6,4)
D) (6,2)
E) (6,4)

12. In the figure below, j is parallel to k. What is the measure of $\angle x$?

F) 60°
G) 120°
H) 140°
J) 160°
K) 240°

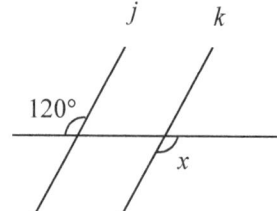

13. Which of the following is an irrational number?

A) $\sqrt{11}$
B) $|-0.34|$
C) 3
D) 10.5
E) 10^{-6}

14. In a math class with 5 tests, the average of Raul's first 4 tests is 78%. If Raul wants to average 80% or above on the 5 tests, what is the minimum score he must make on the 5th test?

F) 86%
G) 88%
H) 94%
J) 98%
K) 103%

15. If the ones digit of 3^2 is 9 and the ones digit of 3^3 is 7 then what is the ones digit of 3^{32}?

A) 0
B) 1
C) 2
D) 3
E) 4

16. In the figure below, A lies on $\overline{CQ}$, P lies on $\overline{BQ}$ and $\overline{AP}$ is parallel to $\overline{BC}$. If $\overline{AP}$ is 7 units long, $\overline{PQ}$ is 5 units long, and $\overline{BC}$ is 14 units long, how many units long is $\overline{BP}$?

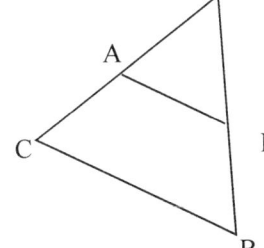

F) 5
G) 8.9
H) 12.1
J) 16
K) 20

17. In the figure below, *j* is parallel to *k*. What is the measure of ∠*x*?

A) 20°
B) 30°
C) 70°
D) 100°
E) 110°

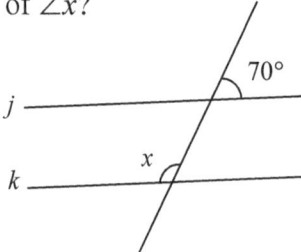

18. A pie selected for dessert is equally likely to have been baked in anyone of five ovens. What is the probability that the pie is from oven two?

F) 0.10
G) 0.20
H) 0.25
J) 0.40
K) 0.60

19. A group of judges rated members of a debate team on a 3-point scale. To member A of the debate team, a rating of 1 was given by 15% of the judges, a rating of 2 by 35%, and a rating of 3 by 50%. To the nearest hundredth, what was the average of the ratings for member A?

A) 1.85
B) 1.95
C) 2.10
D) 2.25
E) 2.35

20. If the product of 7 integers is positive, at least how many if these 7 integers must be positive?

F) 1
G) 2
H) 3
J) 5
K) 7

21. $|4-2| \bullet |6-8| =$

A) -4
B) -3
C) -1
D) 1
E) 4

22. The circumference of the circle below is 108 meters. If the interior angle *n* is 60°, what is the length in meters of arc $\overline{AB}$?

F) 5
G) 9
H) 11
J) 12
K) 18

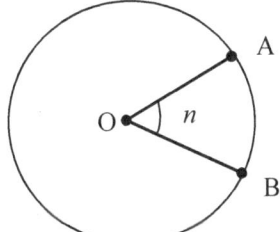

23. The average of a set of five integers is 14. When a sixth number is included in the set, the average of the set decreases to 12.5. What is the sixth number?

A) 4.0
B) 4.5
C) 5.0
D) 5.75
E) 6.25

24. There are *n* students in a class. If, among those students, *p*% play soccer, which of the following general expressions represents the number of students who do NOT play soccer?

F) np
G) $0.01np$
H) $\dfrac{(100-p)n}{100}$
J) $\dfrac{(100-p)n}{0.01}$
K) $100(1-p)n$

25. For what value of c is $x = 4$ the solution to $x+4 = 3x+c$?

A) -8
B) -6
C) -4
D) 2
E) 6

26. What is the value of $x^2-3xy+4y$ when $x = 3$ and $y = -1$?

F) -4
G) -2
H) 4
J) 14
K) 22

27. Gumballs cost $0.50 for m gumballs and jawbreakers cost $0.25 for n jawbreakers. Which of the following is an expression for the cost, in cents, for 4 gumballs and 7 jawbreakers?

A) $7(^{50}/_m) + 4(^{25}/_n)$
B) $(^{50}/_7)m + (^{25}/_4)n$
C) $(50)(4)m + (25)(7)n$
D) $4(^{50}/_m) + 7(^{25}/_n)$
E) $(^{50}/_4)m + (^{25}/_7)n$

28. A balloon expands in volume four cm^3 less than three times its original volume. If its final volume is 46 cm^3, what is the original volume, in cm^3?

F) 12
G) 14
H) 16.67
J) 18
K) 20

29. Which of the points on the (x, y) coordinate plane could be (-4,-6)?

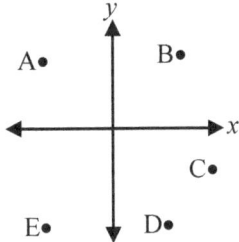

A) A
B) B
C) C
D) D
E) E

30. The lengths of the sides of one triangle are 2, 4, and 12 feet, respectively. What is the perimeter, in feet, of a similar triangle whose longest side is 14 feet?

F) 12
G) 15
H) 18
J) 21
K) 24

31. For ΔABC below, D and E are points on the sides. If $\overline{AB}$ is parallel to $\overline{DE}$, what is the measure of ∠CDE?

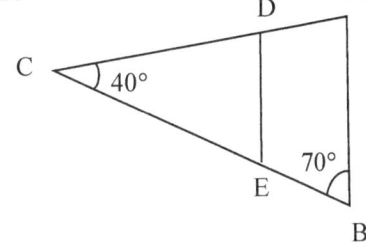

A) 30°
B) 40°
C) 70°
D) 100°
E) 110°

32. A coat bought 5 years ago for $50 is now worth $10. If it deprecated the same dollar value among each year, what percent of its value did it lose in the first year?

F) 4%
G) 16%
H) 20%
I) 30%
J) 80%

33. A visual inspection of t-shirts at a store resulted in the following table. If one T-shirt is selected at random, what is the probability that it contains 3 or more flaws?

Number of Flaws	Proportion of T-shirts
0	0.10
1	0.15
2	0.20
3	0.20
4	0.25
5 or more	0.15

A) 0.20
B) 0.40
C) 0.55
D) 0.60
E) 0.90

34. Find X if $\log_{11} X = 2$

F) 100
G) 121
H) 242
I) 2048
J) 4096

35. $|3-4| - |6-7| =$

A) −2
B) −1
C) 0
D) 2
E) 3

36. Points A(-4,-3) and B(-2,5) determine the line segment $\overline{AB}$ in the standard (x, y) coordinate plane. If the midpoint of $\overline{AB}$ is (-3,b), what is the value of b?

F) -8
G) −1
H) 0
J) 1
K) 8

37. The sun is directly overhead at 12:00 noon and sets at exactly 6:00 PM, 90° later. How many degrees must the sun have moved by 2:00 PM?

A) 20°
B) 30°
C) 40°
D) 50°
E) 60°

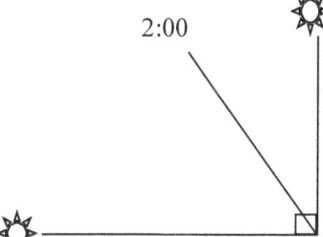

38. The graph of $(x-3)^2 + (y+6)^2 = 100$ describes a circle in the standard (x, y) coordinate plane. What is its area?

F) 10π
G) 20π
H) 50π
J) 80π
K) 100π

39. A young leaning tree needs support to stand upright as it grows. A string can be tied to the tree 3 feet above the ground and staked 3 feet from the tree's base. How much string is required (not considering what is needed to tie the ends)?

A) 3
B) $\sqrt{10}$
C) $3\sqrt{2}$
D) $5\sqrt{2}$
E) 12

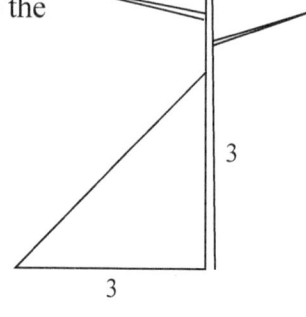

40. Two numbers have a greatest common factor of 3 and a least common multiple of 126. Which of the following could be the pair of numbers?

F) 9 and 12
G) 9 and 18
H) 18 and 21
J) 18 and 24
K) 18 and 27

41. What is the smallest positive integer x such that $4 \leq |2-x|$?

A) 0
B) 1
C) 2
D) 4
E) 6

42. If $x = 5^a$ and $y = 5^{-a}$, what is y in terms of x?

F) $y = 1/x$
G) $y = -1/x$
H) $y = 5/x$
J) $y = x/5$
K) $y = x^{-5}$

43. The amount of force (F) required to accelerate (a) an object of a certain mass (m) is the product of the acceleration and the mass of the object ($F = ma$). If an object weighing 40 kg is dropped and gravity causes it to accelerate 9.8 m/s², how much force, in kgm/s², does the object exert on the ground when it hits?

A) 4
B) 26
C) 196
D) 392
E) 422

44. The density of an object is given by the ratio of an object's mass and its volume. If a kg is a unit of mass equal to 1000g and cm³ is a unit of volume, what is the density, in g/cm³, of an object weighing 0.75 kg and taking up 150 cm³?

F) 0.005
G) 2.5
H) 5
I) 5.2
J) 7.5

45. Point X lies on $\overline{AB}$ and ∠CBX is a right angle. What is the measure of ∠BCX if ∠AXC is 120°?

A) 10°
B) 25°
C) 30°
D) 45°
E) 50°

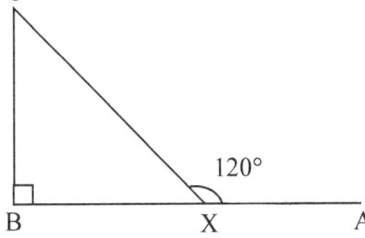

46. If $(x+k)^2 = x^2+18x+k^2$ for all real numbers x, then k is:

F) 3
G) 6
H) 9
I) 12
J) 18

47. In the rectangle below, side $\overline{AB}$ is twice the length of $\overline{BC}$. If point E lies on side $\overline{BC}$ and $\overline{AB}$ is 12 inches, what is the area of $\triangle AED$ in square inches?

A) 144
B) 120
C) 96
D) 72
E) 36

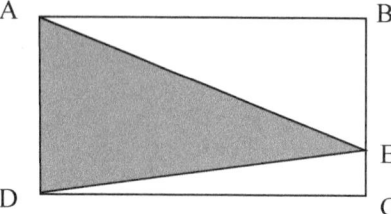

48. Which of the following is equivalent to $\dfrac{2x}{\sqrt{8x+2}}$?

F) $\dfrac{4x^2}{8x+2}$

G) $\dfrac{2x^2}{4x+1}$

H) $\dfrac{16x^2+4x}{8x+2}$

J) $\dfrac{8x^2+2x}{4x+1}$

K) $\dfrac{x\sqrt{8x+2}}{4x+1}$

49. Lengths of the triangle below are given in centimeters. What is the value of x?

A) $\dfrac{0.5}{\sqrt{3}}$
B) 0.5
C) $\dfrac{3}{4}$
D) $\dfrac{\sqrt{3}}{4}$
E) $\dfrac{\sqrt{3}}{2}$

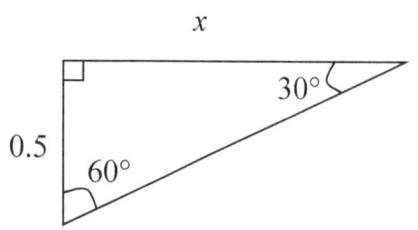

50. When 2 times *x* is decreased by 6, the result is greater than 8. Which of the following is a graph of the real numbers *x* that satisfy this relationship?

F)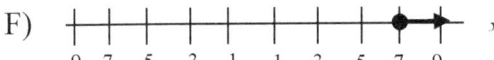

G)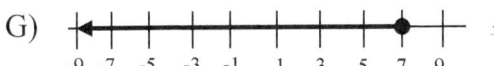

H)

J)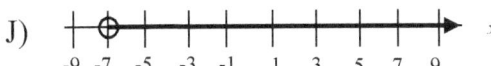

K)

51. If at 12:00 noon the sun is directly overhead and it sets at 6:00 PM, 90° later, what time is it when the sun is 15° before sunset?

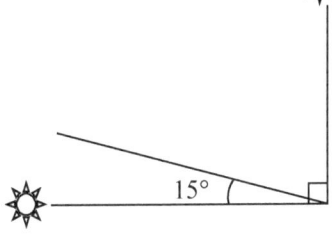

A) 3:00 PM
B) 3:30 PM
C) 4:00 PM
D) 4:30 PM
E) 5:00 PM

52. Suppose a batter hits a ground ball at a 30° angle from the 1st base line. How many degrees will the fielder have to rotate to throw the ball to 1st base?

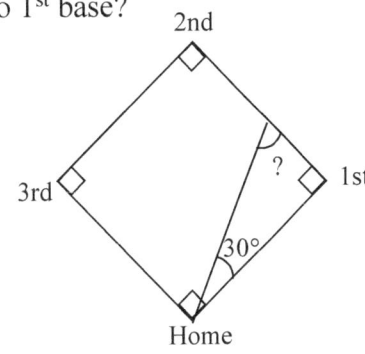

F) 30°
G) 45°
H) 60°
J) 75°
K) 90°

53. The sum of the 3 integers x, y, and z is 200. If $0 \le x \le 20$ and $-10 \le y \le 0$, what is the smallest possible value for z?

A) 170
B) 180
C) 185
D) 190
E) 200

54. If x, y, and z are nonzero real numbers and xy=z, which of the following equations for z must always be true?

F) $z = {}^{x}/_{y}$
G) ${}^{z}/_{x} = y$
H) ${}^{y}/_{z} = x$
J) $z - y = x$
K) $x + y = 0$

55. Which of the following is the graph of the solution set $y \ge -3$?

A) 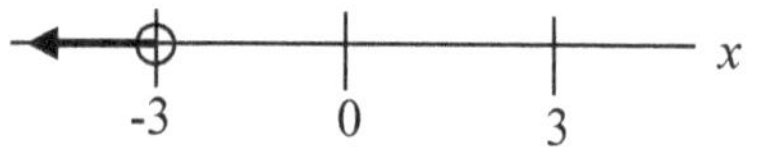

B) 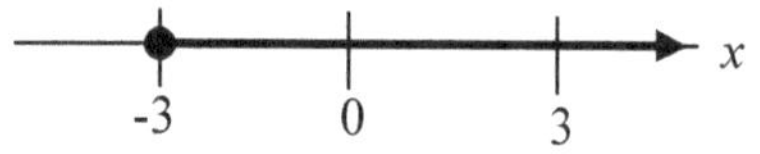

C) 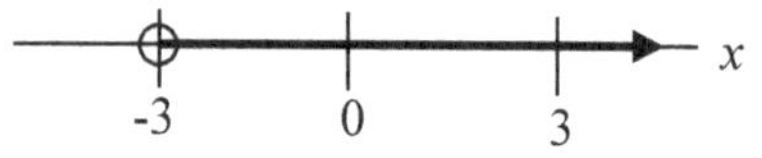

D) 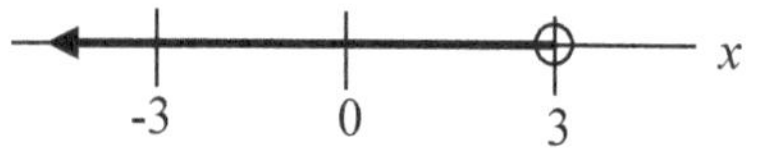

E) 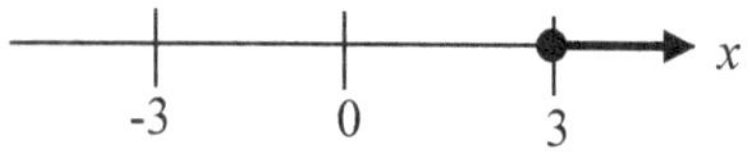

56. △ABC has ∠'s in ratio of 2x:3x:4x, what is the measure of the smallest ∠?

F) 20°
G) 30°
H) 40°
J) 60°
K) 80°

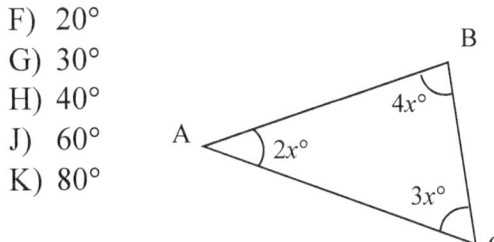

57. An item purchased from Store A costs twice as much the same item purchased from Store B. Store C charges $10 less than twice Store B's price. If n is the price of the item when purchased at Store A, what is the price of the item at Store C?

A) $n/2$
B) $n - 10$
C) $2n - 10$
D) $2n$
E) $n/2 - 10$

58. A list of tasks has been gathered for a Habitat for Humanity project. Each of 12 volunteers agrees to perform two 30-minute tasks from the list. This will ensure that all but 20 minutes worth of tasks will be performed. How many minutes of tasks are on the list?

F) 360
G) 420
H) 710
J) 740
K) 800

59. In the figure below, ∠B is a right angle. If $\overline{BC}$ is 20 units long and the cotangent of angle A is 5, then how many units long is $\overline{AB}$?

A) 5
B) 3/5
C) 40
D) 120
E) 100

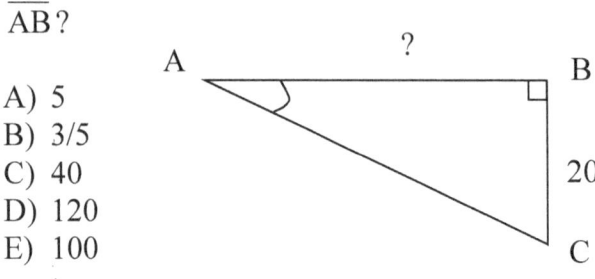

60. Two paths exist from the library to the parking lot. If the angle between the beginning of the two paths is 22° and the direct route is 40 feet, how much farther is the indirect route?

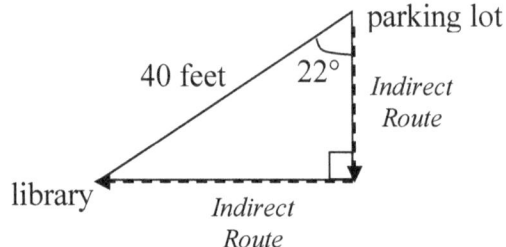

F) 40 sin 22° – 40 cos 22° + 40
G) 40 sin 22° – 40 cos 22° - 40
H) 40 cos 22° – 40 sin 22° - 40
J) 40 cos 22° + 40 sin 22° - 40
K) 40 cos 22° + 40 sin 22° + 40

MATH – WORKSHEETS KEY

Angles add to 180° - p. 230

1. **B** 20+90+x=180
2. **B** ∠A=70   70+10+x=180
3. **A** ∠ACD=65 ∠DAC=25
   ∠CAB=25
   ∠ACB=115 115+25+x=180
4. **A** ∠A=30 ∠CAB= ½ ∠BAD
5. **E** ∠YXZ=65 20+65+x=180
6. **C** 2x+6x+4x=180; 12x=180; x=15; so 2x=30
7. **E** 3x+3x+6x=180 12x=180; x=15; so 3x+3x = 6x = 90
8. **C** (x+40) + (2x+40) + (3x-20) = 180
   6x+60=180; x=20; ∠ABC=60
9. **A** (3x+15) + (2x+10) + (x-25) = 180°
   6x=180°; x=30°
   ∠CAB = x-25 = 30-25 = 5
10. **D** 2x+x+30°=180°; 3x=150°; x=50° (∠ABC)
    ∠ABC=2x=100°
11. **A** x+ $x/4$ +30°=180°; $5x/4$=150°;
    x=120° $x/4$ = 30°

Area of a Triangle - p. 233

1. **B** ½(9)(12)=54
2. **C** Sketch figure; see that area increases as k increases for a set m value
3. **D** ½(14)(14)=98
4. **C** ½(9)(12)=54
5. **C** ½(5)(12)=30
6. **A** ¾(4)=3 (height)
   Base=6
   ½(6)(3)=9
7. **E** Area = ½bh
   30 = ½(3)h
   30 = $3/2$$h$
   h = 20
8. **A** h (or a)= $\sqrt{2}$, c=2, Pythag Thm says $b=\sqrt{2^2 - \sqrt{2}^2} = \sqrt{2}$;
   Area = ½bh = ½($\sqrt{2}$)($\sqrt{2}$) = ½(2) =1
9. **D** ½(10)(10)=50
10. **E** $\overline{BC}$=6 which is ½ of $\overline{AB}$
    ½(6)(12)=36

Area of a Circle - p. 236

1. **E** πr^2=$\pi(5/8)^2$=$25\pi/64$
2. **C** radius=½diameter=½(3)=$3/2$; area = $\pi(3/2)^2$ =$9/4\pi$
3. **E** πr^2=$\pi 6^2$=36π
4. **E** 16 is r^2 in this equation; area =πr^2=16π
5. **B** 4 is r^2 in this equation; area = πr^2=4π
6. **B** area=πr^2 = 9π; 9=r^2; 3=r
7. **C** area=πr^2 = 9/25π ; 9/25=r^2; 3/5=r
8. **B** area=πr^2 = 25π ; 25=r^2; 5=r
9. **A** area of square =2=lw; l=w=$\sqrt{2}$;
   Pythag. Thm: diag of square =$\sqrt{4}$ =2= diameter of circle; radius = 1; area of circle = πr^2 = π
10. **B** area of square is 2=lw; l=w=$\sqrt{2}$;
    circle radius = ½l = ½w=$\sqrt{2}/2$;
    circle area = πr^2 = $2/4\pi$ or $\pi/2$

Midpoint Formula – p. 239

1. **D** ½(-2+8)
2. **E** x=½(6+4), y= ½(-4+8)
3. **D** ½(-6+x)=-2; ½(4+y)=6; -3+½x=-2;
   2+½y=6; ½x=1; ½y=4; x=2; y=8
4. **C** ½(-5+7)
5. **C** x=½(-3+5), y= ½[6+(-4)]
6. **A** ½(3+x)=-1, ½(-4+y)=-2
   $3/2$+½x=-1, -2+½y=-2
   ½x=$-5/2$, ½y=0
   x=-5, y=0
7. **A** y = $(-2+3)/2$ = $1/2$
8. **D** x = $(2+3)/2$ = $5/2$; y = $(12-6)/2$ = $6/2$=3

9. **C** $(7+x_2)/2 = -2$; $x_2 = (2) \cdot (-2) - 7 = -11$;
   $(4+y_2)/2 = -2$; $y_2 = (2) \cdot (-2) - 4 = -8$
10. **A** $a = (1-3)/2 = -2/2 = -1$

Parallel Lines Divided by a Transversal - p. 242

1. **E** α is supplementary angle with 40°; α = 180-40
2. **D** ∠DAC=∠55° since $\overline{DC} \parallel \overline{AB}$
3. **B** ∠DAC=∠ACB since $\overline{DC} \parallel \overline{AB}$; ∠ACB=180-110-30=40
4. **E** $x = 110-30 = 80$
5. **D** $x = 40$ since k ∥ j
6. **D** $x = 180 - 65$
7. **B** since $\overline{AC} \parallel \overline{DE}$
8. **A** ∠1 + ∠4 =180
9. **D** others are supplementary angles
10. **D** ∠1+∠2 = ∠4

Inscribed Angles - p. 245

1. **D** $75/15 = 5$, $\angle m = 360°/5 = 72°$
2. **B** $75/15 = 5$ $\angle m = 360°/5 = 72°$; $\angle n = \frac{1}{2}\angle m = 36°$
3. **A** $\frac{5}{15} = \frac{i}{360}$, so i = interior angle = 120°; inscribed angle = 60°
4. **C** $\frac{15\,cm}{c} = \frac{40}{360}$; $c = \frac{(15\,cm)(360)}{40} = (15\,cm)(9) = 135\,cm$
5. **D** $\frac{7}{60} = \frac{i}{360}$ then $60i = (7)(360)$ and $i = \frac{(5)(360)}{60} = (7)(6) = 42°$
6. **B** $\frac{12}{90} = \frac{i}{360°}$ then
   $90i = (12)(360°)$,
   $i = \frac{(12)(360°)}{90} = (12)(4) = 48°$;
   $j = \frac{i}{2} = 24°$
7. **C** $\frac{2}{9} = \frac{i}{360}$, so i = interior angle = 80°; inscribed angle = 40°.
8. **A** $\frac{32\,cm}{c} = \frac{16}{360}$; $c = \frac{(32\,cm)(360)}{16} = 720\,cm$
9. **B** $\frac{m}{60} = \frac{54}{360}$ then $360m = (54)(60)$ and $m = \frac{(54)(60)}{360} = \frac{(54)}{6} = 9$ minutes
10. **D** $c = \frac{(5\pi)(360)}{200} = 9\pi$, $c = 2\pi r$
    $r = \frac{9\pi}{2\pi} = 4.5$

Percents - p. 248

1. **E** $650.00(1-.15) = $552.50
2. **D** $0.30x = 60$; so $x = 200$
3. **D** $16.99(1+0.07) = $18.18
4. **E** $18(0.07) = 1.26$
5. **C** $0.30x = 83$; so $x=276.67$
6. **D** $0.20(400) = 80$; and $80-10=70$
7. **C** 60% played at least 2 sports
   40%(.75) = 30% played 1 sport
   30% + 60% = 90% played sports
   100% - 90% = 10% didn't play
8. **D** $18/30$=60% of shots made
   $18/36$ = 50% after misses
   $(18+x)/(36+x)=0.60$;
   $18+x=21.6+0.60x$;
   $0.40x=3.6$; so $x=9$
9. **B** $18/48 = 37.5\%$
10. **C** $20\%x = 13$; $0.20x = 13$; so $x=65$
11. **B** $42,000(1+5\%) = 42,000(1+0.05) = 42,000(1.05) = 44,100$

Square Roots - p. 251

1. **E** $\sqrt{2x-8} = 4$; $(\sqrt{2x-8})^2 = 4^2$;
   $2x-8=16$; $2x=24$; $x=12$
2. **D** $\sqrt{2x-5} = 3$; $(\sqrt{2x-5})^2 = 3^2$;
   $2x-5=9$; $2x=14$; $x=7$
3. **A** $x \geq 0$; Square root of a negative number is not real
4. **A** $x \geq -3$; Square root of a negative number is not real
5. **B** $\sqrt{40} = \sqrt{4}\sqrt{10} = 2\sqrt{10}$
6. **B** $\sqrt{32} = \sqrt{16}\sqrt{2} = 4\sqrt{2}$
7. **C** $\sqrt{40}\sqrt{30} = \sqrt{1200} = 34.6 \cong 35$
8. **B** $\sqrt{50}\sqrt{40} = \sqrt{2000} = 44.7 \cong 45$
9. **E** Multiply top and bottom by $\sqrt{4x-z}$
10. **B** Multiply top and bottom by $\sqrt{6a+c}$

Irrational Numbers - p. 254

1. **E** $\sqrt{13}$ is a non terminating and non repeating decimal
2. **C** $\sqrt{6}$ is a non terminating and non repeating decimal
3. **B** non terminating and non repeating decimal
4. **D** $33/7$ is a repeating decimal
5. **C** $\sqrt{5}$ is a non-repeating and non-terminating decimal
6. **C** $\sqrt{4} = 2$
7. **E** $\sqrt{36} = 6$, and $5/6$ is a repeating decimal
8. **A** $\dfrac{2}{\sqrt{8}} = \dfrac{1}{\sqrt{2}}$, which is non-repeating and non-terminating

Similar Triangles - p. 256

1. **C** longest sides of each Δ are 7 and 14, $7/14 = 1/2$. $7+9+14=30$ (perimeter of larger Δ). Similar Δ is half, so $30/2=15$.
2. **D** $8/18 = x/27$; $18x=216$; so $x=12$
3. **A** $7/9=14/x$, where $x = \overline{BQ}$; $7x=126$; $x=18$; so $18-9=9$ ($\overline{BQ} - \overline{PQ} = \overline{BP}$)
4. **B** $6/x=8/20$; where $x = \overline{BC}$
5. **C** $4/8=b'/12$; $8b'=48$; $b'=6$
6. **B** $12/20=x/30$; $20x = 360$; $x=18$
7. **E** $20/28 = 15/x$; $20x = 420$; $x=21$
8. **B** Area of $\Delta = 1/2 bh = 1/2(12)(9) = 54$
9. **C** Δ_2 area = 24; Δ_1 area = $1/2 bh = 1/2(3)(4) = 6$; Δ_2 area = $4 \cdot \Delta_1$ area, therefore Δ_2 sides are $\sqrt{4} \cdot \Delta_1$ sides; Δ_2 shortest side = $\sqrt{4} \cdot \Delta_1$ shortest side = $\sqrt{4} \cdot 3 = 6$
10. **C** Δ_1 area = $9 \cdot \Delta_2$ area, therefore sides of Δ_1 are $\sqrt{9} \cdot$ sides of Δ_2; hypotenuse of = $15/\sqrt{9} = 5$
11. **D** perim(ΔABC) = perim(ΔDEF)/5; perim(ΔDEF) = $2 \cdot$ perim(ΔGHI); perim(ΔABC)=25, therefore perim(ΔDEF) = 125, therefore perim(ΔGHI) = 62.5; $25/62.5 = 5/x$; $x = 12.5$

Common Right Triangles - p. 260

1. **A** $3^2+4^2=c^2$
   $9+16=c^2$
   $25=c^2$; $5=c$
2. **C** $6^2+8^2=c^2$
   $36+64=c^2$
   $100=c^2$; $10=c$
3. **E** $5^2+12^2=c^2$
   $25+144=c^2$
   $169=c^2$; $13=c$

4. **A** $4^2+3^2=c^2$
 $16+9=c^2$
 $25=c^2$
 $5=c$ (direct route)
 Original trip was 7 miles direct route is 5 miles therefore 2 miles saved.
5. **C** $a^2+12^2=13^2$
 $a^2+144=169$
 $a^2=25$
 $a=5$
6. **D** $a^2+6^2=10^2$
 $a^2+36=100$
 $a^2=64$
 $a=8$
7. **E** 3-4-5 then 5-12-13
8. **D** Altitude of isosceles triangle is ⊥ and bisects the base of the triangle.
 $a^2+8^2=10^2$
 $a^2=36$
 $a=6$
9. **D** $a^2+8^2=10^2$
 $a^2=36$
 $a=6$ $6+6=12$
10. **D** $x^2+4^2=5^2$
 $x^2+16=25$
 $x^2=9; x=3$
 $x+y=10$
 $3+y=10; y=7$

Word Problems - p. 263

1. **E** constant = 500, plus 25 per sale
2. **B** worth = 95K plus 15% of 95K
3. **D** product of 2 even integers must be even; $x+y=42$; $xy=?$; for large product multiply numbers that are close together (20 • 22 = 440)
4. **A** C = n; B = $3n$; A = $3n+7$
5. **C** $4(2) + (0.15)432 = \$72.80$
6. **E** $\$30(1-.20) = \$30(.80) = \$24$ (*bodysuit*)
 $\$10(1-.15) = \$10(.85) = \$8.50$ (*tights*)
 $\$24 + (\$8.50 \cdot 3) = \$49.50$
7. **B** $1/67$ $0.5 = x/31.25$
 $62.5x = 31.25: x=1/2$
8. **B** $18/15 = x/60$; $15x = 1080$; $x = 72$
9. **D** $2.6(\$.99) + 0.5(\$1.25) + 3(\$1.98)=$
 $\$2.57 + \$0.63 + \$5.94 = \$9.14$
10. **B** d is distance from stop sign
 @ $t=0$, $d=0$; @ $t=20$, $d=0$
11. **D** $10+35=45$; $45/5=9$
12. **D** $\$5(\#kids) + \$3(\#kids)(\#hours)$
13. **B** $(12)(60)=720$
 $(10)(60)+(6)(60)= 600+360=960$
 $960-720=240$
14. **E** There is nothing in the problem to indicate the length of $\overline{BC}$
15. **E** Put the friends in order of tallest to shortest: Eddie, Monica, Harris, Dave, Kaden; Eddie is tallest.

Geometry - p. 269

1. **B** $90°-65°=25°$
2. **D** $180°-25°=155°$
3. **A** $180°-140°=40°$
4. **C** $60°+40°=100°$; $180°-100°=80°$
5. **C** $180°-45°-85°=55°$
6. **B** $90°-25°-15°=50°$
7. **B** $90°-70°=20°$
8. **D** $180°-85°=95°$
9. **C** 12 o'clock to 3 is 90°; Every 5 minutes is 30°
10. **B** $90°-80°=10°$

Quadratic Equations - p. 272

1. **E** x^2-2x-3
 $(x-3)(x+1)=0$
 $x = 3$; $x = -1$
2. **C** $(x+2)(x-1)=0$
3. **C** $8+8=16$ $8(8)=64$
4. **A** $2(x^2+3x-4) = 2(x+4)(x-1)$
5. **D** $2x^2+12x-4x-24 = 2x^2+8x-24$; then factor out a 2

MATH – WORKSHEETS KEY

6. **C** use FOIL
7. **E** $\dfrac{3(x^2+2x-8)}{x+4} =$
   $\dfrac{3(x+4)(x-2)}{x+4} = 3(x-2)$
8. **B** $\dfrac{(x+5)(x-2)}{x+5} = x-2$
9. **D** $x^2-kx-12=0$
   $3^2-3k-12=0$
   $9-3k-12=0$
   $3k-3=0$
   $-3k=3; k=-1$
10. **A** $x^2-kx+4=0$
    $16-4k+4=0$
    $5-k=0$
    $k=5$
11. **D** $(2x-1)(x+3)=0$
    $2x-1=0;\ x+3=0$
    $2x=1;\quad x=-3$
    $x=\frac{1}{2}$;
    therefore product = $(\frac{1}{2})(-3) = -\frac{3}{2}$
12. **C** $x^2-x-20=0$
    $(x-5)(x+4)=0$
    $x-5=0,\ x+4=0$
    $x=5,\quad x=-4$
    $5+(-4)=1$
13. **C** $(x-3)(x+4)=0$
    $x-3=0;\ x+4=0$
    $x=3;\quad x=-4$
    If $x<0$ then $x=-4$
14. **E** $(x-4)(x-4)=0$
    $x-4=0,\ x-4=0$
    $x=4,\quad x=4$;
    so $4x+16 = 4(4)+16 = 32$

Inequalities – p. 275

1. **A** $8x-18 \geq 6$
   $8x \geq 24$, so $x \geq 3$
2. **C** $|x| \leq 6$, so $x \leq 6$ and $x \geq -6$
3. **D** must be larger than 12
4. **A** $x^3 > 8$, so $x > 2$
5. **E** $x-1 > 5$, so $x > 6$
6. **C** simplifiy $4/n > 2/13$ and $4/n < 2/11$
   $52 > 2n;\ 44 < 2n$
   $26 > n;\ 22 < n$
   3 solutions: 23, 24, 25
7. **B** $-3x < 6$, so $x > -2$
8. **C** $6x+4 < 22;\ 6x < 18$, so $x < 3$
9. **B** If a is greater than 0 and b is greater than a, then b will always be greater than 0.

Logarithms – p. 280

1. **E** $8^2 = 64$
2. **C** $3^4 = 81$
3. **D** $5^4 = 625$
4. **E** $4^3 = 64$
5. **D** $6^3 = 216$
6. **B** $3^5 = 243$
7. **B** $5^3 = 125$
8. **E** $8^3 = 512$
9. **A** $1.5^2 = 2.25$
10. **E** $\left(\dfrac{3}{2}\right)^4 = \dfrac{81}{16}$

Pythagorean Theorem - p. 282

1. **B** $3^2 + 2^2 = c^2$
   $9 + 4 = c^2$
   $13 = c^2$
   $\sqrt{13} = c$
2. **B** $a^2 + \sqrt{407}^2 = 24^2$
   $a^2 + 407 = 576$
   $a^2 = 169$
   $a = 13$
3. **D** $25 + 4 = c^2$
   $29 = c^2$
   $\sqrt{29} = c$ (direct path)
   Original distance 7 miles so miles saved is $7-\sqrt{29}$
4. **C** Altitude of equilateral triangle bisects the base and all sides are

the same length. If x is the length of each side the base is $x/2$.

$\left(\frac{x}{2}\right)^2 + (4\sqrt{3})^2 = x^2$

$\left(\frac{x^2}{4}\right) + (16)(3) = x^2$

$\frac{x^2}{4} + 48 = x^2$

$\frac{x^2}{4} - x^2 = -48$

$(3/4)x^2 = 48$

$x^2 = 64$

$x = 8$

5. **B** $\sqrt{2}^2 + 3^2 = c^2$
   $2 + 9 = c^2$
   $11 = c^2$
   $\sqrt{11} = c$

6. **E** Each side of the square is 9 ($36/4$)
   $c = \sqrt{9^2 + 9^2} = \sqrt{162}$
   $= \sqrt{81} \cdot \sqrt{2} = 9\sqrt{2}$

7. **D** $c = \sqrt{13^2 + 7^2}$
   $= \sqrt{169 + 49} = \sqrt{218}$

8. **B** $d_1^2 = 3^2 + 2^2 = 9 + 4$; $d_1 = \sqrt{13}$;
   $d_2^2 = 4^2 + 1^2 = 16 + 1$; $d_2 = \sqrt{17}$;
   $d_1 - d_2 = \sqrt{13} - \sqrt{17}$

9. **D** $c = \sqrt{4^2 + \sqrt{5}^2} = \sqrt{21}$
   $x = \sqrt{4^2 + \sqrt{21}^2} = \sqrt{37}$

10. **D** $c = \sqrt{\sqrt{7}^2 + 4^2} = \sqrt{23}$

Absolute Values - p. 285

1. **E** $5 \cdot 2 = 10$
2. **C** $-5 + 5 =$
3. **A** $b \neq 5$ (makes left side = 0); a must be negative to make left side < 0
4. **B** $|-3| - |-5| = 3 - 5 = -2$
5. **B** $-|2-4| - |-3-1| = -2 - 2 = -4$
6. **E** $2 \cdot 4 = 8$
7. **C** $-9/3 = -3$
8. **B** $-|6| / |-3| = -6/3 = -2$
9. **D** $3 \cdot 2 = 6$

10. **A** $b \neq 3$ (makes left side = 0); a must be positive to make left side > 0
11. **B** $6x = 10$ so $x = 10/6 = 5/3$; $6x = 4$ so x also $= 4/6 = 2/3$
12. **E** $4x = 2$ so $x = 2/4 = 1/2$; $4x = -8$ so x also $= -8/4 = -2$
13. **C** $x > 0$ and $|7 + y| > 0$ so $y \neq -7$
14. **A** $3a = 4$ so $a = 4/3$; $3a = -12$ so a also $= -12/3 = -4$
15. **D** $2a = 10$ so $a = 10/2 = 5$; $2a = 4$ so a also $= -4/2 = 2$

Averages - p. 288

1. **C** $(36 + 18 + 22 + 24 + 20) \div 5$
   $120 \div 5 = 24$
2. **C** median is middle value = 22
3. **B** $(4 + 4 + 5) \div 3$; $13 \div 3 = 4\ 1/3$
4. **B** $(11/16 + 0.125) \div 2$
   $0.8125 \div 2 = 0.40625$
5. **C** $6.75 = \text{sum}/8$; sum = 54; newavg = [sum - (8)(2)] / 8 = 4.75
6. **B** $(325 + 250 + 400 + 225) \div 4$
   $1200 \div 4 = 300$
7. **D** median is average of middle two numbers when n is even; median = $(250 + 325)/2 = 287.5$
8. **D** $\text{sum}/4 = 13$; sum = 52;
   $(52 + x) / 5 = 15$; $52 + x = 75$;
   $52 + x = 75$; $x = 23$
9. **D** $(1)(0.20) + (2)(0.45) + (3)(0.35) = 2.2$
10. **A** $(11/8 + 0.645) \div 2$
    $2.02 \div 2 = 1.01$
11. **C** $(6 + 3 + 4) \div 3$
    $13 \div 3 = 4.33$
12. **E** $8.25 = \text{sum}/9$; sum = 74.25; newavg = [sum + (9)(8)] / 9 = 16.25
13. **A** mode is the most common number: 2

Trigonometry - p. 292

1. **C** $\tan = o/a$; $\tan C = 2/3$; $o = 2, a = 3$

2. **D** $a^2 + 4^2 = 5^2$; $a + 16 = 25$; $a^2 = 9$;
   $a = 3$ cos A = $a/h = 3/5$
3. **B** sin A = o/h = $13/\sqrt{49+169} = 13/\sqrt{218}$
4. **C** cos θ = $a/h = x/z$
5. **A** sinθ = $o/h = y/z$
6. **B** tan C = $o/a = \overline{AB}/\overline{BC}$
7. **C** tan θ = $o/a = 6/2 = 3$
8. **B** cos A = $a/h = \sqrt{121-49}/11$
9. **B** sin A = $o/h = \sqrt{169-36}/13$
10. **C** $10 \cdot 0.4 = 4$
11. **D** $1/0.2 = 5$
12. **D** $\tan x = \dfrac{o}{a} = \dfrac{2}{a} = 0.5$; $o=2$;
    $a = \dfrac{2}{0.5} = 4$;
    $h = \sqrt{2^2 + 4^2} = \sqrt{20} = 2\sqrt{5}$;
    $\sec x = \dfrac{1}{\cos x} = \dfrac{h}{a} = \dfrac{2\sqrt{5}}{4} = \dfrac{\sqrt{5}}{2}$
13. **C** $0.375 \cdot 8 = 3$

Must know these two trig identities:

$^{\sin}/_{\cos} = \tan$

$\sin^2 x + \cos^2 x = 1$

---

14. **A** $(\sin x)(^{\sin x}/_{\cos x})(\cos x) + (\cos x)(^{\cos x}/_{\sin x})(\sin x) = \sin^2 x + \cos^2 x = 1$
15. **A** $(\sin x)(^{\cos x}/_{\sin x})(\cos x) + (\cos x)(^{\sin x}/_{\cos x})(\sin x) = \cos^2 x + \sin^2 x = 1$
16. **B** $(\cos x)(^1/_{\sin x})(^{\sin x}/_{\cos x}) + (\sin x)(^1/_{\cos x})(^{\cos x}/_{\sin x}) = 1 + 1 = 2$
17. **E** $(\cos x)(^1/_{\sin x})(^{\sin x}/_{\cos x}) + (\sin x)(^1/_{\cos x})(^{\sin x}/_{\cos x}) = 1 + \tan^2 x$

Algebra - p. 298

1. **C** $2^5 - 9(4) = 32 - 9(4) = 32 - 36 = -4$
2. **E** $3.5 \text{ feet} \left(\dfrac{12 \text{ inches}}{1 \text{ foot}}\right) = 42 \text{ inches}$
3. **C** 2
4. **E** $(c+3) - \frac{1}{5}(c+3) = \frac{4}{5}(c+3)$
5. **E** $2(4^2) - 2(4)(2) + 1^2 = 32 - 16 + 1 = 17$
6. **D** $\left(\dfrac{8 \text{ ounces}}{1 \text{ cup}}\right)\left(\dfrac{2 \text{ cups}}{1 \text{ pint}}\right)\left(\dfrac{2 \text{ pints}}{1 \text{ quart}}\right)$
   $\left(\dfrac{4 \text{ quart}}{1 \text{ gallon}}\right)\left(\dfrac{3 \text{ gallons}}{4}\right) = 96 \text{ ounces}$
7. **D** 5; $6 \cdot 7 = 42$; $47 - 42 = 5$
8. **A** $xz + y$
9. **D** $2(2^0) - 2(7)(0) + (2)(7) = 2 - 0 + 14 = 16$
10. **D** $\left(\dfrac{4 \text{ dats}}{1 \text{ dut}}\right)\left(\dfrac{3 \text{ duts}}{1 \text{ din}}\right) 5 \text{ dins} = 60 \text{ dats}$
11. **D** 6; $12 \cdot 5 = 60$; $66 - 60 = 6$
12. **C** $\dfrac{\left(\dfrac{y}{2} + 75\right)}{2} + 75 = \dfrac{\left(\dfrac{y}{2} + \dfrac{150}{2}\right)}{2} + 75 =$
    $\dfrac{y + 150}{4} + \dfrac{300}{4} = \dfrac{y + 450}{4}$

Distance Formula - p. 301

1. **C** $\sqrt{(3-7)^2 + (7-4)^2} = \sqrt{16+9} = \sqrt{25} = 5$
2. **C** $\sqrt{(9-1)^2 + (8-6)^2} = \sqrt{64+4} = 2\sqrt{17}$
3. **D** $\sqrt{(15-10)^2 + (5-8)^2} = \sqrt{25+9} = \sqrt{34}$
4. **A** $\sqrt{(x_A + 8)^2 + (7-3)^2} = \sqrt{52}$;
   $(x_A + 8)^2 + 16 = 52$; $(x_A + 8)^2 = 36$;
   $x_A + 8 = 6$; $x_A = -2$
5. **B** $\sqrt{(x_B + 1)^2 + (2+5)^2} = \sqrt{58}$;
   $(x_B + 1)^2 + 49 = 58$; $(x_B + 1)^2 = 9$;
   $x_B + 1 = 3$; $x_B = 2$

6. **B** $\sqrt{(3-6)^2 + (y_A+2)^2} = \sqrt{25}$;
   $9 + (y_A+2)^2 = 25$; $(y_A+2)^2 = 16$;
   $y_A + 2 = 4$; $y_A = 2$

7. **B** $\sqrt{(3+1)^2 + (y_A+5)^2} = \sqrt{97}$;
   $16 + (y_A+5)^2 = 97$; $(y_A+5)^2 = 81$;
   $y_A + 5 = 9$; $y_A = 4$

8. **A** $\sqrt{(6-2)^2 + (-4--3)^2} =$
   $\sqrt{16+1} = \sqrt{17}$

9. **C** $\sqrt{(-2+5)^2 + (4-2)^2} =$
   $\sqrt{9+4} = \sqrt{13}$

10. **D** $\sqrt{(9-7)^2 + (-8-4)^2} = \sqrt{4+144}$

    Work this quickly by looking at the similar answers to see if they are different from each other. Also, don't calculate the whole distance, just calculate and compare the $(x_A - x_B)$ and (y_A-y_B) terms. For reference:

    $\sqrt{(7-5)^2 + (3--1)^2} =$
    $\sqrt{4+16} = \sqrt{20}$;
    $\sqrt{(3-5)^2 + (3--1)^2} = \sqrt{4+16}$;
    $\sqrt{(0-2)^2 + (-6--2)^2} = \sqrt{4+16}$;
    $\sqrt{(9-7)^2 + (-8-4)^2} = \sqrt{4+144}$;
    $\sqrt{(9-7)^2 + (-8--4)^2} = \sqrt{4+16}$

Equation of a Circle - p. 306

1. **E** $(x-4)^2 + (y+1)^2 = 9$
   Note that $r = {}^6/_2$
2. **A** $(-4, 2)$
3. **D** $(x+7)^2 + (y+1)^2 = 81$
4. **E** $= 8$ is the radius squared; $\sqrt{8}$
5. **A** $(7,5)$ is the center pt. Radius=3
6. **E** $(x+3)^2 + (y-6)^2 = 16^2$
7. **D** $(x+2)^2 + (y+7)^2 = 16$
8. **A** $(8,-5)$ is the center pt. Radius=3
9. **B** $(x-6)^2 + (y-2)^2 = 25$
10. **E** $(x+6)^2 + (y-6)^2 = 4$

Functions & Polynomials - p. 311

1. **E** $f(g(x)) = 0.5(3^4) = 0.5(81) = 40.5$
2. **C** crosses x axis at $x = 6, -3, 7$, and -4
3. **B** leave terms factored and cross out like terms
4. **E** multiply to get
   $(x^2 - 4x - 5) - (x^2 + 4x + 3) = -8x - 8$
5. **D** $2(3x)^3 - 3(3x) =$
   $2(27x^3) - 9x = 54x^3 - 9x$
6. **A** Factor first:
   $(x+0)(x+0)(x+3)(x+1)$; $f(x) = 0$
   when $x = 0, -3$, and -1
7. **A** leave terms factored and combine like terms
8. **C** Multiply through to get:
   $(x^3 - 2x^2 - x + 2) + (x^2 + 5x + 6) =$
   $x^3 - x^2 + 4x + 8$
9. **D** Crosses at $x = -3, -2, -1, 0, 1$, and 2
10. **A** $g(h(x)) = {}^4/_2 = 2$, so $f(g(x)) =$
    $2^4 + 1 = 17$

Greatest Common Factor / Least Common Multiple - p. 313

1. **C** $x = 14$; sum is $1+4 = 5$
2. **C** $10 = (2)(5)$, $12 = (2)(2)(3)$;
   multiply terms that are not in common: all less one 2
3. **A** $105 = (5)(3)(7)$,
   $135 = (5)(3)(3)(3)$;
   greatest factor is $(3)(5) = 15$
4. **E** $6 = (3)(2)$, $14 = (2)(7)$;
   multiply terms that are not in common: all less one 2
5. **D** $x = 25$; sum is $2+5 = 7$
6. **A** $15 = (3)(5)$, $18 = (2)(3)(3)$; multiply terms that are not in common: all less one 3
7. **A** $12 = (4)(3)$, $8 = (4)(2)$; multiply terms that are not in common: all less one 4
8. **D** $x = 16$; sum is $1+6 = 7$

9. **D** 7 and 15 are prime so share no factors; multiply 7 and 15
10. **E** 112 = (2)(56), 56 = (56); greatest factor is 56
11. **C** 2 cycles • 6 yards/cycle
12. **D** common factors: 7 & 35; $x = 35$

General Equation of a Line - p. 316

1. **D** $\frac{7-8}{-3-4} = \frac{-1}{-7} = \frac{1}{7}$
2. **B** $\frac{\text{negative rise}}{\text{positive run}}$; rise is approximately twice the run so -2 is best guess at slope
3. **C** Rearrange into $y = mx+b$ form: $7y = 6x - 3$; $y = \frac{6}{7}x - \frac{3}{7}$; intercept = $b = -\frac{3}{7}$
4. **A** $y = 0$ $0 = \frac{5}{9}x + 7$; $x = \frac{-63}{5}$
5. **B** Substitute and solve for b: $y = -4x + b$; $4 = -4(1) + b$; $b = 4 + 4 = 8$, so $y = -4x + 8$.
6. **E** $m = \frac{1--6}{9-3} = \frac{7}{6}$; $y = \frac{7}{6}x + b$; $1 = \frac{7}{6}(9) + b$; $b = 1 - \frac{21}{2} = -\frac{19}{2}$. $y = \frac{7}{6}x - \frac{19}{2}$
7. **E** negative reciprocal of the slope 8 is $-1/8$
8. **A** line must have the same slope: 8
9. **D** $\frac{4-0}{2-0} = \frac{4}{2} = 2$
10. **E** $\frac{\text{positive rise}}{\text{positive run}}$; rise is approximately the same as the run so +1 is the best guess at the slope
11. **A** Rearrange into $y = mx + b$ form: $3y = 2x - 4$; $y = \frac{2}{3}x - \frac{4}{3}$; intercept = $b = -\frac{4}{3}$
12. **C** Substitute $y = 0$ to obtain: $7x = 1$ and $x = 1/7$
13. **A** for b: $8 = -1/2(3) + b$; $b = 8 + 3/2 = 19/2$, so $y = -1/2x + 19/2$, converting to standard form: $2y = -x + 19$ or $x + 2y = 19$
14. **A** $m = \frac{-4-2}{6-0} = -1$; $y = -x + b$; $2 = -0 + b$; $b = 2$; $y = -x + 2$; rearranging to standard form: $x + y = 2$
15. **A** Obtain slope of line in standard form by rearranging to $y = mx + b$. Notice the relationship between the x and y coefficients: slope is the negative ratio of coefficient of x over coefficient of y: $-8/2 = -4$; perpendicular slope is $1/4$; slope of E is -2; of D is -1; of C is -1; of B is $-1/4$; of A is $1/4$;.
16. **D** Obtain slope of line in standard form by rearranging to $y = mx + b$. Slope of given line is $-8/4 = -2$; slope of E is $4/2$; of D is $-4/2$; of C is $-6/4$; of B is $-6/4$; of A is $6/4$.
17. **B** $y = (2)(4) - 6 = 8-6 = 2$, so the point is (4, 2)
18. **B** Solve for x when $y=0$: $9x+4(0) = 3$; $x = 3/9 = 1/3$.
19. **E** Solve for x when $y=0$: $0 = 3x+27$; $x = -27/3 = -9$.
20. **E** Determine the equation of the line then solve for x when $y=0$: $m = \frac{(1-4)}{(3--2)} = -\frac{3}{5}$. (3, 1) is a point on the line, so $1 = -3/5(3) + b$; $b = 1 + 9/5 = 14/5$. → $y = -3/5x + 14/5$. When $y=0$, $0 = -3/5x + 14/5$; $3/5x = 14/5$; cross multiply to get $x = 14/3$.

Graphing and the (x, y) Coordinate System - p. 322

1. **B** Remember each *x* and each *y* coordinate must be named twice for a rectangle.
2. **D** The fourth point before movement is (-7, -5). Adding +3 to the *x*-coordinate produces -7+3 =-4; subtracting 3 from the y-coordinate produces -5-3 = -8. The final answer is (-4, -8).
3. **D** We know it will be a parabola since the *x* is squared; quickly plugging in *x* values to get *y* and plotting both on a small graph shows the U is upright since *y* values increase as the absolute values of the *x*'s increase.
4. **C** Graph intercepts *x*-axis when y = 0; substituting y = 0 into the equation produces intercepts at $\pm 1/2$, so either is correct.
5. **D** The third point must create a right angle. Since the base is parallel with the *x*-axis, and the two points have the same *x*-coordinate, we know the line given must not be the hypotenuse. This means the *x*-coordinate for the third point doesn't matter and the *y*-coordinate must be either +1 or -10. Answer E is a duplicate of the first point named.
6. **C** Again, the base is parallel with the *x*-axis. However, the two points don't have the same *x* or *y*-coordinates. This line formed must be the hypotenuse, so the coordinates for the third point must have the same *x*-coordinate as one point and the same *y*-coordinate as the other. The possibilities are (-2, 6) and (-7, 8). Now, subtract 1 unit in *x*-direction and 2 units in *y*-direction. Two possible answers are: (-3, 4) and (-8, -2). Whew!
7. **B** The equation is in the straight line form, so we know it's a straight line. Also, the slope is positive 18.
8. **E** Plug *y* = 0 into the equation and get *x* = 25
9. **A** Use the equation of the circle to see what points are possible. Eqn is $(x-5)^2 + (y+3)^2 = 49$.
10. **A** Use the equation of the circle to see what points are possible. Eqn is $(x-7)^2 + (y+9)^2 = 16$.
11. **B** By rearranging the equation into $x^2 + y^2 = 3$. This is the equation for a circle whose center is at (0, 0).
12. **E** Plug *x* = 0 into the equation to get $y = \pm\sqrt{3}$. Or, if you recognize it as the equation for a circle, you know that the radius is $\sqrt{3}$ and the center is at (0, 0).

Perimeter - p. 326

1. **D** 22 (7+4+7+4=22)
2. **B** 5 (Since $\overline{AD}=\overline{BC}$ and $\overline{AB}=\overline{CD}$: $14=\overline{AB}+\overline{BC}+\overline{CD}+\overline{AD} = 2+\overline{BC}+2+\overline{AD}$; $2\overline{AD}=10$ and $\overline{AD}=5$)
3. **B** 24 (6+6+6+6=24)
4. **B** 9 (2+1+1+1+1+2+1=9)
5. **C** 22 (3+3+2+?+2+?+3+6; the ? must sum to 3, therefore, perimeter = 22)
6. **A** 4 (26-2-1-2-2-1-1-2-6-1-1-1-1-1= 4)
7. **E** (1+1+1+1+3+2+1+2+2+1+1+2+5+1=24)
8. **B** 3 (Since the left side of the figure has a total height of 3=1+1+1, *a+b*=3)
9. **D** $20+\pi$; $(1/2)2\pi(1)+2+2+3+4+5+4 =20+\pi$)
10. **E** $18+2\pi$; $(1/2)2\pi(2)+2+2+3+4+5=18+2\pi$)

MATH – WORKSHEETS KEY

Area - p. 331

1. **E** 28 (7 • 4 = 28)
2. **B** 10 (2 • 5 = 10 See *Perimeter Worksheet* #2 for calculation of 2nd side length.)
3. **B** 19 (4 • 4 + ½ • 2 • 3 = 19)
4. **E** (½ • 1 • 4 + 4 • 2 + ½ • 1 • 4 + 2 • 2 = 16)
5. **A** 2 $\sqrt{13-9} = 2$
6. **D** 14 (6 • 1 + 2 • 3 + 2 • 1 = 14 or 6 • 3 − 2 • 2 = 14)
7. **B** $a=2$, (1•1 + 3•3+(3−a)•1 + 2•3; 17 − 1 − 9 − 6 = 3−a; 1=3−a; a = 2)
8. **E** 14 (1•1 + 3•3 + 1•1 + 1•3 = 14 or 5•1 + [3+1] • 2 + 1•1 = 14)
9. **C** $20+\pi/2$ (½•π•1² + 4•4 + 2•2)
10. **E** $24+2\pi$ (½•π•2² + 4•5 + 2•2 =24+2π)

Polygons and Angles - p. 336

1. **D** $\frac{360}{180-120} = 6$
2. **A** angles in a triangle add to 180°
3. **C** $\frac{360}{180-108} = 5$
4. **B** $\frac{360}{180-140} = 9$
5. **E** $\frac{360}{180-150} = 12$
6. **B** $\frac{180(5)-360}{5} = 108°$
7. **E** $\frac{180(10)-360}{10} = 144°$
8. **D** $\frac{180(9)-360}{9} = 140°$
9. **B** $\frac{180}{3} = 60°$
10. **C** $\frac{180(6)-360}{6} = 120°$
11. **E** they are both convex, so the sum of the measures of their interior angles is the same: 180(6) − 360 = 1080°

Simplification and Factoring - p. 339

1. **A** $(x^2 − 3)(x^3 + 3x)$ Multiply to get: $x^5 − 3x^3 + 3x^3 − 9x = x^5−9x$
2. **E** $(x − 3)(x + 6)$
3. **C** Multiply to get: $(x^3 + 3x^2 − 5x − 15)$•$(x−x^2) = x^4 + 3x^3 − 5x^2 − 15x − x^5 − 3x^4 + 5x^3 + 15x^2$, simplify to get $−x^5 − 2x^4 + 8x^3 + 10x^2 − 15x$
4. **A** $4x^8 − 16x^7 + 16x^6$ Multiply to get: $x^6(2x − 4)(2x − 4) = x^6(4x^2 − 16x + 16)$.
5. **B** $\frac{5a^2}{c^2}$
6. **B** $\frac{5a^2}{c^2}$
7. **C** $72x^5y$
8. **E** $\frac{5x^5y^3}{(3xy^2)^2}$
9. **C** $\frac{4x^5(y^3)^2}{2xy^8}$
10. **D** $\left(\frac{4x^5y^3}{2xy^8}\right)^2$

Sequences and Series - p. 343

1. **A** arithmetic, so looking for amount to add; try 4, 3, 6, 8, and 5; 5 is not a factor of the range, test others and eliminate base on how fast the sum increases
2. **E** n^{th} term is $g^{n^2}h^{2n}$
3. **D** create table of ones digits and powers: **9**: 2 & 6; **3**: 3 & 7; **1**: 4 & 8; **7**: 1 & 5; series will repeat and 17 will fall under 7
4. **E** arithmetic; range = 210; 9 and 11, are not factors of 210
5. **C** n^{th} term is $a^{n/2}b^{n+1}$, so 100th term is $a^{50}b^{101}$
6. **D** create table of hundreds digits and powers: **1**: 3 & 5; **6**: 4 & 6; series will repeat and 50 will fall under 6
7. **B** arithmetic; range = 168; 5 and 11 are not factors of 168; terms in D will add up too quickly, A and C are possible *first* three terms, not *last* three
8. **B** $x^{n-2}y^{3n}$
9. **A** $y_n = y_{n-1} + 2(n-1)$, where the nth term is y_n
10. **C** $y_n = y_{n-1} + 3(n-1)$, where the nth term is y_n

Probability and Proportions - p. 346

1. **A** 8 green out of 30 total
2. **A** 8 green out of 29 total
3. **B** $x > 3$, so sum probabilities for $x = 4$ and $x = 5$: 0.05 + 0.30 = 0.35
4. **D** add probabilities of ways to get a hit: 0.20 + 0.15 + 0.10 + 0.05 = 0.50 or subtract prob of getting out from 1: 1 − 0.20 − 0.30 = 0.50
5. **D** 3 of 7 (Jessie is the 7th) will get a spot on the team
6. **E** ways to draw a 7 or a 9 divided by cards remaining: $(2 + 3) / (52 − 4) = 5/48$
7. **B** ways to win more than $100 divided by number of people who enter: $(10 + 5 + 2 + 1) / 100{,}000 = 18/100{,}000$ (Note that odds for a normal lottery are even worse than this; that's why this author doesn't gamble.)
8. **E** number of red, odd pieces / total number of pieces; 7 odd, black pieces, so there must be 8 odd, red pieces; $8/30$ (Again, your odds of winning here are not good.)
9. **C** two ways to solve. 1 minus prob of drawing none: $1 − (10/15)^2 = 1 − 100/225 = 125/225$; OR prob of drawing one plus prob of drawing two: $[(5/15)(10/15) + (10/15)(5/15)] + (5/15)(5/15) = 50/225 + 50/225 + 25/225 = 125/225$
10. **C** use *No Questions* row and *Buy* column to obtain 10 of 50 who don't ask questions; $10/50 = 0.20$.
11. **C** $1 − 0.8 = 0.2$

Expressions - p. 350

1. **E** $\frac{1}{2}(10b)h = 10A$
2. **C** simplify to get $3x \le 3$, so $x \le 1$
3. **D** make sure you add and multiply in the right place.
4. **B** Write out the units; see which cancels out the dollar sign. Also: what if they cost $1 and $5?
5. **C** shows the amount of tax paid
6. **D** nx is the number of points his last n assignments will contribute. Divide by $n+3$ total assignments.
7. **A** if $x = 2$ then $y = \frac{1}{2}$
8. **C** B, C and D x is larger than y; E $x \approx y$ coord.; A has $x \approx \frac{1}{2}y$
9. **C** One is odd, the other is even; squares of odd numbers are even; squares of even numbers are even
10. **A** $10-$4 = $6, +$0 = $6, -$5 = $1, -$10 = -$9, +$15 = $6

TEST 1 - p. 354

1. **B** $180° - 155° = 25°$
2. **F** $180° - 50° - 45° - 60° = 25°$
3. **C** $180° - 45° = 135°$; $135°/2 = 67.5$
4. **G** $(12+2+0+15) \div 4$; $29 \div 4 = 7.25$
5. **E** $39.99(1-.2) = 39.99(.8) = 32$
6. **K** Equilateral – all sides are equal
7. **B** $800{,}000 \cdot 0.3 = 240{,}000$ (income)
   $240{,}000 \div 3 = 80{,}000$
8. **J** area $= \pi r^2 = \pi(15)^2 = 225\pi$
9. **C** (3,4) - Quad I; (-6,4) Quad II
10. **H** $97.5 \div 3 = 32.5$
11. **D** $a+b=3$
    $a=3-b$
    $a^2=(3-b)^2$
    $a^2=(3-b)(3-b)$
    $a^2=9-3b-3b+b^2$
    $a^2=b^2-6b+9$
12. **H** $2.3/50 = 3.1/x$; $2.3x = 155$
    $x = 67.4 \sim 67$
13. **B** $180° - 55° - 35° - 70° = 20°$
14. **J** $1.075(11{,}000) = 11{,}825$
15. **C** $900 - 350 - 325 = 225$
    $225/900 = 0.25 = 25\%$
16. **K** Key – Shape must be a square with all sides 3 units long.
17. **B** Each tick mark is 0.1
18. **F** This coordinate would lie in quadrant II
19. **B** $(5\sqrt{3})^2 + b^2 = 10^2$
    $25(3) + b^2 = 100$
    $75 + b^2 = 100$
    $b^2 = 25$
    $b = 5$
20. **G** height = 4
21. **E** 2+3 is the opposite interior angle of 5 and opposite interior angles are equal
22. **J** $0.20 + 0.15 + 0.10 = 0.45$
23. **D** $\sqrt{13}$ is a non-terminating and non-repeating decimal
24. **K** $60°/360° = 6$; $108/6 = 18$
25. **C** In this formula of a circle 25 is r^2
    Area $= \pi r^2 = 25\pi$
26. **K** Consider 1st point
    +3 in $x = 5$
    -2 in $y = 2$
27. **E** $a(-1)^2 = 3$; $a = 3$
28. **K** (0, 20)
29. **B** $c^2 = 13^2 + (2\sqrt{30})^2$
    $c^2 = 169 + 4(30)$
    $c^2 = 169 + 120$
    $c^2 = 289$
    $c = 17$
30. **J** $c^2 = 6^2 + 8^2$
    $c^2 = 36 + 64$
    $c^2 = 100$
    $c = 10$
31. **A** $3/24 = x/80$
    $24x = 240$
    $x = 10$
32. **H** $\dfrac{y^3 z^2}{x^2}$; y and z are increasing 1; x is decreasing 1
33. **C** $3/12 = x/60$; $7/20 = x/60$
    $180 = 12x$; $420 = 20x$
    $x = 15$; $x = 21$
    $15(4) = 60$; $21(4) = 84$
    $60 + 84 = 144$
34. **J** $1.5w(w) = 2400$
    $1.5w^2 = 2400$
    $w^2 = 1600$; $w = 40$; $l = 60$
35. **B** $x^2 + x^2 = 8^2$
    $2x^2 = 64$
    $x^2 = 32$
    $x = \sqrt{32}$
    $x = \sqrt{16} \cdot \sqrt{2} = 4\sqrt{2}$; Or you can use the common factors for a 45-45 isosceles right triangle.
36. **K** $c^2 = (2\sqrt{6})^2 + 5^2$;
    $c = 4(6) + 25 = 49$; $c = 7$
37. **D** $k = 10$ $(x-5)(x-5)$
38. **G** The angles around 50° are 50° and 80°. Since alternate interior angles are congruent, $x = 80°$.
39. **D** $42/2 = 21$ So use 20 and 22
40. **G** $\triangle_{ABC}$ is 2, 7, 5
    $\triangle_{DEF}$ is 6, 21, 15
    $6/4 = 1.5$

41. **A** $2(2+x) < 6$
    $2+x < 3$
    $x < 1$
42. **K** is the only inequality that must *always* be true. Ex. $a = -4$, $b = 1$
43. **D** $|3|-|-2| = 3-2 = 1$
44. **G** $\dfrac{1+x}{2} = -3$; $1+x = (-3)(2)$; $x = -7$, and $\dfrac{4+y}{2} = 2$; $4+y = (2)(2)$; $y = 0$; $(-7, 0)$
45. **A** $\sin x = o/h = 3/5$
    $3^2 + b^2 = 5^2$
    $9 + b^2 = 25$; $b^2 = 16$; $b = 4$
    $\cos x = a/h = 4/5$
46. **H** Area $= \pi r^2$
    $36\pi = \pi r^2$; $r^2 = 36$; $r = 6$
    diameter $= 2r = 2(6) = 12$
47. **A** $f(-2) = 4(-2)^3 - 2(-2)^2 - 4(-2) + 3$
    $= 4(-8) - 2(4) + 8 + 3$
    $= -32 - 8 + 8 + 3 = -29$
48. **J** $5^2 + b^2 = (\sqrt{34})^2$ (solve for $\overline{DE}$)
    $25 + b^2 = 34$; $b^2 = 9$; $b = 3$
    $\overline{EC} = \overline{AB} - \overline{DE} = 12 - 3 = 9$
49. **B** $\dfrac{3x}{\sqrt{6x-2}} \cdot \dfrac{\sqrt{6x-2}}{\sqrt{6x-2}} = \dfrac{3x\sqrt{6x-2}}{6x-2}$
50. **J** Angles add to 180. Trig only works with right triangles.
51. **C** Multiples are: 8, 16, & 24; and 12 & 24, LCM = 24
52. **J** K works, but 362 is *smallest*
53. **B** $90/2$
54. **K** Let $x = 2$ and $m = 3$ (or any other two values); K doesn't work
55. **B** Add 3^n, so that $4 + 3^1 = 7$; $7 + 3^2 = 16$; $16 + 3^3 = 16 + 27 = 43$
56. **G** $5x + 2 \leq 12$
    $5x \leq 10$
    $x \leq 2$
57. **C** $s^2 = $ Area of a square; $s^2 = 16$; $s = 4$; using 45-45 rules, $r = 2\sqrt{2}$
58. **H** y-intercepts must be the same
59. **B** $\tan 45° = 6/a$; $a = 6/\tan 45°$
60. **G** $1/1.74 = 0.57$; $\csc = 1/\sin$

TEST 2 - p. 370

1. **D** $7 - (-4) = 7 + 4 = 11$
2. **J** $180° - 50° = 130°$
3. **A** $180° - 90° - 40° = 50°$
4. **J** $11.99(1 - .15) = 11.99(.85) = 10.20 \sim 10$
5. **B** $\frac{1}{2}(13)(7) = 45.5$
6. **K** $6^2 + b^2 = 10^2$; $36 + b^2 = 100$
    $b^2 = 64$; $b = 8$; The figure is an isosceles triangle therefore the altitude bisects and is perpendicular to the base.
    $\overline{AB} = 16$.
7. **B** Try each answer
8. **G** radius = 5; center = $(-6, -5)$
9. **B** $230(1 + .14) = 230(1.14) = 262.20$
10. **J** $c^2 = 5^2 + 12^2 = 25 + 144 = 169$; $c = 13$
11. **C** $\dfrac{-3 + (-9)}{2} = \dfrac{-12}{2} = -6$ and
    $\dfrac{2+6}{2} = \dfrac{8}{2} = 4$ so point is $(-6, 4)$
12. **G** Opposite exterior angles are equal
13. **A** Square root of a prime number is a non-repeating and non-terminating decimal
14. **G** $\dfrac{4(78) + x}{5} = 80$ then solve for x:
    $80(5) - 78(4) = x = 88\%$
15. **B** See sequences and series lesson
16. **F** $7/14 = 5/\overline{BQ}$; $\overline{BQ} = 10$; $\overline{BP} = 10 - 5 = 5$
17. **E** Opposite angles are equal, then $180° - 70° = 110°$
18. **G** $1/5 = 0.20$
19. **E** $0.15(1) + 0.35(2) + 0.5(3) = 0.15 + 0.7 + 1.5 = 2.35$
20. **F** Only 1 - if all neg., get neg. result
21. **E** $|2| \bullet |-2| = 2 \bullet 2 = 4$
22. **K** $60°/360° = 1/6$
    $108/6 = 18$
23. **C** $\text{Sum}/5 = 14$, so Sum = 70
    $\text{Sum}+x/6 = 12.5$, so Sum$+x = 75$; and $x = 5$

24. **H** Let $p = 10$ $(100-10)/100 = 0.9$
    $0.9n$ = number who do not play
25. **C** $4+4 = 3(4)+c$; $8 = 12+c$; $c = -4$
26. **J** $3^2-3(3)(-1)+4(-1) = 9+9-4 = 14$
27. **D** Identify unit cost then multiply by the number you are buying
28. **H** $3v-4 = 46$; $3v = 50$; $v = 16.66$
29. **E** Both values are negative it must be in the bottom left - Quad. III
30. **J** $^{12}/_{18} = {^{14}}/_x$; so $12x = 252$, and $x = 21$
31. **C** $\angle CED = 70$ since $\angle CBA = 70$; so $\angle CDE = 180-40-70 = 70$
32. **G** $50-$10 = $40 (total depreciation) $^{40}/_5 = 8$ (depreciation per year) = $^8/_{50} = 0.16 = 16\%$
33. **D** 3 or more; $0.2+0.25+0.15 = 0.6$
34. **G** $11^2 = 121$
35. **C** $|-1|-|-1| = 1-1 = 0$
36. **J** $\dfrac{-3+5}{2} = \dfrac{2}{2} = 1$
37. **B** From noon to 6 pm is 6 hrs; $^{90°}/_6 = 15°$ per hour •2 hours $= 30°$
38. **K** Using equation of a circle $r^2 = 100$, so Area $= \pi r^2 = 100\pi$
39. **C** $c^2 = 3^2+3^2 = 9+9 = 18$
    $c = \sqrt{18} = \sqrt{9}\sqrt{2} = 3\sqrt{2}$
40. **H** Try each choice
41. **E** Try each choice
42. **F** $^1/_{5a} = 5^{-a}$
43. **D** $F = ma = 40•9.8 = 392$
44. **H** $0.75\text{kg}•1000\ ^g/_{kg} \div 150\text{cm}^3 = 750\text{g} \div 150\text{cm}^3 = 5\ ^g/_{cm^3}$
45. **C** 30-60 right triangle
46. **H** 9 since $9+9 = 18$
47. **E** $\frac{1}{2}(bh) = 1/2(6)(12) = 36$

48. **K** $\dfrac{2x}{\sqrt{8x+2}} \cdot \dfrac{\sqrt{8x+2}}{\sqrt{8x+2}} = \dfrac{2x\sqrt{8x+2}}{8x+2}$
    $= \dfrac{2x\sqrt{8x+2}}{2(4x+1)} = \dfrac{x\sqrt{8x+2}}{4x+1}$
49. **E** From calculator, $\tan 30° = 0.577$.
    From memory, $\tan 30° \dfrac{opp}{adj} =$
    $\dfrac{0.5}{x} = \dfrac{1}{2} \cdot \dfrac{1}{x} = \dfrac{1}{2x}$. So $\dfrac{1}{2x} = 0.577$, and $x = {^1}/_{(2)(0.577)} = 0.866$.
    Use trial and error to see that
    $0.866 = \dfrac{\sqrt{3}}{2}$. Whew!
50. **K** $2x-6 > 8$; $2x > 14$; $x > 7$
51. **E** Noon to 6 pm is 6 hours; $^{90°}/_{6\text{ hours}} = 15°$ per hour One hour before 6pm is 5 pm
52. **H** $180°-30°-90° = 60°$
53. **B** Let $x = 20$ and $y = 0$
54. **G** Divide both sides by x
55. **B** Closed circle at -3 and to the right
56. **H** $2x+3x+4x = 180°$; $9x = 180°$; $x = 20°$; Smallest angle is $2x = 2(20°) = 40°$
57. **B** $A = n$ $B = {^n}/_2$ $C = ({^n}/_2)(2) - 10$
58. **J** $\dfrac{x-20}{12} = 60$; $x-20 = (60)(12) = 720$; $x = 720+20 = 740$
59. **E** cot is $^a/_o$ where $o = 20$
60. **J** $\cos 22° = {^{\text{vert dist}}}/_{40}$; $\sin 22° = {^{\text{horiz dist}}}/_{40}$; Vert dist + Horiz dist $= 40\cos 22° + 40\sin 22°$. Subtracting 40 gives distance that direct route is shorter.

READING COMPREHENSION – GENERAL TIPS AND STRATEGIES

40 Questions	35 Minutes

Passage Topics
Prose Fiction
Social Science
Humanities
Natural Science

This test has four passages, one each based on the general topics mentioned above. Each passage has ten questions. In each passage, the questions get progressively harder. This simply means that question one is the easiest and question ten is the hardest. For the next passage, question eleven is the easiest and question twenty is the hardest.

Each ACT Reading test is built around the same kinds of questions. Questions may focus on identifying the main idea of a paragraph or the passage as a whole, identifying the correct sequence of events presented in the passage, identifying and analyzing details from the passage, identifying the meaning of a word or phrase, making a generalization about information or people in the passage, analyzing the way ideas or people are compared or contrasted in the passage, identifying any cause and effect relationships in the passage or analyzing the author's style, writing method or perspective. As you practice this test, you will become very familiar with the common question types. This familiarity will help you know how to answer these questions and what to look for while reading the passage.

The following are some very effective strategies and methods for taking the reading comprehension test.

1. VISUALIZE WHAT YOU READ.

- Use visualization to force yourself to think about what you are reading.
- Visualize things with which you can relate.
- Don't memorize individual facts; memorize the images.
- Limit the number of images in your mind to five.
- Remember the order of your images to make your look-back more efficient.

Have you ever read a book for a while then wondered what you just read? Or maybe you read a little and instead of thinking about the story, your mind was thinking about what you were going to do that evening or what you did the day before. I think we have all experienced that too many times. On the ACT test, this dilemma is all too familiar.

The point is that you read the story, but you didn't have a clue what you just read because you weren't thinking about the story. So how can you prevent this? Visualize what you read as you read it. If you are visualizing the story as you read it, you force yourself to think about it.

There are a few key guidelines for visualization. The first is to visualize things with which you can relate. For example, if the story talks about a girl going to her mailbox to get a letter, I want you to think of someone you know going to her mailbox. I want you to actually see this happening in your mind.

The second key is not to memorize individual facts. See the image. If the paragraph says the girl went to the mailbox to get a small white postcard, then I want you to memorize one single image in your mind that contains all of those facts. Don't memorize a list of facts: girl, mailbox and small white postcard. Just memorize one image that contains those facts. If you do this, you only have to remember one thing, your image, and not several facts. The facts are contained in the image.

The third key is to limit the number of images in your mind. There are very good studies analyzing what normal humans are able to store in short-term and long-term memory. You are limited in the number of facts you can store in short-term memory. Instead of trying to memorize 30 or 40 facts from the story, try to reduce the facts to no more than five images in your mind. Your five images will contain many facts. Now I know you probably will not be able to ascertain all 30 or 40 facts from your five images, but you can retain many more facts from remembering your images than you would from concentrating on individual details.

The final point is that you should try to remember the order of your images as they take place in the story. Have you ever tried to look back in the story to find the answer only to read the entire passage before you come to the answer? There is nothing wrong with looking back through the passage to find the answer, but if you remember the order of your images, then you will have a very good idea about where you can find your answer in the passage. This makes your look-back much more efficient.

An old cliché says that a picture is worth a thousand words. Well, I believe a few images in your mind are worth many questions on an ACT reading comprehension test. Give it a try. I think you will be surprised at the results.

2. DON'T SPEAK WHAT YOU READ.

- Read with your eyes, not with your mouth.
- Read in groups of words rather than reading each individual word.
- Keep your eyes moving through the page.

Many students have a tendency to say what they read as they read it. You may be one of these students. Maybe you don't actually say the words when you read them, but you move your mouth when you read as if you were saying the words. Or, maybe you are extreme and do what I did in high school. I didn't say the words or move my mouth as if I was saying them, I breathed as if I was saying the words. If you do that very long, you'll pass out. If you breathe what you read on a 35 minute test, you will be really fatigued by the end. All of these actions are totally unnecessary.

You should be at peace when you read. You have probably heard your elementary teachers tell you this at some point, but here it is again: read with your eyes, not with your mouth. Reading with your mouth slows you down (as well as irritates the people around you). If you read with your mouth, you only read as fast as you can say the words, and you force yourself to stop at every word on the page until your mouth says it. Your brain can read and comprehend words much faster than your mouth can say them. Almost any speed-reading course will try to teach you to do two key things: read in groups of words rather than individual words and keep your eyes moving through the page. If you have to say every word, you can't read in groups of words and your eyes have to identify each word as you say it. By reading with your eyes and not your mouth, you are able to capture groups of words in an instant and keep your eyes moving through the page.

If you have a tendency to speak what you read, work on correcting that habit. Increasing your reading comprehension speed and reducing the focus on individual words can greatly improve your comprehension. Go to www.chadcargill.com for a free speed reading lesson.

3. GET LOST IN YOUR TEST.

- Ignore everything around you.
- Stay focused.
- Be mentally tough!

I don't mean "get lost" like you have no clue. I mean "get lost" like when you notice no distractions. Have you ever been playing a video game or doing something you really loved, and you look up and notice that an hour has gone by in what seems to be just a few minutes? You became oblivious to the time and your surroundings. That's what I mean by getting lost. It's a good thing.

There are many distractions during the reading comprehension test. I believe reading comprehension is the quietest section of the ACT. There are no calculators being pounded, and most students are not even writing. Everyone in the test center is reading. But because it is so quiet, this test is also the loudest test you take. It is so quiet every little noise is going to be magnified millions of times, and you *are* going to notice it. At some point during your reading comprehension test, I guarantee you someone is going to cough or sneeze. What will be your response? You are going to look and may even offer a "bless you." Let me assure you the person who sneezed will be just fine without your blessing. You need to keep testing. Just do your best to ignore the distractions around you.

I know the stories on the ACT are extremely boring. I know you don't care about these topics, and, frankly, you don't want to read about them. Remember the purpose of these passages is not to entertain you. You are reading them for information so you can answer the questions. When the test administrator says, "You may begin," I want you to make a commitment to do nothing but concentrate on this test. Be mentally tough! You are devoting 35 minutes of your life to a very specific goal. Higher test scores mean more scholarship money for the school you really want to attend. You can do it.

4. LEARN YOUR METHOD.

- Different students comprehend better using different methods.
- You must try each method.
- Mix and match, add to and take away—find what combination works for *you*.

Reading experts have many theories on how high school students should take this test. I am amazed at how many experts tell groups of students they should all use the same method. Typically, these experts tell students they should preview the questions first. However, I believe every student learns differently and every student comprehends what he or she reads differently. I don't think you can give a set method to a group of students and say that this will maximize scores. To defend this, I did a study at Oklahoma State University analyzing what method works best for high school students on the ACT reading test. We had 117 high school students from several different high schools take practice tests. We tried a variety of methods. In the end, I found that 48 percent did score highest on the ACT when they first previewed the questions. That sounds really good, but this result told me that there were 52 percent of today's high school students that need to do something else. Forty-four percent of the 117 students scored highest if they read the passage first at a pace that they could understand and then looked at the questions. The remaining 8 percent actually scored highest if they didn't read the passage at all. These students just went to the questions, then scanned the passage to find the answers. These 8 percent would read small excerpts out of the passage, but in general, they didn't read the passage.

In my work with high school students, I find that approximately 15-20 percent of students feel that not reading the passage works best for them. Typically, students who genuinely score highest using this method, score very well on the ACT reading comprehension test; however, students who use this method just so they don't have to read the passages typically score very poorly.

The key is that you must find what genuinely works for you—not anyone else. Only then will you be able to maximize your score. Here are three general methods that you should try to determine what works best for you.

Method 1:
      Step 1: Preview the questions
      Step 2: Briskly read the passage
      Step 3: Answer the questions, referring back to the passage

Method 2:
      Step 1: Read the questions thoroughly
      Step 2: Find the answers in the passage

Method 3:
      Step 1: Read the passage thoroughly
      Step 2: Find the answers
      Step 3: Quickly answer the questions

There are many variations to these methods. For example, many experts say to underline important words or phrases while you are reading the passage. This works for some students, while others get more confused by this. You should practice this section enough times to not only find the best method for you but also to master it.

5. LEARN TO FINISH IN 35 MINUTES.

- Use all the time available.
- Don't try to finish early.
- Maximize your time; maximize your score.

When you read this bullet, you are probably thinking, "No kidding, it's a 35 minute test." Obviously, you want to finish the test, but let's look at this from a different angle.

Let's say you are thinking you don't need help in reading because you have a 27 and you finish ten minutes early every time. You know you're a really good reader, and you fly through this section. A 27 is a really good score, and you are proud of it, especially considering that it takes you only twenty-five minutes instead of thirty-five minutes. Let's break down these numbers and determine what really happened. Finishing ten minutes early implies that you had on average two and a half extra minutes for each of the four passages. Typically a score of 27 in the reading section means you missed about 12 questions. If each passage has ten questions, then on average you got seven out of ten correct or 70%. Now a 27 is still a great score, but a reader who is this good should get more than 70 percent of the questions correct. Wouldn't you agree that if you had an extra two and a half minutes to look back through the passage to find the answer to one of those three questions you missed, you could probably get one more right per passage? If you are that good of a reader, you could probably get two more right per passage. If you get two of those three that you missed per passage correct, your score would increase from a 27 to about a 33.

If you are at a 27 and finish ten minutes early, you should be scoring about a 33. If your score is a 27 and you finish five minutes early, you should be scoring about a 30 in reading. Maximize your time; maximize your score.

In the three methods given in strategy four, you should notice that the words are very vague. Words like *briskly*, *thoroughly*, and *quickly* are used. How would you define these words? Define the words such that whatever method works best for you allows you to finish in 35 minutes. If you are a method one reader, then how briskly should you read the passage or how long should you preview the questions? You should define them such that you finish in 35 minutes. The specific amount of time you dedicate to each step can only be set by you. Don't take a stopwatch and give yourself one minute to preview the questions, four minutes to briskly read the passage, and four minutes to answer the questions. You should practice your method enough that you have a general feel for how long is appropriate for each step.

Each passage should take you about 8 minutes and 45 seconds to complete. If you finish late, work your pace and method to speed up. If you typically finish the test early and you are not scoring high 30s, slow down.

6. READ FIVE MINUTES A DAY.

- Get a book about something you love.
- Read sliding a notecard from the top down.
- Read three minutes with a card and two minutes without a card.
- Keep your eyes moving down the page.

Do you hate to read? Give me a student who reads every day, and I'll show you a student who usually scores high on standardized tests. I guarantee if you read on a daily basis, your reading will improve. So let's establish a manageable, attainable way a person who hates to read can start reading every day.
1. Choose a book about a topic you love. Specifically for ACT preparation, I like books that have narrow columns about the width of an ACT column.
2. Start a timer on your phone for three minutes.
3. Slide a notecard from the top down at a rate that is slightly uncomfortable for your reading speed.
4. At the end of the three minutes, stop, get up, and stretch.
5. Start a new timer for two minutes.
6. Continue reading without the card, and keep your eyes moving down the page.

7. PASSAGE A / PASSAGE B STRATEGY

- Save this for last of the four reading passages.
- Read Passage A. Answer all Passage A questions.
- Answer any remaining question specifying a line number.
- Check time remaining and determine strategy for Passage B.

One of the four reading passages is now broken into two parts. I skip this one and do it last. I'll explain why in a moment. I start by reading Passage A only. Then I answer each question about Passage A. This is half the material to remember, and my look back is efficient. Next, I answer every question that specifies a line number. These questions say, "in line…" I can answer these quickly by looking back at the lines specified. Now I have 3-4 questions left which are all about Passage B. Using the timing method I recommend (see page 5), I quickly check to see how many minutes remain. Then I make decision if I have time to read Passage B, skim Passage B, or just find answers. Many have used this method after I taught it, and the response has been overwhelmingly positive. I hope you'll give it a try and see if it helps you.

TYPES OF QUESTIONS

Understanding how to answer the standard types of questions that appear on the reading test can improve your score immensely. Following are three passages with questions that illustrate the basic concepts tested on the reading test. Read each passage carefully, then consider each question its explanation.

PASSAGE ONE

HUMANITIES: THE PASSAGE IS EXCERPTED FROM GUSTAV KOBBE'S *THE LOVES OF GREAT COMPOSERS*.

Nearly eight years after Mozart's death, his widow, in response to a request from a famous publishing house for relics of the composer, sent, among other Mozartiana, a packet of letters written to
5 her by her husband. In transmitting these she wrote:

"Especially characteristic is his great love for me, which breathes through all the letters. Is it not true—those from the last year of his life are just as tender as those written during the first year of our
10 marriage?" She added that she would like to have this fact especially mentioned "to his honor" in any biography in which the data she sent were to be used. This request was not prompted by vanity, but by a just pride in the love her husband had borne her and
15 which she still cherished. The love of his Constance was the solace of Mozart's life.

The wonder-child, born in Salzburg in 1756, and taken by his father from court to court, where he and his sister played to admiring audiences, did not, like
20 so many wonder-children, fade from public view, but with manhood fulfilled the promise of his early years and became one of the world's great masters of music. But his genius was not appreciated until too late. The world of today sees in Mozart the type of
25 the brilliant, careless Bohemian, whom it loves to associate with art, and long since has taken him to its heart. But the world of his own day, when he asked for bread, offered him a stone.

Mozart died young; he was only thirty-five. His
30 sufferings were crowded into a few years, but throughout these years there stood by his side one whose love soothed his trials and brightened his life—the Constance whom he adored. What she wrote to the publishers was strictly true. His last
35 letters to her breathed a love as fervent as the first.

Some six months before he died, she was obliged to go to Baden for her health. "You hardly will believe," he writes to her, "how heavily time hangs on my hands without you. I cannot exactly explain
40 my feelings. There is a void that pains me; a certain longing that cannot be satisfied, hence never ceases, continues ever, aye, grows from day to day. When I think how happy and childlike we would be together in Baden and what sad, tedious hours I pass here! I
45 take no pleasure in my work, because I cannot break it off now and then for a few words with you, as I am accustomed to. When I go to the piano and sing something from the opera ["The Magic Flute"], I have to stop right away, it affects me so. Basta!--if
50 this very hour I could see my way clear to you, the next hour wouldn't find me here." In another letter written at this time he kisses her "in thought two thousand times."

1. In the context of the passage, it is most reasonable to infer that the phrase "But the world of his own day, when he asked for bread, offered him a stone" in lines 27-28 means that
    A. Mozart was reduced to begging for food from his neighbors.
    B. Mozart's society rejected his talent.
    C. poverty and starvation were widespread during Mozart's lifetime.
    D. society threatened to stone Mozart to death.

Question 1 asks you to **IDENTIFY THE MEANING OF A PHRASE**. Look for clues in the passage that will help you understand the meaning. The sentence before the phrase you are considering states that the modern world recognizes Mozart for the genius he is. The word *But* at the beginning of the chosen phrase implies some sort of contradiction to another idea in the passage. You can reasonably conclude that society during Mozart's life did not recognize his talent. This assumption is also supported by an earlier sentence in the paragraph: "But his genius was not appreciated until too late." Based on the inferences you can make, given the context clues in the passage, B is the best answer. Mozart was not literally asking his neighbors for bread (the bread is a metaphor for appreciation or recognition), so choice A is incorrect. Nothing in the passage supports the assertion in choice C. If you understand the nuances of the phrase, choice D becomes obviously incorrect.

2. Based on the passage, which of the following statements best describe the relationship between Mozart and Constance?
   F. Constance's health suffered as a result of Mozart's demanding personality.
   G. Mozart believed that Constance was the inspiration for his musical creations.
   H. Mozart relied on Constance for support and encouragement.
   J. The marriage was secondary to Mozart's desire to compose music.

Question 2 asks you to **IDENTIFY AND ANALYZE INFORMATION** from the passage. To answer this type of question, you need to identify clues and details from the passage which give you information about the topic of the question and then form some sort of conclusion based on that information. In this case, look through the passage for details about the relationship between Mozart and Constance. In lines 6-10, Constance talks about the letters from Mozart which illustrate his great, undying love for her. Lines 15-16 identifie Constance as the solace (comfort) of Mozart's life. Lines 31-33 give you an image of Constance as the person who supported him through his "trials and brightened his life." Lines 34-35 tells you that his last letters revealed a "love as fervent as the first." The last paragraph reveals that Mozart would have gladly given up working on his music to be with Constance in Baden.
Based on all of these details, you can reasonably conclude that Mozart depended on Constance for support throughout their time together and that theirs was a true love match. Choice H is the option that best fits this conclusion. The passage does not connect Constance's ill health (mentioned in the last paragraph) to Mozart in any way, which eliminates choice F. It also does not offer evidence that Mozart saw Constance as the direct inspiration for his musical creations, so choice G is incorrect. Because of Mozart's desire to be with Constance instead of working that is expressed in the last paragraph, you can also eliminate choice J.

3. The main point of the passage is that
   A. Constance was proud of the fact that Mozart's love for her had endured and thrived to the end of his life.
   B. Constance was the unwavering love of Mozart's life.
   C. Mozart didn't like Constance to be away from him for any length of time.
   D. Mozart fulfilled his childhood potential and became a music genius.

Question 3 asks you to **IDENTIFY THE MAIN POINT OF THE PASSAGE**. To answer this type of question (or questions that ask about the main idea or main theme), you must consider the passage as a whole. Ask yourself what is the point of the passage? What does the passage talk mostly about? You are looking for the focus of the passage; avoid choosing one detail from the passage to illustrate the main idea. Instead, look for the repetition or emphasis of an idea that is supported by several details. This passage begins by discussing the love letters Mozart's widow is sending to a publishing company; these letters illustrate the strong, abiding love Mozart had for his wife, Constance. Paragraphs 3 and 4 give you some background information about Mozart and end by reaffirming the love he felt for Constance. Paragraph 5 is focused on how much Mozart dislikes Constance being away from him and how much he misses her. The paragraph ends with his desire to kiss her "in thought two thousand times." The clear focus of this passage is how much Mozart loved his wife. That main idea is clearly expressed in choice B. Although choices A and C are true and supported by evidence in the passage, they do not express the main idea of the passage. They are merely details used to support the main idea. Choice D is also true, but it is part of the background information given so that you will understand Mozart's lifestyle and does not express the main idea of the passage.

4. Which of the following statements can NOT be supported by information in the passage?
   F. Mozart's widow approved of the biography to be written about her husband.
   G. Mozart's father believed his children were immensely talented and musically gifted.
   H. Mozart found comfort and enjoyment in Constance's company.
   J. Mozart and his wife lived in poverty because his talent was not acknowledged during his lifetime.

Question 4 asks you to **MAKE A GENERALIZATION** about information given in the passage. You should also notice the capitalized *NOT* in the question stem. Be sure to pay attention to any word that is capitalized in the question stems because it will direct you to think differently about the information you are considering. In this case, you are looking for a statement that is not supported by evidence from the passage. The tricky part is that all of the statements listed may be true; however, the question wants you to focus on what the passage actually talks about. Choice F can be supported by the passage: Constance obviously approved of the biography if she sent materials to be used in the writing of it. Choice G can also be supported by the passage. Lines 18-19 tell you that Mozart's father took his son and daughter from one royal court to another so that they could perform to admiring audiences. Certainly he would not have done that if he did not believe they would be successful. Choice H is amply supported by the passage, so just by the process of elimination, choice J is correct. You may know that the statement in choice J is literally true; Mozart and Constance's financial situation was strained because he could not find a patron, but that statement is not supported by any information in the passage

PASSAGE TWO

SOCIAL STUDIES: THIS PASSAGE IS EXCERPTED FROM HERBERT N. CASSON'S *THE HISTORY OF THE TELEPHONE*

Alexander Graham Bell was a young man, barely twenty-eight, at the time when his ear caught the first cry of the telephone, but he was already a man of some note on his own account. He had been
[5] educated in Edinburgh, the city of his birth, and in London, and had in one way and another picked up a smattering of anatomy, music, electricity, and telegraphy. Until he was sixteen years of age, he had read nothing but novels and poetry and romantic tales
[10] of Scottish heroes. Then he left home to become a teacher of elocution in various British schools, and by the time he was of age he had made several slight discoveries as to the nature of vowel sounds. Shortly afterwards, he met in London two distinguished men,
[15] Alexander J. Ellis and Sir Charles Wheatstone, who did far more than they ever knew to forward Bell in the direction of the telephone.

Ellis was the president of the London Philological Society. Also, he was the translator of
[20] the famous book on "The Sensations of Tone," written by Helmholtz, who, in the period from 1871 to 1894, made Berlin the world center for the study of the physical sciences. So it happened that when Bell ran to Ellis as a young enthusiast and told his
[25] experiments, Ellis informed him that Helmholtz had done the same things several years before and done them more completely. He brought Bell to his house and showed him what Helmholtz had done—how he had kept tuning forks in vibration by the power of
[30] electromagnets and blended the tones of several tuning forks together to produce the complex quality of the human voice.

Now, Helmholtz had not been trying to invent a telephone nor any sort of message-carrier. His aim
[35] was to point out the physical basis of music and nothing more. But this fact that an electromagnet would set a tuning fork humming was new to Bell and very attractive. It appealed at once to him as a student of speech. If a tuning fork could be made to
[40] sing by a magnet or an electrified wire, why would it not be possible to make a musical telegraph—a telegraph with a piano key board, so that many messages could be sent at once over a single wire? Unknown to Bell, there were several dozen inventors
[45] then at work upon this problem, which proved in the end to be very elusive. But it gave him at least a starting point, and he forthwith commenced his quest of the telephone.

As he was then in England, his first step was
[50] naturally to visit Sir Charles Wheatstone, the best known English expert on telegraphy. Sir Charles had earned his title by many inventions. He was a simple-natured scientist, and treated Bell with the utmost kindness. He showed him an ingenious
[55] talking-machine that had been made by Baron de Kempelin. At this time Bell was twenty-two and unknown; Wheatstone was sixty-seven and famous. The personality of the veteran scientist made so vivid a picture upon the mind of the impressionable young
[60] Bell that the grand passion of science became henceforth the master motif of his life.

From this summit of glorious ambition he was thrown, several months later, into the depths of grief and despondency. The White Plague had come to the
[65] home in Edinburgh and taken away his two brothers. More, it had put its mark upon the young inventor himself. Nothing but a change of climate, said his doctor, would put him out of danger. And so, to save his life, he and his father and mother set sail from
[70] Glasgow and came to the small Canadian town of Brantford, where for a year he fought down his tendency to consumption, and satisfied his nervous energy by teaching "Visible Speech" to a tribe of Mohawk Indians.

1. According to the passage, Bell's inspiration to invent what became the telephone began with
   A. the concept of electromagnets transmitting the tones of a human voice
   B. the discovery of de Kempelin's talking-machine
   C. the invention of a musical telegraph
   D. the idea that vibrating tuning forks could generate the intricate nuances of a human voice

Question 1 asks you to **IDENTIFY THE CORRECT SEQUENCE OF EVENTS** in the passage. In answering these questions, keep in mind that the order that events appear in the passage may or may not be the order that they actually happened. Don't assume that just because one event is mentioned before another that it occurred first. Read carefully for clues and details that reveal the correct sequence of events.

According to lines 28-32, lines 39-43 and lines 46-48, Bell connected the ability of the vibration of the tuning fork powered by electromagnets to produce the tones of a human voice to the idea of a device that would transmit several messages at once through a single wire. This new idea was the beginning of research that ultimately resulted in the telephone, so choice D is correct. Choice A is incorrect because, according to the passage, electromagnets did not transmit the sounds themselves; they merely caused the tuning forks to vibrate which then produced the sounds. Choice B is incorrect because de Kempelin's talking machine isn't mentioned until after Bell has already conceived the idea of what became the telephone. Choice C is incorrect because the musical telegraph had not been invented yet; Bell envisions creating one.

One of the keys in answering this question lies in lines 46-48. The pronoun *it* in line 46 is identified as the "starting point" for his "quest of the telephone." Identifying the antecedent of the pronoun *it* will provide you with Bell's inspiration. That antecedent is the idea of using the ability of a tuning fork to produce sounds to create a device that could send multiple messages through a single line.

2. The description of Sir Charles Wheatstone provided in paragraph four serves to emphasize the description of
   F. Bell's youth and inexperience
   G. Bell's stubbornness and desire to succeed
   H. Baron de Kempelin's successful invention
   J. his long and distinguished career

Question 2 asks you to **ANALYZE A COMPARISON** the passage makes between Sir Charles Wheatstone and one of the choices provided. To answer this kind of question, you must first determine if a comparison is truly being made between the items identified. Nowhere in the passage is a comparison made between Wheatstone and Baron de Kempelin, so choice H is incorrect. The fact that Wheatstone had a long and distinguished career is just part of the description of him, not a fact being compared with the description, so choice J is incorrect. Lines 56-57 clearly establish a comparison being made between Wheatstone and Bell, so you have narrowed the potentially correct choices to F or G. Now ask yourself if the description of Wheatstone as an "expert on telegraphy" having "earned his title by many inventions" (lines 51-52) and as "sixty-seven and famous" (line 57) emphasizes Bell's youth and inexperience or his stubbornness. The passage makes no reference to Bell being stubborn, but does say that Bell was "twenty-two and unknown" (lines 56-57), so you can infer that the comparison is made to emphasize Bell's youth and inexperience (choice F).

3. According to the passage, the White Plague caused which of the following?
   I. Bell to develop consumption
   II. the development of a language that used signs rather than sounds
   III. the deaths of Bell's brothers
   A. I only
   B. II only
   C. I and III only
   D. I, II and III

Question 3 asks you to **IDENTIFY A CAUSE AND EFFECT RELATIONSHIP**. To answer this kind of question you must read carefully to make sure a clear relationship exists between the cause (the White Plague) and the effects (the choices offered). Just happening after the cause doesn't guarantee that relationship. The deaths of

Bell's brothers are a direct result of the arrival of the White Plague (lines 64-65), so choice III is correct. Bell does develop consumption as a result of his experience with the White Plague (lines 66 and 72), so choice I is also correct. Although Bell leaves his home and moves to Brantford as a result of his having contracted the White Plague, he doesn't develop a visual language because of that. According to the passage, he **taught** "Visible Speech," but there is no indication that he **developed** it then. Choice C is the correct answer.

PASSAGE THREE

PROSE FICTION: THIS PASSAGE IS EXCERPTED FROM *THE SECRET GARDEN* BY FRANCES HODGSON BURNETT.

When Mary Lennox was sent to Misselthwaite Manor to live with her uncle, everybody said she was the most disagreeable-looking child ever seen. It was true, too. She had a little thin face and a little thin body, thin light hair and a sour expression. Her hair was yellow, and her face was yellow because she had been born in India and had always been ill in one way or another. Her father had held a position under the English Government and had always been busy and ill himself, and her mother had been a great beauty who cared only to go to parties and amuse herself. She had not wanted a little girl at all, and when Mary was born she handed her over to the care of an Ayah, who was made to understand that if she wished to please the Mem Sahib she must keep the child out of sight as much as possible. So when she was a sickly, fretful, ugly little baby she was kept out of the way, and when she became a sickly, fretful, toddling thing she was kept out of the way also. She never remembered seeing familiarly anything but the dark faces of her Ayah and the other native servants, and as they always obeyed her and gave her her own way in everything, because the Mem Sahib would be angry if she was disturbed by her crying, by the time she was six years old she was as tyrannical and selfish a little pig as ever lived. The young English governess who came to teach her to read and write disliked her so much that she gave up her place in three months, and when other governesses came to try to fill it they always went away in a shorter time than the first one. So if Mary had not chosen to really want to know how to read books she would never have learned her letters at all.

1. The relationship between Mary and her mother can best be described as
   A. distant but polite
   B. loving but disciplined
   C. physically abusive and demeaning
   D. unaffectionate and neglectful

Question 1 asks you to **ANALYZE INFORMATION** that is provided in the passage. The paragraph gives several clues as to the relationship between Mary and her mother: Her mother is described as a person "who cared only to go to parties and amuse herself" (line 11) and who "had not wanted a little girl at all" (12). Once Mary was born she "handed her over to the care of an Ayah" (13-14) and told the nurse to "keep the child out of sight as much as possible" (16). The servants are careful to keep Mary happy because they knew her mother "would be angry if she was disturbed by her crying" (24). Based on these details about how Mary's mother acts and feels about her daughter, you can infer that there is little affection between the two because Mary's mother never sees her or thinks about her other than to be annoyed at any distraction she might provide. Choice D clearly describes the relationship and is the correct answer. Choice B is incorrect because neither Mary nor her mother is described as loving, even if the relationship might be described as disciplined. Choice C might sound correct at first glance because the relationship could be described as demeaning for Mary, but the passage doesn't specify how Mary feels about the treatment of her mother. The passage also doesn't offer any evidence that Mary's mother is physically abusive to her. Although their relationship could be described as distant as choice A offers, neither Mary nor her mother are described as polite or even actually interacting with one another.

2. The main purpose of the paragraph is to
   F. describe Mary's background so that the reader will better understand her character
   G. explain why Mary is sent to live with her uncle
   H. show how the servants feel about Mary and her parents
   J. show how uneducated Mary is as compared with her family

In answering questions that ask you to **IDENTIFY THE MAIN PURPOSE** of the paragraph, you must consider the paragraph as a whole. Think about what information the paragraph has given and then decide what conclusion the author wants you to make about that information. Although not all of the information given in the passage is directly about Mary, it does provide a picture of how her life is. Based on what you read in the passage, you understand that both her mother and her father have very little, if any, interaction with her, and that most of her care comes from servants who are unable to discipline her in any way. She has had very little formal education and no apparent friends at all. The result is an unpleasant, spoiled child. The passage also describes Mary's appearance which seems to fit with her personality: "she was the most disagreeable-looking child ever seen" (line 3). After reading the paragraph, you should have a better understanding of Mary and her behavior. Since all of the information given focuses on Mary and her background, you can conclude that choice F is the best option. Choice G is incorrect because although the first sentence of the paragraph mentions Mary being sent to live with her uncle, the rest of the paragraph does not explain why that happens. Choice H is incorrect because the paragraph only briefly and indirectly alludes to the attitude of the servants toward Mary's mother (and not all toward her father) by describing how the servants never disciplined Mary because they did not want to anger her mother. This is merely a detail used to complete the characterization of Mary, not provide the focus of the paragraph. The same logic is applied to choice J: the mention of Mary's lack of education is just a part of the overall characterization, not the focus of the paragraph.

3. As it is used in line 26, the word *tyrannical* most nearly means
   A. angry
   B. demanding
   C. unhappy
   D. self-centered

Question 3 asks you to **IDENTIFY THE MEANING OF THE WORD** *tyrannical*. When answering this type of question, be sure that you consider how the word is used in the passage. Some words may have slightly different meanings based on how they are used in context. Don't just assume that because you think you know what a word means that it will mean the same thing in every situation. Choice B is the best answer because it most nearly describes Mary's attitude toward everyone around her. The servants "always obeyed her" (line 22) and she has been given "her own way in everything" (23); this kind of treatment has caused her to becoming *demanding*. Choice A is incorrect because the paragraph offers no evidence of Mary's anger. While choice C may be true of Mary overall, it doesn't fit with the context given of a child who is accustomed to getting her way. Choice D is incorrect because it would be redundant in context; *self-centered* is too similar in meaning to *selfish*.

4. Which of the following statements most accurately explains why a governess for Mary was so difficult to find?
   F. The pay wasn't sufficient to compensate for dealing with Mary.
   G. The location was too remote for most people.
   H. Mary was unpleasant and difficult to teach.
   J. Mary's parents didn't like any of the candidates for the job.

Question 4 asks you to **MAKE A GENERALIZATION** based on information given in the passage. Choice H is the only choice supported by the passage. The paragraph clearly establishes that Mary is an unpleasant child and her demanding, spoiled behavior would make her a troublesome student. The passage never mentions the remoteness of the location, the amount of money the governesses received or the opinion that Mary's parents had about any of the governesses.

5. As it is used in line 16, the title *Mem Sahib* refers to
   A. Mary's mother
   B. Mary Lennox
   C. Mary's governess
   D. Mary's nursemaid

Question 5 asks you to **IDENTIFY INFORMATION** from the passage. Lines 12-16 establish the identity of Mem Sahib: "She had not wanted a little girl at all, and when Mary was born she handed her over to the care of an Ayah, who was made to understand that if she wished to please the Mem Sahib she must keep the child out of sight as much as possible." The pronoun *She* clearly refers to Mary's mother, so choice A is correct.

Visualization Exercises
(Practice Exercise for General Reading Tip #1)

Directions: The following lists of words could be identified as critical information from paragraphs or groups of paragraphs in an ACT reading passage. Ask someone to read you a list provided below. If no one is available to read the list to you, read the list then cover the words. Instead of memorizing each list of words or facts, create a mental image containing each set of words. Try to remember only one image that contains the list of words or facts. After waiting about 10-15 seconds, see if you can write the words in the order they were given (still using your image).

The more you can train yourself to visualize the text as you read, the more you interact with the text and the better reader you will become.

me dog walk brown park pond 2 birds 2 trees 3 goldfish	girl mailbox card surprised cool sunny leaves on ground	cheering many people painted faces stadium teams cheerleaders bands
preacher choir guitar old solo sing	lawn Trumpet Vine hummingbirds Ruby Red-Throats darting flight patterns protecting food	classroom bulletin board blue pictures presidents constitution Declaration of Independence
podium audience hot tie nervous speech applause	saxophone soprano melody trumpet harmony conductor stop	pond still boat anchor rod reel bass tackle

CONCEPT: SPEED READING

WORD GROUPING

One important aspect of increasing your reading speed is to limit the number of eye fixations. Each eye fixation causes you to stop (even if only for an instant) to read a word. One way to reduce these stops is by reading in groups of words rather than by reading individual words.

EXAMPLE: John and his sister went to the store to buy some candy.

Instead of reading the sentence as 12 individual words, try reading the sentence with word grouping as shown below.

John and his sister   went to the store   to buy some candy.

Instead of twelve eye fixations, now there are only three.

An ACT reading test typically has between 3600 and 4000 words. Using word grouping, you can greatly reduce your reading time by limiting your eye fixations.

STEP 1: Read the following passages using the word groupings provided. Limit your eye fixations to the groupings. You should read the word grouping as a single element instead of reading each individual word. Try to increase your speed as you go.

PASSAGE I

The Devoted Friend

by Oscar Wilde

One morning   the old Water-rat   put his head out   of his hole.   He had
bright beady eyes   and stiff gray whiskers,   and his tail   was like a long bit
of black India-Rubber.   The little ducks   were swimming about   in the pond,
looking just like   a lot of yellow canaries,   and their mother,   who was pure white
with real red legs,   was trying to teach them   how to stand   on their heads
in the water.

"You will never be   in the best society   unless you can stand   on your heads,"
she kept saying to them,   and every now and then   she showed them how
it was done.   But the little ducks   paid no attention to her.   They were so young
that they did not know   what an advantage it is   to be in society at all.
"What disobedient children!"   cried the old Water-rat;   "they really deserve
to be drowned."   "Nothing of the kind,"   answered the Duck,   "every one must
make a beginning,   and parents cannot   be too patient."   "Ah! I know nothing
about the feelings of parents,"   said the Water-rat;   "I am not   a family man.
In fact,   I have never been married,   and I never intend to be.
Love is all   very well in its way,   but friendship is much higher.   Indeed, I know
of nothing in the world   that is either   nobler or rarer   than a devoted friendship."

PASSAGE II
The Young King
      by Oscar Wilde

It was the night before the day fixed for his coronation, and the young King was sitting alone in his beautiful chamber. His courtiers had all taken their leave of him, bowing their heads to the ground, according to the ceremonious usage of the day, and had retired to the Great Hall of the Palace, to receive a few last lessons from the Professor of Etiquette; there being some of them who had still quite natural manners, which in a courtier is, I need hardly say, a very grave offence.

The lad for he was only a lad, being but sixteen years of age was not sorry at their departure, and had flung himself back with a deep sigh of relief on the soft cushions of his embroidered couch, lying there, wild-eyed and open-mouthed, like a brown woodland Faun, or some young animal of the forest newly snared by the hunters.

And, indeed, it was the hunters who had found him, coming upon him almost by chance as, bare-limbed and pipe in hand, he was following the flock of the poor goatherd who had brought him up, and whose son he had always fancied himself to be. The child of the old King's only daughter by a secret marriage with one much beneath her in station— a stranger, some said, who, by the wonderful magic of his lute-playing, had made the young Princess love him; while others spoke of an artist from Rimini, to whom the Princess had shown much, perhaps too much honor, and who had suddenly disappeared from the city, leaving his work in the Cathedral unfinished— he had been, when but a week old, stolen away from his mother's side, as she slept, and given into the charge of a common peasant and his wife, who were without children of their own, and lived in a remote part of the forest, more than a day's ride from the town. Grief, or the plague, as the court physician stated, or, as some suggested, a swift Italian poison administered in a cup of spiced wine, slew, within an hour of her wakening, the white girl who had given him birth, and as the trusty messenger who bare the child across his saddle-bow, stooped from his weary horse and knocked at the rude door of the goatherd's hut, the body of the Princess was being lowered into an open grave that had been dug in a deserted churchyard, beyond the city gates, a grave where, it was said, that another body was also lying, that of a young man of marvelous and foreign beauty, whose hands were tied behind him with a knotted cord, and whose breast was stabbed with many red wounds.

> STEP 2: Re-read the passages. Create your own word groupings as you read. Try not to look back and increase your speed as you go.

PASSAGE I
The Devoted Friend
by Oscar Wilde

    One morning the old Water-rat put his head out of his hole. He had bright beady eyes and stiff gray whiskers, and his tail was like a long bit of black india-rubber. The little ducks were swimming about in the pond, looking just like a lot of yellow canaries, and their mother, who was pure white with real red legs, was trying to teach them how to stand on their heads in the water.
    "You will never be in the best society unless you can stand on your heads," she kept saying to them; and every now and then she showed them how it was done. But the little ducks paid no attention to her. They were so young that they did not know what an advantage it is to be in society at all.
    "What disobedient children!" cried the old Water-rat; "They really deserve to be drowned."
    "Nothing of the kind," answered the Duck, "Every one must make a beginning, and parents cannot be too patient."
    "Ah! I know nothing about the feelings of parents," said the Water-rat; "I am not a family man. In fact, I have never been married, and I never intend to be. Love is all very well in its way, but friendship is much higher. Indeed, I know of nothing in the world that is either nobler or rarer than a devoted friendship."

PASSAGE II
The Young King
by Oscar Wilde

    It was the night before the day fixed for his coronation, and the young King was sitting alone in his beautiful chamber. His courtiers had all taken their leave of him, bowing their heads to the ground, according to the ceremonious usage of the day, and had retired to the Great Hall of the Palace, to receive a few last lessons from the Professor of Etiquette; there being some of them who had still quite natural manners, which in a courtier is, I need hardly say, a very grave offence.
    The lad—for he was only a lad, being but sixteen years of age—was not sorry at their departure, and had flung himself back with a deep sigh of relief on the soft cushions of his embroidered couch, lying there, wild-eyed and open-mouthed, like a brown woodland Faun, or some young animal of the forest newly snared by the hunters.
    And, indeed, it was the hunters who had found him, coming upon him almost by chance as, bare-limbed and pipe in hand, he was following the flock of the poor goatherd who had brought him up, and whose son he had always fancied himself to be. The child of the old King's only daughter by a secret marriage with one much beneath her in station—a stranger, some said, who, by the wonderful magic of his lute-playing, had made the young Princess love him; while others spoke of an artist from Rimini, to whom the Princess had shown much, perhaps too much honor, and who had suddenly disappeared from the city, leaving his work in the Cathedral unfinished—he had been, when but a week old, stolen away from his mother's side, as she slept, and given

into the charge of a common peasant and his wife, who were without children of their own, and lived in a remote part of the forest, more than a day's ride from the town. Grief, or the plague, as the court physician stated, or, as some suggested, a swift Italian poison administered in a cup of spiced wine, slew, within an hour of her wakening, the white girl who had given him birth, and as the trusty messenger who bare the child across his saddle-bow, stooped from his weary horse and knocked at the rude door of the goatherd's hut, the body of the Princess was being lowered into an open grave that had been dug in a deserted churchyard, beyond the city gates, a grave where, it was said, that another body was also lying, that of a young man of marvelous and foreign beauty, whose hands were tied behind him with a knotted cord, and whose breast was stabbed with many red wounds.

CONCEPT: SPEED READING
EYE MOVEMENT

- Keep your eyes moving down the page.
- Use an index card to cover the words as you practice reading. Slide the card slightly faster than you are reading.
- Increase the speed of the card as you become comfortable.
- Go to www.chadcargill.com for free speed reading exercises.

➪ **Not only do you want to limit the number of eye fixations per line but also you want to keep your eyes moving down the page.**

➪ **Avoid look-back.**

➪ **Avoid re-reading the same line multiple times.**

STEP 1: Select a passage from one of the practice reading tests provided. Time yourself as you read the passage at your normal speed. This will provide a base-line time to compare with your increased rate after completing step four.

STEP 2: Turn to another passage from the four practice tests provided. Using an index card or something similar, slide the card over the words (from the top down) as you read the passage. Covering the words from the top downward forces you to keep your eyes moving down the page. Try to move the card slightly faster than the rate you are reading such that the speed of the card makes you very uncomfortable. This will be frustrating but keep reading. As you become comfortable reading at the rate you are sliding the card, slightly increase the speed of the card. Continue to increase the speed of the card as your reading speed increases. After about 15 minutes of reading with the card, remove the card and see how much faster you can read a passage.

If you feel slow reading is really hindering your performance on the reading section, try reading with an index card as described above for 15 minutes a day for two weeks leading up to the test. You will be amazed at how much faster you can read the passages after doing this practice.

READING COMPREHENSION

READING TEST I

35 MINUTES / 40 QUESTIONS

TEST 1 - Passage I

PROSE FICTION: THE PASSAGE IS ADAPTED FROM L. M. MONTGOMERY'S *ANNE OF AVONLEA* (©1909 BY L. M. MONTGOMERY).

A demure little Jersey cow came scuttling down the lane and five seconds later Mr. Harrison arrived, if "arrived" be not too mild a term to describe the manner of his eruption into the yard.

He bounced over the fence without waiting to open the gate, and angrily confronted astonished Anne, who had risen to her feet and stood looking at him in some bewilderment. Mr. Harrison was their new right-hand neighbor and she had never met him before, although she had seen him once or twice.

In early April, before Anne had come home from Queen's, Mr. Robert Bell, whose farm adjoined the Cuthbert place on the west, had sold out and moved to Charlottetown. His farm had been bought by a certain Mr. J. A. Harrison, whose name, and the fact that he was a New Brunswick man, were all that was known about him. But before he had been a month in Avonlea he had won the reputation of being an odd person . . ."a crank," Mrs. Rachel Lynde said. Mrs. Rachel was an outspoken lady, as those of you who may have already made her acquaintance will remember. Mr. Harrison was certainly different from other people. . .and that is the essential characteristic of a crank, as everybody knows.

In the first place he kept house for himself and had publicly stated that he wanted no fools of women around his diggings. Feminine Avonlea took its revenge by the gruesome tales it related about his housekeeping and cooking. He had hired little John Henry Carter of White Sands and John Henry started the stories. For one thing, there was never any stated time for meals in the Harrison establishment. Mr. Harrison "got a bite" when he felt hungry, and if John Henry were around at the time, he came in for a share, but if he were not, he had to wait until Mr. Harrison's next hungry spell. John Henry mournfully averred that he would have starved to death if it wasn't that he got home on Sundays and got a good filling up, and that his mother always gave him a basket of "grub" to take back with him on Monday mornings.

As for washing dishes, Mr. Harrison never made any pretense of doing it unless a rainy Sunday came. Then he went to work and washed them all at once in the rainwater hogshead and left them to drain dry.

Additionally, Mr. Harrison was "close." When he was asked to subscribe to the Rev. Mr. Allan's salary he said he'd wait and see how many dollars' worth of good he got out of his preaching first. . .he didn't believe in buying a pig in a poke. And when Mrs. Lynde went to ask for a contribution to missions--and incidentally to see the inside of the house—he told her there were more heathens among the old woman gossips in Avonlea than anywhere else he knew of, and he'd cheerfully contribute to a mission for Christianizing them if she'd undertake it. Mrs. Rachel got herself away and said it was a mercy poor Mrs. Robert Bell was safe in her grave, for it would have broken her heart to see the state of her house in which she used to take so much pride.

"Why, she scrubbed the kitchen floor every second day," Mrs. Lynde told Marilla Cuthbert indignantly, "and if you could see it now! I had to hold up my skirts as I walked across it."

Finally, Mr. Harrison kept a parrot called Ginger. Nobody in Avonlea had ever kept a parrot before; consequently, that proceeding was considered barely respectable. And such a parrot! If you took John Henry Carter's word for it, never was such an unholy bird. It swore terribly. Mrs. Carter would have taken John Henry away at once if she had been sure she could get another place for him. Besides, Ginger had bitten a piece right out of the back of John Henry's neck one day when he had stooped down too near the cage. Mrs. Carter showed everybody the mark when the luckless John Henry went home on Sundays.

All these things flashed through Anne's mind as Mr. Harrison stood, quite speechless with wrath apparently, before her. In his most amiable mood Mr. Harrison could not have been considered a handsome man; he was short and fat and bald; and now, with his round face purple with rage and his prominent blue eyes almost sticking out of his head, Anne thought he was really the ugliest person she had ever seen

1. According to the passage, which of the following best describes the attitude of the women in Avonlea toward Mr. Harrison?
   A. friendly
   B. judgmental
   C. open-minded
   D. jealous

2. As it is used in line 19, a *crank* most nearly describes a person who is
   F. extremely angry.
   G. different from everyone else.
   H. determined to succeed.
   J. certifiably insane.

3. According to the passage, which of the following justifies the women's opinion of Mr. Harrison as a crank?
   I. He keeps house for himself.
   II. He has no scheduled mealtimes.
   III. He owns a parrot.
   A. I only.
   B. I and II.
   C. II and III
   D. I, II and III.

4. It can be inferred from paragraph six (lines 46-60) that Mr. Harrison can be described as a person who:
   F. is not afraid to speak honestly and bluntly.
   G. wants to assimilate into the community.
   H. is, underneath his gruff exterior, an extremely tenderhearted person.
   J. is very lonely.

5. As it is used in line 46, the word *close* most nearly means
   A. stingy.
   B. generous.
   C. charitable.
   D. destitute.

6. According to the passage, in what order did the following events take place?
   I. Anne returned home from Queen's.
   II. Mr. Harrison angrily confronts Anne.
   III. Mr. Harrison purchases Mr. Bell's farm.
   F. I, II, III
   G. III, I, II
   H. II, I, III
   J. II, III, I

7. It can best be inferred from Mr. Harrison's opinion in lines 52-56 that he feels
   A. benevolent toward the good Christian women of Avonlea.
   B. angry at the treatment he received from the women of Avonlea.
   C. anxious to make friends with the women of Avonlea.
   D. that the so-called women of Avonlea are hypocrites.

8. What were the two purposes of Mrs. Lynde's visit to Mr. Harrison?
   F. to get a charitable contribution and to get a donation for the preacher's salary
   G. to get a charitable contribution and scrutinize the inside of his home
   H. to get a donation for the preacher's salary and to gossip about the old women in Avonlea
   J. to gossip about the old women in Avonlea and to scrutinize the inside of his home

9. All of the following aspects of life at Mr. Harrison's are described EXCEPT
   A. his hired hand.
   B. his pet.
   C. his barn.
   D. his housekeeping.

10. The main purpose of this passage is to
    F. give the reader a clear picture of Mr. Harrison's character.
    G. develop the character of Mr. Harrison as a suitor for Anne.
    H. describe the peaceful, rural setting of Avonlea.
    J. develop the character of John Henry as a foil to Mr. Harrison.

TEST 1 - Passage II

SOCIAL SCIENCE: THIS PASSAGE IS ADAPTED FROM THE 102ND CONGRESS' CONGRESSIONAL RECORD, 1991-1992.

Mr. President, some decades ago, agronomists and entomologists in Brazil wanted to produce a better honey bee. According to those scientists, the old, comfy honey bee common in North and South America was too easygoing, too docile, and too stingy in making honey. Somebody down in Brazil got the notion of crossing their domestic honey bees with African honey bees.

The perfect answer, they said.

Over millions of years, African honey bees had been forced to compete against all kinds of enemies. To survive, the African honey bees had evolved into fierce, strong, and vicious combatants. Lions, hyenas, elephants—it did not matter. Whatever got in the way of the African honey bee got the devil stung out of it. In great swarms, African honey bees would attack a potential enemy and sting it and sting it and sting it until it died. The Brazilians corralled a swarm or two of African honey bees and brought them across the Atlantic. Then, the scientists mated those vicious African honey bees with domestic honey bees.

The result was a disaster.

The new bees made less honey than the old American bees made. Certainly, the new bees lost their domestic docility. But in the place of docility, the new bees had all the meanness and bad temper of their African antecedents. But, worse, one day, somebody let a swarm of the new Africanized bees loose. Out of the laboratory they flew. Outside, these Africanized bees –these "killer bees"—spread throughout Brazil. The killer bees expanded into Venezuela, Colombia, Panama, Costa Rica, into Mexico, and, finally, Mr. President, years later, the killer bees reached Texas. Scores of people have been killed by these bees. Hundreds of people—men, women, and children—and countless cattle have been stung by them. The killer bees so far are unstoppable, and they are probably headed toward Washington.

Mr. President, I tell this story as an example of what can happen when people do not stop to consider the ramifications—the practical results—of something new before they put it into action.

We have a problem—Federal budget deficits, a nearly $4 trillion national debt, and all that those fiscal dilemmas threaten. Some people claim that a balanced budget amendment to the U.S. Constitution will solve those fiscal problems. The balanced budget amendment is being extolled as a panacea for all that ails our economy. If only the Congress will pass this balanced budget amendment, the White House claims, we can end all this wasteful deficit spending and pay off the national debt, and Nirvana will be just around the corner.

Mr. President, at this point, nobody knows what a balanced budget amendment will do to the country. There are all kinds of balanced budget amendments floating around. But what this one, that one, or another one will do, as compared with what an amendment which might ultimately be adopted would do, is anybody's guess. Nobody knows that a balanced budget amendment would solve our fiscal problems or make them worse. But some of us have a pretty good idea. Nobody really knows—because it has not been tried—what the social, political, or economic impact of a balanced budget amendment to the Constitution would be 10 years from now, 50 or 100 years from now.

Mr. President, this balanced budget proposal might just be another "killer bee," a killer bee amendment that we and our children and grandchildren will rue for generations to come and for which we in this Congress would be blamed as long as man remembers our names.

What is the plan to enforce the balanced budget amendment? Where are the teeth in the amendment? Where is the plan to keep the Government going if the money runs out? So far, all of the proposals for a balanced budget amendment are like somebody's "granny"—cute, feisty, but with no teeth. We cannot "gum" the deficit out of existence.

Mr. President, I want to balance the Federal budget, too. I want to pay down the national debt. I do not know anybody in the Senate who is not in favor of cutting deficit spending and reducing the national debt, Republican or Democrat. But the balanced budget amendment to the Constitution, presently making the rounds, is not going to reduce Federal deficits or cut the national debt. The balanced budget amendment that I have seen is a magician's hat with no rabbit in it.

11. According to the passage the author's primary concern is
    A. the African honey bee invasion of Washington
    B. the loss of the American honey bee
    C. the passage of the proposed balanced budget amendment
    D. adding the cost of controlling the killer bees to the national debt

12. According to the passage, the hybridization of the domestic honey bee and the African honey bee produced a bee that
    F. produced less honey and was dangerously aggressive.
    G. produced more honey and retained its domestic behavior.
    H. was less dangerous but sterile.
    J. had a painful but harmless sting.

13. The paragraph eight (lines 68-73) makes what comparison?
    A. congressmen and African honey bees
    B. killer bees and the $4 trillion national debt
    C. killer bees and African honey bees
    D. killer bees and the balanced budget proposal

14. Which of the following sentences connects the analogy of the killer bee to the proposed balanced budget amendment?
    F. The perfect answer, they said. (line 9)
    G. Then, the scientists mated those vicious African honey bees with domestic honey bees. (lines 20-21)
    H. But in the place of docility, the new bees had all the meanness and bad temper of their African antecedents. (lines 25-27)
    J. Mr. President, I tell this story as an example of what can happen when people do not stop to consider the ramifications—the practical results—of something new before they put it into action. (lines 39-42)

15. Judging from the passage, the author's tone is best described as
    A. serious yet witty.
    B. stern and woeful.
    C. authoritative and domineering.
    D. sarcastic and rude.

16. As used in line 48, the word *panacea* most likely means
    A. anecdote.
    G. consequence.
    H. cure.
    J. conflict.

17. According to the passage, which of the following was the prevailing reason for cross breeding the African honey bee and the domestic honey bee?
    A. to market the new bee in Colombia
    B. to extend the life span of the bee
    C. to increase the quantity of honey
    D. to decrease the susceptibility to diseases

18. According to White House claims, the balanced budget amendment will produce which of the following?
    I. end wasteful deficit spending
    II. pay off the national debt.
    III. eliminate individual income tax

    F. I and II
    G. I and III
    H. II and III
    J. I only

19. What figurative language does the speaker use to describe the balanced budget amendment?
    I. a bee with no sting
    II. a feisty granny with no teeth
    III. a magician's hat with no rabbit

    A. I and II
    B. II and III
    C. I and III
    D. I, II and III

20. Which of the following sentences best expresses the main idea of the passage?
    F. Mr. President, some decades ago, agronomists and entomologists in Brazil wanted to produce a better honey bee.
    G. Mr. President, this balanced budget proposal might just be another "killer bee," a killer bee amendment that we and our children and grandchildren will rue for generations to come and for which we in this Congress would be blamed as long as man remembers our names.
    H. The result was a disaster.
    J. The balanced budget amendment is being extolled as a panacea for all that ails our economy.

TEST 1 - Passage III

HUMANITIES: THIS PASSAGE IS ADAPTED FROM INFORMATION ON THE INSTITUTE OF MUSEUM AND LIBRARY SERVICES WEBSITE, 1999.

When children galloped into Oklahoma public libraries two years ago to participate in the "Read Stampede" summer reading program, they probably were not aware that the statewide initiative served 66,000 children. When they made cowboy finger puppets at the library, they were not aware of the librarian workshops that had been held. And when they picked up free pony express book bags and bookmarks, they did not realize that the Oklahoma Department of Libraries had commissioned original artwork for the program. The children also did not know that the program had won a prestigious award of the American Library Association. All they needed to know was that going to the library is fun and that leaving with books is a pleasure.

When school breaks for summer, children anticipate a break from the books with lots of outdoor fun. Librarians, however, are kicking off their annual summer reading drives to put books back into the hands of children. The ubiquitous summer reading program is just one way that public libraries serve children and families. Libraries today have expanded their services to families and children to include a wide array of services, such as homework centers, special programs for at-risk children, and family reading programs. Federal funds, through the Library Services and Technology Act (LSTA), are essential to these special services to help families learn and discover together.

Many other state libraries also prepare summer reading programs. Several states, including Alaska, Idaho, Iowa, Kansas, Michigan, Montana, Nebraska, Nevada, North Dakota, South Dakota, and Utah, form a consortium with LSTA funding to develop annual reading programs. The programs are planned years in advance and in great detail: commissioned artwork, commissioned music, performers, reading lists, workshops for librarians, promotional posters and bookmarks, and manuals for librarians for all sorts of thematic public programming and for publicity.

Public libraries have a well-earned reputation for providing free and equitable service to all. For the poor, libraries' free offerings are especially meaningful as services that may be otherwise out of reach. Sometimes LSTA supports library branches set up in innovative spaces in poverty-stricken areas where library enrichment makes a big difference.

The Blue Springs Branch of the Huntsville-Madison County Public Library in Alabama is a library center in the economically depressed northwest part of town. Housed in a renovated YMCA, the library was created with the Boys and Girls Club as part of an after school homework and recreation center that serves more than 350 kids a day. It received support from a three-year LSTA grant for $17,500. This library is not your typical library. The room exudes promises of "fun" with lively bright purple, gold, and teal green on walls and decorations. It has a mural that was colored in by kids on opening day in June 1997. Books and tapes are shelved on wire video shelving on castors. There are fanciful cartoons hanging from the ceiling. There is seating for about sixteen, where children can read a book, do homework, or play board games and puzzles. The six computer stations are always popular with connections to the Internet and learning games, as well as phonics and publishing software.

Each day of the week, the library hosts a program for the children, such as Friday's movies and crafts. At other times the library is the site for preschool story hours. It buzzes with activity arranged by various community groups. To assist poor families desperately in need of educational resources, the Moristown-Hamblen Public Library in Morristown, Tennessee opened a branch library at the C. Frank Davis Homes Housing Project. The library obtains operational funding from the Morristown Library Board, which pays for staff salary, books, and materials, and from the Housing Authority, which pays for the building and utilities. Three grants from LSTA have provided additional support for computers, a homework center, a Head Start outreach partnership and Spanish language materials.

Many groups make use of the library services, such as "Stepping Out Ministries," an agency for disadvantaged women that sends 3 or 4 women a week to the library to learn computer skills. Other groups take advantage of the library's outreach services. Librarians and volunteers visit low income day care centers and Head Start programs to present story hour, a youth emergency shelter to deliver surplus books and magazines, and senior citizen centers to lend large print books and books on tape.

When it comes to serving children, many library programs go hand in hand with formal education. LSTA funds a variety of innovative programs that help public libraries become a valuable educational community resource.

21. According to the passage, activities such as making finger puppets and gifts of book bags and bookmarks are primarily intended to
    A. encourage children to read.
    B. advertise the new books at the library.
    C. raise funds for the Oklahoma Department of Libraries.
    D. benefit physically disabled children.

22. As it is used in line 20, the word *ubiquitous* most closely means
    F. instantly popular.
    G. heavily attended.
    H. ever present.
    J. extremely successful.

23. As it is used in line 46, the word *innovative* most nearly means
    A. traditional
    B. inferior
    C. superior
    D. uncommon

24. According to the passage, which of the following best describes the Blue Springs Branch library?
    F. traditional arrangement of resources
    G. stark, modern interior
    H. colorful, child-friendly environment
    J. dilapidated, run down atmosphere

25. According to the passage, which of the following is NOT a way libraries assist the people in their communities?
    A. provide computer stations with Internet access
    B. host children's programs
    C. donate reading materials to local organizations
    D. provide free individual subscriptions to magazines and newspapers

26. According to the passage, which of the following are considered characteristics of an exceptional library?
    I. interesting, enjoyable projects for children of all ages
    II. quiet, isolated sections for individualized reading
    III. free access to technology such as the Internet, educational software and word processing.

    F. I and II
    G. II only
    H. I and III
    J. II and III

27. According to the passage, why would incorporating a library into poverty-stricken areas make a difference in the community?
    A. The library provides a place for homeless or displaced people to spend time.
    B. Providing a library in these areas is good publicity for the local politicians.
    C. The library provides services that may otherwise be inaccessible to local community members.
    D. Incorporating a library into disadvantaged neighborhoods improves the appearance of the area.

28. The main point of the final paragraph is that
    F. libraries provide educational services independent and separate from conventional educational institutions
    G. educational services provided by public and private schools are superior to the programs offered by public libraries.
    H. in spite of the federal funding available, most libraries are still traditionally organized and do not offer inventive programs.
    J. through federal funding, libraries can be an integral component of the educational process.

29. It can be inferred that the primary purpose of the passage is to
    A. encourage public librarians to apply for federal funds available in order to connect their computers to the Internet.
    B. celebrate the vital role libraries play in the education and socialization of their surrounding communities.
    C. motivate parents and educators to enroll children in summer reading programs.
    D. influence Congress to allocate additional funds to public libraries.

30. Which of the following best expresses the main idea of the passage?
    F. Libraries must be quiet and orderly, and usually are not child-friendly.
    G. Libraries are places to explore learning, provide needed services to the community, and broaden the horizons of all of their patrons.
    H. Libraries are isolated from their surrounding communities, serving a select clientele.
    J. Libraries are only for people who are strong, proficient readers.

TEST 1 - Passage IV

NATURAL SCIENCE: This passage is adapted from information on the U.S. Fish and Wildlife Services website, 2001.

Coastal barriers are unique land forms that provide protection for diverse aquatic habitats and serve as the mainland's first line of defense against the impacts of severe coastal storms and erosion.
5 Located at the interface of land and sea, the dominant physical factors responsible for shaping coastal land forms are tidal range, wave energy, and sediment supply from rivers and older, pre-existing coastal sand bodies. Relative changes in local sea level also
10 profoundly affect coastal barrier diversity.

Coastal barriers protect the aquatic habitats between the barrier and the mainland which contain resources of extraordinary scenic, scientific, recreational, natural, historic, and economic value.
15 Together with their adjacent wetland, marsh, estuarine, inlet, and near shore water habitats, coastal barriers support a tremendous variety of organisms. Millions of fish, shellfish, birds, mammals, and other wildlife depend on barriers and their associated
20 wetlands for vital feeding, spawning, nesting, nursery, and resting habitat. These habitats are also critically important for many species harvested in the nation's commercial fish and shellfish industries. The barrier and its associated habitats are one ecological
25 system, and the health and productivity of the entire system depend on the rational use of all the component parts.

If a suitable sediment source and sufficient wind, waves, and tidal energy exist, a secondary barrier
30 may occasionally form behind the seaward coastal barrier. Secondary barriers are located in large, well-defined bays or in lagoons on the mainland side of coastal barrier systems. These barriers are maintained primarily by internally generated wind waves rather
35 than open ocean waves. Consequently, secondary barriers are generally smaller and more ephemeral than barriers along the open coast. Nonetheless, these barriers are formed just as most oceanic barriers are and, more importantly, they also protect vital fish and
40 wildlife habitat and provide substantial protection for the mainland during major storms.

Under normal weather conditions, only aquatic habitats immediately adjacent to coastal barriers are exposed to direct wave attack. However, major
45 coastal storms routinely affect the entire landward aquatic habitat. This habitat survives major storms because coastal barriers receive the brunt of the ocean's energies. Storm waves break on the barrier beach, leaving a diminished wave to travel into the
50 wetland. At the same time, the wetland stores storm flood waters, easing the flood pressure on the mainland. Without extensive sand beaches protecting many bluffs and terraces, damages from violent storms would be much greater. Sand acts as a brake
55 or drag on waves. Where there are barrier beaches fronting embayments, the sand absorbs the energy much as it does at the base of cliffs. The principal danger to beaches and barriers is not intense storms but a steady reduction in the sand supply caused by
60 dams on tributary streams and the diversion or interruption of littoral transport along the seaward edge of beaches and barriers by bulkheads, groins, jetties. In some situations, mining of beach sand has contributed to the problem.

65 Spits and low-lying barrier beaches survive severe storms with relatively slight effects as long as there is a supply of sand available to restore the beach. A severe storm is a short-term phenomenon, repeating the annual cycle of changing width and
70 slope of the beach within a few hours. Sometimes a spit is eroded back or shortened and the dunes reduced or moved, but the sand begins to build up again towards its equilibrium condition almost as soon as the storm ends. The entrance to a bay and/or
75 river mouth may be relocated or shoaled, but this sometimes also happens without storms. Shoaling of harbor entrances may be dangerous to navigation and require dredging to restore an entrance channel.

31. As it is used in line 10, *profoundly* most closely means
    A. superficially.
    B. officially.
    C. slightly.
    D. intensely.

32. According to the passage, which factors are NOT responsible for the formation of coastal barriers?
    F. tidal range
    G. wave energy
    H. sediment supply
    J. commercial fisherman

33. The main purpose of the second paragraph is to
    A. show the importance of coastal barriers to the ecological system as a whole.
    B. describe the many types of fish and other wildlife that depend on the barrier.
    C. illustrate how the barrier protects the fish and wildlife near it.
    D. explain the complicated relationship between the barrier and the commercial fishing industry.

34. According to the passage, which of the following statements explains why secondary coastal barriers may be smaller than barriers along the open coast?
    F. Fewer fish seek refuge in the secondary coastal barriers.
    G. Commercial fishing depletes their resources.
    H. Secondary barriers are maintained by interior wind waves rather than open ocean waves.
    J. Their size is diminished by the assault of major coastal storms.

35. What is the most important function of secondary barriers?

    I. to protect fish habitat
    II. to protect wildlife habitat
    III. to provide protection for the mainland

    A. I only
    B. II only
    C. II and III
    D. I, II, and III

36. According to the passage, the prevalent danger to beaches and barriers is
    F. the repetition of intense storms.
    G. sand erosion.
    H. turbulent ocean waves.
    J. the reduction of certain species of fish.

37. According to the passage, which of the following causes most of the destruction to the barriers?
    A. fish and wildlife
    B. humans
    C. storms
    D. natural deterioration

38. Which of the following issues does the passage NOT address?
    F. the specific components that constitute a coastal barrier
    G. the location of coastal barriers
    H. the factors responsible for creating a coastal barrier
    J. the function of coastal barriers

39. Which of the following statements identifies the author's attitude toward coastal barriers?
    A. Too much money is spent protecting them.
    B. They are being irreparably harmed.
    C. They are immensely beneficial to the earth's ecosystem.
    D. They are beautiful to observe.

40. According to the passage, how does the author characterize the relationship between the coastal barrier and its surrounding environment?
    F. competitive
    G. symbiotic
    H. detached
    J. independent

END OF READING TEST ONE

READING TEST II

35 MINUTES / 40 QUESTIONS

TEST 2 - Passage I

PROSE FICTION: THIS PASSAGE IS ADAPTED FROM SAKI'S "THE BLOOD FEUD OF TOAD-WATER: A WEST-COUNTRY EPIC" (©1910 BY SAKI [H.H. MUNRO])

The Cricks lived at Toad-Water; and in the same lonely upland spot Fate had pitched the home of the Saunderses, and for miles around these two dwellings there was never a neighbor or a chimney or
[5] even a burying-ground to bring a sense of cheerful communion or social intercourse. Nothing but fields and spinneys and barns, lanes and wastelands. Such was Toad-Water; and, even so, Toad-Water had its history.

[10] Thrust away in the benighted hinterland of a scattered market district, it might have been supposed that these two detached items of the Great Human Family would have leaned towards one another in a fellowship begotten of kindred circumstances and a
[15] common isolation from the outer world. And perhaps it had been so once, but the way of things had brought it otherwise. Indeed, otherwise. Fate, which had linked the two families in such unavoidable association of habitat, had ordained that the Crick
[20] household should nourish and maintain among its earthly possessions sundry head of domestic fowls, while to the Saunderses was given a disposition towards the cultivation of garden crops. Herein lay the material, ready to hand, for the coming of feud
[25] and ill blood. For the grudge between the man of herbs and the man of livestock is no new thing; you will find traces of it in the fourth chapter of Genesis.

And one sunny afternoon in late springtime the feud came—came, as such things mostly do
[30] come, with seeming aimlessness and triviality. One of the Crick hens, in obedience to the nomadic instincts of her kind, wearied of her legitimate scratching-ground, and flew over the low wall that divided the holdings of the neighbors. And there, on
[35] the yonder side, with a hurried consciousness that her time and opportunities might be limited, the misguided bird scratched and scraped and beaked and delved in the soft yielding bed that had been prepared for the solace and well-being of a colony of seedling
[40] onions. Little showers of earth-mold and root-fibers went spraying before the hen and behind her, and every minute the area of her operations widened. The onions suffered considerably. Mrs. Saunders, sauntering at this luckless moment down the garden
[45] path, in order to fill her soul with reproaches at the iniquity of the weeds, which grew faster than she or her good man cared to remove them, stopped in mute discomfiture before the presence of a more magnificent grievance. And then, in the hour of her
[50] calamity, she turned instinctively to the Great Mother, and gathered in her capacious hands large clods of the hard brown soil that lay at her feet. With a terrible sincerity of purpose, though with a contemptible inadequacy of aim, she rained her earth
[55] bolts at the marauder, and the bursting pellets called forth a flood of cackling protest and panic from the hastily departing fowl. Calmness under misfortune is not an attribute of either hen-folk or womankind, and while Mrs. Saunders declaimed over her onion bed
[60] such portions of the slang dictionary as are permitted by the Nonconformist conscience to be said or sung, the Vasco da Gama fowl was waking the echoes of Toad-Water with crescendo bursts of throat music which compelled attention to her griefs. Mrs. Crick
[65] had a long family, and was therefore licensed, in the eyes of her world, to have a short temper, and when some of her ubiquitous offspring had informed her, with the authority of eye-witnesses, that her neighbor had so far forgotten herself as to heave stones at her
[70] hen—her best hen, the best layer in the countryside— her thoughts clothed themselves in language "unbecoming to a Christian woman"—so at least said Mrs. Saunders, to whom most of the language was applied. Nor was she, on her part, surprised at Mrs.
[75] Crick's conduct in letting her hens stray into other body's gardens, and then abusing of them, seeing as how she remembered things against Mrs. Crick—and the latter simultaneously had recollections of lurking episodes in the past of Susan Saunders that were
[80] nothing to her credit. "Fond memory, when all things fade we fly to thee," and in the paling light of an April afternoon the two women confronted each other from their respective sides of the party wall, recalling with shuddering breath the blots and blemishes of
[85] their neighbor's family record. There was that aunt of Mrs. Crick's who had died a pauper in Exeter workhouse—everyone knew that Mrs. Saunders' uncle on her mother's side drank himself to death— then there was that Bristol cousin of Mrs. Crick's!
[90] From the shrill triumph with which his name was dragged in, his crime must have been pilfering from a cathedral at least, but as both remembrancers were speaking at once it was difficult to distinguish his infamy from the scandal which beclouded the
[95] memory of Mrs. Saunders' brother's wife's mother— who may have been a regicide, and was certainly not a nice person as Mrs. Crick painted her.

1. As it is used in line 54, the phrase *contemptible inadequacy of aim* most nearly means
   A. extremely inferior accuracy.
   B. total incompetence.
   C. blaming someone else.
   D. misdirected anger.

2. The setting of the passage can best be described as
   F. populous.
   G. urban.
   H. rural.
   J. gothic.

3. According to the passage, the relationship between the Saunders and the Crick families can best be described as
   A. amiable.
   B. jovial.
   C. hostile.
   D. jealous.

4. It can be inferred from the passage that the source of the feud was a/an
   F. generational dispute.
   G. upped debt.
   H. misunderstanding concerning the legal boundaries of their lands.
   J. conflict about using the land for plants or animals.

5. According to the passage, why were the onions suffering?
   A. lack of water
   B. the bird's destruction
   C. too much water
   D. poor soil condition

6. According to the passage, in what way are the women and hens similar?
   F. They are both calm under pressure.
   G. They grieve deeply and intensely.
   H. Neither reacts well under pressure.
   J. They burst forth in song.

7. Which of Mrs. Saunders actions prompted Mrs. Crick to use language "unbecoming to a Christian woman" (line 72)?
   A. throwing stones at Mrs. Crick's best hen.
   B. killing Mrs. Crick's best hen.
   C. digging up Mrs. Crick's onions.
   D. defaming Mrs. Crick's name.

8. According to the passage, which of the following were insults used by Mrs. Saunders and Mrs. Crick during their argument?
   I. Mrs. Crick's aunt died poor.
   II. Mrs. Saunders' uncle was a drunk.
   III. Mrs. Crick's cousin was banished from the church.
   IV. Mrs. Saunders' brother committed murder.

   F. I, II, IV
   G. I, II, III
   H. I and II
   J. I only

9. Mrs. Crick's attitude toward Mrs. Saunders could best be described as
   A. indignant
   B. affectionate
   C. indifferent
   D. courteous

10. The tone of the passage may best be described as
    F. morose.
    G. cheerful.
    H. optimistic.
    J. witty.

TEST 2 - Passage II

SOCIAL SCIENCE: This PASSAGE IS ADAPTED FROM INFORMATION ON THE WHITE HOUSE WEBSITE, 2001.

   In spite of all the aids, comforts, and privileges that come to a President and his family, homemaking in a house that is also a national monument has its drawbacks. When President Coolidge arrived at the
5 White House in 1923, he tried to continue his pleasant after-dinner habit of sitting on his front porch—the great North Portico—and watching the people go by on Pennsylvania Avenue. So many pedestrians stopped to stare at him, however, that he
10 gave up his modest form of relaxation. President Coolidge, too, once invited a Missouri Senator friend to accompany him on an evening walk outside the grounds. As they returned to the mansion, the Senator remarked facetiously, "I wonder who lives there."
15 "Nobody," replied the President. "They just come and go."

   Though Chief Executives have moved in and out with regularity, the White House has always been a place of extremely personal living. Indeed, the
20 attention commanded by the Presidency intensifies and exaggerates the normal joys and sorrows of everyday family experience, the high moments of birth and death that are part of life here as in any other home. One of the most endearing aspects of life
25 at the Executive Mansion can be glimpsed from the hundreds of stories that have come down through the years about the many children who have lived there. The very young ones were usually grandchildren, since few men have reached the top rung of the
30 political ladder in their early years. And the first of all children whose shouts and laughter echoed through the mansion was 4-year-old granddaughter of John and Abigail Adams. Jefferson's eight years in the presidency were cheered and brightened by the
35 many visits of his married daughters, Martha Randolph and Maria Eppes. On one of the visits, in the winter of 1805, Mrs. Randolph gave birth to her eighth child—James Madison Randolph—the first baby born in the Executive Mansion.

40   The most photographed presidential grandchild of the 19th century must have been "Baby McKee," who lived in the White House with Grandfather Benjamin Harrison and his four-generation family during the early 1890's. Little Benjamin was often
45 photographed as he drove his own goat cart about the grounds. The goat once ran away with Baby McKee. As the goat darted off with the boy and raced down the White House driveway onto Pennsylvania Avenue, the portly President himself, dressed in top
50 hat and frock coat, followed in hot pursuit. President Lincoln and Mary Lincoln were loving and indulgent parents who often said, "Let the children have a good time." This the children did, and the President's friends and colleagues quite probably felt at times he
55 was too permissive when he failed to punish Tad for bombarding the door with his toy cannon during a Cabinet meeting, or when the boy stopped his father's callers to sell refreshments and wheedle money for war charities at stands he set up at the mansion.

60   The only President's child born in the White House was Esther Cleveland, the second daughter of Grover and Frances Cleveland. Esther's sister Ruth, who had arrived during the interlude between Cleveland's two terms, was almost 2 years old at the
65 time of Esther's birth in 1873. Before the President's second term ended, another girl, Marion, was born at the Cleveland's summer home in Massachusetts. Four and a half years after the departure of the demure little Cleveland girls, the uninhibited children of
70 Theodore Roosevelt came on with the force of a hurricane. The five younger children—ages 3 to 14 when the Roosevelts arrived—slid down the stairways on trays stolen from the pantry, stalked the halls on stilts, and bicycled and skated on newly
75 polished floors. The Roosevelt children also kept a small zoo of pets that included a badger, a bear, raccoons, cats, dogs, rats, guinea pigs, snakes, and a calico pony named Alogonquin. When Archie had the measles, his brothers entertained him by leading
80 the pony into his second-floor bedroom, after riding up the President's elevator.

   Behind the scenes and events, the men and women who have lived in the Executive Mansion have known the same happiness and frustration, pride
85 and misery that come to all of us. Every night, the gruff and lonely warrior, Andrew Jackson, performed a tender ritual. After removing the treasured miniature of his dead wife, Rachel, which he carried next to his heart, he would place it on the bedside
90 table near her worn and faded Bible, so that he might see her face first on awakening in the morning. In another of the family rooms, frail Eliza Johnson, devoted wife of Andrew Johnson for 41 years, rocked and sewed as she awaited word of the Senate vote at
95 her husband's impeachment trial. "I knew he'd be acquitted," she said firmly, but with tears in her eyes, to the official who brought the good news. "I knew it."

11. It can reasonably be inferred from paragraph one that living in the White House
    A. is dangerous.
    B. requires sacrificing privacy.
    C. means giving up friendships.
    D. results in many family difficulties.

12. As it is used in line 58, the word *wheedle* most nearly means to
    F. borrow.
    G. beg.
    H. donate.
    J. steal.

13. The writer's main purpose in this passage was to
    A. discuss a personal side of the lives of U.S. Presidents in the White House.
    B. inform the reader of the common everyday moments that occur with uncommon people throughout the world.
    C. argue for less publicity about the private lives of Presidents and families.
    D. describe the hardships of the private lives of public figures.

14. Which of the following are examples of President Lincoln's permissiveness?
    I. Tad did not get punished for disturbing a cabinet meeting.
    II. Tad peddled refreshments.
    III. Tad raced down the driveway pushing Baby McKee in a carriage.
    F. I only
    G. I and II only
    H. II and III only
    J. I, II, and III

15. According to the passage, the Roosevelt children can best be described as
    A. disciplined and orderly
    B. respectful and polite
    C. rambunctious and mischievous
    D. quiet and rarely seen

16. In terms of the passage as a whole, the most significant aspect of life in the White House is that
    F. White House living offers unbelievable advantages to all its inhabitants.
    G. White House living is very confining and thus offers few advantages.
    H. life in the White House is not without the same problems that affect all families.
    J. despite the prestige of the office of President, the White House is sparsely decorated and exceedingly modest.

17. According to the passage, all of the following had children living in the White House EXCEPT
    A. President Lincoln
    B. Grover Cleveland
    C. Theodore Roosevelt
    D. Calvin Coolidge

18. According to the passage, which of the following is an example of the difficult times White House residents had to endure?
    F. The difficulty in parenting their children under the scrutiny of the press and public.
    G. Mrs. Johnson waiting for news of her husband's impeachment trial.
    H. President Lincoln's desire for an orderly and quiet home.
    J. The lack of comfortable furnishings and rooms in the White House.

19. All of the following aspects of life at the White House are described EXCEPT its
    A. drawbacks.
    B. joyful times.
    C. difficult times.
    D. security advantages.

20. Which of the following statements would best describe life at the White House as illustrated in the passage?
    F. Political concerns prohibit the President from spending much time with his family.
    G. Children in the White House are encouraged to be quiet and out of sight.
    H. Visitors to the White House would never be allowed to interact with the President's family.
    J. Family life is an integral part of life in the White House.

TEST 2 - Passage III

HUMANITIES: This passage is adapted from the 102ⁿᴰ Congress' Congressional Record, 1991-1992.

The lesson I learned from the south central Los Angeles riot in 1992 is that this is a crisis not only of the cities or of race, but is, above all, a crisis of our young people. Not all the rioters were of any one racial or cultural background. But all were young.

I found out exactly the same thing in Watts 27 years ago after the riots there. Yet here we are, nearly 3 decades later, watching another generation of inner-city young people drop out of school into the streets, into drugs, into welfare, into crime, into prison, even into death. I believe we can break that cycle. I believe we know how to do it. We have seen it work in the past. We have pilot programs today in many parts of this country that are working right now, but the time has come for those pilot lights to ignite the whole furnace.

Over the years I have come to believe that major reforms are possible only when two conditions occur: when certain propositions become self-evident and when the lack of action to make them real becomes a scandal.

I believe that work, not welfare, is now a self-evident truth—and we know—we can begin applying that principle to the young. We understand that personal responsibility and self-esteem cannot simply be taught by lectures. They have to be earned. And we need to give young people the opportunity to earn those qualities, which are the same qualities that a good citizen needs and a productive worker needs.

I believe it is a scandal now that we know this, but we sit idly by while another generation of young people falls into alienation, hopelessness, frustration and anger; succumbs to the epidemic of crack cocaine, to the gangs that replace family, church, or any other institution that instills the values of responsible citizenship and productive workmanship. A society with children who need care, with older people who need help, roads that need repair, bridges that need building, cannot afford to allow—and sometimes even pay—able young people to sit idle. It is a scandal, too, that we do not challenge the college-bound young people to move beyond a self-centered life of civic indifference. All our young people, in coming of age in America, must be asked to serve, not to be served. To produce, not just to be consumers.

Today, I want to suggest how we can turn that word "ask" into the strong verb it was when John Kennedy said, "Ask not what our country can do for us, ask what we can do for our country." I see us coming to a new Bill of Rights and Responsibilities for the young with a voucher for a year or two of living expense stipends and educational bonuses that could be used to support work in a wide range of service programs run by local, state or federal governments or by communities, church, student organizations, or nonprofit corporations. Some could be very small, like the best one I know of in the country, the Boston City Year. Some could be larger, like the Pennsylvania Conservation Corps, which I administered in recent years, and the California Conservation Corps, the first of the state conservation corps.

We can go back even further in our history for an older model that worked. What worked best for America in the Great Depression was the Civilian Conservation Corps. Franklin Roosevelt himself said the best thing he ever did was the Civilian Conservation Corps. It enlisted more than 2.5 million young unemployed Americans in a state-based system of residential, Army-run camps in or on the edge of our parks and forests. What worked with FDR was work—not the dole, not welfare, but work. The young men of the CCC were challenged to achieve big goals. They transformed our parks and forests, and then graduated into the national service of World War II.

More importantly, they transformed themselves. Just as the GI bill after the war was one of the best investments America ever made, so is the Civilian Conservation Corps. Such corps are an important part of the answer to the crisis of the young and the problem of welfare dependency. More than 60 such corps are in operation today around the country.

The vehicles for achieving this goal are at hand. Some would not cost any more tax dollars. They would ensure that we make better use of the funds we are now spending on federally mandated youth employment and training programs. And to the extent we do expand our investments in our cities and our young people, the money is already there if we would finally take the step of breaking down the budget wall so we can invest military savings in our pressing domestic needs.

21. The passage compares a pilot light igniting a furnace to
    A. localized rioting spreading into larger areas.
    B. small service programs initiating widespread participation.
    C. one committed young person helping another.
    D. a single community service act passed by Congress that will induce further funding.

22. Which of the following best expresses the main point of paragraph two?
    F. Society is experiencing the same problem it has in the past.
    G. More and more young people are suffering from lack of education and the lure of the streets.
    H. Programs exist to help young people improve their lives and their communities.
    J. The young people of today are similar to the young people of the past.

23. According to the passage, what does the author believe is a scandal?
    A. young people do not believe they can change the world
    B. society knows it needs to teach young people personal responsibility and self-esteem but is not doing it
    C. parents and schools do not adequately support the goals and dreams of their young people
    D. more young people do not have a stable home life, financial security and safe neighborhoods

24. As it is used in line 43, the phrase *civic indifference* most nearly means
    F. a lack of concern about society as a whole.
    G. a focus on their academic goals.
    H. a lack of concern about their families.
    J. a focus on only people in similar economic situations.

25. According to the passage, the formation of youth service programs will NOT
    A. teach young people personal responsibility and self-esteem.
    B. provide a positive alternative to gangs and violence.
    C. allow young people to achieve financial security at an earlier age than otherwise possible.
    D. reduce the welfare dependency of the next generation.

26. According to the passage, which of the following best describes the author's attitude toward young people?
    F. disappointed
    G. cynical
    H. optimistic
    J. contented

27. According to the passage, in which order did the following events take place?
    I. World War II
    II. the Great Depression
    III. the formation of the CCC

    A. III, I, II
    B. II, I, III
    C. II, III, I
    D. I, II, III

28. According to the passage, the most important effect of the Civilian Conservation Corps was that it
    F. prepared the nation's young men to defend the country during World War II.
    G. changed the nation's parks and forests.
    H. provided jobs for many young people during the Depression.
    J. allowed the young men who participated to change their lives for the better.

29. According to the passage, how does the author mean to fund his proposal?
    A. Young people will pay tuition to participate in the program.
    B. Federal funds earmarked for education will be diverted to the program.
    C. Churches and community organizations will offer scholarships to interested young people.
    D. Funds will be taken from the military budget and used to begin the program.

30. Which of the following best expresses the main point of the passage?
    F. If given the opportunities and the skills, the youth of the nation have the potential to change our society.
    G. The future of our society is jeopardized because of the lack of interest young people have in their communities.
    H. Reducing the crime rate and increasing the high school graduation rate will improve our communities.
    J. The riots in Los Angeles and Watts prove that our young people have no focus or discipline

TEST 2 - Passage IV

NATURAL SCIENCE: THIS PASSAGE IS ADAPTED FROM INFORMATION ON THE U.S. FISH & WILDLIFE SERVICE WEBSITE, JANUARY 1998.

When the Endangered Species Act (ESA) was passed in 1973, it represented America's concern about the decline of many wildlife species around the world. It is regarded as one of the most
5   comprehensive wildlife conservation laws in the world.

The purpose of the ESA is to conserve "the ecosystems upon which endangered and threatened species depend" and to conserve and recover listed
10 species. Under the law, species may be listed as either "endangered" or "threatened". Endangered means a species is in danger of extinction throughout all or a significant portion of its range. Threatened means a species is likely to become endangered
15 within the foreseeable future. All species of plants and animals, except pest insects, are eligible for listing as endangered or threatened. As of January 31, 2001, 1,244 U.S. species are listed, of which 508 are animals and 736 are plants.. Groups with the most
20 listed species are (in order) plants, birds, fishes, mammals, and clams/mussels.

The Endangered Species Act is a complex law with a great deal of built-in flexibility. When Congress passed the Endangered Species Act in 1973,
25 it recognized that many of our nation's native plants and animals were in danger of becoming extinct. They further expressed that our rich natural heritage was of "esthetic, ecological, educational, recreational, and scientific value." The purposes of the Act are to
30 protect these endangered and threatened species and to provide a means to conserve their ecosystems.

All federal agencies are to protect species and preserve their habitats. Federal agencies must utilize their authorities to conserve listed species and make
35 sure that their actions do not jeopardize the continued existence of listed species. The U.S. Fish and Wildlife Service (FWS) and the National Marine Fisheries Service work with other agencies to plan or modify federal projects so that they will have minimal impact
40 on listed species and their habitat.

The protection of species is also achieved through partnerships with the states. Section 6 of the law encourages each state to develop and maintain conservation programs for resident federally-listed
45 threatened and endangered species. Federal financial assistance and a system of incentives are available to attract state participation. Some state laws and regulations are even more restrictive in granting exceptions or permits than the current ESA. Working
50 with non-federal landowners, the service provides financial and technical assistance to landowners to implement management actions on their lands to benefit listed and non-listed species.

The protection of federally listed species on
55 federal lands is the first priority of the FWS, yet, many species occur partially, extensively or, in some cases, exclusively on private lands. Policies and incentives have been developed to protect private landowners' interests in their lands while
60 encouraging them to manage their lands in ways that benefit endangered species. Much of the progress in recovery of endangered species can be attributed to public support and involvement.

Listings are made solely on the basis of the
65 species' biological status and threats to its existence. The FWS decides all listings using sound science and peer review to ensure the accuracy of the best available data. The FWS also maintains a list of "candidate" species. These are species for which the
70 service has enough information to warrant proposing them for listing as endangered or threatened, but these species have not yet been proposed for listing. The FWS works with states and private partners to carry out conservation actions for candidate species
75 to prevent their further decline and possibly eliminate the need to list them as endangered or threatened.

The law's ultimate goal is to "recover" species so they no longer need protection under the Endangered Species Act. The law provides for
80 recovery plans to be developed describing the steps needed to restore a species to health. Appropriate public and private agencies and institutions and other qualified persons assist in the development and implementation of recovery plans. Involvement of the
85 public and interested "stakeholders" in development of recovery plans is encouraged. Recovery teams may be appointed to develop and implement recovery plans.

31. The main purpose of paragraph two is to
    A. identify the species which cannot be protected.
    B. identify the agencies which are responsible for protection
    C. explain the responsibilities of non-Federal landowners
    D. explain the concepts of endangered and threatened species

32. As it is used in paragraph two, the term *threatened species* means that
    F. the identified species is at immediate risk for extinction.
    G. the identified species may become at-risk for extinction.
    H. protection of the identified species will be risky for the landowner.
    J. species is at-risk to eliminate itself without intervention from man

33. It can be inferred that some insects will never be on the endangered species list because
    A. their extinction is an impossibility.
    B. they continually evolve into a species more likely to prosper.
    C. they are considered pests to humans.
    D. insects are not essential for other species to survive

34. As it is used in paragraph three, the phrase "our rich natural heritage was of 'esthetic, ecological, educational, recreational and scientific value' " most likely means that species
    F. should be protected for their beauty as well as ecological, social, and scientific concerns.
    G. are already protected because of natural heritage protection laws.
    H. should be protected only in the interest of research and science.
    J. should be protected by relocation to national parks.

35. As indicated in this passage, the purpose of the U.S. Fish and Wildlife Service can best be described as
    A. resentful.
    B. protective.
    C. defensive.
    D. antagonistic.

36. Which of the following best describes the government's attitude towards the relationship between landowners and endangered species?
    I. encourages mutual respect while providing protection for both
    II. places the safety of the endangered species above the landowner's needs
    III. honors landowner's requests

    F. I only
    G. I, II, III
    H. II only
    J. III only

37. The goal of the Endangered Species Act is to
    A. raise public money to use in funding national parks.
    B. relocate endangered species to safer locations.
    C. enable species to recover so that protection is no longer needed.
    D. catalog species that are becoming extinct.

38. Which of the following statements is NOT proven true by the passage?
    F. The FWS maintains a list of species that are protected by the federal government.
    G. The Endangered Species Act is one of the most effective and far-reaching conservation laws in existence.
    H. The FWS partners with state agencies to maintain conservation programs.
    J. The protection of certain species is the exclusive responsibility of the FWS.

39. The partnership between the FWS and state governments would ideally result in
    A. the creation of a state-sponsored list of endangered animals and plants
    B. private landowners establishing programs to protect all species of plants and animals on their land
    C. the prohibition of all projects that modify land status from its completely natural state
    D. the development of an individualized ecologically-friendly plan of improvement for each private landowner

40. The main purpose of this passage is to
    F. explain a comprehensive wildlife conservation law.
    G. argue the merits of preserving all species of wildlife.
    H. explore the consequences of ignoring vanishing wildlife
    J. defend the conservation of water.

END OF READING TEST TWO

READING TEST III

35 MINUTES /40 QUESTIONS

TEST 3 - Passage I

PROSE FICTION: This PASSAGE IS ADAPTED FROM OSCAR WILDE'S "THE YOUNG KING"

It was the night before the day fixed for his coronation, and the young King was sitting alone in his beautiful chamber. His courtiers had all taken their leave of him, bowing their heads to the ground,
[5] according to the ceremonious usage of the day, and had retired to the Great Hall of the Palace, to receive a few last lessons from the Professor of Etiquette; there being some of them who had still quite natural manners, which in a courtier is, I need hardly say, a
[10] very grave offence.

The lad - for he was only a lad, being but sixteen years of age - was not sorry at their departure, and had flung himself back with a deep sigh of relief on the soft cushions of his embroidered couch, lying there,
[15] wild-eyed and open-mouthed, like a brown woodland Faun, or some young animal of the forest newly snared by the hunters.

And, indeed, it was the hunters who had found him, coming upon him almost by chance as, bare-
[20] limbed and pipe in hand, he was following the flock of the poor goatherd who had brought him up, and whose son he had always fancied himself to be. The child of the old King's only daughter by a secret marriage with one much beneath her in station - a stranger, some
[25] said, who, by the wonderful magic of his lute-playing, had made the young Princess love him; while others spoke of an artist from Rimini, to whom the Princess had shown much, perhaps too much honour, and who had suddenly disappeared from the city, leaving his
[30] work in the Cathedral unfinished - he had been, when but a week old, stolen away from his mother's side, as she slept, and given into the charge of a common peasant and his wife, who were without children of their own, and lived in a remote part of the forest,
[35] more than a day's ride from the town. Grief, or the plague, as the court physician stated, or, as some suggested, a swift Italian poison administered in a cup of spiced wine, slew, within an hour of her wakening, the girl who had given him birth, and as the trusty
[40] messenger who bare the child across his saddle-bow, stooped from his weary horse and knocked at the rude door of the goatherd's hut, the body of the Princess was being lowered into an open grave that had been dug in a deserted churchyard, beyond the city gates, a
[45] grave where, it was said, that another body was also lying, that of a young man of marvelous and foreign beauty, whose hands were tied behind him with a knotted cord, and whose breast was stabbed with many red wounds.

[50] Such, at least, was the story that men whispered to each other. Certain it was that the old King, when on his death-bed, whether moved by remorse for his great sin, or merely desiring that the kingdom should not pass away from his line, had had the lad sent for, and,
[55] in the presence of the Council, had acknowledged him as his heir.

And it seems that from the very first moment of his recognition he had shown signs of that strange passion for beauty that was destined to have so great
[60] an influence over his life. Those who accompanied him to the suite of rooms set apart for his service, often spoke of the cry of pleasure that broke from his lips when he saw the delicate raiment and rich jewels that had been prepared for him, and of the almost
[65] fierce joy with which he flung aside his rough leathern tunic and coarse sheepskin cloak. He missed, indeed, at times the fine freedom of his forest life, and was always apt to chafe at the tedious Court ceremonies that occupied so much of each day, but the wonderful
[70] palace - Joyeuse, as they called it - of which he now found himself lord, seemed to him to be a new world fresh-fashioned for his delight; and as soon as he could escape from the council-board or audience-chamber, he would run down the great staircase, with
[75] its lions of gilt bronze and its steps of bright porphyry, and wander from room to room, and from corridor to corridor, like one who was seeking to find in beauty an anodyne from pain, a sort of restoration from sickness.

[80] Upon these journeys of discovery, as he would call them - and, indeed, they were to him real voyages through a marvelous land, he would sometimes be accompanied by the slim, fair-haired Court pages, with their floating mantles, and fluttering ribands; but
[85] more often he would be alone, feeling through a certain quick instinct, which was almost a divination, that the secrets of art are best learned in secret, and that Beauty, like Wisdom, loves the lonely worshipper.

1. As used in line 41-42, the phrase *rude door* most nearly means
   A. insolent.
   B. dysfunctional.
   C. crudely or primitively made.
   D. open and inviting.

2. It can be inferred that the princess
   F. disliked her child and sent him away.
   G. feared for her child's safety.
   H. and her secret husband died of the plague.
   J. may have been killed because of her relationship with a commoner.

3. Which best describes the young king's habit of disappearing?
   A. He escapes into his own world of admiration of Beauty.
   B. He spends hours reminiscing about his former life as a goat-herder.
   C. He goes days without sleeping then sleeps incessantly.
   D. He hides from the other courtiers almost as a game.

4. According to the passage, which of the following may have caused the King to finally acknowledge his heir?
   I. remorse for a great sin
   II. desire that the kingdom stay in his lineage
   III. insistence of the court that he name his legal heir

   F. I only
   G. I and II
   H. I, II, and III
   J. III only

5. As used in line 78, the word *anodyne* most nearly means
   A. a substitute.
   B. anything that soothes or relieves.
   C. anything that causes pain.
   D. a longing for

6. It can be inferred from the passage that the young king
   F. preferred to wear his simple, peasant clothing.
   G. occasionally missed the freedom of his previous life.
   H. disliked the elaborate jewelry and clothing.
   J. is irritated by the disrespectful attitude of the courtiers.

7. Which of the following describes the young king's attitude toward Beauty?
   A. He is less interested in Beauty than in the power he will have as king.
   B. It is best appreciated in solitude.
   C. He believes that nature is more beautiful than the man-made palace and its contents.
   D. He is indifferent to it.

8. According to the passage, the young lad
   F. had always dreamed of being a prince.
   G. fought desperately against being named the heir to the throne.
   H. had always questioned his previous station in life.
   J. was astonished at his new-found position.

9. Based on the passage, the young lad can best be described as
   A. inquisitive and passionate.
   B. rude and ill-mannered.
   C. arrogant and aggressive.
   D. indifferent and lackadaisical.

10. Which of the following is NOT presented as a fact in the passage?
    F. The newly acknowledged prince was sixteen years of age.
    G. The prince had a passion for beautiful objects.
    H. The princess secretly married a lute-playing prince.
    J. The princess was the King's only daughter.

TEST 3 - Passage II

SOCIAL SCIENCE: This passage was adapted from Thomas Holmes' *London's Underworld*.

London's great underworld to many may be an undiscovered country. Drunkenness, debauchery, crime and ignorance are never absent; and in it men and women grown old in sin and crime spend their last evil
5   days. The whining voice of the professional mendicant is ever heard in its streets, for its poverty-stricken inhabitants readily respond to every appeal for help.

Now come fellows, young and middle-aged, who dare not be seen by day, for whom the police hold
10 "warrants," for they have absconded from wives and children, leaving them chargeable to the parish. Here are men who have robbed their employers, here young people of both sexes who have drained Circe's cup and broken their parents' hearts. Surely it is a strange and
15 heterogeneous procession that issues evening by evening from the caves and dens of London's underworld. But notice there is also a returning procession! For as the sun sinks to rest, sad-faced men seek some cover where they may lie down and rest their
20 weary bones; where perchance they may sleep and regain some degree of passive courage that will enable them, at the first streak of morning light, to rise and begin again a disheartening round of tramp, tramp, searching for work that is everlastingly denied them.
25 Hungry and footsore, their souls fainting within them, they seek the homes where wives and children await their return with patient but hopeless resignation.

Take notice of the places they enter, for surely the beautiful word "home" is desecrated if applied to most
30 of their habitations. Horrid places within and without, back to back and face to face they stand. At their doorway death stands ready to strike. In the murky light of little rooms filled with thick air child-life has struggled into existence; up and down their narrow
35 stairs patient endurance and passive hopelessness ever pass and repass. Small wonder that the filthy waters of a neighboring canal woo and receive so many broken hearts and emaciated bodies.

But the procession now changes its sex, for weary
40 widowed women are returning to children who for many hours have been lacking a mother's care, for mothers in the underworld must work if children must eat. So the weary widows have been at the washtubs all day long, and are coming home with two shillings
45 hardly earned. They call in at the dirty general shop, where margarine, cheese, bread, tinned meat and firewood are closely commingled in the dank air. A loaf, a pennyworth of margarine, a pennyworth of tea, a bundle of firewood, half a pound of sugar, a pint of
50 lamp-oil exhaust their list of purchases, for the major part of their earnings is required for the rent.

So they climb their stairs, they feed the children, put them unwashed to bed, do some necessary household work, and then settle down themselves in
55 some shape, without change of attire, that they may rest and be ready for the duties of the ensuing day.

It is one o'clock a.m., and we go down six steps into what is facetiously termed a "breakfast parlor"; here we find a man and woman about sixty years of
60 age. The woman is seated at a small table on which stands a small, evil-smelling lamp, and the man is seated at another small table, but gets no assistance from the lamp; he works in comparative gloom, for he is almost blind; he works by touch. For fifty years they
65 have been makers of artificial flowers; both are clever artists, and the shops of the West End have fairly blazed with the glory of their roses. Winsome lassies and serene ladies have made themselves happy with their flowers.

70 There they sit, as they have sat together for thirty years. Neither can read or write, but what can be done in flowers they can do. Long hours and dark rooms have made the man almost blind.

He suffers also from heart disease and dropsy. He
75 cannot do much, but he can sit, and sit, while his wife works and works, for in the underworld married women must work if dying husbands are to be cared for. So for fifteen hours daily and nightly they sit at their roses! Then they lie down on the bed we see in
80 the corner, but sleep does not come, for asthma troubles him, and he must be attended and nursed.

Two months have passed away, the evil-smelling lamp is still burning, the woman still sits at the table, but no rose-leaves are before her; she is making black
85 tulips. On the bed lies a still form with limbs decently smoothed and composed; the poor blind eyes are closed forever. He is awaiting the day of burial, and day after day the partner of his life and death is sitting, and working, for in this underworld bereaved wives
90 must work if husbands are to be decently buried

11. The word *absconded* in line 10 most nearly means
   A. run away from.
   B. quietly stolen from.
   C. traded for food or money.
   D. murdered.

12. According to the passage, which of the following best describes London's underworld?
    F. affluent and private
    G. clean and healthy
    H. poverty-ridden and dismal
    J. poor but acceptable

13. According to paragraph two, why are the *sad-faced men* disheartened?
    A. They don't want to return to their parents because they have disappointed them.
    B. They are discouraged because they have been unable to find work to support themselves or their families.
    C. They have been fired from their jobs for excessive drinking and have nowhere to live.
    D. Their employers treat them poorly and do not pay them an adequate salary.

14. The main purpose of paragraph three is to
    F. explain the purpose of the canal.
    G. describe the dangers that lurk in the neighborhood.
    H. identify their burial place.
    J. describe the places squalid conditions of the underworld homes.

15. It can be inferred from line 45 that the phrase *hardly earned* most nearly means that the
    A. widows barely worked that day.
    B. widows did not deserve their pay.
    C. widows' intense labor earned barely two shillings.
    D. widows' money has little value.

16. According to the passage, which of the following statements expresses a contrast illustrated in the story?

    I. the beauty of the artificial flowers with the conditions in which they are created
    II. the "beautiful word 'home' " and the inhabitants' current living conditions
    III. the hopelessness of the inhabitants and the wealth of their employers

    F. I only
    G. II only
    H. I and II only
    J. II and III only

17. Which of the following best describes the relationship between the old man and woman?
    A. They are combative and hostile toward each other.
    B. They are loving and attentive.
    C. The woman blames the man for their poor living conditions.
    D. The man is unconcerned about contributing to their financial support.

18. According to the passage, what happened to the old woman as a result of her husband's death?
    F. Her overwhelming workload changed very little.
    G. She was evicted from her home and was unable to work.
    H. Relieved of the burden of caring for her husband, she was able to leave London for the country.
    J. Because she no longer had to pay for his medicines, she was able to reduce the number of hours she worked.

19. The main purpose of the passage is to describe the
    A. squalid conditions and the poverty-stricken inhabitants of London's underworld.
    B. difficult working conditions for the mothers of this neighborhood.
    C. hopelessness of dealing with death on a daily basis.
    D. effect drunkenness and debauchery can have on families.

20. The author's attitude toward the hard-working subjects of the passage could best be described as
    F. sympathetic admiration
    G. justifiably scornful
    H. unfairly derogatory
    J. amused tolerance

TEST 3 - Passage III

HUMANITIES: THIS PASSAGE WAS ADAPTED FROM *THE EXPERIENCES OF A BANDMASTER* BY JOHN PHILIP SOUSA.

During eighteen years spent in playing music for the masses, twelve years in the service of the United States and six in that of the general public, many curious and interesting incidents have come under my
5   observation.

While conductor of the Marine Band, which plays at all the state functions given by the President at the Executive Mansion, I saw much of the social life of the White House and was brought into more or less direct
10 contact with all the executives under whom I had the honor of successively serving—Presidents Hayes, Garfield, Arthur, Cleveland and Harrison. They were all very appreciative of music, and in this respect were quite unlike General Grant, of whom it is said that he
15 knew only two tunes, one of which was "Yankee Doodle" and the other wasn't!

I think I may say that more than one President, relieved from the onerous duties of a great reception, has found rest by sitting quietly in the corner of a
20 convenient room and listening to the music.

Once, on the occasion of a state dinner, President Arthur came to the door of the main lobby of the White House, where the Marine Band was always stationed, and beckoning me to his side asked me to play the
25 "Cachuca." When I explained that we did not have the music with us but would be glad to include it in the next program, the President looked surprised and remarked: "Why, Sousa, I thought you could play anything. I'm sure you can; now give us the 'Cachuca.'"

30 This placed me in a predicament, as I did not wish the President to believe that the band was not at all times able to respond to his wishes. Fortunately, one of the bandmen remembered the melody and played it over softly to me on his cornet in a corner. I hastily
35 wrote out several parts for the leading instruments, and told the rest of the band to vamp in the key of E flat. Then we played the "Cachuca" to the entire satisfaction of Mr. Arthur, who came again to the door and said: "There, I knew you could play it."

40 The Marine Band played all the music for President Cleveland's wedding, which took place in the Blue Room of the White House. The distance from the room up-stairs to the exact spot where the ceremony was to take place was carefully measured by Colonel
45 Lamont and myself, in order that the music might be timed to the precise number of steps the wedding party would have to take, and the climax of the Mendelssohn "Wedding March" was played by the band just as the bride and groom reached the clergyman. A few days
50 before the ceremony I submitted my musical program to Colonel Lamont for the President's approval, and among the numbers was a quartet called "The Student of Love," from one of my operas. Even in the anticipation of his happiness Mr. Cleveland was keenly
55 alive to the opportunities for humorous remarks which this title might afford to irreverent newspaper men; and he said to his secretary: "Tell Sousa he can play that quartet, but he had better omit the name of it." Accordingly, "The Student of Love" was conspicuous
60 by its absence.

In all my experience the acme of patriotic fervor was reached during a reunion of the Loyal Legion at Philadelphia some years ago. The exercises were held in the Academy of Music, and the band occupied the
65 orchestra pit in front of the stage, which was crowded with distinguished veterans. I had strung together for the occasion a number of war-songs, bugle-calls and patriotic airs, and when the band played them, the martial spirit began to stir the people. As we broke into
70 "Marching Through Georgia," a distinguished-looking old soldier stepped to the foot-lights and began to sing the familiar words of the famous song in a loud, clear voice. The entire audience joined in, and as the swelling volume of melody rolled through the house,
75 the enthusiasm waxed more intense.

Verse after verse was sung, interrupted with frantic cheers, until it seemed that the very ecstasy of enthusiasm had been reached. It was only when physically exhausted that the audience calmed down
80 and the exercises proceeded.

21. According to the passage, how did General Grant feel about music?
    A. He only liked patriotic music.
    B. He was disinterested in it.
    C. He disliked classical music.
    D. He felt music should be reserved for funerals and weddings.

22. As it is used in line 18, *onerous* most nearly means
    F. difficult.
    G. secretive.
    H. pleasant.
    J. mysterious.

23. According to the passage, in which order did the following events occur?

    I. A bandsman played the melody softly.
    II. The president asked for the song, "Cachuca."
    III. Mr. Sousa wrote the musical arrangement for the song.

    A. I, II, III
    B. II, I, III
    C. III, II, I
    D. I, III, II

24. Why was the title of the song, "Student of Love" omitted from the musical program?
    F. The bride didn't like the tune.
    G. The president preferred something more traditional.
    H. The president was concerned that the press would ridicule the song's title.
    J. Mr. Sousa couldn't play the song.

25. As it is used in line 61, *acme* most nearly means
    A. the worst example of.
    B. the opposite of.
    C. the lowest point.
    D. the highest point.

26. It can be inferred from the passage that music can be used to
    I. restore order and calm fears.
    II. excite and inspire.
    III. provide relaxation.

    F. I only
    G. II only
    H. II and III only
    J. I, II, and III

27. The main purpose of the passage is to
    A. inform the reader about Mr. Sousa's experiences as a bandmaster.
    B. persuade the reader to play in a band.
    C. describe what music is appropriate for a specific occasion.
    D. identify what music is used in the White House.

28. All of the following describe Mr. Sousa EXCEPT?
    F. thoroughly patriotic
    G. shockingly incompetent
    H. obligingly flexible
    J. calmly unflappable

29. According to the passage, which of the following statements best describes the narrator's attitude toward his work?
    A. He prefers to play for military or state occasions rather than the social or private events of the president and his family.
    B. He is often frustrated at his audience's lack of appreciation of music and works diligently to improve people's understanding and regard for classical music.
    C. Because of his superior talent, he believes that he should only play for significant occasions and audiences.
    D. He takes great pride in his ability to fulfill the desires of the president and his ability to communicate with his audience through the music he and his band play.

30. Which of the following statements best illustrates the purpose of the last two paragraphs in relation to the rest of the passage?
    F. They express the emotions a veteran feels about his military service and his country.
    G. They give an explanation of the impact music can have on an audience.
    H. They function as another example of the "curious and interesting incidents" in Mr. Sousa's career.
    J. They show the bond people share when they have a common, defining experience.

TEST 3 - Passage IV

NATURAL SCIENCE: This passage was adapted from T.H. Huxley's *Coral and Coral Reefs*.

The red coral polyp perches upon the sea bottom. It then grows up into a sort of stem, and out of that stem there grow branches, each of which has its own polyps, and thus you have a kind of tree formed, every branch of the tree terminated by its polyp. It is a tree, but at the end of the branches there are open mouths of polyps instead of flowers. Thus there is a common soft body connecting the whole, and as it grows up, the soft body deposits in its interior a quantity of carbonate of lime, which acquires a beautiful red or flesh color, and forms a kind of stem running through the whole, and it is that stem which is the red coral. The red coral grows principally at the bottom of the Mediterranean Sea, at very great depths, and the coral fishers, who are very adventurous seamen, take their drag nets, of a peculiar kind, roughly made, but efficient for their purpose, and drag them along the bottom of the sea to catch the branches of the red coral, which become entangled and are thus brought up to the surface. They are then allowed to putrefy, in order to get rid of the animal matter, and the red coral is the skeleton that is left.

In the case of the white coral, the skeleton is more complete. In the red coral, the skeleton belongs to the whole; in the white coral there is a special skeleton for every one of these polyps in addition to that for the whole body. There is a skeleton formed in the body of each of them, like a cup divided by a number of radiating partitions towards the outside; and that cup is formed of carbonate of lime, only not stained red, as in the case of the red coral. And all these cups are joined together into a common branch, the result of which is the formation of a beautiful coral tree. This is a great mass of madrepore, and in the living state every one of the ends of these branches was terminated by a beautiful little polyp, like a sea anemone, and all the skeleton was covered by a soft body which united the polyps together. You must understand that all this skeleton has been formed in the interior of the body, to suit the branched body of the polyp mass, and that it is as much its skeleton as our own bones are our skeleton. In this next coral the creature which has formed the skeleton has divided itself as it grew, and consequently has formed a great expansion; but scattered all over this surface were polyp bodies like those I previously described. Again, when this great cup was alive, the whole surface was covered with a beautiful body upon which were set innumerable small polyp flowers, if we may so call them, often brilliantly colored, and the whole cup was built up in the same fashion by the deposit of carbonate of lime in the interior of the combined polyp body, formed by budding and by fission in the way I described. You will perceive that there is no necessary limit to this process. There is no reason why we should not have coral three or four times as big; and there are certain creatures of this kind that do fabricate very large masses, or half spheres several feet in diameter. Thus the activity of these animals in separating carbonate of lime from the sea and building it up into definite shapes is very considerable indeed.

The animals which form coral are scattered over the seas of all countries in the world. The red coral is comparatively limited, but the polyps which form the white coral are widely scattered. There are some of them which remain single, or which give rise to only small accumulations; and the skeletons of these, as they die, accumulate upon the bottom of the sea, but they do not come to much; they are washed about and do not adhere together, but become mixed up with the mud of the sea. But there are certain parts of the world in which the coral polyps which live and grow are of a kind which remain, adhere together, and form great masses. They differ from the ordinary polyps just in the same way as those plants which form a peat bog or meadow-turf differ from ordinary plants. They have a habit of growing together in masses in the same place; they are what we call "gregarious" things; and the consequence of this is, that as they die and leave their skeletons, those skeletons form a considerable solid aggregation at the bottom of the sea, and other polyps perch upon them, and begin building upon them, and so by degrees a great mass is formed. And just as we know there are some ancient cities in which you have a British city, and over that the foundations of a Roman city; and over that a Saxon city, and over that again a modern city, so in these localities of which I am speaking, you have the accumulations of the foundations of the houses, if I may use the term, of nation after nation of these coral polyps; and these accumulations may cover a very considerable space, and may rise in the course of time from the bottom to the surface of the sea.

31. According to the passage the red coral formation on the sea bottom most closely resembles a
    A. multi-branched tree.
    B. completely articulated skeleton.
    C. complicated maze.
    D. many-layered city.

32. All of the following are steps in the collection process of the red coral EXCEPT
    F. the fishermen drag their nets on the bottom of the sea.
    G. the coral is allowed to completely dry out.
    H. the fishermen spray the coral with lime carbonate.
    J. the coral is entangled in the nets.

33. It is reasonable to conclude from the passage that the relationship between the fishermen and the coral can best be described as
    A. parasite and host.
    B. necessary for each to survive.
    C. beneficial to the species but harmful to the individual.
    D. predator and prey.

34. According to the passage, what is the primary difference in the red and white coral?
    F. The red coral contains more lime carbonate.
    G. Their polyps are shaped differently.
    H. The white coral exists in warmer water temperatures.
    J. The white coral consists of multiple skeletons.

35. Which of the following best describes the polyp flowers?
    A. small and nearly colorless
    B. beautiful and often vibrantly colored
    C. complex and poisonous
    D. only red in color

36. As it is used in line 81, *gregarious* most nearly means
    F. threatening and dangerous.
    G. sociable and cooperative.
    H. apathetic and isolated.
    J. infected and deteriorating.

37. Which of the following explains the principal difference between the ordinary polyps and the polyps which tend to produce large masses of skeletons?
    A. The ordinary polyps have a limited life span.
    B. As opposed to the ordinary polyps, the others have a tendency to grow together in the same place.
    C. The ordinary polyps are always red in color.
    D. The polyps in large masses become engulfed in the mud.

38. As it is used in line 83, *aggregation* most nearly means
    F. a group of individual items.
    G. an increase in liquid.
    H. a point of irritation.
    J. the reversal of a procedure.

39. The author offers the illustration of the accumulation of cities on the same site to demonstrate
    A. how the coral formations are created.
    B. how to determine the age of the coral.
    C. how one level of coral is destroyed by the next.
    D. how the levels of coral acquire their different colors.

40. The purpose of this passage is to
    F. inform the reader about the formation of coral reefs.
    G. describe the precarious living conditions of the coral.
    H. persuade the reader to promote conservation efforts.
    J. identify the geographical location of the coral.

END OF READING TEST THREE.

READING TEST IV

35 MINUTES / 40 QUESTIONS

TEST 4 - Passage I

PROSE FICTION: This passage was adapted from Mark Twain's *The Tragedy of Pudd'nhead Wilson*.

In 1830 Dawson's Landing was a snug collection of modest one and two-story frame dwellings, whose whitewashed exteriors were almost concealed from sight by climbing tangles of rose vines, honeysuckle, and morning glories. Each of these pretty homes had a garden in front fenced with white palings and opulently stocked with hollyhocks, marigolds, touch-me-nots, prince's feathers, and other old fashioned flowers; while on the windowsills of the houses stood wooden boxes containing moss rose plants and terracotta pots in which grew a breed of geranium whose spread of intensely red blossoms accented the prevailing pink tint of the rose-clad house front like an explosion of flame. When there was room on the ledge outside of the pots and boxes for a cat, the cat was there—in sunny weather—stretched at full length, asleep and blissful, with her furry belly to the sun and a paw curved over her nose. Then that house was complete, and its contentment and peace were made manifest to the world by this symbol, whose testimony is infallible.

All along the streets, on both sides, at the outer edge of the brick sidewalks, stood locust trees which furnished shade for summer and a sweet fragrance in spring, when the clusters of buds came forth. The main street, one block back from the river, and running parallel with it, was the sole business street. It was six blocks long, and in each block two or three brick stores, three stories high, towered above interjected bunches of little frame shops. Swinging signs creaked in the wind the street's whole length. The candy-striped pole, which indicates nobility, proud and ancient along the palace-bordered canals of Venice, indicated merely the humble barbershop along the main street of Dawson's Landing. On a chief corner stood a lofty unpainted pole wreathed from top to bottom with tin pots and pans and cups, the chief tinmonger's noisy notice to the world (when the wind blew) that his shop was on hand for business at that corner. Dawson's Landing was sleepy and comfortable and contented. It was fifty years old, and was growing slowly—very slowly, in fact, but still it was growing.

The chief citizen was York Leicester Driscoll, about forty years old, judge of the county court. He was very proud of his old Virginian ancestry, and in his hospitalities and his rather formal and stately manners, he kept up its traditions. He was fine and just and generous. To be a gentleman—a gentleman without stain or blemish—was his only religion, and to it he was always faithful. He was respected, esteemed, and beloved by all of the community. He was well off, and was gradually adding to his store. He and his wife were very nearly happy, but not quite, for they had no children. The longing for the treasure of a child had grown stronger and stronger as the years slipped away, but the blessing never came—and was never to come.

Judge Driscoll had retired from the bench and from all business activities and had now been comfortably idle three years. He was president of the Freethinkers' Society, and Pudd'nhead Wilson was the other member. The society's weekly discussions were now the old lawyer's main interest in life. Pudd'nhead was still toiling in obscurity at the bottom of the ladder, under the blight of that unlucky remark which he had let fall twenty-three years before about the dog.

Judge Driscoll was his friend, and claimed that he had a mind above the average, but that was regarded as one of the judge's whims, and it failed to modify the public opinion. Or rather, that was one of the reasons why it failed, but there was another and better one. If the judge had stopped with bare assertion, it would have had a good deal of effect; but he made the mistake of trying to prove his position. For some years Wilson had been privately at work on a whimsical almanac, for his amusement—a calendar, with a little dab of ostensible philosophy, usually in ironical form, appended to each date; and the judge thought that these quips and fancies of Wilson's were neatly turned and cute; so he carried a handful of them around one day, and read them to some of the chief citizens. But irony was not for those people; their mental vision was not focused for it. They read those playful trifles in the solidest terms, and decided without hesitancy that if there had ever been any doubt that Dave Wilson was a pudd'nhead—which there hadn't—this revelation removed that doubt for good and all. That is just the way in this world; an enemy can partly ruin a man, but it takes a good-natured injudicious friend to complete the thing and make it perfect. After this the judge felt more tender than ever toward Wilson and surer than ever that his calendar had merit.

Judge Driscoll could be a freethinker and still hold his place in society because he was the person of most consequence to the community, and therefore could venture to go his own way and follow out his own notions. The other member of his pet organization was allowed the like liberty because nobody attached any importance to what he thought or did. He was liked, he was welcome enough all around, but he simply didn't count for anything.

1. According to the passage, what symbolized the peaceful contentment of the Dawson's Landing?
   A. the terra cotta pots
   B. the intense red geraniums
   C. the lazily sleeping cat
   D. the white-washed exterior of the house

2. The purpose of the description of the business area of town was to
   F. confirm the comfortable, contented setting.
   G. provide contrast to the description of the home.
   H. describe the hurried, noisy life of the town.
   J. show the lack of industrial development.

3. It can be reasonably inferred that Pudd'nhead's downfall can be attributed to his
   A. remark about a dog.
   B. poor upbringing.
   C. slovenly appearance.
   D. association with Judge Driscoll.

4. As it is used in line 63, *blight* most nearly means
   F. a much-needed blessing
   G. an undesired curse
   H. a proven lack of judgment
   J. a physical defect

5. According to the passage, Judge Driscoll's wild opinions were acceptable in the community because
   A. he was a man of importance.
   B. he was a devoutly religious man.
   C. his position as a judge caused citizens to fear retribution.
   D. his wife was wealthy and respected.

6. According to the passage, which of the following statements is true?
   F. The citizens didn't have the mental capacity to understand irony.
   G. The citizens found the calendar to be whimsical and amusing.
   H. A few of the prominent citizens recognized its literary merit.
   J. Dave Wilson was making money on the sale of the calendar.

7. Which can be reasonably inferred about the Freethinkers' Society?
   A. It is a small group because the rest of the community is lower class.
   B. Membership is reserved for only the most brilliant, liberal thinkers.
   C. It is a small group because no one other than the judge and Pudd'nhead are interested in joining.
   D. Membership is expensive.

8. According to the passage, Judge Driscoll's mistake was
   F. trying to prove Pudd'nhead to be above average intelligence.
   G. forgiving Pudd'nhead for his remark about the dog.
   H. marketing Pudd'nhead's calendar.
   J. forming the Freethinkers' Society.

9. Judge Driscoll's status in the community compared to that of Dave Wilson can best be expressed as
   A. illustrious compared to uncelebrated
   B. insignificant compared to eminent
   C. precarious compared to established
   D. infamous compared to prominent

10. It can reasonably be inferred from the passage that the judge does NOT believe that
    F. maintaining tradition is important.
    G. Dave Wilson has an above average intellect.
    H. he has failed his wife because they have no children.
    J. the townspeople have misjudged Dave Wilson.

TEST 4 – Passage II

SOCIAL SCIENCE: This passage was adapted from *Sanitary and Social Lectures* by Charles Kingsley.

This pettiness and dullness of our modern life is just what keeps the modern rage for sensational novels. Those who read them so greedily are conscious, poor souls, of capacities in themselves of passion and action for good and evil, for which their frivolous humdrum daily life gives no room, no vent. They know too well that human nature can be more fertile, whether in weeds and poisons, or in flowers and fruits, than it is usually in the streets and houses of a well-ordered and tolerably sober city. And because the study of human nature is, after all, that which is nearest to everyone and most interesting to everyone, therefore they go to fiction, since they cannot go to fact, to see what they themselves might be had they the chance; to see what fantastic tricks before high heaven men and women like themselves can play, and how they play them.

There are those who cannot read sensational novels, or, indeed, any novels at all, just because they see so many sensational novels being enacted round them in painful facts of sinful flesh and blood. There are those, too, who have looked in the mirror too often to wish to see their own disfigured visage in it any more; who are too tired of themselves and ashamed of themselves to want to hear of people like themselves; who want to hear of people utterly unlike themselves, more noble, and able, and just, and sweet, and pure; who long to hear of heroism and to converse with heroes; and who, if by chance they meet with an heroic act, bathe their spirits in that, as in May-dew, and feel themselves thereby, if but for an hour, more fair.

If any such shall chance to see these words, consider that one word *Hero*, and what it means. *Hero*, *Heroic*, *Heroism*—these words point to a phase of human nature, the capacity for which we all have in ourselves, which is as startling and as interesting in its manifestations as any, and which is always beautiful, always ennobling, and therefore always attractive to those whose hearts are not yet seared by the world or brutalized by self-indulgence.

But let us first be sure what the words mean. There is no use talking about a word till we have got at its meaning. We may use it as a cant phrase, as a party cry on platforms; we may even hate and persecute our fellow-men for the sake of it, but till we have clearly settled in our own minds what a word means, it will do for fighting with, but not for working with. Socrates of old used to tell the young Athenians that the ground of all sound knowledge was to understand the true meaning of the words which were in their mouths all day long, and Socrates was a wiser man than we shall ever see. So, instead of beginning an oration in praise of heroism, I shall ask my readers to think with me what heroism is.

Now, we shall always get most surely at the meaning of a word by getting at its etymology—that is, at what it meant at first. And if heroism means behaving like a hero, we must find out not merely what a hero may happen to mean just now, but what it meant in the earliest human speech in which we find it.

A hero or a heroine, then, among the old Homeric Greeks, meant a man or woman who was like the gods, and who, from that likeness, stood superior to his or her fellow creatures. Gods, heroes, and men, is a threefold division of rational beings, with which we meet more than once or twice. Those grand old Greeks felt deeply the truth of the poet's saying "Unless above himself he can exalt himself, how poor a thing is man."

But more: the Greeks supposed these heroes to be, in some way or other, partakers of a divine nature; akin to the gods; usually, either they, or some ancestor of theirs, descended from a god or goddess. A hero or a heroine was a godlike man or godlike woman.

A godlike man. What varied, what infinite forms of nobleness that word might include, ever increasing, as men's notions of the gods became purer and loftier, or, alas! decreasing, as their notions became degraded. The old Greeks, with that intense admiration of beauty which made them, in after ages, the master-sculptors and draughtsmen of their own, and, indeed, of any age, would, of course, require in their hero, their godlike man, beauty and strength, manners too, and eloquence, and all outward perfections of humanity, and neglect his moral qualities. Neglect, I say, but not ignore. The hero, by virtue of his kindred with the gods, was always expected to be a better man than common men, as virtue was then understood.

The hero was at least expected to be more reverent than other men to those divine beings of whose nature he partook, whose society he might enjoy even here on earth. He might be unfaithful to his own high lineage; he might misuse his gifts by selfishness and self-will; he might, like Ajax, rage with mere jealousy and wounded pride till his rage ended in shameful madness and suicide. He might rebel against the very gods, and all laws of right and wrong, till he perished.

11. According to the passage, why do people read sensational literature?
    I. Their own lives are boring.
    II. They know life could be more than what they live.
    III. Their lives are similar to what is being written.

    A. I and II only
    B. II and III only
    C. I, II and III
    D. I only

12. The main purpose of paragraph one is to
    F. criticize sensationalism in fiction
    G. prove that sensational literature is better than heroic literature
    H. identify the reasons people read sensational literature
    J. show the author's preference for nonfiction literature

13. According to the passage, people read heroic literature because they want to read about
    A. people they dislike.
    B. people more noble and pure than themselves.
    C. common people who live like they do.
    D. sinful flesh and blood.

14. The main idea of paragraph four is that
    F. it is important to completely understand a word before using it.
    G. Socrates was a true hero.
    H. young Athenians do not understand the word *hero*.
    J. heroism should be the battle cry of all young Athenians.

15. As it is used in line 44, *cant* most nearly means
    A. ambiguous or unclear.
    B. insincere or meaningless.
    C. slang or jargon.
    D. proper or formal.

16. The phrase "Unless above himself he can exalt himself, how poor a thing man is" (lines 68-69) is based on the assumption that man
    F. must distinguish himself in some way in order to become heroic.
    G. will always remain in poverty unless he becomes heroic.
    H. will never be greater than the gods.
    J. must rely upon a revelation from the gods in order to be a hero.

17. According to the passage, Homeric Greeks believed a hero
    A. was never a direct descendant of the gods.
    B. had to complete a journey or conquest.
    C. was more powerful than the gods themselves.
    D. was godlike and superior to other humans.

18. As it is used in line 69, *exalt* most nearly means to
    F. become honest.
    G. raise in status.
    H. become rich.
    J. sacrifice himself.

19. Which of the following is NOT a characteristic of ancient Greek heroes?
    A. always virtuous
    B. physically beautiful
    C. physically strong
    D. godlike

20. The main purpose of the passage is to
    F. praise heroism.
    G. prove the need for heroes.
    H. promote sensational literature.
    J. define heroism.

TEST 4 - Passage III

HUMANITIES: This passage adapted from Amy Steedman's *Knights of the Art*.

Sometimes in a crowd of people one sees a tall man, who stands head and shoulders higher than any one else, and who can look far over the heads of ordinary- sized mortals. So among the crowd of painters traveling along the road to Fame we see above the rest a giant, a greater and more powerful genius than any that came before or after him. When we hear the name of Michelangelo we picture to ourselves a great rugged, powerful giant, a veritable son of thunder, who, like the Titans of old, bent every force of Nature to his will.

This Michelangelo was born at Caprese among the mountains of Casentino, and his father, Lodovico Buonarroti, was podesta or mayor of Caprese. Now the day on which the baby was born happened to be not only a Sunday, but also a morning when the stars were especially favorable. So the wise men declared that some heavenly virtue was sure to belong to a child born at that particular time, and without hesitation Lodovico determined to call his little son Michael Angelo, after the archangel Michael. Surely that was a name splendid enough to adorn any great career. It happened just then that Lodovico's year of office ended, and so he returned with his wife and child to Florence. He had a property in a little village just outside the city, and there he settled down.

Most of the people of the village were stonecutters, and it was to the wife of one of these laborers that little Michelangelo was sent to be nursed. In after years the great master often said that if his mind was worth anything, he owed it to the clear pure mountain air in which he was born, just as he owed his love of carving stone to the unconscious influence of his nurse, the stone-cutter's wife.

As the boy grew up he clearly showed in what direction his interest lay. At school he was something of a dunce at his lessons, but let him but have a pencil and paper and his mind was wide awake at once. Every spare moment he spent making sketches on the walls of his father's house. But Lodovico would not hear of the boy becoming an artist. There were many children to provide for, and the family was not rich. It would be much more fitting that Michelangelo should go into the silk and woolen business and learn to make money. But it was all in vain to try to make the boy see the wisdom of all this. Scold as they might, he cared for nothing but his pencil, and even after he was severely beaten he would creep back to his beloved work. How he envied his friend Francesco who worked in the shop of Master Ghirlandaio! It was a joy even to sit and listen to the tales of the studio, and it was a happy day when Francesco brought some of the master's drawings to show to his eager friend.

Little by little Lodovico began to see that there was nothing for it but to give way to the boy's wishes, and so at last, when he was fourteen years old, Michelangelo was sent to study as a pupil in the studio of Master Ghirlandaio. It was just at the time when Ghirlandaio was painting the frescoes of the chapel in Santa Maria Novella, and Michelangelo learned many lessons as he watched the master at work.

But it was like placing an eagle in a hawk's nest. The young eagle quickly learned to soar far higher than the hawk could do, and ere long began to "sweep the skies alone." It was not pleasant for the great Florentine master, whose work all men admired, to have his drawings corrected by a young lad, and perhaps Michelangelo was not as humble as he should have been. In the strength of his great knowledge he would sometimes say sharp and scornful things, and perhaps he forgot the respect due from pupil to master. Be that as it may, he left Ghirlandaio's studio when he was sixteen years old. Thenceforward he worked out his own ideas in his giant strength, and was the pupil of none.

Michelangelo went to study in the gardens of San Marco, where Lorenzo the Magnificent had collected many statues and works of art. Here was a new field for Michelangelo. Without needing a lesson he began to copy the statues in terra cotta, and so clever was his work that Lorenzo was delighted with it. "See, now, what thou canst do with marble," he said. "Terracotta is but poor stuff to work in."

Michelangelo had never handled a chisel before, but he chipped and cut away the marble so marvelously that life seemed to spring out of the stone. There was a marble head of an old faun in the garden, and this Michelangelo set himself to copy. Such a wonderful copy did he make that Lorenzo was amazed. It was even better than the original, for the boy had introduced ideas of his own and had made the laughing mouth a little open to show the teeth and the tongue of the faun. There was nothing that the magnificent ruler loved so much as genius, so Michelangelo was received into the palace and made the companion of Lorenzo's sons. Not only did good fortune thus smile upon the young artist, but to his great astonishment Lodovico too found that benefits were showered upon him, all for the sake of his famous young son.

21. It can be reasonably inferred from the first paragraph that Michelangelo is
    A. an unusually tall man for his time period.
    B. a person of vast significance in the artistic world.
    C. a Titan, descended from the gods.
    D. a giant with power over the forces of Nature.

22. According to the passage, why was the painter named Michael Angelo?
    F. The choice was based on advice from the wise men.
    G. It was a family name from his father's ancestors.
    H. His father believed that naming him after the archangel would bring him good fortune.
    J. The choice was based on the alignment of the stars.

23. Michelangelo attributed his intelligence and passion to which of the following?
    A. his father and his painting master
    B. his friend and his own skill
    C. a spiritual revelation and his formal education
    D. the clear mountain air and the influence of his nurse

24. According to the passage, why did Lodovico oppose Michelangelo's chosen field of work?
    I. The Buonarroti family needed Michelangelo to contribute to the family finances.
    II. Lodovico wanted Michelangelo to continue in the family business of trading silks and woolens.
    III. Lodovico did not believe that being an artist was a proper vocation.

    F. I only
    G. I and II only
    H. II and III only
    J. I, II and III

25. According to the passage, which of the following statements is true?
    A. Michelangelo was determined to fulfill his dream in spite of any obstacles.
    B. Michelangelo learned all his skill from imitating Master Ghirlandaio.
    C. As a young boy, Michelangelo wanted to work in the silk and woolen business.
    D. Michelangelo's wealthy family provided a studio to develop his skill.

26. The author uses the illustration of the young eagle and the hawk to suggest that
    F. the master viciously attacked the pupil.
    G. youth quickly succumbs to experience.
    H. the pupil eventually surpassed the master.
    J. artistic talent results in intense competition.

27. The relationship between Ghirlandaio and Michelangelo can best be described as
    A. friendly and cooperative.
    B. mutually respectful.
    C. tense and competitive.
    D. beneficial and enduring.

28. According to the passage, Lorenzo appreciated Michelangelo because
    F. his father held an important political post.
    G. of his ability to imitate other artists.
    H. of his close friendship and good influence on Lorenzo's sons.
    J. of his amazing artistic talent.

29. According to the passage, how did Michelangelo's copy of the faun statue differ from the original?
    A. He added a sense of life to his copy that wasn't apparent in the original.
    B. He added original touches to the copy using terra cotta instead of marble.
    C. He altered his copy to slightly resemble Lorenzo's youngest son.
    D. He adjusted the design of his copy to show the menacing teeth of the original faun.

30. Which of the following best describe the purpose of the passage?
    F. to argue the need for artistic standards.
    G. to show how Michelangelo's father could have prevented the artist's career.
    H. to prove that Michelangelo's genius is unsurpassed.
    J. to describe the development of a great genius

TEST 4 - Passage IV

NATURAL SCIENCE: THIS PASSAGE WAS ADAPTED FROM STEWART EDWARD WHITE'S *THE MOUNTAINS*.

Six trails lead to the main ridge. They are all good trails, so that even the casual tourist in the little Spanish-American town on the seacoast need have nothing to fear from the ascent. In some spots they
[5] contract to an arm's length of space, outside of which limit they drop sheer away; elsewhere they stand up on end, zigzags each more hair-raising than the last, or filled to demoralization with loose boulders and shale. A fall on the part of your horse would mean a
[10] more than serious accident, but Western horses do not fall. The major premise stands: even the casual tourist has no real reason for fear, however scared he may become.

Our favorite route to the main ridge was by a
[15] way called the Cold Spring Trail. We used to enjoy taking visitors up it, mainly because you come on the top suddenly, without warning. Then we collected remarks. Everybody, even the most stolid, said something.

[20] You rode three miles on the flat, two in the leafy and gradually ascending creek-bed of a canyon, a half hour of laboring steepness in the overarching mountain lilac and laurel. There you came to a great rock gateway which seemed the top of the world. At
[25] the gateway was a Bad Place where the ponies planted warily their little hoofs, and the visitor played "eyes front," and besought that his mount should not stumble.

Beyond the gateway a lush level canyon into
[30] which you plunged as into a bath; then again the laboring trail, up and always up toward the blue California sky, out of the lilacs, and laurels, and redwood chaparral into the manzanita, the Spanish bayonet, the creamy yucca, and the fine angular shale
[35] of the upper regions. Beyond the apparent summit you found always other summits yet to be climbed. And all at once, like thrusting your shoulders out of a hatchway, you looked over the top.

From the ridge, ascending from seaward in a
[40] gradual coquetry of foothills, broad low ranges, cross-systems, canyons, little flats, and gentle ravines, inland dropped off almost sheer to the river below. And from under your very feet rose, range after range, tier after tier, rank after rank, in
[45] increasing crescendo of wonderful tinted mountains to the main crest of the Coast Ranges, the blue distance, the mightiness of California's western systems. The eye followed them up and up, and farther and farther, with the accumulating emotion of
[50] a wild rush on a toboggan. There came a point where the fact grew to be almost too big for the appreciation, just as beyond a certain point speed seems to become unbearable. It left you breathless, wonder-stricken, awed. And in the far distance,
[55] finally, your soul, grown big in a moment, came to rest on the great precipices and pines of the greatest mountains of all, close under the sky.

In a little, after the change had come to you, a change definite and enduring, which left your inner
[60] processes forever different from what they had been, you turned sharp to the west and rode five miles along the knife-edge Ridge Trail to where Rattlesnake Canyon led you down and back to your accustomed environment.

[65] To the left as you rode you saw, far on the horizon, rising to the height of your eye, the mountains of the channel islands. Then the deep sapphire of the Pacific, fringed with the soft, unchanging white of the surf and the yellow of the
[70] shore. Then the town like a little map, and the lush greens of the wide meadows, the fruit groves, the lesser ranges—all vivid, fertile, brilliant, and pulsating with vitality. You filled your senses with it, steeped them in the beauty of it. And at once, by a
[75] mere turn of the eyes, from the almost crude insistence of the bright primary color of life, you faced the tenuous azures of distance, the delicate mauves and amethysts, the lilacs and saffrons of the arid country.

[80] This was the wonder we never tired of seeing for ourselves, of showing to others. And often, academically, perhaps a little wistfully, as one talks of something to be dreamed of but never enjoyed, we spoke of how fine it would be to ride down into that
[85] land of mystery and enchantment, to penetrate one after another the canyons dimly outlined in the shadows cast by the westering sun, to cross the mountains lying outspread in easy grasp of the eye, to gain the distant blue Ridge, and see with our own
[90] eyes what lay beyond.

31. As it is used in line 18, *stolid* most nearly means
    A. completely impassive.
    B. overly talkative.
    C. intensely emotional.
    D. easily excited.

32. Which of the following are reasons casual tourists should not be afraid to travel the trails?

    I. The horses are reliable.
    II. The paths are smooth and clear of debris.
    III. The trails are safe in spite of their dangerous appearance.

    F. I and II
    G. I and III
    H. II and III
    J. I, II and III

33. What was remarkable about the Cold Spring Trail?
    A. the difficulty in reaching the top
    B. the dangerous zigzag trails
    C. the beauty of the lilacs, laurel and chaparral
    D. the suddenness of reaching the top of the trail

34. Which of the following describes the basic geography of the area surrounding the main ridge?
    F. The ridge is completely surrounded by desert.
    G. The ridge is located on an island peninsula.
    H. The ridge is surrounded by a variety of landscapes, including canyons and small ravines.
    J. The ridge leads up to the Rocky Mountains.

35. As it is used in line 56, *precipices* most nearly means
    A. deciduous fir trees.
    B. steep cliffs.
    C. the lowest points of a valley.
    D. the high water marks on the side of the ravine.

36. According to the passage, which trail led back to the small Spanish American town?
    F. Rattlesnake Trail
    G. Cold Spring Trail
    H. Ridge Trail
    J. Coast Range Trail

37. According to the last paragraph, why do the trail guides want to explore the land they see from Ridge Trail?
    A. They are tired of dreaming of the trip but never doing it.
    B. They would like to be the first to explore the canyons and mountains.
    C. They wanted to study the land and its inhabitants for a research study.
    D. They wanted to discover the secrets of the land for themselves.

38. It is reasonable to conclude from the passage that the attitude of the trail guides toward their environment is one of
    F. financial opportunity.
    G. fear and trepidation.
    H. disdain and ignorance.
    J. respect and awe.

39. It is reasonable to infer from the passage that the author would agree with which of the following statements about nature.
    A. Humanity is awed by such natural beauty and grandeur.
    B. Nature is to be conquered and used for man's purposes.
    C. Humanity has no connection with nature.
    D. Nature is only productive if it produces money.

40. The main purpose of the passage is to
    F. describe the life-changing beauty of the land.
    G. encourage tourists to visit the trail ride company.
    H. convince investors to purchase plots of land for development.
    J. prevent the government from reducing funding for natural resources.

END OF READING TEST FOUR

READING TESTS — ANSWER KEYS

READING TEST I
PASSAGE I—PROSE FICTION *Anne of Avonlea*

1. **B** The women of Avonlea are clearly judgmental of Mr. Harrison. They have already labeled him a "crank" (line 19), which is a person who is "certainly different from other people" (line 22-23). The women criticize him for not having set mealtimes (¶ 4) and keeping a filthy house (¶ 5, 6 & 7). The women are also critical of the fact that Mr. Harrison keeps an apparently vicious and foul-mouthed parrot (¶ 8).

2. **G** The word *crank* is defined in lines 22-24: "Mr. Harrison was **certainly different from other people**…and that is the **essential characteristic of a crank**".

3. **D** Keeps house for himself (line 25); no scheduled mealtimes (lines 31-32); owns a parrot (line 65). All of these things make him different from other people in the community which in the women's minds makes him a crank.

4. **F** Mr. Harrison can be described as a person who speaks bluntly because he speaks openly and straightforwardly about not paying Reverand Allan's salary until he decides if his preaching deserves a donation (lines 47-49). He speaks the same way to Ms. Lynde when she asks for a donation to missions, telling her he would be glad to donate if she would consider "Christianizing" the gossips in Avonlea (lines 53-56).

5. **A** The word *close* can be defined by the examples given in the paragraph of Mr. Harrison's behavior: He is hesitant to donate to either the Reverend's salary or the mission group. Because he doesn't part easily with his money, he can be said to be *close* or *stingy*.

6. **G** The sequence of events is established in the following lines: Mr. Harrison purchases Mr. Bell's farm then Anne returns home (lines 11-15); Mr. Harrison confronts Anne (lines 5-8).

7. **D** Mr. Harrison feels that the women of Avonlea should tend to their own problems before they worry about sending money to missions. He clearly feels that the women's behavior is hypocritical. See ¶ 6.

8. **G** "Mrs. Lynde went **to ask for a contribution** to missions—and incidentally **to see the inside of the house**—" (lines 51-52).

9. **C** His hired hand is described in ¶ 4: "He had hired little John Henry Carter of White Sands…" (lines 29-30). His pet is described in ¶ 8: "Mr. Harrison kept a parrot called Ginger." (line 65). His housekeeping is described in ¶ 4 & 5: "he kept house for himself" (line 25); "the gruesome tales it related about his house-keeping and cooking" (line 28-29); "As for washing dishes…" (line 42). His barn is not mentioned in the passage.

10. **F** The passage describes Mr. Harrison, giving the reader a clear picture of his habits, attitudes and lifestyle. After reading the passage, the reader should know that Mr. Harrison cleans only when necessary, eats only when he is hungry and is impatient with the traditions and expectations of the Avonlea women. He is reclusive and bad-tempered. No mention is made of him being a potential suitor for Anne; the passage does not describe Avonlea as peaceful; John Henry is mentioned only briefly and not as the opposite (foil) of Mr. Harrison.

READING TEST I
PASSAGE II—SOCIAL SCIENCE *Congressional Record*

11. **C** The speaker identifies his purpose (primary concern) in lines 39-42: "Mr. President, I tell this story as an example of what can happen when people do not stop to consider the ramifications—the practical results—of something new before they put it into action." The speaker is referring to passing the proposed balanced budget amendment without clearly considering all of the consequences. The killer bee story is used as an illustration to develop his point, not as the main focus of the passage.

12. **F** The new bees are described in ¶ 5, lines 23-27: "The **new bees made less honey** than the old American bees made. Certainly the new bees **lost their domestic docility**. But in the place of docility, the new bees **had all the meanness and bad temper** of their African antecedents." There is no reference in the passage to the sterility of the new bees. The passage clearly describes how dangerous the sting of the new bees can be: "Scores of people have been killed by these bees" (lines 34-35).

13. **D** In lines 68-73, the speaker makes a connection between the proposed amendment and the killer bee when he calls the amendment "another 'killer bee', a killer bee amendment that we and our children and grandchildren will rue for generations." The specified lines never reference congressmen, African honey bees or the $4 trillion national debt.

14. **J** Choice J is the only choice offered that connects the story of the bees to the proposed balanced budget agreement. The other choices only reference the bee story.

15. **A** The speaker is speaking about a serious political issue (passing the amendment), but he does interject some humor and clever statements: "The killer bees so far are unstoppable, and they are probably headed toward Washington" (lines 37-38); "So far, all of the proposals for a balanced budget are like somebody's "granny"—cute, feisty, but with no teeth. We cannot "gum" the deficit out of existence" (lines 77-80). The speaker does not appear woeful—he is not bemoaning the passage of the amendment. He is not authoritative or domineering nor is he sarcastic or rude.

16. **H** The word panacea is seen as a cure because it will "solve those fiscal problems" (line 47) and it will fix "all that ails our economy" (line 49). An anecdote is a story used as an illustration of a point. Panacea is not the consequence or result of the amendment, and it isn't a conflict to the amendment.

17. **C** Lines 4-6 list the problems with the North and South American honey bee that the scientists wish to correct: "too easygoing, too docile, and too stingy in making honey." Choice C is the only potential answer to refer to one of the problems listed.

18. **F** Lines 51-53 list the potential positive results the White House claims the amendment will bring: "we can **end all this wasteful deficit spending** and **pay off the national debt**, and Nirvana will be just around the corner." There is no mention of eliminating individual income tax.

19. **B** Lines 78-79 describe the amendment as "somebody's "granny," cute, feisty, but with no teeth"; lines 89-90 describe the amendment as "a magician's hat with no rabbit in it." The passage does not describe the amendment as a "bee with no sting."

20. **G** The main idea of the passage is that the proposed balanced budget agreement will be just as much of a disaster as the crossing of the African bees with the American bees was. Everything in the passage supports that point. The other choices are supporting details for either the bee story or the explanation of the amendment.

READING TEST I
PASSAGE III—HUMANITIES   Library Services

21. **A** The focus of the activities at the library (finger puppets, book bags, bookmarks) is on encouraging children to read even during the summer. The purpose is stated in lines 13-15: "All they needed to know was that **going to the library is fun and that leaving with books is a pleasure**." The first ¶ does not connect those activities listed to advertising new books (choice B), fundraising (choice C), or physically disabled children (choice D).

22. **H** As it is used in line 20, *ubiquitous* most closely means *ever present*. A context clue appears in line 18: "their **annual** summer reading drives" which means that reading drives are a repeated, familiar event. There is no indication that the drives are instantly popular (choice F), heavily attended (choice G) or extremely successful (choice J).

23. **D** As it is used in line 46, *innovative* most nearly means uncommon. Paragraphs 5, 6 and 7 provide examples of libraries that are different from traditional libraries by having unique set-ups, programs and services. They are effective because they are different. There is no comparison made in the passage, so neither inferior or superior could be correct.

24. **H** Several examples in ¶ 5 offer support for choice H: "The room exudes promises of 'fun' with lively bright purple, gold and teal green on walls and decorations. It has a mural colored in by kids"; "fanciful cartoons hanging from the ceiling"; "seating for about 16, where children can read a book, do homework or play board games and puzzles" (lines 56-64). These examples support the idea of a colorful, child-friendly environment. The library is not a traditional arrangement of resources: "This library is not your typical library" (lines 55-56). There is nothing stark about the colorful decorations and displays. From the description of the library, it seems to be well-maintained and fairly new: "opening day in June 1997" (line 59); nothing indicates that it is dilapidated or run-down.

25. **D** There is no indication in the passage that libraries provide free individual subscriptions to magazines and newspapers. They do provide computer stations with Internet access (line 65), host children's programs (lines 67-68), and donate reading material to local organizations (lines 90-92).

26. **H** Although quiet, isolated settings for isolated reading may be a characteristic of an exceptional library, it is not mentioned in this particular passage. This passage does establish choices I and III as characteristics necessary to exceptional libraries (¶ 5; ¶ 6; ¶7).

27. **C** The library provides "services that may be otherwise out of reach" (lines 44-45). There is no reference in the passage to homeless or displaced people, publicity for local politicians or improving the appearance of the neighborhood.

28. **J** The passage clearly describes libraries as a partnership with formal education: "library programs go hand in hand with formal education" (lines 93-94) not as independent or separate. There is no reference in the passage comparing library services to those provided by public or private schools, and the passage proves that many libraries offer imaginative, innovative programs designed to best serve their clientele.

29. **B** The passage is not intended to persuade anyone to apply for federal funds, to motivate parents/educators to enroll children in summer reading programs or influence Congress to give more funds to libraries. The sole purpose of the passage is to celebrate what is being done in libraries across the nation to improve the education and socialization of their communities. Two statements support this: "libraries' free offerings are especially meaningful as services that may otherwise be out of reach" (lines 43-45); "libraries become a valuable educational community resource" (lines 96-97).

30. **G** According to the passage, libraries are places to explore learning: "computer stations are always popular with **connections to the Internet** and **learning games**, as well as **phonics and publishing software**" (lines 64-66); provide needed services to the community: "an agency for disadvantaged women that sends 3 or 4 women a week to the library to learn computer skills" (lines 84-86); broaden the horizons of all of their patrons: "library branches se up in innovative spaces in poverty-stricken areas where library enrichment makes a big difference" (lines 45-47). Libraries are not necessarily quiet: "It buzzes with activity" (line 70) and are very child-friendly. Libraries are not isolated from their communities and do not serve only a certain clientele: "Many groups make use of the library services, such as women's groups, low income day care centers, Head Start programs, a youth emergency shelter and senior citizen centers (lines 83-92). Library services are available for all levels of readers providing services such as "homework centers, special programs for at-risk children and family reading programs" (lines 24-26).

READING TEST I
PASSAGE IV—NATURAL SCIENCE   Fish and Wildlife Services

31. **D** The first paragraph identifies things that seriously affect the shape of coastal land forms: "tidal range, wave energy, sediment supply" (lines 7-8). Line 9 lists "changes in local sea level" as one more thing that also **profoundly** or **intensely** affects coastal barrier diversity. The local sea level doesn't **superficially** affect the barrier diversity; it changes it deeply. There is no reference to the information being made **official**, and the sea level affects the barriers and beaches more than just **slightly**—it changes it significantly.

32. **J** Lines 5-8 identify the factors responsible for the formation of coastal barriers: "the dominant physical factors responsible for shaping coastal land forms are **tidal range, wave energy, and sediment supply**." Commercial fishermen are not mentioned as a determining factor.

33. **A** Lines 24-27 provide the reader with the answer: "The barrier and its associated habitats are one ecological system, and the health and productivity of the entire system depend on the rational use of all the component parts." Based on this sentence, the reader can infer that the barrier is critical to the ecological system. While the paragraph refers to the fish and wildlife the barrier protects, it does not describe them in any detail (choice B), nor does it describe in detail how the barrier protects that wildlife (choice C). The paragraph does not discuss at all the "complicated relationship between the barrier and the commercial fishing industry" (choice D).

34. **H** Lines 35-37 confirm the answer: "Consequently, secondary barriers are **generally smaller** and more ephemeral than barriers along the open coast."

35. **D** Lines 39-41 provide the answer: "they also **protect vital fish** and **wildlife habitat** and provide substantial **protection for the mainland** during major storms."

36. **G** Lines 57-59: "The principal danger to beaches and barriers is not intense storms but a **steady reduction in the sand supply**."

37. **B** Humans are the most destructive force. The reader may infer this from lines 57-63: "The principal danger to beaches and barriers is not intense storms but a steady **reduction in the sand supply caused by dams** on tributary streams and the **diversion or interruption of littoral transport** along the seaward edge of beaches and barriers **by bulkheads, groins and jetties**." It is assumed that humans created the dams, bulkheads and jetties and are therefore responsible for the loss of sand. The passage does not discuss any damage fish and wildlife might cause to the barrier; it does state that the barrier is able to recover from storms and natural deterioration.

38. **F** The passage identifies locations of coastal barriers: "Located at the interface of land and sea" (line 5). It identifies the factors responsible for creating the barrier: "the dominant physical factors responsible for shaping coastal land forms are tidal range, wave energy, and sediment supply" (lines 5-8). It also identifies the function of barriers: "barriers protect the aquatic habitats between the barrier and the mainland" (lines 11-12). The passage does not identify the specific components or makeup of a coastal barrier.

39. **C** The author never mentions any amount of money being spent to protect the barriers, nor does he indicate that they are being irreparably harmed. While the barriers may be beautiful, the author does not discuss that specifically. The author does make the point that the barriers are beneficial to the ecosystem: "Coastal barriers protect the aquatic habitats" (line 11); "coastal barriers support a tremendous variety of organisms" (lines 16-17); "wildlife depend on barriers…for feeding" (lines 19-20); the barriers are also "critically important for many species harvested in the nation's commercial fish and shellfish industries" (lines 22-23). Based on his descriptions of the barriers, the reader can see the importance of them to the earth's ecosystem.

40. **G** In lines 24-27, the author calls the barrier and its associated habitats "one ecological system." There is no evidence that the barrier is **competitive** with its surroundings, and based on the lines listed above, they cannot be **detached** or **independent**.

READING TEST II
PASSAGE I—PROSE FICTION "The Blood Feud of Toad-Water"

1. **A** The phrase "contemptible inadequacy of aim" is linked to Mrs. Saunders' actions as she "rained her earth bolts at the marauder" (lines 54-55) and is referring to her inability to hit the hen with the dirt clods. The passage never describes Mrs. Saunders as feeling incompetent or that her anger is misdirected. The phrase does not apply to any blame Mrs. Saunders might be assigning.

2. **H** The Cricks and the Saunders live in a rural spot: "lonely upland spot" (line 2); "Nothing but fields and spinneys and barns, lanes and wastelands" (line 6-7). These lines clearly show that the setting is not populous or urban and does not have characteristics of a gothic environment (dark atmosphere, fantastic architecture, etc).

3. **C** Several phrases in the passage give clues to the type of relationship between the Cricks and the Saunders: "There was never a neighbor or a chimney or even a burying-ground to bring a sense of cheerful communion or social intercourse" (lines 4-6); "it might have been supposed that that these two detached items of the Great Human Family would have leaned towards one another in a fellowship…but the way of things had brought it otherwise" (lines 11-17). The altercation between Mrs. Crick and Mrs. Saunders firmly establishes the hostile relationship. The interaction between the two families is not amiable (friendly) nor is it jovial (cheerful). The passage does not indicate that the two women have any reason to be jealous of each other.

4. **J** The source of the feud is identified in lines 17-25: "Fate…had ordained that the Crick household should nourish and maintain…sundry head of domestic fowls, while …the Saunderses…the cultivation of garden crops. Herein lay the material, ready to hand, for the coming of feud and ill blood." There is no indication that the families have been fighting for years, that they owe each other money, or that they are confused about the boundaries of their lands.

5. **B** The garden bed is described as having been "prepared for the solace and well-being of a colony of seedling onions" (lines 38-59). Based on that description, the onions are obviously being well cared for, so choices A, C and D are incorrect. Immediately after the description of the garden bed comes the description of the destruction the chicken causes to the onion seedlings (lines 40-43). That description is followed by the statement: "The onions suffered considerably" which the reader can infer is the **result of the bird's destruction**.

6. **H** Choice F is proven incorrect in line 59-60: "Calmness under misfortune is not an attribute of either hen-folk or womenkind." There is no indication of the hen or the women grieving intensely or bursting into song. Choice H is proven correct by the reaction of the hen to having dirt clods thrown at her: the "fowl was waking the echoes of Toadwater with crescendo bursts of throat music which compelled attention to her griefs" (lines 62-64); in other words, the chicken was crowing loudly because Mrs. Crick tried to hit her with dirt clods. The women react in a similar way when they begin yelling at each other, complaining about throwing stones and letting hens go where they aren't welcome.

7. **A** The answer is established in lines 67-72: "when some of her ubiquitous offspring had informed her…that her neighbor had so far forgotten herself as to heave stones at her hen…her thoughts clothed themselves in language 'unbecoming to a Christian woman.'" This statement shows that the inappropriate language is the result of discovering Mrs. Saunders had thrown stones at her hen. Choice B is incorrect because Mrs. Saunders didn't kill the hen. Choice C is incorrect because the hen dug up Mrs. Crick's onions, not Mrs. Saunders. Although Mrs. Saunders did defame Mrs. Crick's name, it wasn't the initial cause of the inappropriate language.

8. **H** Choice I is found in lines 85-86: "aunt of Mrs. Crick's who had died a pauper." Choice II is found in lines 87-88: "Mrs. Saunders' uncle on her mother's side drank himself to death." Choice III is incorrect based on lines 89-95: "Bristol cousin of Mrs. Crick's! From the shrill triumph with which his name was dragged in, his crime must have been pilfering from a cathedral at least, but as both remembrancers were speaking at once it was difficult to distinguish his infamy from the scandal which beclouded the memory of Mrs. Saunders' brother's wife's mother." The reader does not know what Mrs. Crick's cousin's actual crime was, only that by the tone of voice of the women, it must have been serious (like stealing from a church). Choice IV is also

proven incorrect by these lines because the passage refers to Mrs. Saunders' brother's wife's **mother**, not Mrs. Saunders' **brother**.

9. **A** The best way to answer these kinds of questions if you do not know what one or more of the choices mean is by process of elimination. Choice B is wrong; Mrs. Crick and Mrs. Saunders are clearly not affectionate toward one another. Choice C is also wrong because their angry confrontation could not be defined as indifferent (not caring). Choice D is really wrong because courteous (polite) people certainly wouldn't treat each other like the women do. Choice A is correct because Mrs. Crick feels indignant (displeased) toward Mrs. Saunders for throwing dirt clods at her hen.

10. **J** The author gives several **witty** (or clever) descriptions in the passage: "One of the Crick hens, in obedience to the nomadic instincts of her kind, wearied of her legitimate scratching-ground" (lines 30-33); "with a hurried consciousness that her time and opportunities might be limited, the misguided bird scratched and scraped and beaked and delved in the soft yielding bed" (lines 35-38); "she rained her earth bolts at the marauder" (lines 54-55); "the Vasco da Gama fowl" (line 62). The overall tone of the passage is lighthearted, so choice F is incorrect. Morose means gloomy or depressed. Although the passage is lighthearted, it is describing the very serious feud between the two women, so choice G is incorrect. The passage does not offer any hope that the feud may be resolved, so choice H is incorrect.

TEST II
PASSAGE II—SOCIAL SCIENCE   The White House

11. **B** Lines 8-10 describe how President Coolidge practiced his habit of sitting on the front porch after dinner: "So many pedestrians stopped to stare at him, however, that he gave up his modest form of relaxation." The passage does not indicate that the occupants of the White House are in any danger, nor does it indicate that they have to sacrifice any relationships because they live in the White House. The passage also does not discuss any security issues.

12. **G** Tad is begging money from his father's callers to donate to war charities. He is not borrowing the money because there is no indication that he intends to pay it back. He is not donating money; he is soliciting it from others. There is no indication that he is stealing money.

13. **A** The passage discusses the personal aspects of living in the White House as opposed to the public aspects. The passage only discusses the lives of former United States Presidents, so choice B is incorrect. Although the passage mentions the loss of privacy, it does not call for any action about that issue, so choice C is incorrect. Choice D is incorrect because the passage is not primarily focuses on the hardships of public figures; it discusses both joys and sorrows.

14. **G** Choices I and II are supported by lines 55-58: "Tad for bombarding the door with his toy cannon during a Cabinet meeting, or when the boy stopped his father's callers to sell refreshments." Choice III is incorrect because Tad didn't push Baby McKee in a carriage (lines 46-50).

15. **C** The Roosevelt children can best be described as rambunctious and mischievous based on lines 72-81. They "slid down stairways on trays," "stalked the halls on stilts," "bicycled and skated on newly polished floors," and took a pony in the elevator to visit their sick brother.

16. **H** The passage points out in two places that the occupants of the White House have the same experiences as other people: "the normal joys and sorrows of everyday family experience, the high moments of birth and death that are part of life here as in any other home" (lines 22-24); "the men and women who have lived in the Executive Mansion have known the same happiness and frustration, pride and misery that come to all of us" (lines 82-85). The passage does not focus on the resulting advantages or lack of advantages connected to living in the White House. The passage also does not focus on the decoration of the White House.

17. **D** President Lincoln's children are discussed in lines 51-59. President Cleveland's children are discussed in lines 60-69. President Roosevelt's children are discussed in lines 70-81. All were inhabitants of the White House during their fathers' terms.

18. **G** Lines 92-98 discuss Mrs. Johnson waiting for news of her husband's impeachment. The passage never discusses the difficulty they had raising their children or the lack of comfort in the White House. According to the passage, President Lincoln preferred the children have fun rather than maintain an orderly home.

19. **D** The security advantages of living in the White House are never discussed in the passage. The passage does identify the drawbacks (lack of privacy), its difficult times (President Jackson missing his deceased wife), and the families enjoying their stay in the White House.

20. **J** Most of the examples discussed in the passage illustrate the importance of family life in the White House. The passage doesn't discuss the challenges the President may face in balancing his job with his family. Based on the examples of the Lincoln and Roosevelt children, being quiet and out of sight, and not interacting with visitors was not emphasized.

TEST II
PASSAGE III—HUMANITIES   Congressional Record

21. **B** Lines 13-16 establish the answer: "We have pilot programs today in many parts of this country that are working right now, but the time has come for those pilot lights to ignite the whole furnace." The pilot lights that the author refers to are the small youth centered programs that are currently active. The author's focus is expanding those programs into nation-wide participation. Choice A is incorrect because the author is clearly against continued violence. Although it may be an accurate statement, choice C does not fit with the author's metaphor. The passage does not reference a single community service act, so choice D is incorrect.

22. **H** Paragraph 2 begins by listing several problems young people face. These examples lead into the main idea of the paragraph, found in lines 13-16: "we have pilot programs today in many parts of this country that are working right now, but the time has come for those pilot lights to ignite the whole furnace." These lines express the speaker's call to action or his focus for the whole speech. Choices F, G and J are expressions of the problems listed in the beginning of the paragraph.

23. **B** Lines 24-28 establish the answer: "We understand that personal responsibility and self-esteem cannot simple be taught by lectures. They have to be earned. And we need to give young people the opportunity to earn those qualities." The other choices are incorrect because although they may be accurate statements according to the passage, they are not linked to line 30 as choice B is.

24. **F** Civic is defined as relating to a city or citizenship; in other words, civic refers to society. Civic indifference would be a lack of concern about **society as a whole.** That reasoning would make the other choices incorrect.

25. **C** The speaker believes that having young people participate in some sort of service program will break the cycle of gangs, welfare and violence (lines 8-11), and that these programs will provide opportunities for young people to develop personal responsibility and self-esteem (lines 25-29). The passage never connects financial security at a young age to the service programs.

26. **H** The author clearly believes that young people's lives can be changed: "I believe we can break that cycle [of drugs, welfare, crime, prison]. I believe we know how to do it" (lines 11-12). He may be disappointed in the system, but he does not express that feeling in connection with young people. Because he is optimistic about the future, he cannot be cynical (unbelieving). He is certainly not contented with young people because he wants to change the way they act and are treated.

27. **C** President Roosevelt established the CCC to combat the effects of the Great Depression (lines 64-75). That would place the Depression occurring before the formation of the CCC. Lines 75-77 tell us that after a generation of young men worked in the CCC, they moved on to serve in WWII.

28. **J** Although all of the other choices are accurate statements and important effects of the CCC, according to the passage, only choice J is the most important effect. The passage establishes that in line 78: "**More importantly**, they transformed themselves."

29. **D** The correct answer is given in the last paragraph of the passage: "take the step of breaking down the budget wall so we can invest military savings in our pressing domestic needs." (lines 92-94)

30. **F** Everything the speaker says in the passage is leading up to or supporting his main point: If given the opportunities and the skills, the youth of the nation have the potential to change themselves and society. Although choices G, H and J are accurate, they are not the focus or main point of the passage.

TEST II
PASSAGE IV—NATURAL SCIENCE   US Fish and Wildlife Service

31. **D** The paragraph begins by identifying the purpose of the ESA and then goes on to define two terms included in that purpose: *endangered* and *threatened*. The rest of the paragraph is expanding on the definitions of those two terms. Choice A is incorrect because the paragraph identifies species which can be protected. Choice B and C are incorrect because the paragraph does not discuss individual agencies or non-federal landowners.

32. **G** Lines 13-15 define the term *threatened species*: "Threatened means a species is likely to become endangered within the foreseeable future." Choice F is incorrect because it defines *endangered* rather than *threatened*. Choice H is incorrect because the term does not refer to the landowner in any way. Choice J is incorrect because man's intervention (of lack of) is not inherent in the definition of the term.

33. **C** Lines 15-17 provide the answer: "All species of plants and animals, **except pest insects**, are eligible for listing as endangered or threatened."

34. **F** The phrase indicated lists several reasons that "our rich natural heritage" should be preserved; choice F covers more than the other choices: beauty, ecological, social and scientific concerns. Choice G is incorrect because there are no natural heritage laws; choice H is incorrect because it identifies only two of the reasons listed in the passage: research and science. Choice J is incorrect because the phrase indicated does not discuss specific geographical placement of any species.

35. **B** Lines 54-55 identify the primary purpose of the Fish and Wildlife Service: "The protection of federally listed species on federal lands is the first priority of the FWS." The FWS is not described as resentful, defensive or antagonistic; rather they are described as cooperative and proactive, trying to compromise and find solutions before a listed species is threatened.

36. **F** Lines 57-61 identify the government's attitude toward the relationship between landowners and endangered species: "Policies and incentives have been developed to protect private landowner's interests in their lands while encouraging them to manage their lands in ways that benefit endangered species." According to the passage, the government does not favor one group over the other, so choices II and III are incorrect.

37. **C** Lines 77-79 identify the purpose of the ESA: "The law's ultimate goal is to 'recover' species so they no longer need protection under the Endangered Species Act." According to the passage, the law does not provide for fundraising. Although the enforcement of the ESA may result in relocation of certain species or a catalog of extinct species, that is not the main focus of the law.

38. **J** Choice F is supported by lines 66-69: "The FWS decides all listings using sound science and peer review to ensure the accuracy of the best available data. The FWS also maintains a list of 'candidate' species." Choice G is supported by lines 4-6: "It is regarded as one of the most comprehensive wildlife conservation laws in the world." Choice H is supported by paragraph 5, the first lines of which follow: "The protection of species is also achieved through partnerships with the states" (lines 41-42). The passage never indicates that the FWS is responsible for only specific species or that that protection is exclusive to the FWS.

39. **B** Paragraph five (lines 41-53) explains the interaction the FWS has with state governments. Lines 50-53 specify how the FWS woks with private landowners. The passage never suggests that states should create a list of targeted species, prohibit all development projects or create individual plans for each landowner.

40. **F** The main purpose of the passage is to explain the Endangered Species Act and the role of its enforcing agency, the Fish and Wildlife Service. The passage does not try to persuade the reader to support the

preservation of wildlife nor does it explain the consequences of ignoring needed preservation. The passage's discussion is limited to wildlife and plants and does not mention water conservation at all.

TEST III
PASSAGE I—PROSE FICTION   "The Young King"

1. **C** It can be inferred from the passage that a goatherd would live in a poor, shabby home, thus the hut is crude or primitively made. The hut cannot be insolent (disrespectful) and doesn't seem to be dysfunctional in any way. There is no indication that the goatherd's home is welcoming; rather, the messenger seems to be bringing the child in secret.

2. **J** Lines 22-49 describe the rumors about the princess and her relationships, the abduction of the child, and the subsequent death of the princess. The cause and effect relationship between the birth of the child and the suspicious, secretive death of the princess is established in that paragraph. The reader can infer that the princess died as a result of her relationship with a commoner or someone considered inappropriate. The child was stolen against her will as she slept, so choice F is incorrect. The princess may have feared for the child's safety, but that isn't the reason she was killed, so choice G is incorrect. The rumor was that the princess died of the plague not her secret husband, so choice H is incorrect.

3. **A** Lines 72-79 support choice A: "as soon as he could escape from the council-board or audience-chamber, he would run down the great staircase…like one who was seeking to find in beauty…a sort of restoration from sickness." The passage gives no indication that he missed being a goatherd or that he has sleeping issues. The passage doesn't describe him hiding from the courtiers as a game.

4. **G** Lines 52-54 support choice G: the king "whether moved by remorse for his great sin, or merely desiring that the kingdom should not pass away from his line." There is no indication in the passage that the king's court insisted that he name a legal heir.

5. **B** Lines 78-79 describe the prince as seeking in beauty a "sort of restoration from sickness." He is not substituting beauty for something else in his life, nor does it cause him pain, so choices A and C are incorrect. Choice D does not work either because the prince is not longing for pain—he longs for beauty.

6. **G** Lines 66-67 support choice G: "He missed, indeed, at times the fine freedom of his forest life." Both choice F and H are incorrect based on lines 62-66: "the cry of pleasure that broke from his lips when he saw the delicate raiment and rich jewels that had been prepared for him and of the almost fierce joy with which he flung aside his rough leathern tunic and coarse sheepskin cloak." Because nothing in the passage discusses his opinion of the courtiers that accompany him, the reader doesn't know if they irritate him or not, so choice J is incorrect.

7. **B** Choice B is supported by lines 85-89: "but more often he would be alone, feeling through a certain quick instinct, which was almost a divination, that the secrets of art are best learned in secret, and that **Beauty**, like Wisdom, **loves the lonely worshipper**." The passage doesn't reveal how the prince feels about his potential power or how he feels about nature as opposed to his palace, so choices A and C are incorrect. Based on his response to the clothing, jewels, and surroundings he now has, (lines 62-66; 69-72), he cannot be described as indifferent.

8. **J** The reader can infer that the young prince is astonished at his new-found position because of the true delight he takes in his surroundings. He is not cynical; instead he is appreciative. The passage does not indicate the young man ever dreamed of the possibility that he might become a prince or had been unhappy with his station as a goatherd, so choice F and H are incorrect. The passage does not indicate that the young man argued against being named the king's heir, so choice G is incorrect.

9. **A** The prince can be considered *inquisitive*: "Upon these journeys of discover, as he would call them—and, indeed, they were to him real voyages through a marvelous land" (lines 80-82) and *passionate*: "it seems that from the very first moment of his recognition he had shown signs of that strange passion for beauty" (lines 57-

59). The passage does not offer any evidence that the prince is *rude* and *ill-mannered* or *arrogant* and *aggressive*. His passion about art and beauty would prove that he is not *indifferent* and *lackadaisical*.

10. **H** The passage lists two rumors about the princess' secret husband: "a stranger, some said, who, by the wonderful magic of his lute-playing, had made the young Princess love him; while others spoke of an artist from Rimini, to whom the Princess had shown much, perhaps to much honour" (lines 24-28). The identity of the princess' secret husband is unknown and much speculated on by the citizens. Choice F is presented as a fact: "lad, being but sixteen years of age" (lines 11-12), as is choice G: "he had shown signs of that strange passion for beauty" (lines 58-59) and choice J: "the child of the old King's only daughter" (lines 22-23).

TEST III
PASSAGE II—SOCIAL SCIENCE   *London's Underworld*

11. **A** *Absconded* most nearly means *run away from*. Lines 10-11 tell that in absconding from their wives and children, the men have left "them chargeable to the parish." In other words, the community is now responsible for supporting the women and children because their men have left them behind. There is no indication that the men have stolen anything from the women and children, traded them for food or money, or murdered them.

12. **H** The inhabitants of London's underworld are described as "poverty-stricken" in line 6; the third paragraph (lines 28-38) describes the conditions they live in: "the beautiful word 'home' is desecrated if applied to most of their habitations. Horrid places within and without…At their doorway death stands ready to strike…the murky light of little rooms filled with thick air." The conditions are obviously dismal. Based on that description, choices F, G and J are clearly wrong.

13. **B** Lines 18-27 describe the unending circle of misery these men are suffering because they have been "searching for work that is everlastingly denied them." Their souls are "fainting within them" as they return home to the their families who "await their return with patient but hopeless resignation." Although they may be reluctant to return to their families, that is not the specific reason they are "sad-faced." They are sad because they cannot provide for themselves or their families. The parents of these men are not mentioned, so choice A is incorrect. These particular men are currently unemployed and have not worked for some time, so choices C and D are incorrect.

14. **J** Lines 28-30 establish the purpose of the paragraph: "Take notice of the places they enter, for surely the beautiful word 'home' is desecrated if applied to most of their habitations." The details found in the rest of the paragraph support that statement by relating why the places they live are so bad. Although the canal is mentioned, it is only a supporting detail, not the main focus of the paragraph. The same argument applies to choice H: the description of their burial place (possibly the canal) is not the main focus of the paragraph. Lastly, although their homes do seem dangerous, the author does not go into great detail about the surrounding neighborhood.

15. **C** The phrase "hardly earned" can best be described as barely earned. In other words, the widows have worked hard for many hours and have little to show for it. They only earned two shillings for all their work. Choice A is incorrect because line 43-44 tell the reader that the "weary widows have been at the washtubs all day long." Choice B is incorrect because the reader can assume that if the women have been working hard for that long, they most likely deserve their pay. Choice D is incorrect because the phrase "hardly earned" doesn't refer to the value of the money (it is the same as any other shilling); rather it refers how the money was gained.

16. **H** Lines 57-69 describe the elderly couple creating their beautiful flowers, "the shops of the West End have fairly blazed with the glory of their roses" in the squalid place they call home, which includes a "small, evil-smelling lamp," while the old man works in "comparative gloom, for he is almost blind; he works by touch." Lines 28-36 describe the way the "beautiful word 'home' is desecrated by applying it to the places these people live. In both of these situations, beauty is contrasted with squalor. Although the inhabitants are hopeless and some of their employers certainly rich, no direct mention is made of the employers' wealth, so choice III is incorrect.

17. **B** Paragraphs 6-9 (lines 57-91) describe the elderly couple. They seem to be loving and attentive based on how hard his wife works in order to care for him (lines 75-77), how she takes care of him when he is sick (lines 80-81), and how she prepares his body for burial after his death (line 85). The paragraph makes no mention of any

hostility between them or of any blame from the woman for their living conditions. The man does not seem unconcerned about their survival; in fact, although he is very ill, he still does what he can (lines 75-77).

18. **F** Her workload changed very little because the husband was unable to do much even when he was alive due to his poor health and vision. Lines 82-84 describe the woman as still sitting at the table working. She is still in her home, so choice G is incorrect. The passage makes no mention of her leaving London or reducing the number of hours she works.

19. **A** Although the passage does mention the difficult working conditions, the hopelessness of death and the effect of drunkenness and debauchery, they are only supporting examples to the main purpose of the passage established in the first paragraph: "London's great underworld to many may be an undiscovered country" (lines 1-2). The function of the rest of the paragraph is to describe the underworld for the reader.

20. **F** Reading the question carefully lets you know that you are to consider only the **hardworking** people in the passage. These people are the "sad-faced men" (lines 18), the widowed women (line 40), the elderly couple (line 59). The author seems to admire their hardworking attitude and persistence in refusing to give up. He doesn't make fun of them or look down on them, nor is he amused by their situation.

TEST III
PASSAGE III—HUMANITIES   *The Experiences of a Bandmaster*

21. **B** Lines 12-16 establish General Grant's attitude toward music: "They were all very appreciative of music, and in this respect were quite unlike General Grant, of whom it is said that he knew only two tunes, one of which was "Yankee Doodle" and the other wasn't!" The impression of those lines is that he wasn't interested in music as a whole. Choices A, C and D are incorrect because there is no support in the passage for his opinion of specific music genres or when he believed music should be played.

22. **F** Lines 17-20 imply that the responsibilities of a great reception could be difficult because the President could find "rest by sitting quietly…listening to the music." The reader can infer that the music allows the President to relax and take a break from his duties. This line of reasoning would make the other three choices incorrect: the duties do not seem secretive or mysterious, and if they were pleasant, the President would most likely not need a break from them.

23. **B** Line 24-25: the President "asked me to play the 'Cachuca.'" Lines 32-34: "one of the bandmen remembered the melody and played it over softly to me on his cornet in a corner." Lines 34-35: "I hastily wrote out several parts for the leading instruments."

24. **H** "Mr. Cleveland was keenly alive to the opportunities for humorous remarks which this title might afford to irreverent newspaper men" (lines 54-56). There is no indication that the President wanted something more traditional or that the bride didn't like the song. Mr. Sousa is able to play the song because it comes from an opera that he himself wrote.

25. **D** Line 61 begins a description of a reunion at which Mr. Sousa and his band played. Lines 76-78 describe how enthusiastic the crowd becomes from the music: "Verse after verse was sung, interrupted with frantic cheers, until it seemed that **the very ecstasy of enthusiasm was reached**." The enthusiasm of the audience increases as the music continues. The experience at the reunion was an example of the *acme* or the *highest point*.

26. **H** Choice II is supported by the description of the audience's enthusiastic response to the patriotic music (lines 61-80). Choice III is supported by lines 17-20 as the President relaxes to the sound of Sousa's music. The passage doesn't offer any evidence of music restoring order or calming fears.

27. **A** The purpose of the passage is stated in the first paragraph, lines 1-5: "During my eighteen years…many curious and interesting incidents have come under my observation." All the examples that follow (the President relaxing to the music (lines 17-20), President Arthur asking for the song "Cachuca" (lines 21-39), President Cleveland's wedding (lines 40-60) and the concert for the veterans (lines 61-80) provide support for the first sentence of the paragraph.

28. **G** Based on his experiences and talent, Mr. Sousa is seen as an excellent musician and bandmaster, so he could not be called incompetent. Based on the passage, he is patriotic (he enjoys playing patriotic music and enjoys his service to the president), flexible (quickly writes out the music for a song the President wanted to hear), and unflappable (instead of panicking because he doesn't know the song the President asks for, he listens to his bandman and writes out the music for the band to play).

29. **D** The narrator clearly feels great pride in his ability to fulfill his duties to the President and he thoroughly enjoyed the responses of his audiences to his music. He makes no statements about preferring one occasion over another, or that he is frustrated by his audience's lack of music knowledge. He also never appears to be arrogant because of his talent.

30. **H** The focus of the passage is given in the first paragraph: the passage is about Mr. Sousa's interesting career. The last two paragraphs provide a final example of that career. The other choices are true statements about the last two paragraphs, but they do not describe how those paragraphs function in relation to the entire essay.

TEST III
PASSAGE IV—NATURAL SCIENCE   Coral and Coral Reefs

31. **A** Lines 1-6 describe the red coral formation: "The red coral polyp perches on the sea bottom…have a kind of tree formed, every branch of the tree terminated by its polyp." Although the red coral does have a type of skeleton, that is not what the entire structure resembles. The red coral is not compared to a maze. It is the manner in which the white coral grows that is compared to a city, not the red coral.

32. **H** Lines 15-23 describe the steps in the collection of the red coral: "the coral fishers…take their drag nets…along the bottom of the sea to catch the branches of the red coral, which become entangled…They are then allowed to putrefy, in order to get rid of the animal matter, and the red coral is the skeleton that is left." Spraying the coral with lime carbonate is never mentioned.

33. **D** The fishermen are predators; the coral is their prey. Parasite and host does not describe the relationship because one is not physically connected and living off the other. While the fishermen may need the coral to survive, the same cannot be said for the coral. The fishermen are not described as beneficial to the coral in any way.

34. **J** The primary difference between the red and white coral is established in lines 24-25: "In the case of the white coral, the skeleton is more complete" than that of the red coral. Both types of coral contain lime carbonate; the quantities are not identified (line 10; 31). Both corals have "polyps;" the design of which is not compared (lines 6-7; 51-52). The white coral is not limited to warm waters: "The animals which form coral are scattered over the seas of all countries in the world. The red coral is comparatively limited, but the polyps which form the white coral are widely scattered" (lines 64-67).

35. **B** The polyp flowers are described as beautiful and often vibrantly colored (lines 37; 51-52). This description proves that they are not small and colorless. The polyp flowers are never described as poisonous and can be white instead of red.

36. **G** The coral polyps can be described as sociable and cooperative in the sense that they often grow close together and "form great masses…They have a habit of growing together in masses in the same place" (73-81). They are not considered dangerous or threatening. Because they are actively growing in a large mass, they cannot be considered apathetic or isolated. The passage does not indicate that the coral is infected or deteriorating in any way.

37. **B** When the polyps grow together in the same place, they tend to "adhere together and form great masses" (lines 75-76). A specific time limit to the life of coral is not given, nor is their color limited to red. The passage's reference to polyps engulfed in mud was about the individual polyps as they die, not the large masses of polyps.

38. **F** According to the way it is used in the passage, *aggregation* most nearly means a group of individual items. Lines 79-86 support this definition: "They have a habit of growing together in masses in the same place…as

they die and leave their skeletons, those skeletons form a considerable solid aggregation on the bottom of the sea, and other polyps perch upon them, and begin building upon them, and so by degrees a great mass is formed." This great mass is formed of individual skeletons. It does not indicate that there is an increase in liquid or that it is a point of irritation. The formation of the large mass is not a reversal of procedure.

39. **A** Lines 86-93 connect the analogy of the cities to the formation of the coral: "And just as we know there are some ancient cities in which you have a British city, and over that the foundations of a Roman city, and over that a Saxon city, and over that again a modern city…you have the accumulations of the foundations of the houses, if I may use the term, of nation after nation of these coral polyps." These lines illustrate the formation of the coral polyps not how to determine their age or how they acquire their colors. The new layers of coral do not destroy the previous, they merely "perch upon them" (line 84).

40. **F** The main purpose of the passage is to explain to the reader how coral formations are created. The living conditions of the coral are not described as particularly precarious, and although the geographic location of the coral is generally discussed, it is not the focus of the passage. The passage does not attempt in any way to persuade the reader to promote conservation attempts.

TEST IV
PASSAGE I—PROSE FICTION   *The Tragedy of Pudd'nhead Wilson*

1. **C** Lines 13-19: "When there was room on the ledge outside of the pots and boxes for a cat, the cat was there—in sunny weather—stretched at full length, asleep and blissful, with her furry belly to the sun and a paw curved over her nose. Then that house was complete, and its contentment and peace were made manifest to the world by this symbol."

2. **F** By describing both the peaceful, neatly kept homes and the productive, prosperous business area, the author provides a complete picture of the town. There is no contrast between the residential and business area; both have a sense of contentment and completeness. The town is not hurried and busy. The passage describes several businesses and does not indicate a problem with industry.

3. **A** Lines 61-64: "Pudd'nhead was still toiling in obscurity at the bottom of the ladder, under the blight of that unlucky remark which he had let fall twenty-three years before about the dog."

4. **G** As it is used in the passage, *blight* is connected to Pudd'nhead's obscure social status "at the bottom of the ladder" (line 62) because of the "unlucky remark" (line 63) he had made earlier. That description would make *blight* an undesired curse, not a blessing. Although making the remark about the dog might have shown a lack of judgement, that does not define *blight*. There is no indication of any physical defect in the passage.

5. **A** Lines 91-95: "Judge Driscoll could be a freethinker and still hold his place in society because he was the **person of most consequence to the community**, and therefore could venture to go his own way and follow out his own notions."

6. **F** Lines 79-80: "But irony was not for those people; their mental vision was not focused for it."

7. **C** The citizens of the town do not seem interested in being a freethinker. The last paragraph of the passage establishes that Judge Driscoll is allowed to think differently because he is so important in the community; Dave Wilson is allowed because he is so unimportant.

8. **F** Lines 65-66 establish Judge Driscoll's mistake: the judge was Pudd'nhead's friend and "claimed that he had a mind above the average." Lines 70-72 reinforce this point: "If the judge had stopped with bare assertion, it would have had a good deal of effect; but he made the mistake of trying to prove his position."

9. **A** Judge Driscoll is described as the "chief citizen" (line 42) and he is "respected, esteemed and beloved by all of the community. He was well off…" (lines 49-50). This description would make the Judge seem illustrious (high in social standing). Dave Wilson is seen as "toiling in obscurity at the bottom of the ladder (line 62) and is described as a "pudd'nhead" (line 83). The townspeople didn't attach "any importance to what he though or

did" (lines 96-97) and thought he "didn't count for anything" (line 98-99). This description fits with being uncelebrated.

10. **H** Although the judge and his wife do not have the children they have long desired, the passage does not indicate the judge's specific feelings about that (lines 51-55). He does believe that tradition is important (line 46) and that Dave Wilson is smart (lines 65-66) and has bee misjudged by the town (lines 88-90).

TEST IV
PASSAGE II—SOCIAL SCIENCE   *Sanitary and Social Lectures*

11. **A** Their own lives are boring: "for which their frivolous humdrum daily life gives no room, no vent" (lines 5-6). They know life could be more than what they live: "to see what they themselves might be had they the chance" (lines 14-15). According to the passage, people who "have looked in the mirror too often to wish to see their own disfigured visage in it any more; who are too tired of themselves and ashamed of themselves to want to hear of people like themselves" (lines 22-25) do not read sensational novels.

12. **H** The purpose of the paragraph is given in the first sentence: "This pettiness and dullness of our modern life is just what keeps the modern rage for sensational novels" (lines 1-3). The rest of the paragraph gives examples of the specific reasons people read sensational literature. The paragraph is merely presenting examples not criticizing the type of literature. At this point in the passage, no comparison is made between sensational literature and heroic literature. Nowhere in the passage does the author indicate a preference for nonfiction.

13. **B** "who want to hear of people utterly unlike themselves, more noble, and able, and just and sweet, and pure; who long to hear of heroism and to converse with heroes" (lines 26-29).

14. **F** The purpose of the paragraph is established in lines 43-44: "There is no use talking about a word till we have got at its meaning."

15. **B** The author speaks of using the word hero in a casual way, "as a party cry on platforms" (lines 44-45) where it would apparently have little real meaning. It would be insincere since politicians seem to say anything to get their listeners support.

16. **F** The phrase *above himself he can exalt himself* means that man must distinguish himself in some way, make himself a better person, or he will never become truly heroic. Remaining in poverty (or not) has nothing to do with a person being heroic; the phrase does not refer to material wealth. The phrase doesn't imply a comparison with the gods or any interaction on their part.

17. **D** Lines 62-65: "A hero or a heroine, then, among the old Homeric Greeks, meant a man or woman who was like the gods, and who, from that likeness, stood superior to his or her fellow creatures." Homeric Greeks generally believed their heroes or "some ancestor of theirs, descended from a god or goddess" (lines 72-73). The passage does not mention that the hero must undertake a journey of any kind, so choice B is incorrect. Homeric Greeks did believe that a hero was "expected to be more reverent than other men to those divine beings of whose nature he partook" (lines 89-91). In other words, he would be respectful of the gods not more powerful than they are.

18. **G** If a hero must stand "superior to his or her fellow creatures" (lines 64-65), he must raise himself in stature. That is not defined as becoming honest, becoming rich or sacrificing himself.

19. **A** Lines 82-85: Greeks would "require in their hero, their **godlike** man, **beauty** and **strength**…and **neglect his moral qualities**."

20. **J** The main purpose of the passage is to define heroism: "Instead of beginning an oration in praise of heroism, I shall as my readers to think with me what heroism is" (lines 53-55). The entire passage centers around getting to that definition.

TEST IV
PASSAGE III—HUMANITIES   *Knights of the Art*

21. **B** Lines 4-7 establish that the term *giant* is referring to Michelangelo's artistic skills, not his physical stature: "So among the crowd of painters traveling along the road to Fame we see above the rest **a giant, a greater and more powerful genius** than any that came before or after him."

22. **H** Lines 19-22: "without hesitation Lodovico determined to call his little son Michel Angelo, after the archangel Michael. Surely that was a name splendid enough to adorn any great career."

23. **D** Lines 29-34: "So in after years the great master often said that if his mind was worth anything, he owed it to the clear pure mountain air in which he was born, just as he owed his love of carving stone to the unconscious influence of his nurse, the stonecutter's wife."

24. **F** "But Lodovico would not hear of the boy becoming an artist. There were many children to provide for and the family was not rich" (lines 40-42). The silk and woolen business is not described as the family business. Although Lodovico obviously didn't want Michelangelo to become an artist, his opinion of the particular career isn't given.

25. **A** "But it was all in vain to try to make the boy" give up his art (line 45) even after he had been severely beaten (lines 46-50). Michelangelo's skill was already evident before he worked with Ghirlandaio, so although he did learn much from him, he soon progressed past what Ghirlandaio could teach him (lines 58-75). Michelangelo completely resisted working in the fabric business (lines 43-49) and his family wasn't wealthy (41-42).

26. **H** Eagles are generally considered to be more powerful, more cunning, more majestic than hawks. By comparing Michelangelo to an eagle and his master to a hawk, the author automatically gives those characteristics to each man. Eventually, Michelangelo surpasses his master in strength, talent and vision.

27. **C** Lines 65-69: "It was not pleasant for the great Florentine master, whose work all men admired, to have his drawings corrected by a young lad, and perhaps Michelangelo was not as humble as he should have been." In his young and perhaps arrogant way, Michelangelo became a competitor of Ghirlandaio and eventually left his studio to become his own master.

28. **J** After Michelangelo creates a sculpture of a faun from Lorenzo's garden, Lorenzo is amazed. "There was nothing that the magnificent ruler loved so much as genius" (lines 93-94).

29. **A** Michelangelo's copy was "even better than the original, for the boy had introduced ideas of his own and had made the laughing mouth a little open to show the teeth and the tongue of the faun" (lines 90-92). He didn't use terra cotta (line 85) nor did he make his copy look like Lorenzo's son. The faun copy is described as laughing, not menacing.

30. **J** The passage relates the journey of Michelangelo from a young child who loves drawing to a man famous for his artistic skills. The passage does not discuss any need for artistic standards. Although the passage does describe how Michelangelo's father tried to divert his son's artistic interests, that is only one incident in the journey of the artist not the focus of the passage. Also, although it could be argued that Michelangelo's genius is unsurpassed, the purpose of the passage is not to persuade the reader of that.

TEST IV
PASSAGE IV—NATURAL SCIENCE   *The Mountains*

31. **A** As it is used in the passage, *stolid* most nearly means impassive. Stolid and impassive both mean someone who is not demonstrative or openly emotional. According to the author, "Everybody, even the most stolid, said something" when they reached the top of the main ridge (lines 18-19). In other words, even the most undemonstrative person is moved to react by the sight at the top of the trail. That reasoning would make choice B, C and D incorrect.

32. **G** Choice I is supported by lines 9-11: "A fall on the part of your horse would mean a more than serious accident, but Western horses do not fall." Choice III is supported by lines 11-13: "The major premise stands: even the casual tourist has no real reason for fear, however scared he may become." Choice II is proven incorrect by lines 8-9: the trails are "filled to demoralization with loose boulders and shale."

33. **D** The correct answer is supported by lines 15-17: "We used to enjoy taking visitors up it, mainly because you come on the top suddenly, without warning." Although the other three choices are characteristics of the trail, they are not what make the trail remarkable.

34. **H** Lines 39-43 support choice H: "From the ridge, ascending from seaward in a gradual coquetry of foothills, broad low ranges, cross-systems, canyons, little flats, and gentle ravines, inland dropped off almost sheer to the river below." These lines also prove choice F and G to be incorrect. The ridge does not lead to the Rocky Mountains; it leads to the Coast Ranges, so choice J is incorrect as well.

35. **B** According to lines 48-49, the tourist's eyes follows the mountains "up and up, and farther and farther" to the very top of the mountains. This description implies the vast height of the mountains and focuses on the steep cliffs or sides of the mountains, the precipices. This reasoning eliminates choice C. Although the mountains have pine trees, the description does not specifically mention fir trees, and the description of the mountains does not mention any high water line which eliminates both A and D.

36. **H** Lines 61-64: "you turned sharp to the west and rode five miles along the knife-edge Ridge Trail to where Rattlesnake Canyon led you down and back to your accustomed environment." The lines refer to Rattlesnake Canyon not Rattlesnake Trail. Cold Spring Trail led up to the main ridge not down to the town. The passage doesn't mention a Coast Range Trail, only Coast Range mountains.

37. **D** The guides would like to "see with our own eyes what lay beyond" (lines 89-90).

38. **J** The guides speak of their surroundings in respectful, awestruck terms: "vivid, fertile, brilliant and pulsating with vitality" (lines 72-73); "It left you breathless, wonder-stricken, awed" (lines 53-54). Although they are certainly making money from showing the land to the tourists, the guides are not described as focusing on that. Although the guides have a healthy respect for the land, they do not overly fear it. They certainly are not ignorant or disdainful of the land.

39. **A** The surrounding landscape is described in glowing, majestic terms, while the humans in the story are described as "breathless, wonder-stricken, awed" (lines 53-54). There is no indication in the passage that the author is in favor of conquering nature, only admiring it. A very strong connection is established in the passage between humanity and nature; the guides (and occasional tourists) are inspired and renewed by the natural world. The passage focuses on the beauty of nature for its own sake, not for any material gain.

40. **F** The main purpose of the passage is stated in lines 80-81: "This was the wonder we never tired of seeing for ourselves, of showing to others." That wonder is the beauty of the landscape. The entire paragraph focuses on describing that beauty. Although the passage may encourage more visitors, that isn't the main purpose. The passage doesn't discuss investors or the government.

SCIENCE REASONING – GENERAL TIPS AND STRATEGIES

40 Questions	35 Minutes

This test contains six passages. Each passage is designed to be approximately equal length and equal difficulty. Notice that six passages over the 35-minute period implies that you should average completing one passage every five-minutes and 50 seconds. When the five-minutes remaining announcement is made, just ignore it. At that announcement, you should just have started the last passage. So don't start guessing. Keep testing. When taking the science reasoning test, have a working knowledge of how to read and interpret information portrayed in the form of a graph or table. Also, be familiar with the basic concepts of geology, genetics, chemistry, physical science, and biology. These fields of science are the primary subjects covered in the passages. Very seldom will they ask you a science question that you must have had previous knowledge of the subject. If they do ask a question of this nature, generally it will not be too difficult. Certainly, your familiarity with these subjects helps on this test, but it is not absolutely necessary to get the correct answer.

So, if the science reasoning test is not a test of content, what is it? There are passages to read, so is it a test of science comprehension? No. This test is called science, but it really is still the test of its former name Science Reasoning. The key word is *reasoning*. This is unlike any science test you have probably ever taken. The answers usually aren't obvious. For example, the passage will never tell you that the apple is red, then ask you for the color of the apple. That is comprehension. The passage or data table may indicate that the color of the apple is somewhere between pink and purple, and you would have to reason that red would be a valid answer.

To reason means you don't look for the right answer. You use the clues to eliminate the wrong answers. Be willing to pick the least wrong answer rather than the right answer. Many times you simply will not know the right answer, but through reasoning you can find the least wrong answer. The least wrong answer will be the best answer.

For a given passage, the questions get progressively harder as they are asked. Don't take too much time on any one question. If you can't figure out an answer, circle the question number in the test booklet and come back to it if you have time. At the end of the section, if you realize you are not going to have time to work the problem, guess.

Many experts say you should preview the questions before you read the passages. As with all sections of the ACT, you must find out what works best for you.

<u>Primary Question Types</u>
1. Read and interpret information from graphs and tables.
2. Make conclusions and predict results.
3. Compare opposing views or compare different experiments.

SCIENCE REASONING – GENERAL TIPS AND STRATEGIES

1. Stay Focused.

- Science is the last test – Resist wanting to quit because you are tired and don't care anymore.
- Everything bad you can possibly imagine will start happening to you.
- Take a few 5-10 second breaks to stretch and help you stay awake.
- Try your best on every question – Don't guess because you are tired and don't care.
- The difference in a 26 and a 32 is as few as 5 questions.
- This is the most important quarter of the test: the fourth quarter.
- This is the easiest section to raise your score.

The most difficult aspect of the science reasoning section of the ACT is simply staying focused. Those of you who have taken the test may relate to the following chronology of a typical test day. It's Saturday morning, and you are at a school, of all places, taking a very long test that started too early in the morning. First, you survived a 45-minute English test at 8am. Then you struggled helplessly through the 60-minute math test that made you feel really frustrated. Then after an awfully short break you endured a 35-minute reading comprehension test. During the reading test, the people around you may have started getting on your nerves with sneezing, coughing, blowing their noses, etc. Your mind is spent. There just isn't anything left in the emotional bank to withdraw. Then it's time for science which is the one section where you don't even really know if you're getting the questions right or wrong.

Everything bad you can possibly imagine will start happening to you. If something can go wrong, it will. The problem may not be that bad, but it seems much worse than it actually is. For example, remember the guy that was coughing during the reading test? When science gets here, his sickness has turned into full-scale pneumonia. On top of all the noise distractions, the fellow next to you may not have showered after Friday night's game. You'll be testing, and all you can think about is how bad the guy smells. In addition to that, he is so hungry his stomach sings a tune to you. These examples may sound extreme, but just wait and see how bad the little things start affecting you during science.

I encourage you to take a few 5-10 second breaks to stretch and help you stay awake. About half-way through the science reasoning test, just take a quick look around the test center. Notice how many of your friends are taking the test with their heads on their desks asleep. It's amazing how many students just quit.

For those of you who have taken the test, how many of you have guessed on a least one question in science because you were tired or just didn't really care anymore? Out of over 150,000 students I have asked at my workshops, over 80% say they guess on at least one question in science because they are tired or don't care. Over half the students that take this test guess on several questions in science for the reasons stated above.

Consider this scenario to prove the value of a question in science:

SCIENCE REASONING – GENERAL TIPS AND STRATEGIES

Let's say you guess on 5 questions because you are tired and just want the test to be over. You miss all 5, but you actually score a 26 in science. Your composite score for the ACT ends up at a total of 112 subscore points or a composite of a 28. (112 / 4 = 28.0)

Now let's say you get to go back in time and actually try on the 5 questions that you guessed. If you get all 5 of them correct, what do you think your 26 would be? Your 26 would increase all the way to a 31 or 32. The difference in a 26 and a 32 in science is as few as 5 questions.

Taking this one step further, if you scored a composite of 28.0 and increased your science score 6 points, your composite would increase to a 30. Under these conditions, the difference in a 28 and a 30 on the ACT is as few as 5 science questions. How important is the science reasoning section? Huge!

If you have a 26 in English while guessing on 5 questions and missing them, then you retake the 5 questions and get them right, your English score would increase from a 26 to a 28. That is just two points in English and six points in science. One main difference is that the English test has 75 questions and the science test has 40. Each question in science has greater value. You can't afford to give less than your best effort on every question in science. Although it would be ridiculous to guess on the English test, I would rather you guess in English than science. If you wouldn't guess in English, don't guess in science. Each section counts an equal ¼ of your composite score.

Let's assume you are playing a basketball game, and you come out in the first period and get a nice lead. During the second period you start to wear down a little, but you work really hard and maintain the lead. At halftime you get a little break and listen to the famous pep talk by the coach. One of my high school basketball coaches Curt Knox always said, "No one's going to ask you who was winning at halftime." He was right. Knowing it is only the final score that counts, you come out and play hard in the third quarter and still maintain your lead. In the fourth quarter you say, "Man, I'm really tired now. I think I'll just not try so hard anymore." You lose. There is no reason to play the first three quarters, if you are going to quit in the fourth quarter.

I didn't just describe a basketball game, I described the ACT test. The first quarter is English. Most students will try in English because it is the first test, and you are relatively fresh. The second quarter is a long, tiring quarter. It is a 60-minute math test. Many of you will have a tendency to already quit, but press on to halftime. When halftime comes, you will get a 15-minute break. Take advantage of this time. Get out of the testing room. Get a snack. Use the bathroom. And make sure you get back to your seat on time. Don't be late for the start of the 3rd quarter. When the 3rd quarter begins, you will start the reading comprehension test. A common dilemma in sports is called the "3rd quarter letdown." This is where you come out of halftime not ready to play. You end up blowing any lead you had and losing all momentum you built in the first half. DON'T HAVE A "3RD QUARTER LETDOWN!" Be ready to play when they say, "Go." Most of you will grind through the reading test, and then comes the fourth quarter – the science test. Just like the basketball game, you are tired and ready for this thing to end, but you have to press all the way to the end. Most coaches say the fourth quarter is the most important quarter of any game. The fourth quarter of the ACT is the most important quarter of the test. Yes, science is the most important test you will take. This game is won or lost in the fourth quarter.

This is the easiest section to raise your score. Why? Most guess on at least one problem in science because you give up. If you try on every question, you will probably raise your score. And most are not staying focused. Be committed to stay focused for the entire 35 minutes of this section.

You must try your best on every question. Remember that if a 6-point increase in science is as few as five questions, you must give each question your very best.

I know this is a very long discussion to tell you to stay focused, but the length of the discussion is appropriate for its importance. Staying focused in science is the most important rule for you to follow. In fact, the two most important words in this whole book is to "STAY FOCUSED." This applies to the entire test, especially in science reasoning.

2. Don't waste time on long confusing words.

- This is not a science vocabulary test.
- They never ask you questions like "Were you able to pronounce this word" or "What is the proper pronunciation of this word?"
- Focus on the prefixes, suffixes, and root words for general meaning.
- Don't sound out a single big science word.

The science reasoning test is notorious for putting big science words that you have never heard of nor have little chance of pronouncing correctly. Yet, students continually try to sound out these words thinking that is what they are supposed to do.

When I was in high school taking this test, I always sounded out these big science words because I believed it was the right thing to do. After I took about 10 ACTs in high school, I finally discovered that they never ask you questions like "Were you able to pronounce this word" or "What is the proper pronunciation of this word?" Those questions just aren't on the test. So, I changed my strategy.

If they have the word *pneumonoultramicroscopicsilicovolcanoconiosis* (officially the longest word in the English language according to my son's McDonalds Happy Meal) or the words *polysystemic chronic candidiasis* in the passage, don't sound it out. Just call it *that word* or *volcano*. This takes very little time. Anytime you see a big science word or set of words, you can continue testing without wasting time trying to sound it out. I don't care what you call it as long as you don't sound it out. Certainly, familiarity with the subjects, words, prefixes, and suffixes helps, but knowing these words rarely is required to get a single question correct. There was a national test where you had to know what the word *homogeneous* meant to get the questions correct. You just had to know that the prefix meant *the same* or *alike*. If you knew that, you could get the question correct. Although you had to know the meaning of this word, this is rare for the ACT science reasoning test. Instead of trying to sound out the big words, just glance at any common prefixes, suffixes, or root words and move on. In my example, *polysystemic chronic candidiasis*, you could focus on the prefix *poly* which means *many* and the root words *systemic* and *chronic* to give you an idea of the meaning. I guarantee you will not have to be able to say this word to get a question right.

3. Preview the associated graphs and tables.

- Before reading an experiment, study, or passage, preview the associated graph or table.
- Focus on the trends.
- Use arrows or symbols to identify trends where possible.
- If they ask about a specific number, then you read it left to right.
- Focus on the axis labels and legend in a graph and column headers or row titles in a table.

There are a wide variety of graphs and tables on the ACT science reasoning test. All graphs and tables will be preceded by some written explanation. The ACT test always has at least one sentence telling you generally what is in the graph or table.

Before you read the associated study, experiment, or passage, preview the table or graph. Consider a passage where there is an introduction and two experiments each with a table. Work through the passage as follows: read the introduction, preview the first table, read experiment one, preview table two, then read experiment two. Notice that for each experiment you previewed the associated graph or table first.

When previewing a table or graph, focus on the trends. When students look through a table, they usually read through the data left-to-right. Consider the following example:

Let's say that I am your chemistry teacher, and we are going to do an experiment where I give each of you a flask filled with an unknown gas. The flask has a cork in the top trapping the gas. A thermometer and a pressure gage extend through the cork into the gas in the flask. I ask you to alter the temperature of the gas and measure the effects of the pressure. You produce the following table:

Temp (°F)	Pressure (atm)
75	0.2
125	0.5
175	0.9
225	1.5

If your experiment yielded this data, what conclusion would you make about the relationship between temperature and pressure? General Answer: As the temperature increased, the pressure increased. The specific numbers are not important to remember.

Typically in an experiment like this example, a general conclusion based on the trends is all that is needed. We don't need to read the numbers left to right. Instead, you should read tables vertically to begin. As you go down the temperature column, what do those numbers do? They get bigger. The trend is that they are increasing. Simply put an up arrow up and 50 by *Temp* to signify that the temperature is increasing by 50. As the temperature increased, what did the pressure do? It increased as well. Put a curved up arrow by *Pressure* signifying that it is increasing at an increasing rate. From our arrows, we quickly conclude that for the conditions of this experiment, as the temperature increases the pressure also increases at a growing rate.

Arrows usually work well for identifying trends in basic number tables. I encourage you to use whatever works for you. Obviously if the numbers in the table are not sorted or appear random, you will not be able to use the arrows. Still, try to quickly identify any trends in your preview.

If they ask a specific question about a number, we read the table left to right. For example, let's assume a question reads "for the conditions of experiment one, if you set the temperature at 150°F, what would you predict the pressure to be?" Then you would estimate where in the table 150°F would be and read left to right. In general, the only time you should read left to right is if they ask about a specific number within the table.

After you preview, you will read the associated experiment, study, or passage. In every passage, they will tell you what is in the graph. For the example above, they would have had at least one sentence that would have said something like "the temperature was changed, and the associated pressures were measured and recorded in table one." If you preview the table, you already know this. You don't need to read that sentence again.

For every graph or table, start with the thought *in general what is happening here?* Focus on the trends not the details.

4. Identify critical elements in passages.

- Constants should go in a box of constants for quick reference.
- Make notes to the side or below the passage, experiment, or study for anything critical.
- Look for things that are changing or are causing something else to change.
- Values (numbers) are usually critical.
- Keep underlining and circling to a minimum.

Students typically read the passages, studies, and experiments, then continually look back and re-read hoping to find the answer. By the end of a passage, you may have read it five or more times. The goal is to never re-read the passages. The primary way of making this possible is to extract all of the critical information from the text.

The following are a few guidelines for identifying and extracting the question critical information:

If a constant is given, write it to the side or below the experiment. After you have identified all the constants, I recommend putting a box around them to set them apart from any other notes you will make.

Comparing experiments or opposing views is a huge part of the science test. In order to quickly compare experiments, you will need to be able to easily identify the conditions of an experiment. The conditions will be the constants. By writing them out to the side or below, you will not have to search for the sentences with constants, then re-read the sentences containing them. Instead, you will be able to quickly glance at your notes, and in a fraction of the time, you will know exactly the conditions of any experiment.

When you identify something critical, you should
1. **Underline or circle.**
2. **Make notes (preferred).**

Critical simply means the information is a clue possibly needed to answer a question. This information is question critical. Identifying question critical information can be a challenge. The following are a few basic guidelines to use:

1. **If something is changing or causing something else to change, it is critical.**
2. **Values (numbers) are typically critical.**

Critical elements need to be easily and quickly identified. These elements are usually buried in a passage, study, or experiment. Since the goal is to not re-read, you will need to make a few notes to the side or below the text.

You could underline or circle something critical in the passage; however, this is not the preferred method. The main reason for this is if you underline too much, you will end up re-reading the passage. Limited underlining and/or circling is excellent. A good guideline is if the critical element can be quickly represented with a note, make the note. Also, the number of underlined/circled items should not exceed two in a given passage, study, or experiment. There may be exceptions to this. As always, you must find out what works best for you. As with everything in this book, remember these are guidelines, and you must spend some time finding out what works best for you.

SCIENCE REASONING – GENERAL TIPS AND STRATEGIES

When making notation, there are two key rules to follow:
1. **Be simple.**
2. **Abbreviate and use symbols for key words.**

Making notes is very effective in reducing the amount of time you spend re-reading. With a glance at a good note, you will know what is contained in many sentences without re-reading them. Being simple in your notes is the key. If you make elaborate notes, you will waste more time making them than re-reading. Notes should contain letters, symbols, arrows, and most importantly abbreviations. Abbreviate everything you can. For example, pressure should just be P. Since you won't be abbreviating that many things in a passage, be extreme with your abbreviations. You will remember what the letters represent. Simple pictures are also excellent. For example, use stick figures not portraits.

When done correctly, making notes is the most effective tool to improving your science score. If you have trouble finishing this test, making notes as well as previewing your graphs and tables to identify trends may be what it takes to finish and increase your score.

SCIENCE REASONING

LOGICAL REASONING

Directions: Answer the following questions based on the given problem/situation. Use logical reasoning to help establish and defend your answers.

Exercise #1 – Basic Logic
(Sample Answers on p.502)

Problem/Situation: **Do you want to be a 1 or a 10?**

Initial Answer, Why?

What questions could you ask to determine more information?

What answers to your questions might cause you to change your initial answer?

Provide an example where your initial answer would still be your answer.

Provide an example where your initial answer would not be your answer.

Provide an example where the answer could reasonably be either depending on the person answering, and tell why it depends on the person answering.

LOGICAL REASONING
Exercise #2 – Investment Challenge
(Sample Answers on p.503)

Problem/Situation: **Two investors compare results from the previous year. One investor makes $1500 profit and another investor makes only $500 profit. Who did better and why?**

Initial Answer, Why?

What questions could you ask to determine more information?

What answers to your questions might cause you to change your initial answer?

Choose one answer from the above question and create at least three points why your initial answer could be wrong.

LOGICAL REASONING
Exercise #3 - The Stock Market
Part 1
(Sample Answers on p.504)

Problem/Situation: **An investment advising company gives stock suggestions to clients. At the end of the month they posted their results. Of the 37 stocks they recommended, 22 (59%) were up, 20 (54%) hit or exceeded targets. How did they do?**

Initial Answer, Why?
_____
_____
_____
_____
_____

What questions could you ask to determine more information?
_____
_____
_____
_____
_____
_____
_____

What answers to your questions might cause you to change your initial answer?
_____
_____
_____
_____
_____
_____
_____

[After you complete this worksheet, go to the next page for additional information]

SCIENCE REASONING

LOGICAL REASONING
Exercise #3 - The Stock Market
Part 2
(Sample Answers on p.505)

Additional Information: **Of the 37 stocks recommended, the average increase was only 0.4%. Now how did they do?**

Initial Answer, Why?

___

What questions could you ask to determine more information?

___

What answers to your questions might cause you to change your initial answer?

___

[After you complete this worksheet, go to the next page for additional information]

LOGICAL REASONING
Exercise #3 - The Stock Market
Part 3
(Sample Answers on p.506)

Additional Information: During the same period the NASDAQ was down 30%. Now how did they do?

Initial Answer, Why?

What questions could you ask to determine more information?

How did your answer change over the 3 questions?

What can be learned from this example?

SCIENCE REASONING

LOGICAL REASONING
Exercise #4 – Win/Loss Records
(Sample Answers on p.507)

Problem/Situation: **Team one has a record of 23-7 and team two has a record of 19-11. Team one should receive the higher seed since they have the best record. Do you agree?**

Initial Answer, Why?

What factors might be considered in order to determine a correct answer?

What would some answers be that might cause you to change your initial answer?

Identify another situation where one team may have a better record, but the team/individual/program/etc. with the lower record may actually be better. Why?

LOGICAL REASONING
Exercise #5 – The Quiz
(Sample Answers on p.508)

Problem/Situation: **You take a 10-question quiz where the more correct you get, the better. Your teacher hands out the papers one by one showing the entire class the grades. The teacher hands you your paper first, and everyone sees that you got 3 out of 10 correct. How did you do?**

Initial Answer, Why?

What factors or questions might be considered in order to determine a correct answer?

Now let's assume that the teacher hands out the remaining papers and every other student got 1 or 0 correct. Now how did you do?

Based on the discussion above, if you complete this course with a 63% average, how did you do?

LOGICAL REASONING
Exercise #6 – Get Home Quick
(Sample Answers on p.509)

Problem/Situation: **You have to get from point A to point B as fast as you possibly can. You are offered two means of transportation that start from the same position. The first is a jet airplane that can transport you at 700 mph. The second option is a Ferrari capable of near 200 mph. Based on your objective to get from point A to point B as fast as you can, which is the best means of transportation?**

Initial Answer, Why?

What factors might be considered in order to determine a correct answer?

What would some answers be that might cause you to change your initial answer?

From the logical reasoning exercises, it is clear that the correct answer is not always obvious. List a few things you have learned from doing these problems.

TABLE TREND EXERCISES

(Sample Answers on Page 510)

On the ACT Science reasoning section, there are many tables. Most tables relate trends.

Directions: Identify the trends in the hypothetical tables below. Place arrows or symbols by each column header to represent the trend.

Table 1

Temperature (°F)	Pressure (atm)	Humidity
75	0.10	65%
100	0.20	64%
140	0.25	66%
200	0.28	65%

Table 2

HCL (ml)	Color
10	Pink
20	Pinkish Blue
30	Bluish Pink
40	Blue

Table 3

Depth (m)	Salinity of Water (g/l)	Quantity of Fish (Est. # Fish / 10m^3)
50	1.0	30
100	1.2	25
150	1.4	12
200	1.6	5

Table 4

Hour	# Mosquitoes Caught in Trap	# of Bat Sightings
Midnight	16	8
1 am	11	3
2 am	7	2
3 am	8	2
4 am	12	6
5 am	18	11

Making Notes Exercise

(Sample Answers on Page 511)

Directions: Make notes for the following being as simple and abbreviated as possible.

Excerpt from Passage	Notes
1. As the temperature increased, the pressure increased	
2. 3 dogs and 2 cats	
3. The current increased to 50 amps then decreased	
4. The water mixed with solution A but not with solution B	
5. Brown eyes and Black hair	
6. 4 carnivores and 2 herbivores	
7. 2 three-leaf clovers	

Making Notes - con't

8. Hydrogen and Oxygen produce water	
9. Yellow and blue make green	
10. Temperature was held constant at 75 degrees Celsius.	
11. As the nitrogen increased the oxygen decreased	
12. The rate of paddling was directly proportional to the frequency of the waves	
13. The pollen is on the anther, and it needs to get to the pistol	
14. The power was held constant at 100 watts	

Making Notes - con't

15. The coefficient of friction was measured to be 0.27.	
16. The limestone and the sandstone came together at the fault	
17. Brown eyes are dominant and green eyes are recessive	
18. There were five cases of carpal tunnel syndrome	
19. The nitrogen instantly turned it white. Whereas, solution A turned it purple.	
20. The cotton was measured at 84 degrees Fahrenheit. Wool was measured at 95 degrees Fahrenheit.	

Making Notes - con't

21. The air conditioner blew 20 cubic feet per minute.	
22. As sugar is added, the number of calories exponentially increases	
23. As the lumination increases, the chlorophyll production increases. Once the lumination exceeds 1000 lumens, the chlorophyll production decreases.	
24. When the pressure is sustained over four hours, the diameter begins to increase	
25. As the lactic acid increases the pain increases.	
26. Yeast causes fermentation	

Making Notes - con't

27. The more viscous the oil, the more expensive it costs.	
28. Porous rock lined the oil reserve	
29. The hatchlings become fledglings at about 17 days	
30. The battery was made from nickel and cadmium	
31. The feeder was most visited by finches, then by chickadees, and least by sparrows.	
32. The puck flew at 105 miles per hour and was deflected at a 30 degree angle into the dasher	
33. The breakeven point was measured to be 2 years and 6 months	

Comprehensive Science Activity
(Sample Answers on p.516)

This project is designed to teach you how to collect data and present the data in the form of graphs and tables. You will learn how to group data for clarity, create four different graphs, and present your data. Below you will find concepts taught in the lesson, a general outline of the lesson, and a 10-step plan to complete the project. An example problem is provided for you. Good luck!

Concepts Taught or Reinforced by Lesson
- Collecting Data
- Grouping and Combining Data for Meaning
- Graphically Representing Data
- Creating and Understanding a Variety of Graph Types
- Interpreting Data from Graphs and Tables
- Predicting Results
- Percents and Averages
- Project Management
- Presentation Skills
- Writing and Grammar Skills

General Outline of Lesson
1. Pick a topic (some ideas are listed below)
2. Collect at least 20 pieces of data
3. Create each of the following from your data:
   - Table
   - Line Chart
   - Bar Chart
   - Pie Chart
   - Pareto Chart
4. Present conclusions

Steps to Follow
Step 1: Pick a Topic
Step 2: Collect Data
Step 3: Sort the Data for Clarity
Step 4: Determine Factors for Grouping
Step 5: Create a Table
Step 6: Create a Line Chart
Step 7: Create a Column Bar Chart
Step 8: Create a Pie Chart
Step 9: Create a Pareto Chart
Step 10: Present

Example Topics To Do:

Brands of shoes being worn (20 people at least)
Length of arms
Shoe size
Number of cavities
Color of Shirts
Birthday Month
Number of touchdowns scored in last 20 games
Number of birds you see at a feeder in 5-minute increments
Number of cars that pass in 5-minute increments
Number of shots taken during a basketball game by a player

EXAMPLE PROBLEM

Step 1: Pick a Topic

The number of passes thrown by a football team over the last 20 games

Step 2: Collect Data

Raw data

Game #	# Passes
1	13
2	19
3	21
4	14
5	24
6	16
7	10
8	8
9	15
10	13
11	26
12	22
13	31
14	18
15	27
16	19
17	13
18	12
19	6
20	10

Step 3: Sort the Data by Number of Passes From Most to Least.

Game #	# Passes
13	31
15	27
11	26
5	24
12	22
3	21
16	19
2	19
14	18
6	16
9	15
4	14
1	13
10	13
17	13
18	12
7	10
20	10
8	8
19	6

The first key point is we have to make this data usable. We can do this by listing the number of occurrences. There were 3 games (occurrences) in which 13 passes were thrown. There were 2 games in which 10 passes and 19 passes were thrown. The remaining games had varying numbers of passes thrown. In order for the data to make sense, we have to determine how to group.

Step 4: Determine Factors for Grouping

Combine the data so that the information can be represented more clearly. The data can be combined many different ways. The groups should be set to allow a clear story to be told with a minimum of data. Look at this example to determine how to group. We'll do this with a pie chart.

1st Option: Minimal Grouping *(Only times with more than one occurrence as mentioned above)*

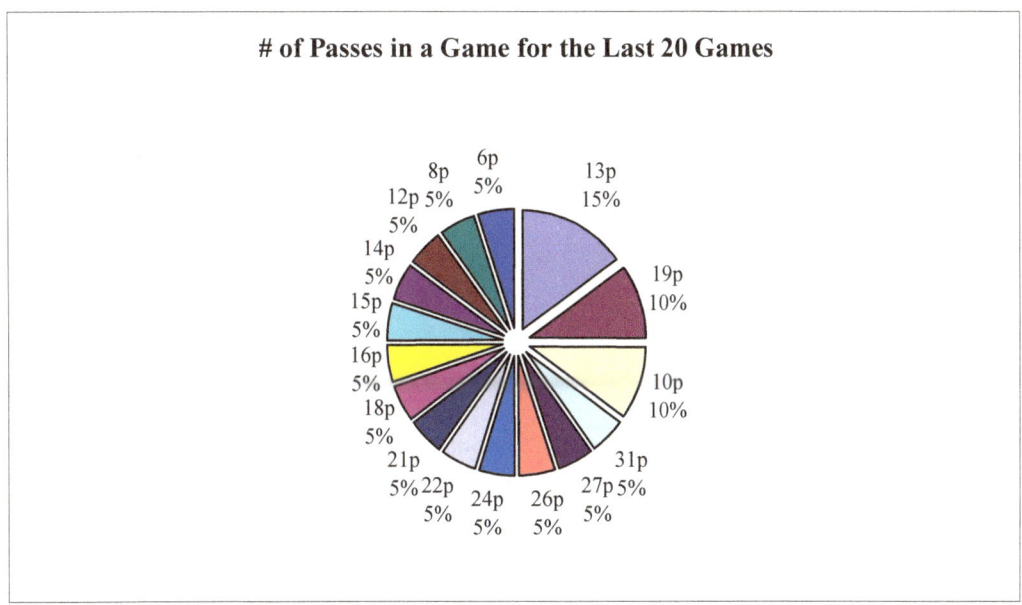

Can you see how busy this graph is? Many data labels make it seem confusing. To make the graph clearer, the pie slices are slightly separated and the number of passes has the letter *p* after it. With the data labels nearly overlapping, you should probably try to remove them and use a legend. A better alternative would be to increase the groupings or change to a different type of graph. The graph below is a column bar chart that makes the data more clear.

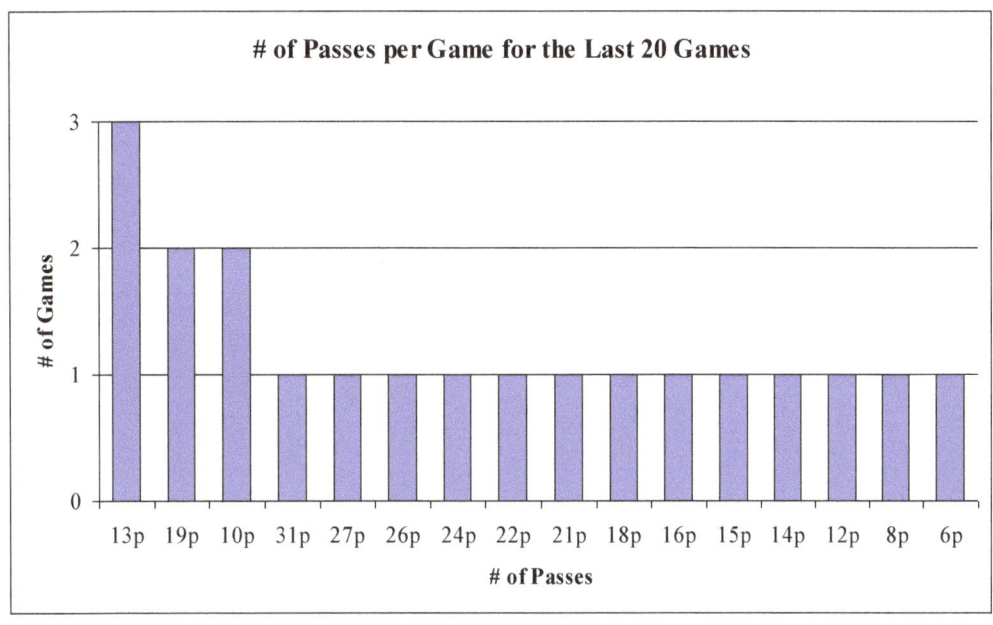

2nd Option: Mid-Level Grouping *(1-5, 6-10, 11-15,...)*

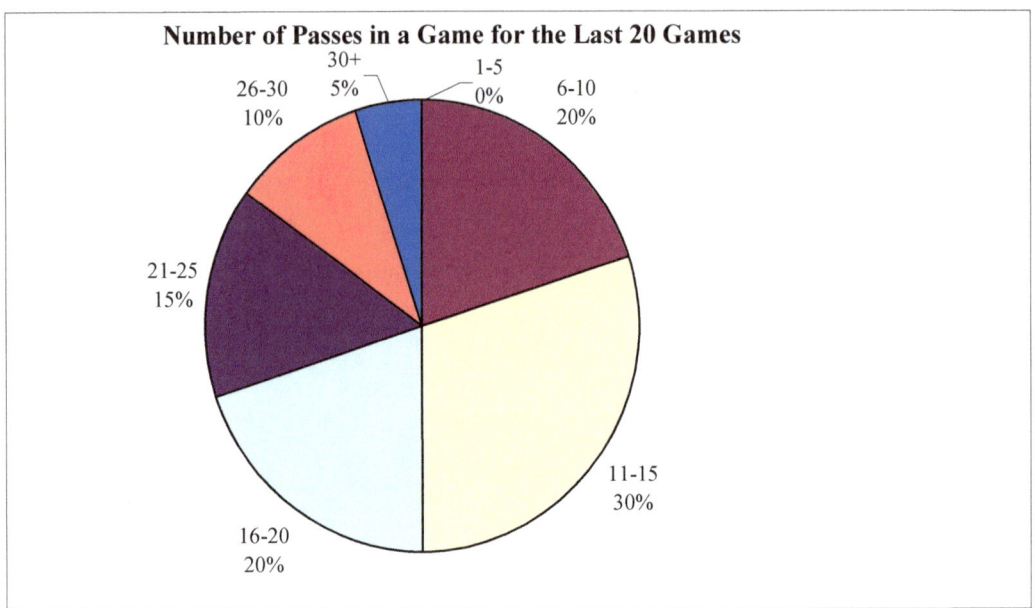

This graph appears much more clear and concise while still telling a complete story. Assume that this graph simply does not provide enough detail (meaning the grouping hides some important data). Since the minimal grouping pie chart is confusing, you should change to a different type graph like the column bar chart.

3rd Option: Large Grouping *(1-10, 11-20, 21-30, 30+)*

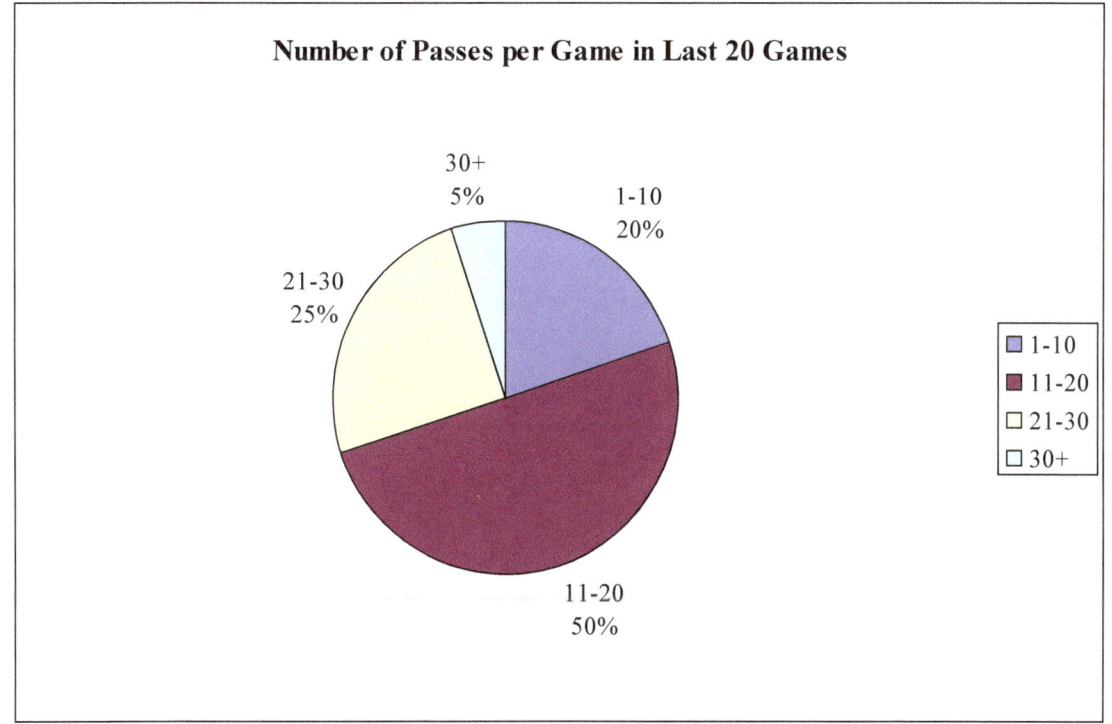

This graph is very clear and concise. The question you must ask is whether this graph has enough detail to tell the full story. The answer totally depends on the situation. This graph would be adequate for certain applications. This study will use the mid-level grouping as the best alternative.
Note: You can add the legend to the right for pie graphs just like other graphs.

Conclusion
Assume that the second option provides a clear and concise picture of the data and best meets the needs of this study. The key is that you just have to do what makes sense for your situation. Each one of the options could work, but you need to identify the option that works best for your purpose.

Step 5: Create a New Table by Your Groupings

Number of Passes per Game for Last 20 Games

Grouping	# of Occurrences
1-5	0
6-10	4
11-15	6
16-20	4
21-25	3
26-30	2
30+	1

Once this is created, you have finished your table of data.

Step 6: Create a Line Chart

A line chart is just like the "dot to dot" game.
- Place your grouping on one axis
- Place the number of occurrences on the other axis
- Plot the dots
- Connect the dots

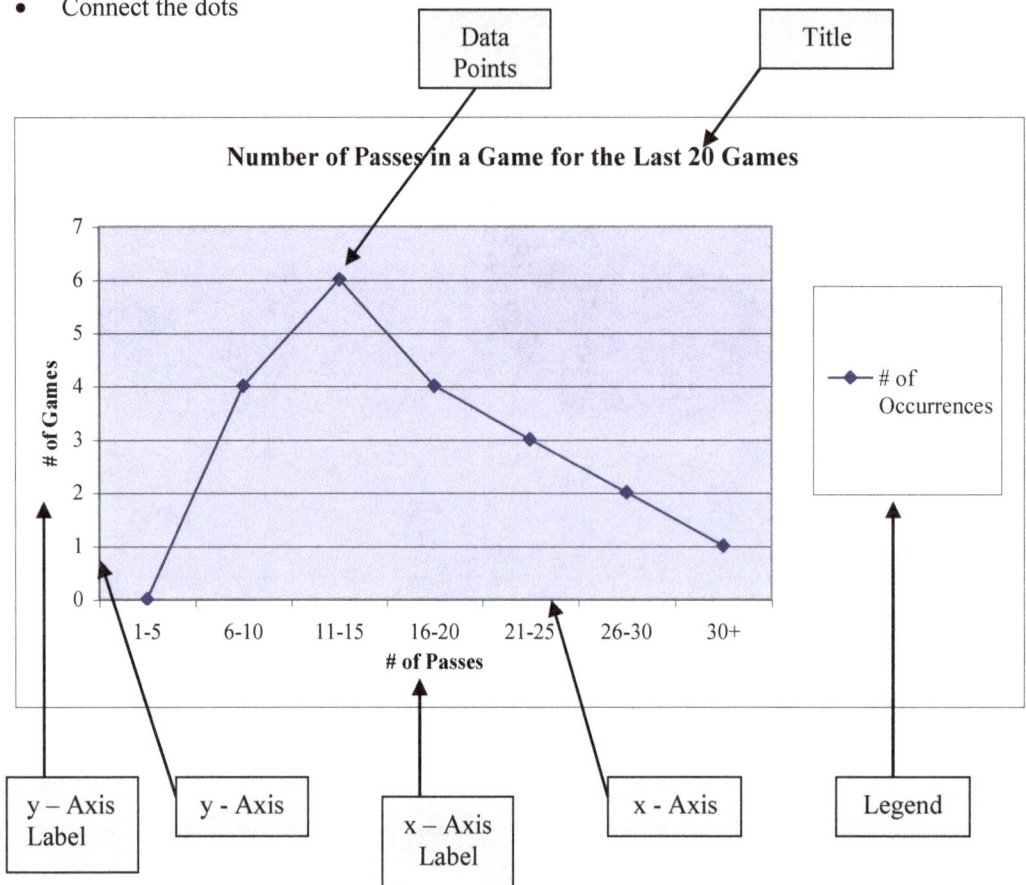

Step 7: Create a Column Bar Chart

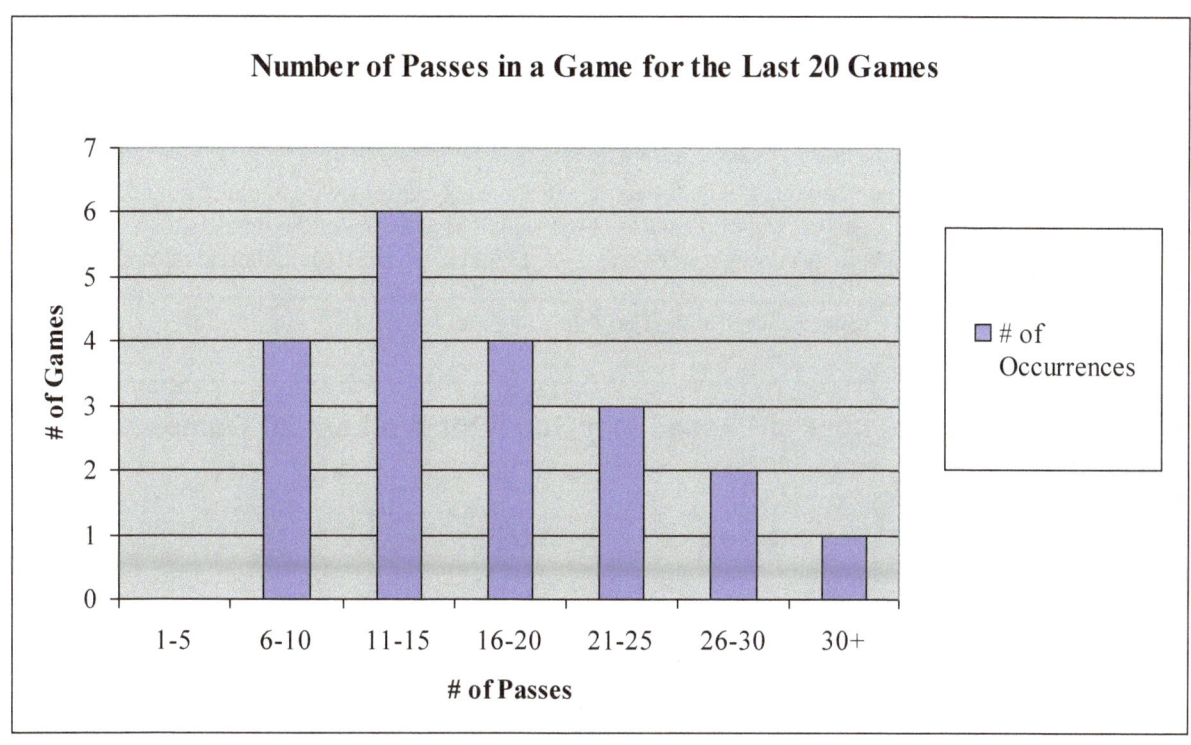

Step 8: Create a Pie Chart
Note: Value labels can be placed with each slice of the pie or as a legend.
Percent values are optional on a pie chart. For this exercise include them with each slice.

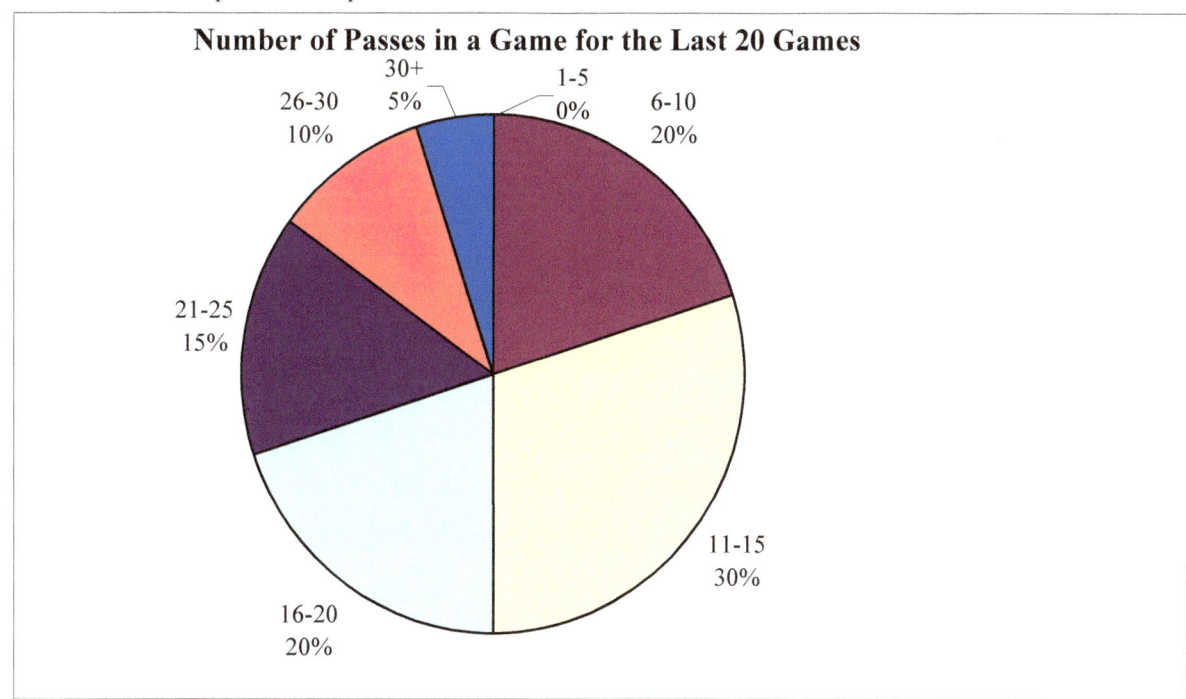

Step 9: Create a Pareto Chart

The Pareto chart is a very confusing chart the first time you view it. A Pareto chart's purpose is to identify the most frequently occurring factors and show the associated percent of the whole. Pareto charts are commonly used in industry to identify the most common defects or factors affecting the outcomes of a process or system.

How would this graph be interpreted? The following are some conclusions we can make from the graph.
- The most frequently occurring # of passes is 11-15, which occurs 30% of the time.
- The two most frequently occurring # of passes is 11-15 and 6-10, which cumulatively account for 50% of the occurrences
- Over 80% of the occurrences were in the first four categories.

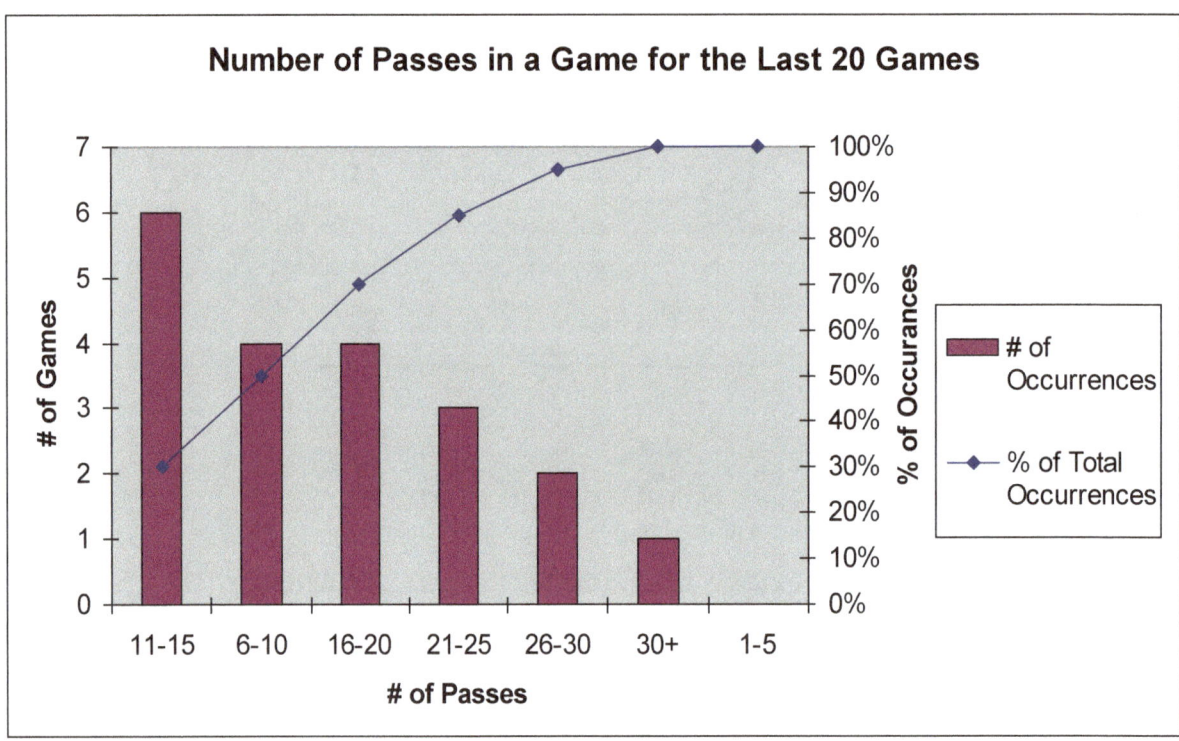

Since Pareto charts are confusing, consider another example that is much simpler.

Another Pareto Example Application - Cleaning for a Party

Let's assume you are hosting a party at your home for many of your friends. Some may have never seen your home and may want a quick tour. Based on an eight-hour day, you have four days of cleaning to do and only 2 days to complete it. If you can't increase the number of hours you work to clean the house and you can't have outside help, what would you do during the two days?

Let's assume you make a list of the areas that need cleaning:
- Living Room
- Bathroom
- Master Bedroom
- Kid's Bedroom
- Kitchen
- Dining Room
- Porch
- Backyard
- Study

Many would just start cleaning and get as much done as possible, but using logical reasoning we could ask some pointed questions to identify the most efficient use of time.

Some valuable general questions might be the following:

- ✓ What is the purpose of the visit?
- ✓ Where are the friends going to spend the most time?
- ✓ Is one room so dirty that it requires more cleaning than the others?
- ✓ Is one room's dirtiness more critical than another room's dirtiness?

Let's assume these are the answers

- ✓ What is the purpose of the visit?
  This is a pool party for my friends.
- ✓ Where are my friends going to spend the most time?
  Since this is a pool party, guests will spend most of their time in the backyard, on the porch, in the kitchen, and the hall bath.
- ✓ Is one area so bad that it must be cleaned over the others?
  It is definitely the backyard.
- ✓ Is one room's dirtiness more critical than another room's dirtiness?
  The hall bath is critical.

Based on the answers above, we can prioritize our cleaning efforts. Let's assign a percent gain for each task trying to reach 100% clean as the ultimate goal. (There are some other considerations such as size of the room and type of cleaning; therefore, there may be some variation in how you would prioritize these functions.) Then we can create a Pareto chart to illustrate this.

Priority by Cleanliness Table

Priority	% Cleanliness Gained	Cumulative % Cleanliness
Backyard	25	25
Kitchen	20	45
Bathroom	15	60
Porch	13	73
Living Room	12	85
Dining Room	6	91
Kid's Bedroom	5	96
Master Bedroom	3	99
Study	1	100

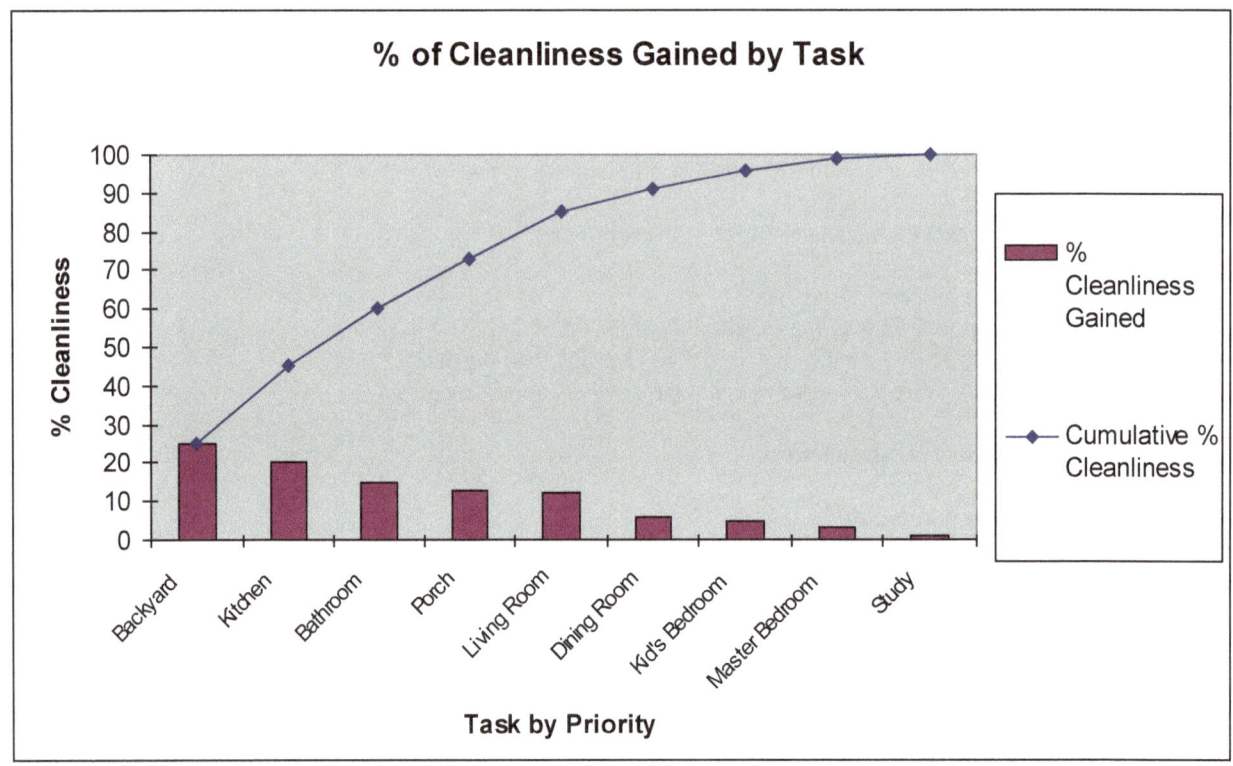

From this Pareto chart we can identify that completing the first four tasks gets us nearly 75% of the cleanliness we need. This also shows that the kid's bedroom, master bedroom, and study really don't contribute that much. So instead of making a list with all the rooms to clean, we can start with the biggest priorities and work down to the less important rooms.

Step 10: Presenting

Prepare a brief presentation of your data including your conclusions and predictions from the data. Complete the worksheet, graphs, and tables on the following page. Although answers will vary and this will not be graded, see if you can complete the worksheet as reinforcement of lessons learned in this book.

Science Data Collection and Presentation Project Report

Topic: _____

1. Where did you find your data (what resources did you use)? _____
   _____

2. How did you collect the data? _____
   _____

3. Which graph best applies to your data? _____ Why? _____
   _____

4. Based on the results of your data, if you were to take 10 more samples of data what would you predict the results to be? _____
   _____

5. By looking at the graphs, can you identify any trends in the data? If so, explain. _____
   _____
   _____

6. What was the average (mean) value of the data you collected? _____ Show your work below.

7. What percent of the total occurrences was the average data value you collected? _____ Show your work here.

8. Write four complete sentences about the data you collected explaining what information you learned from collecting the data and the information in the graphs.
   _____
   _____
   _____
   _____
   _____
   _____
   _____
   _____

LOGICAL REASONING KEY
Exercise #1 - Basic Logic
p. 476

Problem/Situation: **Do you want to be a 1 or a 10?**

Initial Answer, Why?
10. Because everyone wants to be a perfect 10

What questions could you ask to determine more information?
- What are we measuring
- Which is better

What answers to your questions might cause you to change your initial answer?

If 1 is better, I would change.
If we are measuring something like the number of kids you are going to have, then I'm a 10. If we are measuring shots over par, number of wives/husbands you are going to have, number of speeding tickets, or number of times you have to take a class to pass, then I want to be a one.

Provide an example where your initial answer would still be your answer.

Rating in a diving competition

Provide an example where your initial answer would not be your answer.

Place I finished in a contest

Provide an example where the answer could reasonably be either depending on the person answering, and tell why it depends on the person answering.

Having Kids. Some people want to be a one. They don't want a bunch of kids.
Other people want a bunch of kids. They would much rather have ten kids, than just have one kid. And yes, I have 8 kids.

SCIENCE REASONING

LOGICAL REASONING KEY
Exercise #2 - Investment Challenge
p. 477

Problem/Situation: **Two investors compare results from the previous year. One investor makes $1500 profit and another investor makes only $500 profit. Who did better and why?**

Initial Answer, Why? $1500 – More Money

What questions could you ask to determine more information?
- Did they start with the same amount of money
- Were they able to invest in the same markets
- Did they get to invest over the same period of time

What answers to your questions might cause you to change your initial answer?

If the investor that made $1500 profit started with $10,000, then he made 15%.
If the investor that made $500 profit started with only $1000, then he made 50% profit.

Based on the $10,000 and $1,000 assumption above:
If the investor that made $1500 profit was limited to investing in the Nasdaq which increased 15% in the investment period, he performed even with his investment opportunity.
If the investor that made $500 profit was limited to investing in the NYSE which increased 10% in the investment period, he performed 40% better than his investment opportunity.

Choose one answer from the above question and create at least three points why your initial answer could be wrong.

If the investor that made $1500 profit started with $10,000, then he made 15%.
If the investor that made $500 profit started with only $1000, then he made 50% profit.

1. 50% vs. 15% is better if you are trying to maximize your % profit
2. Although $1000 more in absolute dollars is better, the percent return is better for the investor starting with $500.
3. The investor making only $500 may have been limited to certain stocks or a certain number of transactions.

LOGICAL REASONING KEY
Exercise #3 - The Stock Market
Part 1
p. 478

Problem/Situation: **An investment advising company gives stock suggestions to clients. At the end of the month they posted their results. Of the 37 stocks they recommended, 22 (59%) were up, 20 (54%) hit or exceeded targets. How did they do?**

Initial Answer, Why?
Good. If 59% were up, then more than half made money.
If 54% hit or exceeded targets (which was 20 of the 22), then they really did well.

What questions could you ask to determine more information?
What were the targets?
How bad did the 15 stocks do that didn't go up?

What answers to your questions might cause you to change your initial answer?
- If the targets are only to increase 1%, then that may not be that good.
- If the 15 stocks went down more than the 22 stocks went up, then the net result would be a loss.

[After you complete this worksheet, go to the next page for additional information]

LOGICAL REASONING KEY
Exercise #3 - The Stock Market
Part 2
p. 479

Additional Information: **Of the 37 stocks recommended, the average increase was only 0.4%. Now how did they do?**

Initial Answer, Why?
Not good. A return of less than 1% is unacceptable.

What questions could you ask to determine more information?

What was the goal of the investor?
What was the market conditions during the investing period

What answers to your questions might cause you to change your initial answer?

If the goal of the investor was to not lose money, then he succeeded.

[After you complete this worksheet, go to the next page for additional information]

LOGICAL REASONING KEY
Exercise #3 - The Stock Market
Part 3
p. 480

Additional Information: **During the same period the NASDAQ was down 30%. Now how did they do?**

Initial Answer, Why?
- If the market was down 30% and their stocks were up 0.4%, then they beat the market by over 30%.

What questions could you ask to determine more information?
Were they limited to just NASDAQ stocks?
Were there other factors not mentioned in this study?

How did your answer change over the 3 questions?
Initially they did well considering more positive than negative. It was also good that they hit targets on more than half of their stocks.
Then it appeared that they didn't do so well, since the overall increase was only 0.4%.
Finally, they did really good assuming they were invested in NASDAQ stocks since the NASDAQ was down over 30% during the same time period.

What can be learned from this example?
You have to look at the entire situation to determine a good answer.
Previous knowledge of the subject really helps in asking the right questions and making the right conclusions. In this case, knowledge of the stock market is a nice advantage. This is also true of science subjects. Although the ACT science test is not a content test, your general knowledge of a variety of science topics such as chemistry and advanced biology can really help. This is why it is so important to take a third and fourth unit of science in high school.

In conclusion, reasoning goes beyond looking at the obvious. It involves looking beyond the surface, asking good questions, and determining the relation between factors to reach a good conclusion.

SCIENCE REASONING

LOGICAL REASONING KEY
Exercise #4 – Win/Loss Records
p. 481

Problem/Situation: **Team one has a record of 23-7 and team 2 has a record of 19-11. Team one should receive the higher seed since they have the best record. Do you agree?**

Initial Answer, Why?

The team with a record of 23-7 deserves the better seed since they have the better record

What factors might be considered in order to determine a correct answer?

Who did the teams play – common opponents
Did they play in the same conference?
Home record vs. road record
Last 10 games
Strength of schedule

What would some answers be that might cause you to change your initial answer?

If the team with a record of 23-7 played very weak teams as compared to the other team, then the team with the lower record might be better.

Identify another situation where one team may have a better record, but the team/individual/program/etc. with the lower record may actually be better. Why?

Injury. A star player may have just gotten injured causing the team with the better record to no longer be the best team.

LOGICAL REASONING KEY
Exercise #5 – The Quiz
p. 482

Problem/Situation: **You take a 10-question quiz where the more correct you get, the better. Your teacher hands out the papers one by one showing the entire class the grades. The teacher hands you your paper first, and everyone sees that you got 3 out of 10 correct. How did you do?**

Initial Answer, Why?
Terrible. 30% is a terrible percentage on a test in school.

What factors or questions might be considered in order to determine a correct answer?

What is considered good?
What did the other students make on the test?
Was it a valid test?

Now let's assume that the teacher hands out the remaining papers and every other student got 1 or 0 correct. Now how did you do?

Outstanding. If the other students could only get 0 or 1 correct, then 30% is 3 times better than the nearest student.

Based on the discussion above, if you complete a course with a 63% average, how did you do?

It all depends on how everyone else does. If 63% is the highest grade in the class, then you probably did pretty well.

LOGICAL REASONING KEY
Exercise #6 – Get Home Quick
p. 483

Problem/Situation: **You have to get from point A to point B as fast as you possibly can. You are offered two means of transportation that start from the same position. The first is a jet airplane that can transport you at 700 mph. The second option is a Ferrari capable of near 200 mph. Based on your objective to get from point A to point B as fast as you can, which is the best means of transportation?**

Initial Answer, Why?
Jet. 700 vs. 200 is an easy selection to get me home the fastest.

What factors might be considered in order to determine a correct answer?

Where am I going?
Is this conducive to an airplane?
Where is the nearest airport?
Are there roads on which I can drive?
What are the conditions of the roads?
How far do I have to go?
Do I have to cross terrain not suitable to a car?

What would some answers be that might cause you to change your initial answer?

If I am traveling one mile, then I don't need the jet. Getting to an airport would be longer than getting home. If I need to cross an ocean, I need the jet.

From the logical reasoning exercises, it is clear that the correct answer is not always obvious. List a few things you have learned from doing these problems.
Answers will vary. Hopefully you have realized a few things about reasoning. The answer isn't always obvious. Also, you should look at numbers a little bit differently now. Be a scientist by questioning and reasoning. We are all scientists. So practice your talent in everyday life and on the ACT.

TABLE TREND EXERCISES KEY – p. 484

Table 1

Temperature (°F) ↑	Pressure (atm) ↑	Humidity •—•
75	0.10	65%
100	0.20	64%
140	0.25	66%
200	0.28	65%

Table 2

HCL (ml) ↑	Color
10	Pink
20	Pinkish Blue
30	Bluish Pink
40	Blue

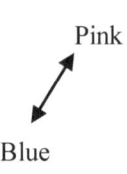

Pink ↕ Blue

Table 3

Depth (m) ↑	Salinity of Water (g/l) ↑	Quantity of Fish (Est. # Fish / 10m³) ↓
50	1.0	30
100	1.2	25
150	1.4	12
200	1.6	5

Table 4

Hour ↑	# Mosquitoes Caught in Trap ⌣	# of Bat Sightings ⌣
Midnight	16	8
1 am	11	3
2 am	7	2
3 am	8	2
4 am	12	6
5 am	18	11

MAKING NOTES EXERCISE KEY – p. 485

Your answers will vary. The key is to be simple, to use abbreviations, and to use symbols. You are the only one who needs to understand your notes. Just make sure that you are able to interpret the excerpt from the notes. The key is only to be used as an example.

Directions: Make notes for the following being as simple and abbreviated as possible.

Excerpt from Passage	Notes
1. As the temperature increased, the pressure increased	T↑ = P↑
2. 3 dogs and 2 cats	3d 2c
3. The current increased to 50 amps then decreased	C ↗ 50a ↘
4. The water mixed with solution A but not with solution B	H2O + A H2O ≠ B
5. Brown eyes and Black hair	BR 👁 / BL 〰〰
6. 4 carnivores and 2 herbivores	4c 2h
7. 2 three-leaf clovers	♣ ♣

8. Hydrogen and Oxygen produce water	$H + O = H_2O$
9. Yellow and blue make green	$Y + B = G$
10. Temperature was held constant at 75 degrees Celsius.	$T = 75°C$
11. As the nitrogen increased the oxygen decreased	$N\uparrow = O\downarrow$
12. The rate of paddling was directly proportional to the frequency of the waves	R (paddle) = F (waves)
13. The pollen is on the anther, and it needs to get to the pistol	A (pollen) ⇒ P
14. The power was held constant at 100 watts	$P = 100W$

15. The coefficient of friction was measured to be 0.27.	μ=.27
16. The limestone and the sandstone came together at the fault	L+S @ Flt
17. Brown eyes are dominant and green eyes are recessive	B g
18. There were five cases of carpel tunnel syndrome	5 - CTS
19. The nitrogen instantly turned it white. Whereas, solution A turned it purple.	N – W Sol A – Pur
20. The cotton was measured at 84 degrees Fahrenheit. Wool was measured at 95 degrees Fahrenheit.	C = 84°F W = 95°F

21. The air conditioner blew 20 cubic feet per minute.	20 cfm/min
22. As sugar is added, the number of calories exponentially increases	S⇑ = cal ↗
23. As the lumination increases, the chlorophyll production increases. Once the lumination exceeds 1000 lumens, the chlorophyll production decreases.	L↑ = C↑ L > 1000 C↓
24. When the pressure is sustained over four hours, the diameter begins to increase	P —4h→ D↑
25. As the lactic acid increases the pain increases.	LA↑ = P↑
26. Yeast causes fermentation	Y ⟶ Ferm

27. The more viscous the oil, the more expensive it costs.	V↑ = $↑
28. Porous rock lined the oil reserve	P - Rk ⌒ Oil
29. The hatchlings become fledglings at about 17 days	h ⇒ f @ 17d
30. The battery was made from nickel and cadmium	Ni + Cd
31. The feeder was most visited by finches, then by chickadees, and least by sparrows.	1-Fin 2-Ch 3-Sp
32. The puck flew at 105 miles per hour and was deflected at a 30 degree angle into the dasher	105 mph → ↗ 30°
33. The breakeven point was measured to be 2 years and 6 months	↗ 2 1/2 yrs →

COMPREHENSIVE SCIENCE ACTIVITY KEY– p. 490

Use the example as a guide. Your answers will vary depending on your topic. When you finish this project, try presenting your findings to a teacher, friend, or family member. See if your results make sense.

After this project is completed, you should have a very good understanding of collecting data, grouping data, graphically representing data, and presenting findings.

Concepts Taught or Reinforced by Lesson
- Collecting Data
- Grouping and Combining Data for Meaning
- Graphically Representing Data
- Creating and Understanding a Variety of Graph Types
- Interpreting Data from Graphs and Tables
- Predicting Results
- Percents and Averages
- Project Management
- Presentation Skills
- Writing and Grammar Skills

General Outline of Lesson
1. Pick a topic (some ideas are listed below)
2. Collect at least 20 pieces of data
3. Create each of the following from your data:
- Table
- Line Chart
- Bar Chart
- Pie Chart
- Pareto Chart
4. Presentation

Steps to Follow
Step 1: Pick a topic
Step 2: Collect Data
Step 3: Sort the data by # of Passes from most to least
Step 4: Decide what to group by if necessary (e.g. 1-5, 6-10, 11-15,…)
Step 5: Create a New Table by Your Groupings
Step 6: Create Line Chart
Step 7: Create a Column Bar Chart
Step 8: Create a Pie Chart
Step 9: Create a Pareto Chart
Step 10: The Presentation

Science Data Collection and Presentation Project Report – Answers will vary

PRACTICE TEST 1

Passage 1

Two scientists discuss the effects of pressure, chemicals, and temperature on fruit. They perform a simple experiment to study the short-term effects of several factors on a random selection of red apples.

Experiment 1
Scientist one does an experiment on the random selection of red apples where she studies the effects of chemicals on the apples. She holds the pressure constant at 1 atm (atm = atmosphere). She finds that if she submerges the apple in liquid nitrogen, the apple instantly turns white. If she submerges the apple in liquid ammonium, depending on the temperature of the ammonium the color of the apple varies somewhere between pink and purple.

Experiment 2
Scientist two continues the study performed in experiment one. He selects red apples randomly from the same group of apples used in experiment one. He holds the temperature constant at 100°F. He varies the chemical and pressure to view the effects of the color of the apples. The results of the experiment are recorded in table 1.

Table 1

Chemical	Pressure (atm)	Color of Apple
Nitrogen	0.5	White
Nitrogen	1.0	White
Nitrogen	2.0	White
Ammonium	0.5	Red
Ammonium	1.0	Red
Ammonium	2.0	Red

1. Which chemical in experiment two has the greatest affect on the color of the apples?

A. Nitrogen
B. Ammonium
C. Not enough information to determine
D. Too much information to determine

2. Which factor is **NOT** included in the first experiment?

F. Temperature
G. Pressure
H. Color
J. Time

3. According to experiment one, ammonium affects the apple differently due to what factor?

A. Time
B. Pressure
C. Temperature
D. Size of the apple

4. If you wanted to study the affects of time the apple is submerged in the liquid, which one of the following would be the best design of the experiment?

F. Hold time constant and vary all other factors.
G. Hold chemical constant and vary time and pressure.
H. Vary time and hold all other factors constant.
J. Vary all factors.

5. The results of experiment two would lead one to conclude that which of the following is true?

A. As the pressure changes the color changes.
B. Nitrogen and ammonium do not affect the color of the apples
C. The constant temperature affects the color of the apples when using nitrogen.
D. The pressure has little if any affect on the color of the apples.

6. For the conditions of experiment 1, if you submerge an apple in liquid ammonium at 50°F, what color would you predict the apple to be?

F. White
G. Black
H. Red
J. Green

Passage 2

A chemistry class was assigned to perform an experiment to measure the density of saltwater for two given solutions known as solutions A and B. The following are the experiments and associated results of two different groups.

Group 1
One liter of solution A was given to group one. The students decided to use a standard glass beaker and burner to heat the solution. The students first weighed the beaker and found that it weighed 10.0 grams. The students rapidly stirred the solution prior to placing it over the burner. After several minutes the water was evaporated leaving a white residue in the beaker. The students again weighed the beaker and found that the beaker and residue weighed 13.6 grams.

Group 2
One liter of solution B was given to group two. The students used a similar beaker and burner as group one. The weight of the beaker was 10.0 grams. The students decided that it would be important to hold the temperature constant at 250°F. In order to maintain the constant temperature they adjusted the output of the burner and kept a thermometer in the solution throughout the experiment. After several minutes the solution was evaporated and the residue remained. The students removed the thermometer and weighed the beaker and residue resulting in a measurement of 12.5 grams.

---

7. Based on the results of group one, what should the reported concentration of the water be? (g=grams; l=liters)

   A. 10 g/l
   B. 13.6 g/l
   C. 3.6 g/l
   D. 23.6 g/l

8. If the teacher claims the solutions were the same, which of the following might be a reason the outputs were different?

   F. Some of the residue in group 2 may have been on the thermometer causing it to be removed from the beaker.
   G. Group two rounded to the nearest whole number whereas group one rounded to the nearest tenth.
   H. It took a different amount of time to evaporate the water in the solution.
   J. The students used the same scale at the beginning of the experiment as they did at the end of the experiment.

9. Group two wants to do more experimenting before concluding the density of solution B. Which of the following supports their goal?

   A. Ignore the result of their first trial and use the result of their second trial.
   B. Repeat the experiment using solution A.
   C. Vary all factors then repeat the experiment.
   D. Repeat the experiment multiple times under the same conditions and take an average of the outputs.

10. Based on the information provided in the passage and assuming the results of the experiments are accurate, one can conclude which of the following?

    F. The constant temperature causes the density to be less.
    G. Stirring the solution causes the solution to be denser.
    H. The use of a thermometer causes the solutions to be different.
    J. The salinity of solution A is more than the salinity of solution B.

11. Assuming a new solution C was to be measured, which of the following would produce the most accurate results?

    A. Have group one watch group two perform the experiment.
    B. Have group two watch group one perform the experiment.
    C. Have both groups perform the experiment on solution C and compare results
    D. Estimate the salinity of solution C based on the results of the earlier experiments.

Passage 3

Gregor Mendel is considered by most to be the father of modern genetics. This title was largely earned from his work over many years on the garden pea. Mendel identified seven different chromosome pairs with dominant and recessive characteristics possible on each pair. He found that yellow seeds were dominant to green seeds and that round seeds were dominant while wrinkled seeds were recessive. In the following test cross, capital letters are used for dominant and small case letters are used for recessive.

Parents

RRYY   rryy

Kinds of Gametes   Kinds of Gametes
RY, RY, RY, RY   ry, ry, ry, ry

F1 generation   RrYy

Kinds of Gametes   Kinds of Gametes
RY, Ry, rY, ry   RY, Ry, rY, ry

F2 generation

Male Gametes of F1

	RY	Ry	rY	ry
RY	RRYY	RRYy	RrYY	RrYy
Ry	RRYy	RRyy	RrYy	Rryy
rY	RrYY	RrYy	rrYY	rrYy
ry	RrYy	Rryy	rrYy	rryy

Female gametes

---

12. Given the results from Mendel's cross, which of the following statements is true?

    F. The parents that produce the f1 generation are capable of donating 4 different combinations of genes.
    G. The parents that produce the f1 generation are capable of donating only two different combinations of genes
    H. The parents that produce the f1 generation have only one possible gene combination they may pass on to offspring
    J. The parents that produce the f1 generation have an infinite number of possible gene pairs that could arise from this test cross

13. Offspring produced in the f1 in this cross will:

    A. Exhibit only dominant characteristics
    B. Exhibit both dominant and recessive characteristics
    C. Possess both dominant and recessive characteristics
    D. Both A & C are correct

14. In the f2 generation the greatest percentage of the seeds will be:

    F. Round and green
    G. Round and yellow
    H. Wrinkled and yellow
    J. Wrinkled and green

15. The seeds that are yellow and wrinkled would most likely exist in the following amounts.

    A. 1/4 of those produced
    B. 3/16 of those produced
    C. ½ of those produced
    D. 9/16 of those produced

16. If Mendel had gone into his garden and had actually gathered 9012 seeds that were round and green the number closest to the actual amount of wrinkled and green seeds should be about.

    F. 1004
    G. 2998
    H. 6021
    J. 8992

17. Assuming the laws of genetics shown in Mendel's experiment hold true for all seeds, which of the following can not be true?

A. Plants will vary depending on their chromosomes
B. Plants will always be the same
C. Chromosomes are a factor in future plant characteristics
D. Chromosomes play no part in plant characteristics

Passage 4

Probability could best be described as the mathematics of the predictability of occurrences, in other words the chances of something happening. The probability can be calculated as one out of the opportunity. The chances of a coin be tossed and being a heads is then one out of two and the chances of two coins being tossed and both being heads is one out of two times one out two or one out of four. The rules of probability apply to many things from games of chance to inheritance of genetic characters.

A single die from a pair of dice has six sides with numbers one through six on the sides. The following chart shows the possible number combinations from a throw of both dice.

Two dice totals	Possible combinations to produce totals
2	1&1
3	1&2 or 2&1
4	1&3 or 2&2 or 3&1
5	1&4 or 2&3 or 3&2 or 4&1
6	1&5 or 2&4 or 3&3 or 4&2 or 5&1
7	1&6 or 2&5 or 3&4 or 4&3 or 5&2 or 6&1
8	2&6 or 3&5 or 4&4 or 5&3 or 6&2
9	3&6 or 4&5 or 5&4 or 6&3
10	4&6 or 5&5 or 6&4
11	5&6 or 6&5
12	6&6

18. What is the probability of the number 6 coming up one any throw of a single die?

F. 16 2/3%
G. 33 1/3%
H. 50%
J. 83 1/3%

19. When two die are thrown the best chances for a total number to come up are for the number seven. The probability of a total number of seven is ___.

A. 16 2/3%
B. 33 1/3%
C. 50%
D. 83 1/3%

20. Of the five answers given in this problem the total number with the lowest probability of happening is the number ___.

F. Two
G. Five
H. Eight
J. Ten

21. Assuming the same rules of probability apply to selection for male or female offspring in humans, what is the probability of a family having three consecutive female children?

A. 1/2 or 50%
B. 1/3 or 33 1/3%
C. 1/4 or 25%
D. 1/8 or 12 ½%.

22. Now using the dice analogy given above assume for the moment that a new dice is developed with eight equal sides and with the numbers one through eight placed on each dice. When a pair of these dice are thrown the odds of both coming up with the number eight for a total of sixteen is ___.

F. 1/64
G. 1/32
H. 1/16
J. 1/8

Passage 5

Homeostasis is the process in the human body that is responsible for the regulation of many of the important ions and chemicals in the body. The most important human organ in this process is the kidney. It is the kidney that controls composition of the blood including those important ions and dissolved chemicals mentioned above in homeostasis. During this regulation by the kidney, urine is produced with some chemicals being eliminated and others being retained for use by the body.

A doctor takes blood from a patient before the blood enters the kidney and also takes urine from the same patient after the urine leaves the kidney. The following table shows what percentages of certain chemicals he found on analysis.

Chemical	% in blood	% in urine
Glucose	0.15	0.00
Potassium	0.02	0.25
Protein	7.03	0.00
Sodium	0.35	0.30
Urea	0.03	2.74
Water	91.25	96.50

23. Other than water the highest % for a chemical substance in the blood is ___.

A. Glucose
B. Protein
C. Urea
D. Sodium

24. The chemical other than water whose % raises the most as it moves from blood to urine is ___.

F. Glucose
G. Protein
H. Urea
J. Sodium

25. The only chemicals in this patient that were present in blood but not in urine were ___.

A. Protein and sodium
B. Protein and urea
C. Glucose and sodium
D. Glucose and protein.

26. The chemical that showed the greatest stability in terms of percentage (before and after the kidney) in this patient was ___.

F. Water
G. Protein
H. Sodium
J. Urea.

27. Assuming that the analysis of this patient is the norm rather than abnormal one might deduce that ___.

A. Protein and glucose are necessary for the body
B. Urea and potassium are necessary for the body
C. Urea and potassium need to be removed from the body
D. Both A & C.

28. Furthermore if the results of this patient are normal then if protein and/or glucose were found in the urine one might deduce that ___.

F. The kidney is working better than expected
G. The patient probably just had too much protein and/or glucose in the blood
H. The kidney was working normally
J. There was a malfunction in the operation of the kidney.

Passage 6

An adventurer discovers a statue that is very old and beautiful and of a weight that suggests it may be made of pure gold. Gold has a density (weight per volume) of 19.3 grams (g)/cubic centimeter (cm^3) and all elements have different densities. Since the shape is irregular the volume cannot be determined by simple measurements. So another method is devised.

Relationships between units of weight:

1 kg	2.2 pounds (lb.) or 1000 grams (g)
1 lb	454 grams or 16 ounces (oz)
1 g	1000 milligrams (mg)
1 oz	28.35 grams (g)

Relationships between units of volume:

1 qt (quart)	.946 l (liter)
1 ml (milliliter)	1.0 cubic centimeter (cm^3)
1 gal (gallon)	3.78 l (liter)
1 l (liter)	1000 ml (milliliter)

29. The first step is to weigh the statue and he finds it weights about 1.8kg. This would be equal to ___.

A. 18000 g
B. 396 g
C. 1800 g
D. 9988 g

30. Next the statue is submerged in a full tub of water and the overflow is captured and measured. The overflow is found to measure 110 ml. This amount is an equivalent to ___.

F. 110,000 cm^3
G. 110 cm^3
H. 454 cm^3
J. 9060 cm^3

31. Knowing how density is calculated, he determines the density of the statue to be ___.

A. 16.36 g/cm^3
B. 163.6 g/cm^3
C. 1.636 g/cm^3
D. None of these

32. From his calculations he determines the statue ___.

F. Cannot be pure gold
G. Is pure gold
H. Is too dense to be gold
J. Has not given enough information to determine if it is gold.

33. If the calculations determined the density of the statue was 19.3 g/cm^3 then ___.

A. It could be pure gold.
B. It could be made of a pure element that is close to gold in density
C. It could not be pure gold.
D. It was most likely a heavy element such as lead covered with pure gold.

34. If the adventurer wanted to measure volume in kg

F. He would have to multiply by 2.2
G. He would have to divide by .946
H. He would have to convert ml to kg
J. kg is not a measure of volume

Passage 7

Pressure is defined as the amount of force applied per unit of area. On the earth the amount of pressure applied to everything at sea level is considered to be one atmosphere. One atmosphere can be expressed as 14.7lb./sq inch or 101.3 kPa. Meteorologists typically measure pressure in millimeters of mercury(Hg) where one atmosphere is 760 mm of Hg. As we move upward in the atmosphere the pressure decreases and as we move down it increases. The same is true as we penetrate the surface of the ocean and dive to deeper depths.

This chart represents different pressures for different depths under water.

Depth (M)	Pressure (Atm)
0	1.0
25	3.5
50	6.0
75	8.5

This chart represents the measurement of air pressure as one goes up into the atmosphere.

Altitude	Air pressure
Sea level	760 mm Hg
10 km	200 mm Hg
25 km	50 mm Hg
50 km	1 mm Hg
100 km	2.3×10^{-3} mm Hg
200 km	1.0×10^{-6} mm Hg

35. As one descends into water the rate of pressure increase for each equivalent distance is ___.

A. Faster
B. Slower
C. The same
D. Variable.

36. Five atmospheres of pressure would most likely occur at a depth of ___.

F. 30 meters
G. 40 meters
H. 45 meters
J. 60 meters.

37. If a person dived to a depth of 100 meters the atmospheres of pressure should be about ___.

A. 10 atm
B. 11 atm
C. 11.5 atm
D. Not enough information to determine.

38. If a U.S. nuclear submarine had engineering specifications that showed it could withstand 25 atmospheres of pressure and it dived to a depth of 500 meters, we would reasonably expect it to ___.

F. Explode
G. Be crushed
H. Be just fine
J. Not enough information to calculate.

39. On a piece of standard graph paper, depth versus pressure would graph as ___.

A. A straight line
B. A wavy line
C. A hyperbola
D. Not enough information to calculate.

40. After viewing how pressure changes below water and in the atmosphere, it would be reasonable to state that ___.

F. In water pressure changes as a direct relationship to depth
G. In the air pressure change does not occur the same amount for each equivalent distance
H. Air pressure change and water pressure change would not graph the same
J. All are true (A, B, C).

PRACTICE TEST 2

Passage 1

The atmosphere of the earth contains roughly 78% N_2 (free nitrogen gas). Nitrogen is utilized by most living things and is found in chemicals of those organisms as well as chemicals in nature. The flowchart at the bottom of the page shows the movement of the element.

1. Nitrates (NO_3^-) in soil water are supplied from ___.

    A. Nitrogen dioxide (NO_2^-) as a gas in the atmosphere picked up by rain
    B. Gaseous nitrogen (N_2) from the atmosphere
    C. Nitrites (NO_2^-) from soil water
    D. All of the above (A, B, & C)

2. Nitrogen containing protein in animals comes directly from ___.

    F. Gaseous nitrogen (N_2) in the air
    G. Protein material from plants
    H. Decomposers
    J. All of these

3. Decomposers convert nitrogen compounds found in the proteins of plants and animals to ___.

    A. Nitrites (NO_2^-) in soil water
    B. Nitrates (NO_3^-) in streams, rivers, and lakes
    C. Nitrogen dioxide (NO_2^-) in the atmosphere
    D. Ammonia (NH_3) and ammonium salts (NH_4^+) in soil water

4. Free nitrogen (N_2) in the atmosphere comes directly from all of the following except ___.

    F. Nitrates (NO_3^-) in soil water
    G. Decomposers
    H. Nitrites (NO_2^-) in soil water
    J. Ammonia (NH_3) and ammonium salts (NH_4^+) in soil water

5. For plants to utilize nitrogen, the nitrogen must come directly from ___.

    A. From soil water
    B. From animal protein
    C. From ammonia (NH_3) and ammonium salts (NH_4^+)
    D. From both A & C

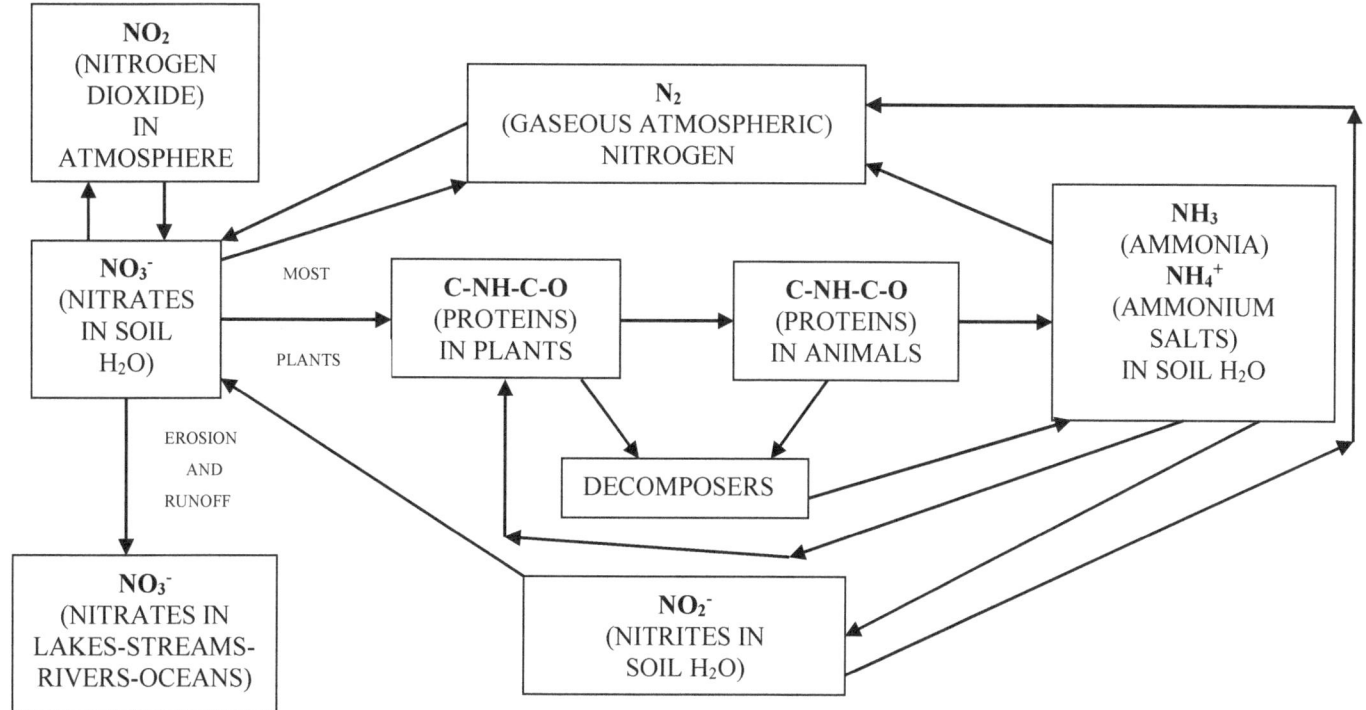

Passage 2

Organic molecules that contain only hydrogen and carbon atoms are termed hydrocarbons. Those molecules that have only single bonds are members of the alkane series, while those with one double bond are members of the alkene series and those with one triple bond are members of the alkyne series. There are also many more hydrocarbons that are made up with different numbers and kinds of bonds including rings, double rings, and chains.

The following chart shows members of the three series mentioned above with their simple molecular formula, their graphic formula and their structural formula. Each line represents a single pair of shared electrons, two lines represent two pair and three lines represents three pairs.

Name	Simple Molecular	Graphic Formula
Methane	CH_4	CH_4
Ethane	C_2H_6	CH_3-CH_3
Propane	C_3H_8	CH_3-CH_2-CH_3
Butane	C_4H_{10}	CH_3-CH_2-CH_2-CH_3
Pentane	C_5H_{12}	CH_3-CH_2-CH_2-CH_2-CH_3
Hexane	C_6H_{14}	CH_3-CH_2-CH_2-CH_2-CH_2-CH_3
Heptane	C_7H_{16}	CH_3-CH_2-CH_2-CH_2-CH_2-CH_2-CH_3
Octane	C_8H_{18}	CH_3-CH_2-CH_2-CH_2-CH_2-CH_2-CH_2-CH_3
Ethene	C_2H_4	CH_2=CH_2
Propene	C_3H_6	CH_2=CH-CH_3

Name	Simple Molecular	Graphic Formula	Structural Formula
1-Butene	C_4H_8	$CH_2=CH-CH_2-CH_3$	
2-Butene	C_4H_8	$CH_3-CH=CH-CH_3$	
3-Butene	C_4H_8	$CH_3-CH_2-CH=CH_2$	
1-Pentene	C_5H_{10}	$CH_2=CH-CH_2-CH_2-CH_3$	
2-Pentene	C_5H_{10}	$CH_3-CH=CH-CH_2-CH_3$	
3-Pentene	C_5H_{10}	$CH_3-CH_2-CH=CH-CH_3$	
4-Pentene	C_5H_{10}	$CH_3-CH_2-CH_2=CH=CH_2$	
Ethyne	C_2H_2	$CH=CH$	
Propyne	C_3H_4	$CH=C-CH_3$	
1-Butyne	C_4H_6	$CH=C-CH_2-CH_3$	
2-Butyne	C_4H_6	$CH_3-C=C-CH_3$	
3-Butyne	C_4H_6	$CH_3-CH_2-C=CH$	

6. The total number of bonds that every carbon atom shares with other atoms in an organic molecule is _____.

F. 1
G. 2
H. 3
J. 4

7. The simplest of all the represented hydrocarbons is ___.

A. Propyne
B. 1-butene
C. Pentane
D. Methane

8. The same prefix in each series represents the same number of ___.

F. Hydrogens
G. Carbons
H. Bonds
J. Both A & B

9. From the same simple molecular formula the ___.

A. Graphic formulas are always the same
B. The names are always exactly the same
C. The number of carbons and hydrogens are always the same
D. The order of the bonds are always the same

10. The best general formula for the alkene series is ___.

F. $C_nH_{(2n-2)}$
G. C_nH_{2n}
H. $C_nH_{(2n+2)}$
J. None of these

11. Of those formulas in the above chart, the only one that does not fit the prescribed formula for its particular series is ___.

A. Heptane
B. 3-butene
C. 4-pentene
D. 2-butyne

Passage 3

Many breakfast cereals are advertised as being the one that is the healthiest for your diet. Observe the following information that has been taken from each cereal's own nutrition facts label and make determinations on which is the best for a person's diet. Many times the factual information is presented in such a matter that it makes it difficult to compare foods so take all factors into account where needed.

Remember that calories are a measurement of the amount of heat produced from a food and this comes from a combination of carbohydrates, sugars and fats. Fiber is most frequently associated with proper digestion and excretion while vitamin A is necessary for good vision, vitamin C for healthy bones and iron for healthy blood. RDA refers to recommended daily amount.

Type of cereal	Serving size	Calories/ serving	Carbo- hydrates	Fat/ serving
Bran with fruit	59 g	190	46g	1g
Oat cereal	30 g	120	24g	1.5g
Sugared cereal	32g	120	28g	1g
Wheat & barley	58g	200	47g	1g

Fiber	Sugars	Vitamin A	Vitamin C	Iron
8g	20g	15% RDA	0% RDA	60% RDA
2g	11g	10% RDA	10% RDA	25% RDA
1g	15g	15% RDA	25% RDA	25% RDA
5g	7g	15% RDA	0% RDA	45% RDA

12. The cereal that gives the greatest amount of calories per gram of serving while the least amount of carbohydrates is ___.

F. Bran with fruit
G. Oat cereal
H. Sugared cereal
J. Wheat and barley cereal

13. The cereal that gives the greatest amount of fiber per gram of serving size is ___.

A. Bran with fruit
B. Oat cereal
C. Sugared cereal
D. Wheat and barley cereal.

14. The number of servings of oat cereal necessary to reach 100% of the RDA of vitamins A & C would be

F. 4
G. 8
H. 10
J. not enough information to determine.

15. In terms of calories, carbohydrates, fiber and vitamin content which pairs of cereals appear to be most alike?

A. bran & oats
B. oats and sugared
C. sugared and wheat-barley
D. bran and sugared.

16. The cereal that would appear to include the greatest amount of material necessary for healthy blood is

F. bran with cereal
G. Oat cereal
H. sugared cereal
J. wheat-barley cereal.

17. Considering all the information given the most healthy cereal would be

A. Bran with fruit
B. Oat cereal
C. Wheat-barley cereal
D. not enough information to determine.

Passage 4

Glucose sugar, $C_6H_{12}O_6$, is the principal chemical from which living things release energy for both the anaerobic process fermentation and the aerobic process respiration. Although the processes start with the same molecule they differ widely in terms of the sequence of the release, the amount of energy released (measured in ATP's), and the molecules that are left at the end of the sequence. The two diagrams below represent simplified views of these two energy release processes.

RESPIRATION

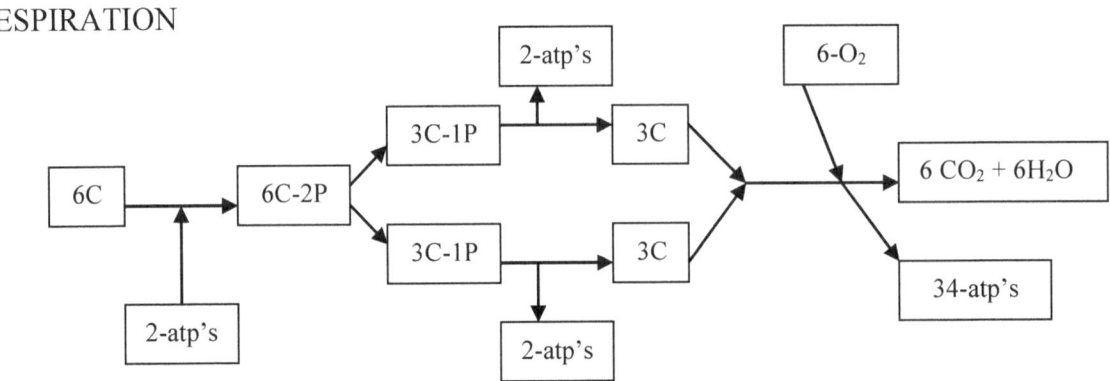

$C_6H_{12}O_6 + 6O_2 \rightarrow 6 H_2O + 6 CO_2$

Glucose + oxygen → Water + Carbon Dioxide

FERMENTATION

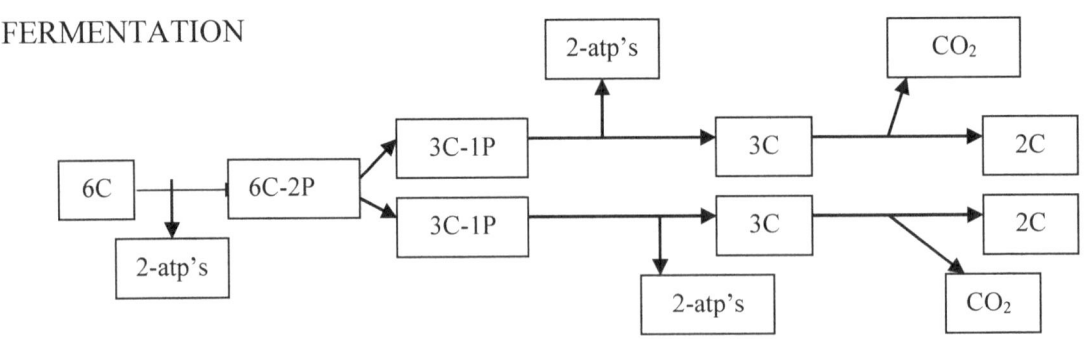

$C_6H_{12}O_6 \rightarrow 2C_2H_5OH + 2CO_2$

Glucose → Ethyl Alcohol + Carbon Dioxide

18. The process that shows a net gain in atp's of energy released is ___.

F. Fermentation
G. Respiration
H. Both processes
J. Neither process

19. The end product of both processes that is the same is ___.

A. Water
B. Carbon dioxide
C. Ethyl alcohol
D. All three are released by both

20. Atp's of energy are

F. input in fermentation only
G. input in both processes
H. output in both processes
J. both b&c

21. The process that shows the most complete breakdown of glucose is

A. fermentation
B. respiration
C. both the same
D. not enough information available

22. The process that is most efficient in terms of material used, net energy released and products produced is

F. fermentation
G. respiration
H. both are equally efficient
J. not enough information to calculate

23. The respiration process starts with 6C and atp's going into the system. What does this mean?

A. atp's are traveling over the path of the 6Cs
B. atp's are searching for other atp's
C. atp is being added to the system to fuel the process
D. atp has no bearing on the process

Passage 5

Growth in all organisms occurs at different rates depending on a variety of factors including available food, sometimes temperature, sometimes age, genetics and many more. The following table shows average size and weight of both sexes of humans at different times in their lives.

	MALE		FEMALE	
AGE	WEIGHT POUNDS	HEIGHT INCHES	WEIGHT POUNDS	HEIGHT INCHES
8	55	49	55	48
9	62	51	62	51
10	68	53	68	53
11	81	55	77	55
12	84	57	88	58
13	95	60	103	61
14	110	64	110	63
15	125	66	119	63
16	136	68	125	64
17	143	69	128	64
18	150	70	128	64

24. Growth rate in height seems to be similar in both sexes until about age ___.

F. 10
G. 11
H. 12
J. 13

25. Girls show the greatest gain in weight between ages

A. 10-11
B. 11-12
C. 12-13
D. 14-15

26. Boys are both shorter and weigh less than girls from ages ___.

F. 11-14
G. 12-13
H. 11-13
J. Not enough data to calculate.

27. On the average growth in height has stopped in girls by age ___.

A. 14
B. 16
C. 18
D. The chart does not indicate stopping point.

28. Boys enjoy the greatest differential over the girls in height and weight at age ___.

F. 11
G. 14
H. 17
J. 18

29. Assuming the trends on the chart continue from the data given one would calculate that at age 20 the differential in height and weight between boys and girls would be ___.

A. Approaching no difference
B. The same
C. Larger than at age 18
D. The data indicates no clear answer.

Go to next page.

Passage 6

Solubility is the amount of a substance that can dissolve in a given amount of solvent. Although there are many different materials that can act as solvents water is considered by most to be the universal solvent. It has this designation because it can dissolve so many different substances. Even though it dissolves many substances there are varying amounts of materials that can be dissolved based on temperature and material to be dissolved.

TEMP.	SOLUBILITY g/100g H_2O
0	12
10	19
20	30
30	44
40	61
50	83

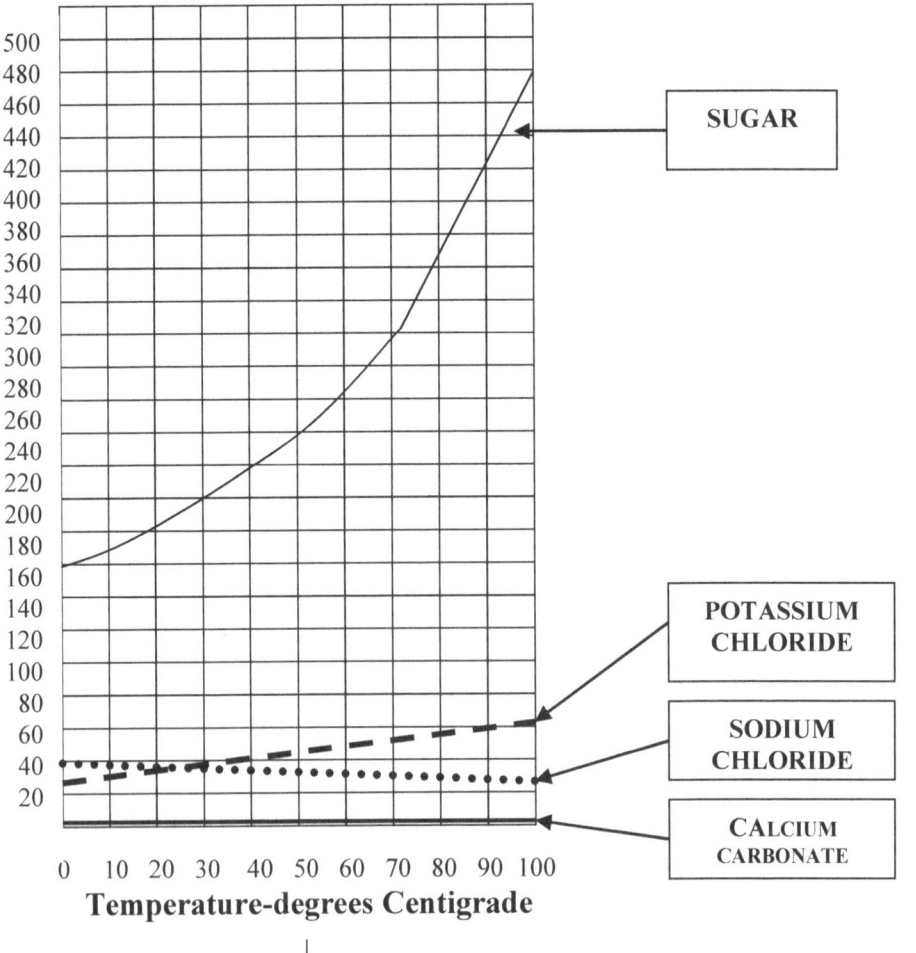

30. The chemical shown which shows the greatest amount of solubility in water is ___.

F. Calcium carbonate
G. Sodium chloride
H. Potassium chloride
J. Sugar

31. The only chemical that shows a decrease in solubility as the temperature increases is ___.

A. Calcium carbonate
B. Sodium chloride
C. Potassium chloride
D. Sugar

32. As temperature increases it is possible for solubility to ___.

F. Increase
G. Decrease
H. Remain about the same
J. All of the above

33. The two factors varying amounts of materials that can be dissolved are

A. temperature and humidity
B. temperature and material to be dissolved
C. time and temperature
D. time and material to be dissolved

34. In table I the solubility ___.

F. Shows to increase by larger amounts as temperature increases
G. Shows to increase by the same amount as temperature increases
H. Shows to increase by smaller amounts as temperature increases
J. Shows a decrease with temperature increase

35. One would postulate based on the given data in table I that at a temperature of 70 degrees the solubility would approximate ___.

A. 44 g
B. 100 g
C. 113 g
D. 142 g

Passage 7

The average temperature in an area plus the amount of precipitation (rain, snow, etc.) that an area receives determines biomes or ecological communities. Although most areas do not receive the same moisture each year, the average over a period of time, helps to dictate the type of biome that exists. Of course other factors such as wind, evaporation and soil depth and type also play important factors.

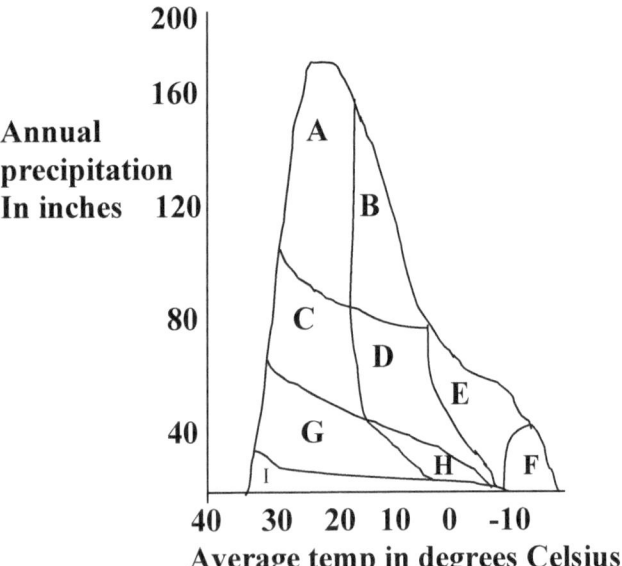

A. Tropical rain forest
B. Temperate rain forest
C. Tropical seasonal forest
D. Temperate forest
E. Taiga
F. Tundra
G. Savanna thorn scrub
H. Grassland
I. Desert

36. Based on the above graph which type of biome receives the greatest annual rainfall?

F. Temperate rain forest
G. Tropical rain forest
H. Tropical season forest
J. Taiga

37. The biome with the greatest variation in temperature is ___.

A. Temperate forest
B. Savannah thorn scrub
C. Taiga
D. Desert

38. The only biome that consistently shows a temperature below freezing is ___.

F. Taiga
G. Tundra
H. Savannah
J. Desert

39. Of the following four which biome has both the highest possible temperature and the highest possible rainfall?

A. Tropical seasonal forest
B. Temperate forest
C. Taiga
D. Not enough information given.

40. The highest possible temperatures and lowest possible rainfall combine to create a ___.

F. Taiga
G. Tundra
H. Desert
J. Grassland

SCIENCE REASONING KEY – PRACTICE TEST 1
p. 517

PASSAGE 1 – Pressure/Temperature/Chemicals on Fruit p. 517

1. A – it changes the apple from red to white
2. J – time
3. C – depending on the temperature
4. H – only vary factor considering
5. D – as the pressure changes, the color stays the same
6. H – red is between pink and purple

PASSAGE 2 – Saltwater p. 518

7. C – 13.6g less 10g for the beaker = 3.6g in one liter
8. F – if residue were on the thermometer, it could have been removed
9. D – keeping everything the same will allow them to verify their results
10. J – key phrase in the question is "results are accurate"
11. C – both try it and compare

PASSAGE 3 – Mendel p. 519

12. H – only one combination from each parent
13. D – both a&c they will possess both but show only dominant
14. G – round and yellow 9/16 to be exact
15. B – yellow and wrinkled 3/16
16. G – 2998 if 9012 is 3/16 then 1/16 would be approx. 3000
17. C – Plants will be different based on their chromosomes

PASSAGE 4 – Probability p. 521

18. F – 16 2/3 % one out of possible six
19. A – 16 2/3 % six out of possible 36
20. F – 2 one out of 36
21. D – 1/8 or 12 ½ % ½ x ½ x ½=1/8
22. F – 1/64 1/8 x 1/8= 1/64

PASSAGE 5 – Homeostasis p. 522

23. B – protein 7.03%
24. H – urea from .03 to 2.74
25. D – glucose and protein both went to 0
26. H – sodium only .05% variation
27. D – both a&c no glucose or protein is eliminated potassium and urea are
28. J – kidney should not eliminate useful substance-if it is, something is wrong

PASSAGE 6 – Gold p. 523

29. C – 1800 g   1kg=1000g so 1.8 x 1000 = 1800
30. G – 110cm^3 1ml=1cm^3
31. A – 16.36 g/cm^3 d=wt/vol   so 1800 g/110 cm^3 is 16.36
32. F – cannot be pure gold density of gold is 19.3
33. A – it could be gold-if it is pure it would be gold
34. J – kg measures weight not volume

PASSAGE 7 – Pressure p. 524

35. C – The same. 2.5 atmospheres for each 25 meters
36. G – 40 meters 3.5 for 25 meters +3/5 of another 25 meters would be 3/5 of 2.5 atmospheres
37. B – 11 atmospheres. 1 atm at sea level + 2.5 for each additional meters
38. G – be crushed. 500 meters would be 51 atmospheres more than twice the safety specs for the sub
39. A – straight line. equal amounts on both axis plots straight line
40. J – all are true per the graph data

SCIENCE REASONING KEY – PRACTICE TEST 2
p. 525

PASSAGE 1 – Nitrogen p. 525

1. D – all of these provide materials for nitrates in soil water
2. G – animals only get nitrogen from plants
3. D – decomposers convert both plants and animal waste and remains to NH_3 and NH_4^+
4. G – decomposers change to NH_3 and NH_4^+ before it becomes N_2
5. D – both a & c produce materials plants can utilize

PASSAGE 2 – Hydrocarbons p. 526

6. J – 4 bonds carbon has 4 outer electrons therefore always shares 4
7. D – methane only compound with just 1 carbon
8. G – number of carbons eth(2) pro(3) but(4) pent(5)
9. C – carbons and hydrogens the same
10. G – always two times as many hydrogens as carbons
11. C – 4-pentene should have only one double bond

PASSAGE 3 – Breakfast Cereals p. 529

12. F – incorrect 190 divided by 59= 3.22 cal/g
    G – correct 120 divided by 30=4.0 cal/g
    H – incorrect 120 divided by 32= 3.75 cal/g
    J – incorrect 200 divided by 58= 3.44 cal/g

13. A – correct 8 divided by 59= .135
    B – incorrect 2 divided by 30= .06
    C – incorrect 1 divided by 32= .03
    D – incorrect 5 divided by 58= .086
14. F – incorrect 4 x 10% =40%
    G – incorrect 8 x 10% = 80%
    H – correct 10 x 10% = 100%
    J – incorrect data given says one serving = 10% therefore it is very simple to calculate 100% see answer c.
15. A – incorrect calories are 190-120, carbohydrates are 46-24, fiber is 8-2 and vitamins are 0% to 10% and 15%-10%
    B – correct calories are identical at 120, carbohydrates very close at 28-24 fiber is almost the same at 2-1 and vitamins a&c close at 10% compared to 15% and 25%
    C – incorrect calories are 32-58, carbohydrates are 28-47, fiber is 1 g to 5g and vitamins are alike at vit A but widely different at vitamin c at 0% to 25%
    D – incorrect calories way off at 190-120, carbohydrates also wide difference at 46-28, fiber the widest at 8-1, and vitamins shows 0% and 60% for bran while sugared shows 25% on each
16. F – correct most important material for blood is iron & iron is at 60% RDA
    G – incorrect oats only have 25% RDA of iron
    H – incorrect sugared cereal only 25% RDA of iron
    J – incorrect wheat and barley has 45% RDA but less than Bran
17. A – incorrect while bran is high in iron, carbohydrates and sugar there has been no method given for overall health comparison
    B – incorrect oats are highest in cal/g but again no method has been given or proposed for overall health comparison
    C – incorrect high in iron and fiber but no vitamin c and again no method given for overall health determination
    D – correct while each cereal has its highs and lows no method was given for overall determination therefore more information is needed

PASSAGE 4 – Fermentation and Respiration p. 530

18. F – fermentation has input of 2 and output of 4-net gain 2
    G – respiration has input of 2 and output of 38-net gain 36
    H – Correct because both a and b show gain
    J – Incorrect-both processes show gain
19. A – incorrect-water only produced in respiration
    B – correct-fermentation produces 2-CO_2 respiration produces 6-CO_2
    C – incorrect-ethyl alcohol produced only in fermentation
    D – incorrect-explanation above in A,B,&C
20. F – incorrect-atp's are input in fermentation but not only
    G – true-atp's are input in both
    H – true-atp's are output in both
    J – correct-atp's are input and output in both processes

21. A – incorrect- end product of fermentation is 2-CO_2 and 2-Ethyl alcohol(C_2H_5OH) a 2-carbon high energy product
     B – correct-respiration produces 6-H_2O and 6-CO_2 completely separating the 6 carbons of glucose and releasing more energy
     C – incorrect-not the same-see A7B above
     D – incorrect-all necessary information given
22. F – incorrect-only 2 net atps are gained and chemicals only partially broken down
     G – correct-more atp's gained and chemicals broken down to simpler substances
     H – incorrect-efficiency obviously different- see above A&B
         Editor's note: Some micro-organisms such as yeast and bacteria depend on energy from fermentation –higher organisms including plants and man depend on respiration.
     J – incorrect-all pertinent information to draw conclusion is given
23. C – atp's provide energy thus fuel the system

PASSAGE 5 – Growth p. 532

24. H – age 12 girls outgrow boys by one inch
25. C – ages 12-13 girls gain 15 pounds
26. G – 12 and 13 girls are bigger both measurements
27. B – age 16,17, 18 all the same
28. J – age 18 22 pounds heavier and 6 inches taller
29. C – key words are assuming trends continue girl's trend-no change boy's trend increase

PASSAGE 6 – Solubility p. 534

30. J – sugar up to 480g/100 g of water
31. B – sodium chloride – shows a decrease from 40g to about 35g
32. J – all - each chemical reacts differently with heat although usually increasing
33. B – Passage specifically states this answer
34. F – each increase in temp brings a bigger increase in solubility
35. D – 142 g calculate the increase per step + the rate of increase per step

PASSAGE 7 – Ecosystems p. 536

36. G – tropical rain forest-up to 200 inches per year
37. D – desert from around 35 degrees down to –5 degrees
38. G – tundra average temp around –10 degrees
39. A – tropical season forest up to 120 inches rain and up to 30 degrees
40. H – desert lowest rainfall of all with temperature up to 35 degrees

REVIEW PAGE

This page should be reviewed prior to taking the test to confirm knowledge of key content areas.

ENGLISH
- Comma
- Dash
- Colon
- Semicolon
- Apostrophes
- Adjective
- Adverb
- Conjunction
- Verb
- Subject/Verb Agreement
- Pronoun and Antecedent Agreement
- Who and Whom
- Dangling and Misplaced Modifiers
- Parallel Structure
- Substandard English
- Conjunctions
- Irregular Verbs
- Transitions

MATH
- Angles Add to 180°/Equilateral/Isosceles/Right Area of a Triangle/Terms: Altitude, Median, Base
- Area of a Circle/Radius/Diameter/Circumference
- Perimeter
- Area of Trapezoid
- Midpoint Formula
- Parallel Lines Divided by a Transversal
- Inscribed Angles/Interior Angles
- Percents
- Trigonometry & Identities
- Square Roots and Exponents
- Rational and Irrational Numbers
- Similar and Right Triangles
- Word Problems General Strategy
- Equation of a Circle
- Distance Formula
- Geometry- Acute, Obtuse, Right, Complementary and Supplementary Angles
- Quadratic Equation
- Inequalities
- Pythagorean Theorem
- Absolute Values
- Averages/Terms: Sum, Difference, Product, and Quotient
- General Equation of a Line
- Graphing and the (X,Y) Coordinate System
- Polygons and Angles
- Greatest Common Factor/Least Common Multiple
- Functions/Polynomials
- Probability and Proportions
- Sequences and Series
- Logarithms

READING
- Reading Method
- Visualize
- Don't Speak What You Read
- Get Lost in Your Test
- Speed Reading
- Finish in 35 Minutes

SCIENCE
- Stay Focused
- Don't Worry About Long Words
- Interpret a Variety of Graphs and Tables
- Identifying Trends
- Making Notes